SMALL PRIVATIZATION

CEU PRIVATIZATION REPORTS | VOLUME 3

SMALL PRIVATIZATION

THE TRANSFORMATION OF RETAIL TRADE AND CONSUMER SERVICES IN THE CZECH REPUBLIC, HUNGARY, AND POLAND

JOHN S. EARLE
ROMAN FRYDMAN
ANDRZEJ RAPACZYNSKI
JOEL TURKEWITZ

With contributions from Carla Kruger, Jan Mládek, Tatiana Nemeth, Anthony Sinclair

CEU

CENTRAL EUROPEAN UNIVERSITY PRESS
BUDAPEST • LONDON • NEW YORK

Published by Central European University Press
H-1021 Budapest, Hűvösvölgyi út 54
Distributed by Oxford University Press, Walton Street, Oxford OX2 6DP
Oxford New York Toronto
Delhi Bombay Calcutta Madras Karachi
Kuala Lumpur Singapore Hong Kong Tokyo
Nairobi Dar es Salaam Cape Town
Melbourne Auckland Madrid
and associated companies in Berlin Ibadan
Distributed in the United States by Oxford University Press Inc., New York

First published 1994

British Library Cataloguing in Publication Data
A CIP catalogue record for this book is available from the British Library.

ISBN 1 85866 006 8 Hardback
ISBN 1 85866 007 6 Paperback

ISSN 0968 5278

Library of Congress Cataloging in Publication Data
A CIP catalog record for this book is available from the Library of Congress.

Typeset by Mayhew Typesetting, Rhayader, Powys
Printed and bound in Great Britain by SRP, Exeter

CONTENTS

About the CEU Privatization Project

The volume of reports presented here is the third in a series produced by the Privatization Project of the Central European University. The Project has created a regional framework for the promotion and improvement of public policies in the area of privatization in Eastern Europe (including former Soviet republics). In particular, the Project aims at the following four objectives:

- the creation of a forum for the collection and exchange of research and information concerning the progress of privatization in all the countries of the region;
- the establishment of a center for policy analysis and advice for the governments in the region;
- the training of local government and academic personnel, as well as other forms of upgrading the human capital required for the successful completion of the privatization process;
- the definition and elaboration of the emerging corporate governance issues in the Eastern European economies, including the development of standards of professional and ethical conduct of corporate directors in the privatized sector and the training of corporate directors in the region.

It is the policy of the Project to involve local personnel as much as possible in its activities. This policy is based on the belief that local participants have special access to information and unique knowledge of the conditions in the region, which, when conjoined with the Western expertise provided by the Project, will greatly enhance the ultimate quality of the Project's activities.

The headquarters of the Project are located in Prague, with offices in New York and all the countries of the region. The Central European University in Prague provides facilities for some of the educational and training programs of the Project. It also serves as a regional clearing-house for information, and a meeting place for the Project participants.

At this stage, the Project operates in the following countries: Belarus, Bulgaria, the Czech Republic, Estonia, Hungary, Latvia, Lithuania, Macedonia, Poland, Romania, Russia, Slovakia, Ukraine, and has approximately sixty East European participants and collaborators.

THE ACTIVITIES OF THE PROJECT

1. Research

The Project's research lies at the core of its activities. The Project is currently conducting, in cooperation with the Research Division of the World Bank, an extensive empirical and theoretical study of the emerging corporate governance structures in the region, including a survey of 600 enterprises in the Czech Republic, Hungary, Poland, and Russia, a study of the postcommunist ownership structure, and a study of investment financing in several countries of the region.

In addition, the Project conducts research under two specialized programs. The Program on Labor Markets in Transition Economies examines labor mobility, the effects of trade unions and worker ownership, and the welfare and policy implications of adjustment costs. The Program on Macroeconomics in Transition Economies studies the impact and propagation of macroeconomic policies under the institutional arrangements in transition, as well as the way in which new institutions at the firm level evolve in response to the economic environment created by these policies.

2. CEU Privatization Reports

The *CEU Privatization Reports* present the results of research and analysis conducted by Project participants. The purpose of the *Reports* is to provide policymakers and analysts in Eastern Europe, as well as Western official, academic, and professional circles with reliable and comprehensive information and analysis concerning the state of privatization in the region.

The individual *Reports* are based on research carried out by the Project teams in each country. The information is collected on the basis of a questionnaire containing a large number of standardized categories and, beginning with this volume, on empirical surveys of East European establishments. The preparation of each report involves several iterations during which issues and answers are further clarified. The first two volumes of the *Reports*, *The Privatization Process in Central Europe* and *The Privatization Process in Russia, Ukraine, and the Baltic States*, have been published by Central European University Press (in association with Oxford University Press) in the first half of 1993.

Future issues of the *Reports* will cover new corporate governance arrangements in Eastern Europe, the development and privatization of the banking system and other financial institutions, mass privatization programs, and labor market dynamics. The Project will also publish, under the title *State and Market Monitor*, a series of shorter pamphlets on special issues, such as labor unions, central banks, and social protection in Eastern Europe.

The *CEU Privatization Reports* are widely disseminated among policymaking, business, and academic circles in the East and in the West. They are translated into several East European languages, including Polish, Russian, and Ukrainian.

3. Educational and training programs

The Project is engaged in several educational programs, both in the public and the private sector, aimed at upgrading the human capital necessary for a successful execution of ambitious privatization plans in the region. Among other initiatives, the Project has been involved in a massive training program for approximately 5,000 territorial and local privatization officials in Russia and the training of the members of corporate boards of directors in the Czech Republic, Hungary, Poland, Romania, and Slovakia.

4. Technical assistance and policy advice activities

The Privatization Project undertakes, upon request from government officials or international organizations active in the participating countries, specially targeted technical assistance and policy advice initiatives. Among other initiatives, Project participants have worked on the revisions of the small privatization program in Russia, and advised on mass privatization programs and other aspects of the transition process the governments of Bulgaria, Poland, Romania, and Ukraine. The Project is also involved in the preparation of a code of professional ethics and responsibilities of corporate directors, which is expected to become a model for adoption in a number of countries in the region.

5. Other Project publications

In addition to *CEU Privatization Reports,* the Privatization Project also sponsors the publication of the results of research conducted under its auspices. Books by Project authors include:

R. Frydman and Andrzej Rapaczynski, *Privatization in Eastern Europe: Is the State Withering Away?* CEU Press, Budapest, London, New York, 1994.

J.S. Earle, R. Frydman, A. Rapaczynski (eds), *Privatization in the Transition to a Market Economy: Studies of Preconditions and Policies in Eastern Europe,* Pinter Publishers and St. Martin's Press, London and New York, 1993.

PROJECT DIRECTORS AND EXECUTIVE OFFICERS

Roman Frydman and Andrzej Rapaczynski, Project Directors
John S. Earle, Deputy Director and Head of the Program on Labor Markets in Transition Economies
Joel Turkewitz, Deputy Director
Fabrizio Coricelli, Head of the Program on Macroeconomics in Transition Economies
Marek Hessel, Head of the Corporate Governance Program
Jan Mladek, Assistant Director and Head of the Czech Team
Kenneth Murphy, Editor-in-Chief of *State and Market Monitor*
Katharina Pistor, Senior Research Associate
Tatiana Nemeth, Research Associate
Karin R. Schumann, Project Officer
Simon Nellis, Assistant Editor of *State and Market Monitor*

The Privatization Project is a part of the Central European University, which is a private, independent, and non-partisan educational institution. Although some Project participants are government officials, the opinions expressed in the *CEU Privatization Reports* and other Project publications are exclusively those of the authors, and do not reflect the views of the respective governments or other organizations.

ACKNOWLEDGEMENTS

The authors would like to thank the Central European University Foundation for providing substantial funding for this study. The Governments of the Czech Republic, Hungary, and Poland generously provided time, information, and support to the research teams.

Kevin Young, John Nellis, and April Harding have contributed ideas and provided the initial impetus for this study.

Local teams, which greatly contributed to the research effort, were comprised of the following members of the CEU Privatization Project: Richard Bures, Karel Cermak, Anton Marcincin, Michal Mejstrik, and Emanuel Sip in the Czech Republic; Laczo Ferenc, Erzsebet Lukacs, Monika Lukacs, Maria Mora, Gabriella Pal, Laszlo Szakadat, Istvan Janos Toth, and Laszlo Urban in Hungary; Ewa Appenheimer, Jaroslaw Gora, Wojciech Maciejewski, Piotr Makowski, Agnieszka Pecura, Krzysztof Rybinski, and Wanda Wojciechowska in Poland.

We are also grateful to PENTOR (and especially to Eugeniusz Smilowski) and ECOMA for assistance in the preparation and carrying out of the country surveys in Poland and the Czech Republic, respectively. George Ftaya provided invaluable computer assistance, and Frances Pinter greatly helped us expedite the completion of this study. Steven Friedman and Karin Rebecca Schumann provided organizational support for the project.

C.V. Starr Center for Applied Economics at New York University and Columbia University School of Law provided institutional support for Roman Frydman and Andrzej Rapaczynski. The National Council for Soviet and East European Research, through the Center for Economic Policy Research at Stanford University, provided partial funding for this study. The Pew Charitable Trusts and Lynde and Harry Bradley Foundation supported our activities in Eastern Europe.

The authors would like to express their special gratitude to George Soros for his unfailing support of the CEU Privatization Project and his continuing faith in the importance of research as an instrument of change in Eastern Europe.

PREFACE

The study presented here constitutes the third volume of the *CEU Privatization Reports*, prepared by the Privatization Project of the Central European University. The first two volumes[1] gave a general overview of the privatization process in ten countries of Central and Eastern Europe, and their focus was on the comprehensiveness, rather than the depth, of the coverage. With the studies contained in this volume, the research of the Privatization Project is moving to its next stage, oriented toward much more intensive and detailed analyses of particular aspects of the privatization process, based in part on large empirical surveys conducted in the region by the Project participants.

While increasing the depth of its coverage, the study of small-scale privatization in the Czech Republic, Hungary, and Poland also has a more policy-oriented objective than the general overview presented in the earlier volumes. The three "Western rim" countries are clearly the most advanced in terms of their reforms of the retail trade and consumer service sectors – in the Czech Republic and Poland, small privatization is essentially complete, while in Hungary the growth of the new private stores and restaurants has dwarfed the importance of the still non-privatized establishments. Thus, one of the aims of this study was to make available to the policymakers in the other countries of Eastern Europe the results of the small privatization programs pursued in the more "advanced" economies, so that appropriate lessons and conclusions could be drawn from their experience in designing the policies for the rest of the region.[2]

The significance of any potential policy conclusion is underlined by

[1] R. Frydman, A. Rapaczynski, J.S. Earle, *et al.*, *The Privatization Process in Central Europe*, and R. Frydman, A. Rapaczynski, J.S. Earle, *et al.*, *The Privatization Process in Russia, Ukraine, and the Baltic States*, CEU Press, Budapest, London, New York, 1993.

[2] An abridged version of this *Report*, together with policy implications and recommendations, has appeared as a World Bank CFS Discussion Paper, under the title *Eastern European Experience with Small Scale Privatization*, Washington, DC, 1994.

the welfare consequences of the performance of the retail trade and consumer services sector. In their zeal for industrial development, central planners typically assigned the consumer a very low weight, and apportioned few resources to both the production and the distribution of consumer goods. Shortages of many commodities and allocation through non-price mechanisms, such as queuing, connections, and corruption, were normal facts of life. The privatization of retail trade and consumer service establishments, and more generally the policies affecting the development of this sector, thus represented an area with tremendous potential for improving everyday standards of living.

1. DEFINITION OF SMALL PRIVATIZATION: THE FOCUS ON RETAIL TRADE AND CONSUMER SERVICES

The term "small privatization," as used in this study, refers exclusively to the processes of ownership transformation in the retail trade, catering, and service sectors, and not to the privatization of all kinds of smaller enterprises – which, in the context of Eastern Europe, may mean manufacturing firms with as many as two hundred employees. As such, the term has both a broader and a narrower meaning than in common use. On the one hand, the retail trade and service sectors in Eastern Europe were organized by the communist regimes in an extremely concentrated manner, with a few huge enterprises and cooperatives often controlling the whole market for a number of consumer goods and services. Their transformation, therefore, may not easily fit the description of "small-scale" privatization; not only because it might involve the initial breakup of very large trade empires, but also because some portions of the trade and service sectors might be privatized as larger units, without being broken up into individual stores, restaurants, etc. Consequently, a part of what we call here "small privatization" in fact involves portions of "large-scale privatization" programs in certain countries, notably Hungary and the Czech Republic. On the other hand, the problems generated by the privatization of shops, restaurants, and service outlets are quite different from those involved in the transformation of manufacturing enterprises, even if the latter are relatively small. The main reason for this is that the break-up of the larger organizational units into individual stores and restaurants employing just a few people is nearly always an option in the retail trade and consumer service sectors, while the very technology and inherent organizational requirements of even small manufacturing firms imposes a certain size constraint, which gives rise to a series of special problems. Among the most important of these are the relatively high capital requirements involved in any sale of larger enterprises and the ubiquitous presence of agency problems linked to the greater size of most manufacturing firms.

There is a certain bias inherent in this way of drawing the line between "small" and "large" privatizations – namely that the presence or absence of agency problems is the key to the choice of a privatization strategy, and that the possibility of avoiding these problems in the retail trade and service sectors is, in and of itself, a powerful argument for the breakup of large enterprises and a quick disposal of individual stores, restaurants, and service outlets. A number of former sectoral insiders in Eastern Europe, as well some independent observers, have pointed to the increasingly concentrated and integrated organizational structure of the retail trade and consumer service sectors in the advanced economies, and argued that it should provide a model for the development of Eastern Europe. As against this argument, we believe there is more merit to the view that the most important objective of privatization in the retail trade and service sectors is a speedy establishment of a large number of relatively small, owner-managed businesses. Such individual or family-run units can quickly adapt to changing circumstances, reallocate the existing stock of consumer goods, find new and better suppliers, as well as make room for numerous entrepreneurial individuals and create an important middle-class constituency for the new regime. Privatization of larger organizational units, on the other hand, involves the very difficult effort of restructuring the old, inefficient institutions, finding, under conditions of acute capital shortage, a manageable number of new owners for the sizeable assets involved, and establishing a new structure of corporate governance assuring the congruence of many conflicting interests, including those of the new owners, old managers, employees, and a number of other parties, such as the state or the suppliers linked to the old enterprise by a host of personal and structural connections. In the case of many manufacturing firms, these distinctive "large-scale" corporate governance problems are most often unavoidable. But one of the keys to quick success in the transformation of the retail trade and service sectors is precisely the possibility of avoiding these complex and intractable problems. Whatever consolidation of the retail trade and service sector firms is needed in the future might best be accomplished not through the initial privatization programs, but through later secondary-market corrections. While we have, to some extent, started from this hypothesis, it has been largely confirmed by the results of our research.

2. DEFINITION OF SMALL PRIVATIZATION: THE FOCUS ON REAL ESTATE

Another, still more important redefinition of the very concept of small privatization was not among our initial hypotheses. Instead, it came about as a result, indeed, perhaps the most important result, of our study. Most shops under communism had very little value as going concerns. In the system characterized by endemic shortages of most goods, and consumer goods in particular, the inventory of most stores was of limited value; very often, it merely consisted of those things that no one wanted to buy in the first place, so that forcing a new owner to take them over, especially at the time when new, often imported goods were becoming widely available, may have meant trying to sell him something of negative worth. The equipment of most stores was also of negligible value: the idea of trying to attract customers by pleasing aesthetic appearance or other modern accoutrements was quite foreign to the socialist concept of retail trade. Finally, given the constant shortages, long lines, shoddy goods, and poor quality of service, the goodwill of a socialist business was, most often, an oxymoron. Although shops in some countries may have fitted this description better than in others – Hungary being the most obvious exception – generally speaking, there was only one asset that was of unquestionable value in most cases: the premises on which the businesses were located.

There are many important consequences of this observation, and we shall bring them out presently. At this point, we only stress its "definitional" importance with respect to the concept of small privatization. First, it implies that the truly essential aspect of the privatization of most state stores in Eastern Europe is not the transfer of a business, but the conveyance of ownership or use rights in the real estate on which the businesses are located. Second, the shift of emphasis from the privatization of a business to the conveyance of real estate blurs the distinction between what is conventionally referred to as the "privatized" stores and the new "start-up" businesses. For the new start-ups are also very often located on premises that had been previously owned or controlled by the state, and the essence of the change in both cases is the transfer of rights to commercial real estate. The observation thus refocuses the whole concept of small privatization and has significant practical consequences.

3. THE IMPORTANCE OF THE ECONOMIC ENVIRONMENT

A rapid ownership transformation in the retail trade and service sectors offered an excellent opportunity for the new regimes in Eastern Europe to gain, in a very short period of time, a large amount of political capital and goodwill. As a result of longstanding neglect, the consumer sector of most communist economies was even more inefficient than the heavy industry and most other areas of manufacturing. Even more significantly, precisely because the transformation of that sector could be accomplished in a very decentralized manner, involving a large number of small entrepreneurs, each of whom needed only a small amount of initial capital, the privatization of most trade and service establishments could deliver a nearly immediate improvement in the satisfaction of the basic needs of the large masses of East European consumers. And yet, in most postcommunist countries – indeed, perhaps in all of them except for the three examined in this study – progress has been tortuously slow and sometimes nonexistent. Often quite a slight improvement in the availability of goods has been offset by a dramatic rise in prices, which has sent many goods beyond the means of the majority of the population. Very little change may be observed in the appearance of, or the quality of service in, most state-owned stores, even if, as in Russia, many of them have been nominally "privatized."[3] And the growth of the new private sector, while not always negligible, did not produce the expected degree of improvement in the provision of consumer goods and services. To explain fully this difference between the three "Vysehrad countries," where the transformation of the retail and service sectors has been, on the whole, a great success, and the rest of the postcommunist world, a separate study of such countries as Russia or Ukraine would be necessary. But it is a central objective of the present volume to provide at least a partial

[3] Mostly through a leasing of the premises and preferential sales of other business assets to the employees.

answer as to what were the key elements of the success of small privatization in the Czech Republic, Hungary, and Poland, and which of these elements may be transferable to the other countries of the region.

The first element, undoubtedly central to the success of small privatization, is the macroeconomic and regulatory environment in which small businesses operate. Indeed it may be argued that policies concerning monetary stabilization, price liberalization, taxation, employment, foreign trade, entry barriers, and other operating regulations so strongly affect the profitability, and indeed the whole *modus operandi*, of a small business that they may outweigh the effect of a mere transfer of ownership or most other policies usually associated with the privatization process.[4] Indeed, it is not impossible that the quite spectacular success of the transformation of the retail and service sectors in the Czech Republic, Hungary, and Poland is, in fact, primarily attributable to the roughly similar general economic policies pursued by all three countries, such as price liberalization, monetary stabilization, and the relaxation of import restrictions, and that the impact of particular privatization policies was of only secondary importance. The fact that the three countries have been more or less equally successful despite their pursuit of quite different privatization policies may strengthen this impression.

Unfortunately, our present information does not permit us to measure the relative effect of particular general policies on the speed of the transformation of the sector under study in this volume. While we obviously believe that privatization policies, especially if understood broadly enough to encompass the disposition of commercial real estate, have a very significant impact on the development of small business, it is also clear that a number of other policies have been more successfully pursued in the Czech Republic, Hungary, and Poland than in any other postcommunist countries, and that the effect of these policies is certainly not negligible. Since they are largely left out of the account that follows, it may be useful to point to the most important differences between the general economic environment of the three countries studied here and most of the other postcommunist economies

[4] It is possible, of course, to view many of the broader policies as, in fact, pertaining to the scope of available property rights, such as the right to set prices or wages in a given business or the right to purchase supplies from any source. Under this interpretation, the inclusion of the broader macroeconomic and regulatory issues may be understood as enriching the very notion of privatization to encompass all the various constraints on the exercise of property rights over transferred assets.

and explain briefly their relevance for the development of the retail trade and service sectors.

The first of these differences concerns the degree of effective *price liberalization*. Although the three countries studied here followed quite different paths toward price decontrol, with Poland adopting the "big bang" policy, while both the Czech Republic and especially Hungary followed a more gradual route, the differences among them were more a matter of tactics than overall strategy. Hungary began with a much more rational price structure for most consumer goods and services than either Poland or the Czech Republic, and could thus avoid a more rapid pace of change. The slower pace of Czech liberalization may have somewhat decreased the pain, while prolonging the period of adjustment. But ultimately, in all three countries most consumer prices were quite quickly and completely decontrolled. Not so in most of the other postcommunist countries. Although significant progress was made nearly everywhere, in many countries price controls have been retained by the central government or imposed by local authorities through a panoply of formal and informal means. It needs no explanation that without a decentralized and relatively unrestricted process of price determination, prices do not convey the necessary information about relative scarcities, and fail to induce a more efficient allocation of resources. Shortages, speculation, and general uncertainty are the most common results. But price controls also require the imposition of all kinds of other regulations that defeat the very purpose of most privatization policies. Thus, for example, if the price of bread is controlled, and profit margins are too low, the privatization of bakeries will quickly lead to their conversion to other types of stores that sell goods which are not controlled or with respect to which the permitted profit margins are higher. Faced with this prospect, the authorities quite naturally follow up with restrictions on the change of the line of business, which seriously limit the property rights of the new owner. With the proliferation of such restrictions (some of which are induced by price controls, others by wage regulations), the meaning of property rights is quickly undermined and the incentives for the new owners to restructure their businesses in a socially desirable direction are severely compromised. It is quite likely that the ineffectiveness of many privatization policies in countries such as Russia is, at least in part, due to factors of this type.

Perhaps the clearest difference between the three countries studied here and most of the other postcommunist countries is the degree of success in *monetary stabilization* and the control of inflation. While the level of inflation is still significant in both Poland and Hungary, prices have remained relatively stable in all three countries.[5] Even in the more equilibrated systems with a long tradition of market pricing, inflation creates noise in relative price signals, limiting the ability of economic agents to respond appropriately to changes in demand or cost conditions and to plan long-term investments. In the postcommunist economies, which begin the reform process with a grossly distorted price system and need a great amount of initial adjustment, inflation makes the task of restructuring so much more difficult. Moreover, the levels of inflation in some countries of the region are so high as to make many people escape from their currencies altogether and undermine the general level of confidence in the future of economic development. This in turn increases the short-termism of most small businessmen, who become more interested in arbitrage and speculation than in genuine investment.

Another important difference concerns the *foreign trade* regime. Again, while Hungary, Poland, and the Czech Republic may have followed somewhat different policies, all three achieved relatively open borders, with lower tariffs and the elimination of most quantitative restrictions. Allowing freer importation of foreign goods had a tremendous impact on the transformation of the retail sector. Shortages that could not be filled by quick adjustments in the domestic manufacturing sector were eliminated by imported goods, and stiff competition was provided to domestic suppliers, forcing them to change product assortment, speed of delivery, quality of service, etc. In fact, many small businessmen became their own suppliers, importing a large number of products from the neighboring advanced economies. Price adjustments were greatly facilitated in this process, with Western price ratios being "imported" together with the Western goods.

The effect of foreign trade was very much strengthened by the realistic *foreign exchange rates* resulting from a combination of current account convertibility, control of inflation, and the availability of stabilization funds provided by international monetary institutions. In the unstable situation prevailing in most other postcommunist countries and with the increasing flight from domestic currencies, the value of the latter on foreign exchange markets falls so low that most imported goods are beyond the means of the overwhelming majority of the

5 This is not to deny that some other countries, above all Estonia, have also successfully stabilized their currencies.

population.[6] Much of the foreign trading activity concentrates therefore on a few luxury items with very high profit margins, but foreign goods cannot effectively compete with the shoddy but extremely cheap products bought by most consumers. Moreover, the unrealistic exchange rates, again, force the governments to introduce a host of otherwise noxious foreign trade regulations, such as restrictions on exports of many commodities (some of which are additionally subsidized), which in turn negatively influence the balance of payments and further contributed to the erosion of the value of domestic currency. By contrast, in the three more advanced postcommunist countries, exchange rates have been set at much more realistic levels, allowing for a gradual penetration of foreign products into most consumer markets, providing increased levels of competition and better satisfaction of consumer needs.

There are certainly other important differences, such as those concerning tax structure, the entry regulations for small businesses, the efficiency of state bureaucracy and the judicial system, or even the general quality of infrastructure and the transportation system. It is likely, however, that the already listed factors were of the greatest significance, and the reluctance of many postcommunist regimes to undertake bolder general economic reform measures constitutes a serious limit on what may be achieved by the more narrowly understood privatization policies alone.

4. THE POLITICS OF SMALL PRIVATIZATION

There is another reason why the task of drawing lessons from the experiences of the Czech Republic, Hungary, and Poland is not straightforward. The three countries examined in this study reveal a great variety of privatization policies used to transform the trade and service sectors of their economies, and the process itself took very different forms in each country. Poland, which started the post-communist reform process with the most devastated consumer trade sector, experienced the fastest and probably the most far-reaching changes. But, strangely enough, Poland did not have any "small privatization" program, nor did its privatization legislation have any

[6] The average wage in some countries of the former Soviet Union has been as low as $10 or $20 per month.

major impact on the retail trade and service sector. Instead, the transformation followed an extremely decentralized pattern, with every municipality pursuing its own policies and a large number of real estate owners acting independently to dispose of the most important assets of the old trade and service establishments. The Czech Republic, by contrast, had the most centralized series of programs, imposing uniform procedures throughout the whole country and conducting formal auctions to dispose of the great majority of shops and restaurants. Finally, Hungary, after a spate of uncontrolled, "spontaneous" privatizations and other organizational changes, has relied primarily on the growth of new stores, with only a fraction of the old state stores being privatized as individual establishments, and the rest still remaining part of larger organizations which the state intends to restructure and sell over a longer period of time.

While all three countries have overall been successful in their transformation efforts, the methods successfully applied in one country would have almost certainly failed in the others. The reasons for this are related to a host of historical circumstances, and particularly the history of reforms during the communist period, which determined the very different starting points for the postcommunist changes. Thus, for example, the Czech Republic may have profited from what Alexander Gershenkron called the "advantage of backwardness."[7] Its communist regime had been the most repressive and the most successful of the three in avoiding any significant reforms. As a result, no significant interest groups, such as labor or local managers, could crystallize, let alone organize, under the conditions of a strictly centralized economic command system. When the regime fell, in 1989, the central authorities were therefore firmly in control of both the political and economic reform process. As a result, the Czech government was able to enact a privatization program that was not designed to appeal to the special interests of sectoral insiders, but rather relied on the support of wide masses of the population for a very open and competitive privatization process, using primarily market mechanisms, such as auctions, to allocate the existing stock of assets to new private owners. The Czech government also relied heavily on restoring a portion of sectoral assets

[7] A. Gerschenkron, *Economic Backwardness in Historical Perspective*, Harvard University Press, 1962. The application of the idea of the advantage of backwardness to the context of Eastern Europe first appeared in R. Frydman and A. Rapaczynski, "Insiders and the State; Overview of Responses to Agency Problems in East European Privatizations," *Economics of Transition*, vol. 1, 1993, reprinted in R. Frydman and A. Rapaczynski, *Privatization in Eastern Europe: Is the State Withering Away?*, CEU Press, 1994.

to precommunist owners through a large-scale restitution program, which freed a significant portion of real estate which could be used for new stores, restaurants, and service establishments.

While the broad use of auctions and a generally open and competitive system was successful in the Czech Republic, it is unlikely that it would have succeeded in either Hungary or Poland. In fact, the central government in Poland strongly encouraged the use of such methods, but the overwhelming majority of shops and restaurants were ultimately privatized through insider-dominated proceedings. Similarly, most attempts at opening the Hungarian privatization process to outsider purchasers, without offering a "special deal" to the insiders, led to repeated delays and, in most cases, an explicit or implicit compromise with the interests of sectoral insiders.

Nor were the methods used in Hungary applicable in Poland or *vice versa*. Hungary entered the postcommunist period after a prolonged period of relatively successful communist reforms which greatly empowered the managers of state enterprises. Also, the performance of the retail trade and service sectors was sufficiently good – certainly better than in any other country of the communist block – for the managers to gain a certain amount of credibility in their claim to remain in charge of the reform process, so long as the blatant abuses of "spontaneous privatization" were curtailed. As a result, neither the state nor the public insisted on breaking up the already significantly restructured retail trade organizations, and the managers were able to retain control, or at least a sort of veto power, over much of the process of small privatization. The policy of large-scale restructuring prior to privatization, favored by the Hungarian managers and the State Property Agency (which supervises the processes of ownership transformation), resulted in a slowing down of the privatization of a significant portion of the old state sector and seriously complicated the property relations pertaining to most sectoral assets. Still, a rapid growth of new private businesses, together with a relatively competitive performance of the (wholly or partially) state-owned stores, combined together to create a very vibrant and dynamic trade and service sector.

If the state was a dominant force in the Czech privatization process, and the managers maintained their upper hand in Hungary, small privatization in Poland, with its history of labor unrest and the political strength of the Solidarity union, was dominated by the employees of the sectoral establishments, often acting in concert with local authorities and other institutional owners of real estate. Unlike in Hungary, the disastrous state of consumer trade and services throughout the last decade of the communist regime, with its endemic shortages, long lines, and drab, empty stores, left the large retail trade empires of the communist era and their *nomenklatura* management with no legitimacy in Poland. But neither did the government, weakened by a long series of decentralizing reforms, have the economic power comparable to its Czech counterpart; communist Poland's reforms failed to improve the economic situation, but succeeded in destroying the old command planning system. In this situation, which boded ill for the government's ability to effect a successful privatization program in general, the Polish authorities have managed an amazing transformation of the retail trade and service sector by more or less consciously focusing on the privatization of *premises* rather than *businesses*, and pitting the interests of real-estate owners (primarily local municipalities and housing cooperatives) and shop employees against those of the old, centralized retail trade organizations.

If one is to draw any lessons from the three Vysehrad countries for the rest of the region, these historical and political considerations cannot be ignored. It has been common for Western advisers and many liberal reformers in Eastern Europe to insist on open privatization processes, with a heavy reliance on auctions as a primary allocation mechanism, without fully considering the costs of this approach in terms of delays and inefficiencies that may be generated by insider resistance. This threat is especially clear in the countries of the former Soviet Union, where the insiders are generally very strong and the government often very weak. Looked at from this perspective, Poland, despite the largely unique strength of the labor movement there, may perhaps be viewed as the most apt model, since its starting point seems to have been similarly disadvantaged, both in terms of the initial economic collapse and the weakness of the government *vis à vis* the special interests of the insiders. But then insider privatization, with special privileges for the employees of the privatized stores, has been tried in Russia on a rather large scale, so far with much more modest results. If Poland is to serve as a model, what is it about its small privatization that allowed it to succeed?

5. THE ELEMENTS OF SUCCESS IN SMALL PRIVATIZATION

To answer this question, a broader issue must be addressed. Despite the variety of privatization methods that may need to be used to take into account the peculiar historical and political conditions of each country, there are, after all, some factors that stand out as conditions of success in any small privatization program. In fact, our empirical survey of three hundred shops, restaurants, and service establishments in the Czech Republic, Hungary, and Poland was specifically designed to isolate those conditions of success from the diversity of particular approaches. While the reader must refer to the survey itself for more detailed results, a summary of some of its main points may be useful at this stage.

We have mentioned already the first, and probably the most important, result of the whole study: that *small privatization is primarily a conveyance of interests in real estate* on which small businesses are or may be located and that the other commercial assets controlled by state retail trade and service units are of very limited value. Approximately 70 percent of the privatized businesses in our sample did not take over any movable assets from their predecessors, and this may have been one of the important conditions of success. Indeed, considering the disadvantages of the organizational structure of the old state sector, its inefficient routines and, above all, the vested interests of its central *nomenklatura* management, the value contributed by the business assets other than real estate may well be negative. Transferring the premises together with the remaining assets, and especially an enforced continuation of the old line of business – a very common condition inserted into the privatization contracts in Russia and the other countries of the former Soviet Union – may thus lower the value of the most productive asset transferred in the process, and this burden may seriously lessen the chances of genuine restructuring.

Shifting the emphasis of small privatization from the privatization of businesses to a transfer of ownership and use rights in real estate may be one of the keys to a successful transformation of the retail trade and service sectors in the remaining countries of the communist bloc. In addition to avoiding the burdening of new businesses with additional liabilities, the focus on real estate has two other important consequences, both of which may have been critical to the success of Polish small privatization. First, in most communist countries, the ownership of businesses involved in retail trade and services was separated from the ownership of real estate on which these businesses were located, and the premises were usually made available to state businesses at well below their market value. Consequently, the interests of the owners of the premises, who, under the new conditions, would like to relet their real estate at much higher rates or at least control its disposition, are quite different from the special interests of the old retail trade empires that stand in the way of change and restructuring. The focus on real estate thus allows for an end-run around the existing structures of retail trade and services, and the enlisting of the real-estate owners, with their interest in a better utilization of their assets, in the struggle for sectoral reform. Second, the focus on real estate makes it clear that small privatization is by no means limited to the privatization of existing state shops, restaurants, etc. In fact, the release of state-controlled real estate for the purpose of allowing *new* businesses to open may be at least as important as the transformation of the old retail trade sector. A dramatic rise in the number of new businesses was clearly crucial for the success of small privatization in the three Vysehrad countries, and, for reasons that will soon become clear, it is likely to be of even greater importance in the countries of the former Soviet Union.

That an increase in the number of new businesses may be important in fostering competition and contributing to better satisfaction of consumer needs is not a surprising conclusion. But there is a special aspect of this phenomenon in the former communist countries that requires particular attention, and it is linked to the second most important finding of our study, one concerning the role of outsiders in small privatization. Our empirical survey attempted to measure the significance of a large number of factors, such as the method of transfer, the type of new owner, and the conditions attached to the transfer, on the levels of postprivatization investment and restructuring. While it is difficult to measure exactly the success of restructuring, we have used the levels of postprivatization investment in the remodeling of premises as a proxy for the degree of desirable change. In analyzing the results, we have found clear evidence that *the entry of new entrepreneurs, not connected with the predecessor retail establishments, is the most significant factor in increasing the levels of postprivatization investment*. In other words, new owners bring in the much needed capital, engage in significantly more restructuring, and generally serve as the agents of change in the sector.

But bringing in new owners is not an easy matter, especially when insider resistance is strong, as it is likely to be in light of the fact that the security of the insiders' jobs (especially the managerial positions) is directly threatened by the change of ownership. To be sure, open privatization processes, such as public auctions, will result in a significant degree of entry of outsiders, and this method was very successfully used in the Czech Republic. As we have already explained, however, when the government is not strong enough to impose a widespread use of open competitive procedures on the reluctant insiders, as was the case in Poland and Hungary, excessive insistence on this feature of the privatization program may lead to significant delays and effective opposition – Hungary may be a good example of this. It is at this point that the importance of the focus on real estate, together with its shift of emphasis from traditional privatizations of businesses to the increased transfers of commercial real estate and the consequent growth of new private businesses, becomes evident. For to the extent that the entry of new owners into the sector does not occur primarily through their purchase of the already existing stores, even a numerically successful strategy focusing on the privatizations of existing businesses may lead to an insider-dominated sector and low levels of post-privatization restructuring – this is exactly what may have happened in Russia. When small privatization concentrates on transfers of commercial real estate, on the other hand, of which the privatization of existing stores and restaurants is only a part, the overall increase in the number of businesses may constitute the primary means for the entry of new entrepreneurs.

We have mentioned already that the importance of this factor may be particularly significant in the countries of the former Soviet Union. The main reason for this is that the general density of stores and restaurants in the former Soviet Union is several times smaller than in the more advanced Vysehrad countries. In Poland, for example, the number of stores per one thousand inhabitants was 4 in 1989 and 9.3 in 1992, as compared with between 7 and 10 in most Western European countries. In Russia, by contrast, the corresponding number in 1993 was between 2 and 2.5.[8] What these figures indicate is that even if all the existing stores in Russia were to be privatized today, and even if privatization were to be followed by significant restructuring, the level of service provided to consumers would probably remain pitifully inadequate. Only a concentration on making available very significant amounts of additional commercial real estate will, therefore, be able to bring countries like Russia into line with the advanced economies, and the increase in the overall number of retail trade establishments, rather than traditional privatizations, should probably be seen as the main way of bringing the necessary new entrepreneurs into the sector.

[8] See Part III, section I. The Russian figures are calculated by the Small Business Development Commission of the State Committee for the Management of State Property of the Russian Federation.

Finally, our empirical survey makes it clear that *the nature of the rights to real estate conveyed in the privatization transaction makes a great deal of difference with respect to the levels of postprivatization restructuring*. Thus, people who buy the premises on which their businesses are located invest more than people who rent, and people who rent for more than five years invest significantly more than people whose leases are shorter. While, given our sample, other results are less robust, restricting the use of premises in various ways, such as prohibiting changes in the line of business, restricting the transferability of the lease, or imposing limitations on the owner's ability to fire the employees or change the sources of supply, is clearly detrimental to the degree of post-privatization restructuring. And while leases are of rather short duration in most postcommunist countries, the restrictions seem much more long-term and burdensome in Russia than in any of the three Vysehrad countries, and this may further contribute to the weaker effect of privatization on the degree of transformation of the retail trade and consumer service sector.

6. THE PLAN OF THE VOLUME

We have attempted to give as timely and complete a picture as possible of the transformation of the retail trade and consumer service sectors in the three countries, so that our study could be used by both scholars in economics and by policymakers still facing problems similar to those tackled by the Czech, Hungarian, and Polish reformers. The volume is divided into four parts. The first three deal with privatization programs in each country: while they complement each other, they can also be read independently of one another. We also believed it was important for the reader to be able to understand the point of departure of the postcommunist reforms, especially since the organization and functioning of the retail trade and consumer service sector under communism had been for the most part neglected in scholarly literature. We have accordingly provided a rather detailed inquiry into the structure and *modus operandi* of the sector prior to the demise of the communist regime in the Czech Republic, where the purest form of the command system had been in effect. Given the similarities among the communist countries during their "classical" period, it would be quite tedious to repeat the same study for the other two countries. Instead, in the parts devoted to Hungary and Poland, we have focused mainly on the departures from the classical model and the effects of the communist reform efforts in the retail trade and consumer service sector. Finally, in Part IV, we describe the empirical survey of 300 enterprises in the three countries and analyze its results. Again, while the survey's results are best understood in the context of the aggregate data and the country reports presented in the first three parts of the book, the survey may also be read independently of the earlier, more descriptive materials.

PART I: THE CZECH REPUBLIC

A. CZECH RETAIL TRADE AND CONSUMER SERVICES UNDER SOCIALISM

1. INTRODUCTION

Although they are critically important for the welfare of ordinary citizens, the retail trade and services sectors have been relatively neglected in studies of "centrally planned" economies, at least those published in the West.[1] This section attempts to redress this omission, in the case of the Czech economy,[2] with an account of how these sectors functioned prior to the beginning of the transformation to a market system. After an overview of the role retail trade and consumer services played in the Czech version of socialism and an account of the nominal ownership as well as the sub-branch composition of these firms, we emphasize key issues for the behavior of economic agents in the sector, particularly focusing on retail trade. We are interested in portraying the incentives and constraints faced by agents at every level of the hierarchy as they make economic decisions about the allocation of goods and the use of labor and capital. Finally, we attempt to characterize possible mechanisms by which the system responded to malfunctions and shocks.

Analysis of the functioning of this sector under socialism is not only of intrinsic interest, but also crucial for understanding the subsequent

[1] Kornai's otherwise remarkably comprehensive account in *The Socialist System* (Clarendon Press, Oxford, 1992), for instance, consciously omits services from its discussion of planning and coordination mechanisms.

[2] We attempt throughout to focus on the Czech Republic, although it is sometimes difficult, particularly in this section, to present data for the Czech Republic alone. We sometimes, therefore, must refer to Czechoslovakia as a whole.

privatization process. For instance, it is necessary to understand what factors were exogenous to the shop under the former system, and which decisions were out of the hands of the shopkeeper, in order to formulate hypotheses about the subsequent effects of the various types of liberalization, decentralization and "small privatization" policies. Indeed, we can draw inferences about the meaning of various behavioral changes if and only if we have some systematic understanding of how the sector worked before. We must understand the *empirical regularities* of the former "system," including its systemic distortions, for if we are only able to view it as randomly distorted then the magnitude and direction of current changes would be meaningless. The meaning of a particular change may also be difficult to interpret due to the general equilibrium effects of numerous other changes. But this only lends greater importance to the attempt to come to some systematic understanding of the sector as it operated under socialism.

The problems of analyzing retail trade and services are legendary, even in a developed capitalist economy, but exponentially so under socialism. The usual difficulties in measuring output are aggravated by the low priority placed on retail trade and consumer services in the official ideology, resulting in their neglect by the statistical authorities. The heterogeneity of the sector, in terms of the types of goods and services sold and organizational modes, is further confounded in socialist economies by the simultaneous presence of state, cooperative, and private administration and ownership, and by the illegal or semilegal character of much of private activity. Finally, the conceptual difficulties in defining the organization and boundaries of the retail trade sector may appear to be ameliorated by the clarity of "central planning." But the characteristics of "real socialism," including the lack of clarity in the distribution of decision-making powers, the overlapping and nonexclusive division of authority, and the ever-presence of bargaining between adjacent hierarchical levels, greatly complicate any attempt to uncover the ways in which goods and services were allocated for consumption by the population.

Our data and analysis primarily concern the several years immediately preceding the "Velvet Revolution" in 1989. In fact, the economic institutions of Czechoslovakia changed rather little over the last two decades of the socialist period. By contrast with the regimes in Hungary and Poland, the Czechoslovak communist leaders managed to preserve an economic system conforming relatively closely to the classic centrally planned model, through to the eve of the Velvet Revolution. Although the 1968 "Prague Spring" introduced reforms designed to decentralize the system and establish various forms of self-management, the Soviet invasion of 1968 successfully reinstated the most conservative forces.[3] As a result, reform movements under way in the 1980s in Hungary and Poland, and later those represented and encouraged by *glasnost'* and *perestroika* in the Soviet Union, had only marginal effects on the Czech system. Czechoslovakia is clearly distinguished from its neighbors in that the changes that occurred after November 1989 were almost completely abrupt, with little earlier foreshadowing.

The structure of Part IA is as follows. The next section adopts a highly aggregated perspective portraying the position of retail trade and consumer services within the Czech economy, including a discussion of the communist ideology regarding the consumer and "global equilibrium" between consumption and production. Next, we characterize the sector on a more disaggregated basis, particularly focusing on its composition according to nominal ownership, organization, and sub-branch. The succeeding sections then consider more closely the micro-economic functioning of the retail trade sector. We attempt to identify constraints and incentives in the process that determined the allocation of goods and the use of labor and capital. A separate section is devoted to privately organized retail trade and consumer services, including the minimal reforms adopted towards the end of the communist era.

2. TRADE AND SERVICES IN THE CENTRALLY PLANNED CZECH ECONOMY[4]

This section views the retail trade and services sector from an aggregate perspective. We start by recounting the pejorative ideology regarding

[3] Under the 1968 reforms, managers in state companies received partial rights to decide about suppliers, the number of plan targets was reduced, workers councils were created, and leasing arrangements with individual proprietors were commenced in small shops and restaurants. The process was reversed step-by-step after the Soviet-led invasion: workers councils were dissolved, the number of plan targets was increased, leases were terminated, and the right to decide about suppliers was once more gradually limited.

[4] We will sometimes follow the Western convention of including all "eating and drinking places" under the classification of retail trade. Where we have separate data and wish to distinguish catering from other retail trade, the text indicates this intention. In Western parlance (for instance, in V. Fuchs' classic, *The Service Economy*, National Bureau for Economic Research (Washington, DC), 1967), the "service sector" includes all transportation, communication, and utilities, as well as wholesale and retail trade, finance, insurance, and real estate, and a group known as "services industries" (hotels, personal and business services, repair, entertainment, health, legal, and education). In this sense, we are concerned throughout this study with only part of the larger service sector.

this sector under communism. We then present measures of the size of retail trade and services relative to the aggregate economy. Finally, we evaluate the proposition that the Czech authorities were fairly successful in maintaining a "global equilibrium" between the aggregate incomes and spending of consumers.

2.1. Socialist ideology regarding consumption

The communist ideology held that retail trade was simply an outlet for the distribution of consumer goods produced by manufacturing industries and agriculture. It was a subject of vigorous and unresolved disputes among Marxist theoreticians to what extent and even whether retail trade contributed to national output. Investigating the origins of this view would lead us far from our topic, but it should be recalled that the legitimacy of communist regimes in large part depended on their claim that socialist systems would quickly overtake the industrialized world's level of growth and material well being. Thus, the ideological foundations on which these regimes based their investment policies repeatedly called for rapid expansion of the "means of production."[5] The low prestige of retail trade had the consequence that the branch officials represented a very weak lobby by comparison with the captains of heavy industry. Planners and party ideologists viewed the "category of consumer demand" with suspicion also because it was impossible to dictate and difficult to manipulate. Services, aside from those provided directly for goods production and transportation (for instance the repair of industrial facilities), were treated with still greater disfavor. Not only was the output invisible, the association of certain services with capitalism (financial services) and with intellectuals (health, legal, education) surely worked to the detriment of the sector in the official ideology.

[5] An alternative, more cynical argument (from J. Winiecki, "Large Industrial Enterprises in Soviet-type Economies: The Ruling Stratum's Main Rent-seeking Area," *Communist Economies*, Vol. 1, No. 4, 1989) is simply that opportunities for rent-seeking were greater in industrial enterprises, thus the *nomenklatura* stressed industrial development. A related view, which does not stress the contrast with consumer goods, however, is that socialist economies were essentially mercantilist, so that the rulers raised revenue through limiting competition and selling the right to operate monopolies. See P. Boettke and G. Anderson, "Socialist Venality: A Rent-seeking Model of the Mature Soviet-style Economy," mimeo, 1992.

These attitudes were reflected in the methodology for the measurement of aggregate output under socialism, the "Material Product System." Only a portion of value-added in trade was supposed to be counted in "Net Material Product" (NMP), and most services were excluded from the "productive" sector (and thus from NMP) entirely. It was actually a chronic problem for Marxist theoreticians to define the notion of "material services," the subject of debate starting in the USSR in 1920s and continuing until the recent past.[6] Among the most problematic cases were transport and communication, where only those services used for the production of material goods were supposed to be counted in NMP, while those for personal use were not.[7] Regarding retail trade, the activity of improving the quality of the material product (for instance, through packaging, storing, or finishing) was supposed to be counted in NMP, while other costs (such as advertisement and marketing) were considered nonproductive. It was, however, difficult to implement this distinction in practice; the statistical office therefore added the whole mark-up into NMP.

2.2. The size of the trade and service sectors

Table I.A.1 presents some measures of the size of retail trade and services in the aggregate Czech economy in 1989. Retail trade accounted for 8.2 percent of total NMP and 9.2 percent of total employment, but only 2.6 percent of total investment. Average wages in trade were 80 percent of national average wages. The total "nonproductive sector" (roughly corresponding to the Western service sector less retail trade and the services provided for the transport of goods and communication) accounted for just over one quarter of total employment.

The enormous degree of vertical integration in socialized enterprises may impart a downward bias to estimates of the size of the business services sector, and the provision by enterprises of some services (for

[6] See, for instance, V. Nachtigal, "O pojetí národního důchodu a produktivní práce" ("About the Concept of Net Material Product and Productive Labor"), *Politická ekonomie*, No. 6, pp. 597–616, 1987, or J. Rypota, *Politická ekonomie – socialismus* (Political Economy – Socialism), Svoboda (Prague), 1980.

[7] J. Pudlák, *Kategorie produktivní práce v ekonomii* (The Category of Productive Labor in Economics), Academia (Prague), 1985.

Table I.A.1 Retail trade and services in the Czech economy in 1989

	Total economy	Retail trade (including catering)	Share in retail trade
Produced NMP (Csk bln)	402.0	33.0	8.2%
Investment (Csk bln)	120.9	3.2	2.6%
Fixed capital (Csk bln)	2,605.2	65.7	2.5%
Employment ('000)	5,343.0	491.4	9.2%
Average wage (Csk)	3,170	2,539	80.0%
*Whole non-productive sector (services)**			
Employment ('000)	5,343.0	1,371	25.7%
Average wage (Csk)	3,170	2,880	90.9%

Source: *Statistical Yearbook of CSFR 1990*, SNTL-ALFA (Prague), pp. 142, 143, 193, 204, 238.

* "Nonproductive" branches in the MPS included science, housing management, accommodation services, services to tourism, municipal services, schooling, culture, health care, trade and technical services, finance, insurance, administration and courts, other social organizations, and part of transport (passenger) and communications.

instance, entertainment, travel, and day-care) to employees does likewise for the size of the consumer services sector. This problem is probably somewhat smaller in Czech data than it is for other countries, however, because of the Czech practice of using more establishment rather than firm level data in estimating employment *by activity*. Furthermore, estimates that take into account the occupational composition within branches indicate that, although service employment was certainly larger than official figures, the sector was still underdeveloped by Western standards.[8]

[8] See A. Nesporova, "The New Role of Services in Czechoslovak Economy and Society," mimeo, Czech Academy of Sciences (Prague), 1989. Another international comparison may be interesting. The percentage of employees in the US on nonagricultural payrolls in retail trade in 1989 was 18.0, and average weekly earnings in retail trade as a percentage of average weekly earnings in private nonagricultural industries was 56.6. The percentage of nonagricultural employees in services was 24.9 (*Economic Report of the President*, Government Printing Office (Washington, DC), 1992). The self-employed are, of course, excluded from these numbers, but their inclusion would greatly magnify the measured difference in the proportions in these sectors in the US compared with the Czech Republic.

The negative ideology regarding trade, however, did not imply a complete lack of interest in the production of consumer goods. Official Communist Party policy statements sometimes treated consumer goods production only as a necessary complement to heavy industrial production and sometimes as a justifiable end in itself. While production of the "means of production" was always a high priority, especially for military purposes, the relative weight placed on consumer goods fluctuated cyclically throughout the socialist period.

The Party's main motivation for not entirely neglecting consumer goods was political. In the early communist years, until 1953, rapid industrialization was emphasized to the exclusion of everything else. The supply problems that developed during this "dual economy," when certain quantities of goods were rationed at controlled prices while the remaining supply was sold freely at high prices, resulted in open public discontent which had to be forcibly repressed.[9] In the years 1954–5, production of consumer goods became a high priority target for the first time in the official pronouncements of the Czechoslovak Communist Party. Thereafter, periodic upswings in the priority given to consumer goods occurred in the early 1960s, when reform communists tried to show that the "needs of the people" could and should be better served, and after the "crisis period" of 1968–9, when at least some popular support for the reimposition of orthodox communism was required.

2.3. "Global equilibrium"

Besides the level of consumption goods to be made available to consumers, the central planners had also to plan, in the absence of an alternative allocation mechanism, the so-called "balance" or "global equilibrium" between personal incomes and total spending. It is sometimes argued that Czechoslovak central planners were relatively successful in achieving such an overall balance in the consumer market, avoiding the characteristic accumulation of monetary overhang in socialist economies and the choice between open inflation and deep,

[9] Public discontent also followed from the drastic monetary reform in 1953, which wiped out most personal savings. The biggest expression of dissatisfaction came in the SKODA factories in Plzen; it was broken by the "People's Militia" and secret police forces.

widespread shortages.[10] This goal was explicitly stated in the state plan, which took into account the many possible sources and uses of income, as shown in Table I.A.2.

In addition to the production plan for consumer goods and the regulation of wages, a variety of techniques could be used to regulate the balance between disposable personal income and the supply of consumer goods. Although prices were almost never directly adjusted to clear markets, they could be implicitly affected in two ways. First, the very low interest charged on consumer loans indicates that credits were essentially equivalent to price reductions; credit policy thus could be and was used to regulate consumer demand. Second, the authorities could encourage a wave of "quality improvement" resulting in price increases. This policy was never practiced as openly as in Poland, where it is rumored that the Central Committee explicitly instructed enterprises to raise prices based on fictitious innovations. But in Czechoslovakia as well, enterprises selling shortage goods were making

[10] There was much literature concerning "shortage phenomena" in Czechoslovakia, most of which is concerned more with aggregate "equilibrium" than with shortages particular commodities. See for instance: V. Dlouhý, "On the Problem of Macroeconomic Equilibrium in Centrally Planned Economies," paper presented at World Econometric Congress (Madrid), 1984; V. Dlouhý, "Nerovnováha a inflace v československé ekonomice" ("Disequilibrium and Inflation in the Czechoslovak Economy"), *Finance a úvěr*, No. 11, 1988; V. Dlouhý, "Disequilibrium Models of Czechoslovak Economy," in W. Charemza and A. Davis (eds), *Modelling of Disequilibrium and Shortage in CPEs*, Chapman and Hall (London), 1989; B. Dolejší, *Rovnováha vnitřního spotřebitelského trhu* (The Equilibrium of the Internal Consumer Market), Academia (Prague), 1984; J. Hlaváček, "Homo se assecurans," *Politická ekonomie* (Prague), 1987; K. Janáček and H. Zelenková, *K rovnováze vnitřního spotřebitelského trhu* (On the Equilibrium of the Internal Consumer Market), EÚ ČSAV (Prague), 1988; J. Klacek and V. Klaus, "Inflační nerovnováha na trhu spotřebních předmětů" ("Inflationary Disequilibrium on the Market for Consumer Goods"), *Politická ekonomie*, Vol. 16, No. 11, 1968; J. Klacek, V. Klaus, and M. Toms, "Inflace, mzdy a trh" ("Inflation, Wages and the Market"), Research Paper No. 54, EÚ ČSAV (Prague), 1968; V. Klaus, "Nepravidelnost spotřebních výdajů domácnosti v sedmdesátých letech" ("Irregularities in Consumer Outlays of Households in the 1970s"), *Politická ekonomie*, Vol. 27, No. 5, pp. 455–67, 1979; J. Mládek, "Globální rovnováha na vnitřním trhu" ("Global Equilibrium on the Internal Market"), *Politická ekonomie*, Vol. 36, No. 9, 1988; J. Mládek, "Selected Problems of Modelling Consumption in a CPE: The Case of Czechoslovakia 1955–1986", *Jahrbuch der Wirtschaft Osteuropas*, Vol. 13, No. 2, Günter Olzog Verlag (Munich), pp. 195–206, 1989; E. Šíp, J. Žůrek, "Problematika kvantifikace uspokojení poptávky a nedostatkovosti na vnitřním spotřebitelském trhu na makroekonomické úrovni" ("Demand Satisfaction and Deficiency on the Domestic Consumer Market: The Problems of Macroeconomic Quantification"), *Politická ekonomie*, Vol. 35, No. 4, 1987; D. Tříska, "Model rozhodování spotřebitele při trvalém převisu poptávky" ("The Model of Consumer Decision Making during permanent Demand Overhang"), *Politická ekonomie*, Vol. 37, No. 4, pp. 475–87, 1989.

Table I.A.2 Balance of income and outlays of population

Income	Outlays
1. Wages from state	1. Purchase of goods in state and cooperative retail trade
2. Wages from agricultural cooperatives	2. Payment for services
3. Free sales of agricultural products	3. Financial payments (taxes, loans paid back, etc.)
4. Social insurance	4. Savings
5. Credits provided to the population	
6. Interest from savings	
7. Other sources	

Source: K. Rozsypal, *Uvod do teorie a praxe narodohospodarskeho planovani* ("Introduction to the Theory and Practice of National Economy Planning"), SNTL-ALFA (Prague), p. 287, 1981.

frequent applications for price increases on this basis. Thus, the Czech authorities could use "innovation control" as a policy instrument, by varying the ease with which such permission could be obtained.

On the supply side, planners could increase imports to make more goods available to consumers. Interestingly, import campaigns appeared with some regularity, related to the five-year planning cycle. At the beginning of each Five Year Plan, investment was stressed at the expense of consumption, and exports were boosted to cover investment imports. A crisis in the consumer market generally occurred about two years later, for instance in 1973 and 1978. The Party and Government then shifted the composition of imports in the direction of more consumer goods, to try to improve the situation before the new Party Congress. In the 1980s, this crisis and subsequent response was delayed due to the fact that the new Five Year Plan was not approved until late 1982, rather than as scheduled in 1980. Shortages became worse beginning in 1986, and relatively large quantities of consumer goods were imported with increasing frequency from China, Yugoslavia, Egypt, and even from South Korea thereafter.

Another action intended to improve consumer goods supply was the campaign in the middle and late 1980s for so called "1 percent to the consumer market." Launched in 1984, the plan was meant to compel large industrial enterprises that did not regularly supply the consumer market to produce some shortage commodity in addition to their normal output. This policy's low level of success was partly due to the fact that many companies chose to produce the same products, which then led to surpluses of those goods.

Table I.A.3 Planned and realized personal income, consumption and saving (in current prices, Csk)

	1961–5	1966–70	1971–5	1976–80	1981–5
Planned income	3.61	–*	5.70	4.32	3.03
Realized income	4.78	8.16	5.23	4.09	3.15
Consumption	4.33	7.89	5.44	4.24	3.00
Saving	28.41	15.13	0.48	–0.30	7.54

Sources: V. Dlouhý, "Disequilibrium Models of Czechoslovak Economy," in W. Charemza and A. Davis (eds), *Modelling of Disequilibrium and Shortage in CPEs*, Chapman and Hall (London), 1989; *Statistical Yearbook of ČSSR 1986*, SNTL-ALFA (Prague), 1986.

* There was no Five Year Plan in the late 1960s due to the Prague Spring reform movement.

We discuss some of these instruments for addressing the problems of balance and shortage at the microeconomic (individual commodity) level later, in section 4.4; here we consider only the evidence for the existence of aggregate or "global" balance. Table I.A.3 displays the rates of growth in planned and realized personal income, consumption, and saving for five-year periods from the early 1960s to the early 1980s.

For this entire period, the growth of actual income stayed very close to the plan (i.e., there was little "wage drift"), and personal consumption expenditures also kept pace with income. Although it is difficult to know whether the high rates of growth of personal saving in the 1960s and early 1980s reflect an increase in desired (as opposed to "forced") saving, there seems to have been little forced saving in the 1970s. Of course, this measure of "global equilibrium" ignores microeconomic adjustment through forced substitution.[11]

Further evidence on this appears in Table I.A.4, which presents the results of surveys of shortages, conducted at the retail establishment level.[12] This measure, sometimes referred to as the "Index of Demand

[11] In *The Socialist System*, Kornai refers to global equilibrium as "forced adjustment equilibrium."

[12] Similar indicators for particular goods will be presented in section 4 below. Here again, we focus only on the aggregate index and the measures for broad commodity groups.

Table I.A.4 Shortage indicators for main consumer goods

Year	All goods	Food	Non-food	Durables*
1977	–13	–9	–17	–
1978	–16	–5	–25	–
1979	–15	–4	–25	–
1980	–12	–6	–16	–
1981	–10	–8	–12	–
1982	–10	–11	–10	–
1983	–3	+4	–8	–8
1984	+1	+10	–8	+3
1985	+1	+10	–7	+0
1986	–2	+11	–11	–18
1987	–7	+4	–15	–17
1988	–14	–2	–23	–53

Sources: J. Šlechtová, "Odvětvová sumarizace výsledku konjunkturních testů za 4. čtvrtletí 1984", VÚO (Prague), 1985; J. Šlechtová, "Roční odvětvová sumarizace výsledků konjunkturních testů za rok 1988", VÚO (Prague) 1989; J. Mládek, "Shortage – the Barrier of Modelling Consumption in a Centrally Planned Economy", *Ekonomicko-matematický obzor*, Vol. 23, No. 2, p. 168, 1987.

* The exact wording of the name of this group is "Household Equipment", e.g. furniture, refrigerators, washing machines, small electronic devices, etc.

Satisfaction",[13] is based on a subjective evaluation by shopkeepers of the existence of shortages of goods in their establishments according to a five-level scale. "Very unsatisfied demand" was assigned the value –100, "partly unsatisfied" the value –50, "partly satisfied" the value 0, "quite satisfied" the value 50, "quite satisfied, with problems in sales" the value 100. The optimum was supposed to be in the range of 0 to 50, while values down to –25 were considered "bearable."

According to this measure, Czechoslovak planners seem to have been able to maintain average shortages at "bearable," "near equilibrium"

[13] See E. Šíp, J. Žůrek, "Problematika kvantifikace uspokojení poptávky a nedostatkovosti na vnitřním spotřebitelském trhu na makroekonomické úrovni" ("Demand Satisfaction and Deficiency on the Domestic Consumer Market: The Problems of Macroeconomic Quantification"), *Politická ekonomie*, Vol. 35, No. 4, 1987.

levels, at least between the years 1977 and 1989.[14] It is noteworthy that some of Czechoslovakia's neighbors were relatively unsuccessful in this effort. In Poland, for example, central planners steadily increased wages, although they probably knew full well that it would not be possible to supply a corresponding quantity of consumer goods and services. The result was inflation – open, repressed, or hidden – and growing levels of shortages. By contrast, Dlouhý estimated that hidden CPI inflation in Czechoslovakia averaged only 2 percent and Johanovský estimated hidden PPI inflation at between 2.5 and 4 percent in the 1980s.[15] As is clear from the differences in the degree of shortage across commodity groups, however, the apparent success of Czechoslovak "global equilibrium" at the aggregate level may well mask many shortages for particular items. This theme is pursued in greater depth in section 4 below.

The reported growth rates of real wages and real per capita consumption in Czechoslovakia were the slowest in any East European centrally planned economy. But these narrow measures of real wages and consumption exclude such factors as the ease of finding goods and the amount of waiting time expended in making purchases, clearly important determinants of consumer utility.

3. FORMAL OWNERSHIP, ORGANIZATION, AND COMPOSITION OF RETAIL TRADE AND CONSUMER SERVICES PRIOR TO 1989

This section examines retail trade and services from a more disaggregated viewpoint. The first part describes the pattern of formal ownership in the sector. We emphasize that formal ownership was often not very meaningful in practice, and indeed that the very concept of ownership is ambiguous in a socialist economy. The second part

[14] Some indirect evidence for this statement is the fact that Czechoslovakia was the only communist country where not only was there little waiting time to purchase cars, but after 1974 it was even the case that credits were made available to consumers in an attempt to stimulate sales of certain types of car. Subsection 4.4 contains further discussion of shortages of particular goods.

[15] V. Dlouhý, "Nerovnováha a inflace v československé ekonomice" ("Disequilibrium and Inflation in Czechoslovak Economy"), *Finance a úvěr*, No. 11, 1988; K. Johanovský, "Problematika investic v prognóze" ("The Issue of Investment in the Forecasting"), mimeo, Prognostický ústav ČSAV (Prague), 1987.

describes the formal administration of the sector through a number of inter-relating hierarchies, which had an unclear distribution of decision-making rights. The discussion of decision-making and the determination of important economic variables, however, is reserved for the following section 4. Finally, this section portrays the sub-branch composition of retail trade and services.

3.1. Ownership

Table I.A.5 shows the share of Net Material Product, employment, and fixed assets (capital at book value) in the state, cooperative, and private ownership sectors of the aggregate Czechoslovak economy in 1983. The dominance of the state sector and the relatively small importance of both the cooperative and the private sectors are clear.

The term "ownership" is taken here to mean the formal title to assets; in fact, it is arguable that "ownership rights" in the conventional sense of enforceable entitlements to use, enjoy the fruits of, and dispose of property did not exist under socialism. None the less, the identity of the formal owner has assumed critical importance in the current privatization process; distinctions that were essentially meaningless in the past have suddenly become decisive. Moreover, as we will discuss shortly, there may have been some significant differences in the administration of state as opposed to cooperative property.

By contrast with its share in the economy as a whole, cooperative ownership was much more important in retail trade, catering, and services, and its relative importance grew throughout the socialist period. Table I.A.6 shows the number of establishments, turnover, and employment in retail trade and catering. Although cooperatives accounted for 43 percent of the total number of establishments in both sectors in 1989, their share of turnover was only 22 percent and of employment only 26 percent: the majority of cooperative units were small and located in rural areas. At the same time, official[16] private activity in retail trade and catering was insignificant during Czechoslovakia's communist years. All enterprises in the trade sector were either state or cooperatively owned.

The Czechoslovak government achieved this ownership structure in

[16] We stress the word "official", because unofficial private activity was probably quite widespread in this sector. We discuss this further in section 4, below.

Table I.A.5 Share of sectors in NMP, employment, and fixed assets in 1983

Sector	NMP	Employment	Fixed assets
State	86.6%	90.2%	82.9%
Cooperative	10.1%	9.6%	9.9%
Private	3.3%	0.2%	7.2%
Total	100%	100%	100%

Sources: *Historical Statistical Yearbook of CSSR*, SNTL-ALFA (Prague), pp. 424, 425, 1985; *Statistical Yearbook of CSSR 1985*, SNTL-ALFA (Prague), p. 132.

Table I.A.6 Trade (including catering) in the Czech Republic, 1989

	State	Cooperative	Total
Number of establishments	33,848	25,388	59,236
Share in total	(57%)	(43%)	
Employment	316,000	110,568	426,568
Share in total	(74%)	(26%)	
Turnover (Csk bln)	160.2	45.4	205.6
Share in total	(78%)	(22%)	

Source: *Statistical Yearbook of CSFR 1990*, SNTL-ALFA (Prague), pp. 517, 530.

the late 1940s and early 1950s, both through large-scale nationalizations and through pressure on private owners either to join cooperatives or to close their businesses or "sell" them to the state (the "dry way" of nationalization, as Lenin put it). Table I.A.7 shows that the size of the private sector had become negligible in Czech retail trade within ten years after the communist accession to power. Also apparent from the table is the consolidation of the retail sector throughout the socialist period. The number of shops declined by nearly 50 percent, the consequence of a policy to simplify the supply-distribution system.

The service sector in the socialist Czech Republic included a small amount of legal private activity,[17] as well as state and cooperative

[17] According to A. Nešporová ("The New Role of Services in Czechoslovak Economy and Society," mimeo from the Institute for Forecasting (Prague), 1989), the USSR and Czechoslovakia went the farthest in the eradication of artisans, craftsmen, and tradesmen. None the less, some freelancing artists, musicians, guides, interpreters, farmers, etc., remained. In 1980, there were 13,476 such individuals registered; of these, 6,184 were farmers, and 7,292 were "other." (*Statistical Yearbook of CSSR 1985*, SNTL-ALFA (Prague).)

Table I.A.7 The ownership structure in retail trade in the Czech Republic: historical development

	1945	1947	1952	1959	1987	1989
Number of establishments	–	–	76,146	57,877	43,770	39,757
Sector			Structure in %			
State	3.0	7.0	68.6	61.7	61.2	59.7
Cooperative	8.0	13.0	26.7	38.0	38.8	40.3
Private	89.0	80.0	4.7	0.3	0.0	0.0

Source: unpublished data from the Ministry of Internal Trade and Tourism.

Table I.A.8 Establishments providing services in the Czech Republic, 1985

Sector	Number	Employment
State	3,729	203,577
Share in total	12%	57%
Cooperative	282	127,368
Share in total	1%	36%
Private	27,423	27,423
Share in total	87%	7%
Total	31,434	358,368

Source: *Statistical Yearbook of CSFR 1986*, SNTL-ALFA (Prague), p. 532.

ownership. State enterprises involved in services were typically controlled at the local level, as described below. The cooperatives in this sector were producer cooperatives, by contrast with the consumer cooperatives dominant in trade.

Unfortunately, the Czech data do not permit a precise quantification of the relative importance of the different ownership forms at a disaggregated level. Local state enterprises and productive cooperatives also engaged in the production of goods as well as the provision of services, but the relative proportion of these various activities is unknown. Table I.A.8 contains the numbers of establishments in the service sector, rather than the actual number of service units.

Some indication of the relative size of the various providers of services can be gleaned from Table I.A.9, showing the revenue of cooperatives and local enterprises, which supplied both goods and

Table I.A.9 Revenue of companies which were active in the Czech service sector in 1989*

		Local state companies	Productive cooperatives	Total
Revenues total (Csk bln)		22.8	18.6	41.4
Revenues from population (Csk bln)		6.8 (100%)	3.9 (100%)	10.7
of which:	Revenues for services	5.8 (85%)	2.4 (62%)	8.2
	Revenues for goods	1.0 (15%)	1.5 (38%)	2.5

Source: *Statistical Yearbook of CSFR 1990*, SNTL-ALFA (Prague), pp. 517, 530, 577.

* Private establishments are not included in this table.

services to other enterprises and to the population at large. Separate data are available on the revenue from services sold to consumers; this revenue amounted to 62 and 85 percent of total revenue for cooperatives and local enterprises, respectively. Such data, however, are not available for the division of revenue between goods and services sold to other enterprises. Assuming the same proportional division for these sales as for those to consumers, the state sector would account for about 70 percent of total revenue derived from the provision of services, with the remaining 30 percent captured by cooperatives.

3.2. Organization

Although formally owned by the state and cooperatives, administrative responsibilities for retail trade fell under a number of ministries and state organs.[18] Most important was the Ministry of Internal Trade and Tourism, which was responsible for the bulk of retail trade and to which the term "state trade" was usually applied. The other two main categories were cooperative trade and "other state trade," the latter defined as trade companies owned by the state but controlled by other ministries and state organs. The relative importance of these three categories is shown in Table I.A.10.

[18] The source for most of the information in this section is: *Seznam obchodnich organizaci v CSR a SSR* ("List of Trade Organizations in CSR and in SSR"), Ministry of Internal Trade and Tourism (Prague), 1984.

Table I.A.10 Number of shops and employment in Czech retail trade (excluding restaurants), 1989

Sector	Shops	Employment
State trade	20,770 (52.2%)	226,211 (60.7%)
Other trade	2,605 (6.6%)	59,308 (15.9%)
Cooperatives	16,014 (40.3%)	80,167 (21.5%)
Coal stores	368 (0.9%)	7,040 (1.9%)
Total	39,757	372,726

Sources: *Statistical Yearbook of CSFR 1990*, SNTL-ALFA (Prague), 1990, p. 530; "Ukazatele maloobchodni site" ("The Variables of the Retail Trade Network"), mimeo, Ekoma (Prague), 1993.

Under the heading of "other state trade," fell a wide variety of products. The Ministry of Culture was responsible for retail and wholesale trade of books, tapes and records. The Ministry of Industry was responsible for all petrol stations and trade in musical instruments. The Ministry of General Engineering managed trade in cars and spare parts. The Ministry of Communications was responsible for trade in newspapers and in collectable stamps. The Ministry of Health administered wholesale pharmaceutical trade, while retail pharmacies were governed by District Institutes of National Health. Retail and wholesale trade of coal was administered by regional governments.[19] Each of these organs administered enterprises that organized the distribution, including final sale, of the goods in question. Other individual enterprise shops, where manufacturing enterprises sold their products directly, also fell under the category of "other state trade."

The hierarchical structure under the Ministry of Internal Trade and Tourism was more complicated. There were five "trusts," which were legal persons, each specializing in a certain commodity group: fruits and vegetables, other food, tourism, textiles, and manufactured goods. The trusts administered enterprises, again legal persons, each of which controlled trade in the commodity group in one of the eight regions (*kraj*) in the Czech Republic. Usually, each enterprise had a local division in each district (*okres*) of its region. Wholesale trade was organized as a

[19] The Slovak Ministry of Trade and Tourism also had a trust administering some department stores in the Czech Republic.

branch either of the regional enterprise or the district division. Individual units (shops) were under the direct control of the district divisions.

Besides trusts, there also existed branch enterprises, which were responsible for regional divisions in jewelry, footwear, and furniture. These branch enterprises functioned essentially like the trusts, and the regional divisions functioned like the enterprises under the trusts in the other branches. However, these three branches had no district divisions. Finally, there was also a category of enterprises controlled directly by the Ministry of Internal Trade and Tourism, including activities such as publishing, computers, architecture, etc. These were services for the other agencies within the ministry and for other ministries; their activity was not in retail trade. In total, there were eighty-four enterprises, 272 local divisions, and over 21,000 shops under the Ministry in 1988.

Cooperative trade was organized under the aegis of the Union of Cooperatives. There were seventy-three local consumer cooperatives organized on a district level involved in both retail trade and catering; the same legal person with the same membership handled both activities. Agricultural and producer cooperatives also had their own shops.

3.3. Composition

Table I.A.11 classifies retail trade units in 1989 according to the principal types of goods sold. Retail trade of food was predominantly in the hands of state and cooperative establishments. On the other hand, in some branches of retail trade, such as petrol stations, newspaper and tobacco kiosks, fuel distribution (coal) and industrial shops (books, records, cars), "other state trade" played an important role.

Local governments and consumer cooperatives were responsible for the administration of restaurants.[20] While the former concentrated their activity in towns, the latter were active mostly in rural areas. The eighty-two companies named "Restaurants," "Restaurants and Eating Places," or "Restaurants and Hotels" were administered by district governments. One company, named "Restaurants of Prague," was administered by the city of Prague. Seventy-three local cooperatives controlled the rest of the

[20] The members of these consumer cooperatives were any Czechoslovak citizen who applied for membership, was accepted by the local cooperative, and paid Csk 100 as a fee. Most members were not employees.

Table I.A.11 Composition of retail trade establishments in the Czech Republic (December 31, 1989)

	State trade	Other state	Cooperatives	Total
Food shops	10,650	21	4,290	14,961
Supermarkets	227	0	2	229
Variety	4,363	1	2,006	6,370
Specialty food	6,060	20	2,282	8,362
Mixed shops	409	1	8,029	8,439
Department stores	39	1	37	77
Cooperative buying centers	0	0	725	725
Industrial goods	9,672	2,572	2,525	14,769
Fuels	0	368	0	368
Construction materials	0	10	408	418
Fixed kiosks	390	2,556	307	3,253
Petrol stations	0	758	0	758
Mobile shops	26	6	555	581
Total	21,186	5,529	16,876	43,591

Source: "Ukazatele maloobchodni site" ("The Variables of the Retail Trade Network"), mimeo, Ekoma (Prague), 1993.

Table I.A.12 Restaurants in the Czech Republic (December 31, 1989)

Sector	Turnover (Csk bln)	Employment	Establishments
Local Governments	20.6 (75.2%)	82,749 (73.1%)	10,105 (51.9%)*
Cooperatives	6.8 (24.8%)	30,401 (26.9%)	9,374 (48.1%)
Total	27.4	113,150	19,479

Source: *Statistical Yearbook of CSFR 1990*, SNTL-ALFA (Prague), pp. 517, 518, 530.

* This figure also includes 836 restaurants controlled by other state organizations.

catering network, on the district level. The relative size of the two types of organization is shown in Table I.A.12.

The service sector of the Czech economy was quite decentralized under communism. As in catering, the most important organizations were local governments and producer cooperatives. Among those under local government authority, three types of service establishments existed.

Table I.A.13 Companies of local economy and productive cooperatives providing services, 1989

	Establishments	Average employment	Revenues (Csk bln)
Local production and service enterprises	272	646	22.9
Budgetary and non-profit organizations	252	92	3.1
Petty economic units of local governments	2,088	11	2.7
Productive cooperatives*	290	450	18.6
Industrial	224	468	15.4
Construction	38	420	2.3
Service	28	347	0.8

Source: *Statistical Yearbook of CSFR*, SNTL-ALFA (Prague), 1990, p. 577.

* The classifications "industrial," "construction," and "service" represent primary activities.

First, Enterprises of Local Production and Services, somewhat larger establishments on average, were usually controlled by district governments. Second, "Petty Units" of Local Governments, much smaller establishments, were controlled by municipal governments. Both of these types provided the following kinds of services: repairs for consumers and industrial companies, laundry and dry cleaning, hair cutting, cosmetic and personal hygiene, photography, house cleaning, hire of durable goods, mortuaries, taxies, freight transport, construction and renovations, and gardening (flower and vegetable production). There was no clear division of labor between the larger and smaller companies; however, the larger tended to be more involved in manufacturing, construction, and freight transport. The third kind of service establishment was the category of "Non-profit Organizations of Local Governments for Public Services," which were responsible for repairing and cleaning local roads, sewage systems, etc. Although all three of these types were legally state owned, local authorities exercised control over most of their operations. Producer cooperatives were also involved in providing services. As mentioned above, however, the available statistical data does not indicate how much of their activity was dedicated to manufacturing or construction, and how much to services. Table I.A.13 summarizes the available information about the local enterprises and cooperatives at least partially involved in providing services.

Due to the integration of services with other activities, few data are available concerning the composition of services by type of activity. There seems to be some evidence, however, that the composition of services was distorted in multiple senses.[21] First, the planners' emphasis on "productive" activities implies that services to industry were given higher priority than those to consumers. Second, even among the so-called "material" services, those activities most closely associated with the production process itself, for instance maintenance and repair services, were emphasized. Arguably, an aging capital stock and low incentives for workers to maintain equipment properly contributed to a greater need for repair services. Third, central planning suppressed certain branches of the service sector, particularly financial, legal, and advisory services.[22] Finally, some services, particularly in health, computers, and telecommunications, and nearly all personal services, simply received an extremely low priority.

4. THE ECONOMICS OF RETAIL TRADE UNDER CZECH COMMUNISM

In this section, we address the principal economic questions of the retail trade sector: what was distributed, how, and for whom? Despite their obvious importance for an evaluation of living standards, these issues have been neglected in nearly all analyses of socialist systems. While the picture of empty shelves and lengthy queues has dominated the view of East European socialism in the Western popular press – and represented a major factor in the lives of most individuals in the East – scholars have instead chosen to focus on the industrial sector, and little systematic inquiry into the functioning of retail trade under socialism has been undertaken. Yet the experience of individuals as consumers, together with their participation in the labor market, essentially defines their

[21] See Nesporova, "The New Role of Services in Czechoslovak Economy and Society."

[22] On the other hand, Nesporova, "The New Role of Services in Czechoslovak Economy and Society," points out that detailed central planning required a larger bureaucracy, including financial and legal "services." In this sense, these activities were less suppressed than they were extremely centralized.

economic well-being; an examination of trade is thus a critical missing piece in our understanding of socialism. Moreover, as we argued in section 1 above, the changes in behavior subsequent to the adoption of economic reforms can be interpreted only in light of the starting point given by the socialist system.

As in the other branches of the economy, "central planning" played a significant role in the allocation of goods to consumers through the retail trade network. But the difficulties faced by planners in obtaining information and making decisions were still much greater in the case of the many thousands of shops and many millions of consumers in the retail trade sector than in the highly concentrated industrial branches. Perforce, therefore, the sector could not be managed in a purely centralized fashion; the argument that allocation by means of central planning alone was infeasible applies *a fortiori* to retail trade.

Our analysis, therefore, must go well beyond a description of formal organization to consider the informal institutions, the real practice of allocative decisions. It goes without saying that this is an extremely difficult undertaking, insofar as many of these practices were illegal, frowned-upon, or at least officially unrecognized, even if they constituted in many cases primary methods of allocation. Moreover, the boundaries between what was permitted, what was discouraged, and what was punished (or would be, if apprehended) were seldom clear.

But the retail trade sector was not only non-transparent because of the unavoidable failure of pure central planning, but also because of the basic fact of shortage of consumer goods, which created powerful incentives for a multiplicity of rent-seeking activities. Shortage in retail trade had a different origin from shortage in the industrial sector. The basis for excess demand for producer goods and factors of production was the soft budget constraints of enterprises, but households operated under hard budget constraints. The explanation is rather more conventionally economic: many consumer prices were held below market-clearing levels. The resulting disequilibrium implied both that consumers ultimately paid more, in a variety of ways, than the official prices for many goods, and that alternative allocational mechanisms had to be found.

This section attempts to disentangle the roles of the different agents and institutions at all levels of the hierarchy in the retail trade sector in the determination of goods allocation, prices and consumer credit, employment and wages, and investment and innovation. For the fundamental issue of goods allocation, it is useful to distinguish among various types of practices. First, some actions were explicitly and precisely planned: the central authorities directed the production and distribution of some goods, and these commands were disaggregated and passed down the hierarchy. Second, more approximate directives were handed down in the form of plans for financial aggregates or as "methodological guidelines." Third, there were a variety of customary ways of doing business which were not constrained by directives from above, but which were also not illegal. Finally, illegal maneuvering could be motivated either to fulfill an impractical plan or by personal aggrandizement.

To these ways of organizing transactions must be added the role of consumers as unofficial employees of the trade sector. Families were forced to adjust to the unavailability of goods by organizing their members to wait in queues; in particular, retired people and children often received this assignment. Enterprises also adjusted, allowing their workers time off during the day to search for ingredients for the evening meal. Part of the customary, if unstated, duties of many junior workers was to procure shortage goods (especially perishables) for her or his supervisor. Because so many transactions were conducted on a barter basis, everyone was continually engaged in a search for the discovery of a "double coincidence of wants" or a possibility to arrange triangular trade among a number of different consumers; sometimes the chains were quite long. No understanding of trade under socialism would be complete without an acknowledgment of the unusually active role played by consumers in organizing allocation.

4.1. Planning, commands, and guidelines[23]

The organization of trade under socialism was extremely concentrated, relative to the dispersed structure of this branch of a capitalist economy. Despite the desire of central planners to hoard decision-making powers as much as possible, however, the technical infeasibility of centralization in trade meant that a wide variety of agents, from top-level political decision-makers down to the level of shops, participated in allocation decisions.

[23] We are indebted to Emanuel Sip for much of the information in this section.

Figure I.A.1 depicts these agents and some of the important relationships among them in the Czech Republic around the mid-1980s.[24] The three columns, below the level of the planning commissions, represent the three important channels for goods to consumers: state trade, organized under the Ministry of Trade; "other state trade," organized under production ministries; and cooperative trade, organized under the Union of Consumer Cooperatives. As discussed in the previous section, the division of labor among these three organizations was partly functional, partly geographic. Certain goods (e.g., automobiles, gasoline, books, newspapers, coal, and furniture) were supplied directly by production ministries to their own outlets, while others were allocated to the Ministry of Trade and the Union of Consumer Cooperatives. For simplicity, the diagram places all production ministries in a single column, although some of them had their own subordinated shops, while others supplied state and cooperative trade. The division between the Trade Ministry and the Cooperatives Union was largely along geographic lines, with the former dominant in urban areas and the latter dominant in rural areas.

The diagram shows the "vertical" and "horizontal" command, co-ordination, and bargaining relationships, as well as the flows of goods, among the various organizations.[25] The command relationships included directions of varying precision from higher levels, including specific orders in physical units, somewhat vaguer aggregations in financial terms (for instance for turnover or profits), and rather less exact "guidelines" for the lower levels to follow. Indeed, all sets of targets combined "soft" with "hard" elements. In the other direction, from bottom to top, was supposed to come information, proposals, and appeals.

Starting from the top, political leaders established aggregate targets for the economy in the Five Year Plan. The party organs, the ultimate loci of power, were closely intertwined with the government and the

[24] To a large extent, this analysis holds for most of the communist period. Although there were some re-organizations of the structure of the trade sector, mostly focused on the intermediate units between the ministries and the enterprises, they affect little of the essence of what follows. The minor developments towards the end of the 1980s are discussed in section 5 below.

[25] The "vertical" versus "horizontal" metaphor is commonly employed in discussions of socialist economy, but must be distinguished from the use of these terms in industrial organization literature.

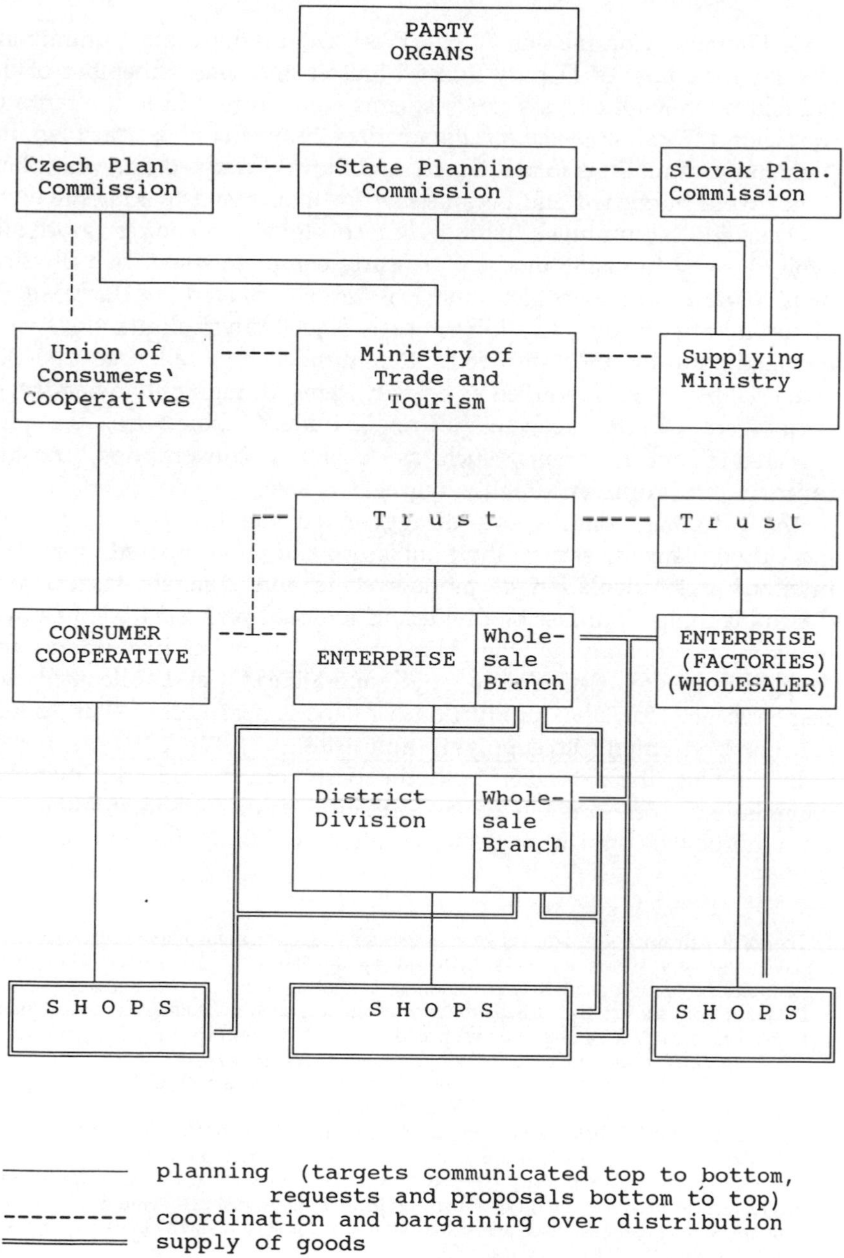

Figure I.A.1 Organization of allocation in trade in the Czech Republic (ca. 1985)

State Planning Commission.[26] The President of the State Commission also held the post of Deputy Prime Minister and was a member of the Politburo, while all of his Vice-Presidents were chosen from the ranks of the Central Committee *nomenklatura* cadres. From the Five Year Plan, the planning commissions (State, Czech, and Slovak) derived one-year plans which were published and became law for their respective jurisdictions.

Over the communist period, Czechoslovak planning gradually evolved away from the model of a nearly completely specified physical plan toward one in which financial targets played an increasingly important role. In the early 1950s, nearly 50,000 physical quantities were specified, but by the late 1980s, the number had fallen to 200–300 "material balances" identified as priority items, though only a handful of these were directly relevant to retail trade.[27] Otherwise, the plan specified financial targets, such as levels of consumption, income, revenue and profits at a highly aggregated level.

The planning commissions disaggregated the one-year plans into individual plans for each of their ministries and subordinated units. This involved the articulation of more specific and concrete targets. The Czech Planning Commission divided its national plan for trade turnover between instructions to the Ministry of Trade and Tourism and "suggestions" to the Union of Cooperatives,[28] and allocated the responsibility for the production of goods earmarked for public consumption among its supplying ministries.

In defining these targets, both the party organs and the planning commissions were influenced by pressures from public opinion and from particular branch or sectoral interests. Public opinion was not

[26] The formal distinction made between government agencies and party organs does not reflect the very strong influence exercised by the latter on the former. Though the examples of connections between personnel in the highest party organs and the State Planning Commission are perhaps the most dramatic, such interrelations were standard in all organizations of any importance. Nearly all nongovernmental organizations, including enterprises and cooperatives, included party groups, whose responsibility it was to ensure that the "party line" was followed in every aspect of the organization's activity.

[27] As discussed further below, these included both "hard" and "soft" targets: of the total, only approximately 50–100 were really obligatory, though on paper they were all represented with equal priority. The physical targets relevant in the retail trade sector included meat products, poultry, clothes, underwear, leather shoes, cement, construction material, stone pipelines, black and brown coal, briquettes, and coke. Some imports were also precisely planned in physical units.

[28] Due to the pervasive influence of the Communist Party and the nearly exclusive control of the state sector over supply, the "suggestions" to the Cooperatives' Union hardly differed in practice from the "commands" to the Ministry of Trade.

usually a decisive force, but there were exceptions, for instance during times of severe shortage when planners might be compelled by political considerations to divert resources from other sectors of the economy into retail trade, perhaps even creating explicit targets for the goods in short supply.[29] The struggle among what we may call "branch lobbies" composed of ministries and enterprises from all sectors of the economy (industrial, agricultural, and military), on the other hand, usually worked to the disadvantage of retail trade, and of consumer goods more generally. Investment hunger, labor and resource shortage, and soft budgets encouraged these lobbies to apply constant pressure on planning commissions and party organs. The ideological favor toward industrial sectors of the economy left the retail trade lobby considerably weaker than its competitors, and it usually lost battles of this sort.

The retail trade plan received by the Ministry of Internal Trade and Tourism contained "orientation targets" for aggregate turnover and profit, compulsory targets in physical quantities of a few specific goods, and compulsory limits on investment, materials usage, employment, wages, and training. But it was also accompanied by much more specific "guidelines" on the plan's implementation. Within the framework given by these guidelines, the Ministry divided the targets by commodity group into separate figures for each of the five trusts, three branch enterprises, and all other enterprises directly controlled by the Ministry.[30] The turnover and profit targets became compulsory at this level, and orientation targets for transportation facilities, health and safety improvements, and technological progress were added. The Ministry also coordinated the allocation of responsibilities with the actions planned by the Union of Cooperatives and the supplying ministries.

The trusts or other intermediate organs then disaggregated the plan regionally among their subordinated enterprises. Until 1988, trade

[29] Although the Czech political system under socialism did not distinguish itself from other communist systems by any particularly greater responsiveness to public demands, it did make reference to improvements in standards of living as one of its goals. Political careers within the Communist Party could be decisively influenced by success or failure on this score.

[30] The "branch enterprises," discussed in section 3 above, functioned essentially identically to the trusts. Thus, nearly everything that follows may also be applied to them. The only exception worth noting is that the shoe, furniture, and jewelry retailers under this category did not employ district divisions. The Ministry of Trade also provided guidelines to the local restaurant enterprises and regulated their activities, for instance with a published volume called *Recipes for Warm Dishes*, which ensured the uniformity of taste and portion size across restaurants.

enterprises received about fifty indicators, including revenues, costs, profit, turnover, employment, new investment, and number of apprentices, together with a number of guidelines. The targets were furthered disaggregated by the enterprises among their wholesale units, district divisions (and their wholesale units), and shops. Shops received a turnover target plus ceilings on materials usage, wages, and employment.

Although in theory most orders flowing down the chain were supposed to be compulsory, in practice they were often subject to negotiation. The agencies receiving these commands very often bargained with their superiors over the precise volume and composition of the trade for which they were responsible, suggesting reductions and alternatives in the process. The importance of pure commands was diminished and the bargaining power of upper levels in the hierarchy was weakened by the asymmetric distribution and general distortion of information, which gave lower level agencies discretion over many decisions and the ability to manipulate outcomes to their own advantage.[31]

Furthermore, although there was a formal division of authority from top to bottom of the vertical hierarchies, it was impractical for the higher levels to plan every last detail, and decisions were often made at levels lower than the formal responsibilities dictated. Such decentralization was tacitly permitted in normal times, but periodically retracted in moments of crisis when the lower levels were criticized for overstepping their competencies.

The result was that, at all levels of the hierarchy, some of the targets were indeed obligatory, in the sense that the "party line" gave them real priority and their achievement would be strictly monitored. But failure to meet others might be overlooked, or they might be negotiable. Still others were critical, but remained unstated or as mere hints in the formal instructions, for instance that imported fruit should be delivered directly to Party demonstrations or congresses. The distinction between merely nominal targets and those which were genuinely compulsory was nowhere made explicit, though any talented apparatchik made it her or his business to learn the priorities of her or his superiors.

Indeed, it was a notable feature of this system that the basic incentives

[31] This is a standard argument about centrally planned economies, for instance in M. Mejstřík and J. Hlaváček, "Preconditions for Privatization in Czechoslovakia in 1990–92", in J. Earle, R. Frydman, and A. Rapaczynski (eds), *Privatization in the Transition to a Market Economy*, Pinter Publishers (London), 1993, and in Kornai, *The Socialist System*.

in the relationships between adjacent levels shared consistent features regardless of their absolute position in the hierarchy: the planning committee had essentially the same relationship with a branch ministry as a trust had with its subordinate enterprise. Even within the trade enterprise (a legal person which included a central management, district divisions, and shops), bargaining among levels had the same features as bargaining between independent legal persons.[32] Each had strong incentives to distort information systematically when communicating with the level above and below it. Communications with superiors were characterized by deliberate under-estimation of performance capacity; those with subordinates, with conscious exaggeration of the urgency of fulfilling targets.

4.2. Supply and distribution of goods

The vertical hierarchies represented by the Ministry of Trade and the Union of Consumer Cooperatives were also engaged in horizontal relationships with supplying ministries and enterprises, as shown in Figure I.A.1, above. The Ministry of Trade was responsible for the coordination of the distribution of priority goods, the targets for which often had been calculated in physical terms and included instructions specifying from which ministry (and later down the hierarchy, which trust and which producing enterprise) that good should be obtained. The supply of other goods was organized by horizontal relationships between corresponding hierarchical levels. For instance, trusts under the Ministry of Trade would identify which of its trade enterprises should be responsible for fulfilling the different parts of its target and would negotiate supply contracts with industrial trusts.

Retail trade enterprises were responsible for matching their plan turnover requirements with sufficient supplies of goods produced by supplying enterprises (or their wholesale divisions). Quarterly contracts were signed for deliveries of the specified quantities, qualities, and assortments of goods. In negotiating these contracts, however, retail trade enterprises had only minimal degrees of choice, since the

[32] Kornai (*The Socialist System*) makes this observation for the industrial hierarchy. A related notion is that the "boundaries of the firm" were essentially meaningless under socialism. See J. Zieleniec, "Microeconomic Categories in Different Economic Systems: The Firm", in R. Quandt and D. Triska (eds), *Optimal Decisions in Markets and Planned Economies*, Westview Press (Boulder), 1990, for an interesting discussion.

foundation for these contractual agreements had already been established through negotiations between trusts, and the options which supplying enterprises could offer were, to a great extent, prescribed by external conditions: supplies of inputs, past investments in assortment and quality, and demands from other enterprises on their production capacity.

Furthermore, most of the options available to retail trade enterprise managers were functions of the organization and composition of retail trade in previous years. To calculate targets for the one-year plan, planning agents at all levels applied growth coefficients (supposedly based on expectations of increased productivity to the previous year's "achievements.")[33] In much the same way, relationships between retail trade and manufacturing enterprises were based on past relationships. The planners' desire to economize on the complexities of planning, coupled with the disincentives for product variation inherent in socialist managed industry, also greatly inhibited growth in the assortment of consumer goods. This further limited the options from which retail trade organizations could choose.

Given the circumscribed choices faced by both parties, it is interesting to ponder the functions of the written contracts through which all horizontal transactions with suppliers were established. In some ways, they seem to have been similar to explicit contracts in a capitalist economy, where their primary function is to create enforceable expectations of future behavior. All contracts, for instance, included special clauses stipulating penalties to be paid if the terms of the delivery agreement were violated.[34] Contract disputes were brought before an arbitrator or communicated to the relevant trusts and ministries, which .would then take appropriate steps to solve them. Contract regulations were issued by every branch ministry, and the body of law was so extensive that specialized arbitrators were required for each sector.

[33] This practice of "indexed planning" based on actual results of the previous plan period also created a "ratchet effect," whereby over-fulfilling the plan raised the next period's targets. The incentive effects were obviously negative and gave rise to self-protective behavior on the part of enterprise managers. For discussions of this subject in the Czech economy, see J. Hlavacek, "Homo se Assecurans," *Politicka Ekonomie*, No. 6, 1986.

[34] These could be of various types and were sometimes quite complicated due to competing and ever-changing objectives. For instance, if a producing enterprise received priority instructions to divert the supply of its goods away from the retail trade, thus disrupting deliveries to the retail trade enterprise with which it had a contractual agreement, it might dispute the validity of the clause requiring it to pay penalties.

But it is not clear that managerial incentives, particularly under the condition of a soft budget constraint, were often decisively influenced by the prospect of a fine, which would at most affect salaries through the bonuses which were tied to profits. Rather, contracts served foremost as formal documentation of responsibilities in a system in which avoidance of blame for malfunctions was uppermost in most managers' minds. Indeed, respecting formal contracts always yielded to more important priorities such as supplying the military and heavy industry, and the main criterion in the arbitration of contract disputes was plan fulfillment. If a trade enterprise could not reach its turnover goals because some of its supply had not been delivered, a signed contract could serve as evidence before the enterprise manager's superiors that he/she was not to blame for malfunctions or shortages resulting from the enterprise's non-performance.

It is, therefore, difficult to assess the degrees of freedom possessed by retail trade enterprise managers in negotiating contracts with suppliers and distributing goods. But that there existed incentives to pursue particular outcomes is not in doubt. To start, the power to allocate goods across wholesale units and shops – not to mention on a discretionary, individual basis – could be quite lucrative. For this reason, enterprise managers had strong incentives to bargain with their production counterparts for a product assortment with a higher average price (as long as they could be sold), better quality, or greater degree of shortage. Not only would this make it easier to meet the turnover target,[35] but it also created stronger possibilities of eliciting any of a vast array of different types of favors or methods of compensation. The retail trade managers' subordinates were also interested in obtaining a higher proportion of shortage, high quality, or high price goods, and they were usually willing to "pay" for it. Thus, there was a chain of negotiations from factory to shop, or better, a web of haggling, once the participation of various upper levels and the numerous possibilities for horizontal arrangements and side-deals had been exploited. People in control of the movement of consumer goods were among the most influential members of Czech socialist society.[36]

The length of the wholesale chain, and thus the scope for various

[35] As discussed in subsection 4.5 below, fulfillment of targets and plan directives was rewarded with bonuses at all levels of the distribution hierarchy.

[36] This is perhaps most true for managers of industrial monopolies, especially of those which produced shortage goods. None the less, it applies to trade enterprise managers as well.

participants to share in rents, depended on the kind of goods being distributed. Consumer durables, such as appliances, shoes, and clothing, passed through only one level of wholesale distribution before they were distributed to shops: from the production enterprise, to the wholesale branch of the trade enterprise, to the shop. However, in other cases, for instance hand tools, building materials, and books, shipments were sent first to the wholesale unit of the producing trust, then to the wholesale branch of the retail trade enterprise, and only then to the shop.

The distribution of food followed a somewhat different pattern. Stored foodstuffs like flour, oil, sugar, and canned goods, were delivered from the manufacturer to the wholesale branch of the district division of the retail trade enterprise, then to the shop. On the other hand, perishables were typically delivered from the enterprise or farm directly to the shop. Factors that may account for these variations in wholesale organization include the concentration of production, the presence of scale economies in warehousing, and the perishability of goods.

The lower an agent was in the distribution hierarchy, of course, the less the bargaining power and influence over the assortment, quality, or quantity of the goods they received. The strength of the trust's bargaining position was greater than that of the wholesale unit, since the degree to which other units in the distribution network depended on trusts was greater than the degree to which other units depended on wholesalers. But all levels had avenues for participation in the second economy. Even shops, which were simply administrative extensions of enterprise wholesale operations and for the most part engaged in no official negotiations, had many opportunities. Although they exercised little control over which goods would be delivered to them or which goods they would be required to sell, they had direct control over which goods their customers would have the opportunity to buy. "Under the counter" sales of shortage goods for higher than official prices, exchange of shortage goods with other stores, and outright pilfering, all helped to supplement the typically below average wages in retail trade.[37]

Although most shops had little room to manipulate their allocation of goods, shops which sold perishable goods and received their supplies directly from producers were responsible for establishing contracts and agreements directly with supplying enterprises or farms.

[37] Some Czech party and planning officials are said to have observed that there was no need to increase the wages of retail shop employees, since they managed to compensate themselves so well through shadow activities.

Skillful negotiation of these contracts and a wide portfolio of personal connections could enable a shopkeeper to obtain supplies of better quality and assortment. Likewise, the managers and employees of such shops had even greater access and opportunity to profit from extralegal, entrepreneurial activity. For instance, unpackaged goods sold to the shop as second class (meat, for instance) would be sold by the shop for first class prices, the profits going to the manager and employees. It was also common to sell smaller portions for full portion prices.[38]

These interdependent connections in the chain of the planning and administration of the allocation of goods distributed decision-making powers throughout the hierarchy. Although, as we have emphasized, many important allocation decisions were determined by bargaining, to some degree each agent was confined to making decisions left to it by the enterprise or wholesaler supplying it with goods. Thus, each level lost some of the options available to the level above it. The last arm of this network, the shop, had very little influence over quantity, assortment, and quality, and played virtually no role in determining the sources from which it received goods. Nor did it have much control over many of the other factors which affect shop performance. Retail and wholesale prices, capital investment, employment levels, and very narrow wage ranges were all dictated by state planning bodies who, in turn, were constrained by the general conditions of shortage economy.

4.3. Determination of prices and consumer credit

In communist Czechoslovakia, prices for virtually all consumer goods were administratively set by Price Bureaus.[39] In consultation with the federal government and the party Politburo, the Federal Price Bureau determined the prices of the most important (e.g. priority) agricultural and industrial products, for instance meat, bread, and automobiles. The Czech Price Bureau was responsible for setting prices of other less important consumer goods. For many commodities, prices were set

[38] According to contemporary newspaper accounts, between 40 and 60 percent of control checks by the Trade Inspection Agency found violations involving cheating of customers. Selling reduced portions for the full price was especially common in eating and drinking places. It is said, for example, that a skillful waiter in a *pivnice* (beer bar) was able to produce 120 half-liter glasses of beer out of a 50 liter barrel of beer.

[39] Those prices which were not administratively set are discussed in section 5, below.

during the first five-year plan in the early 1950s. The basic principle of price determination was to mark up costs by a percentage which varied according to the type of good.

The Price Bureaus were assisted with their work by ministries, trusts, and various other agencies. Production ministries monitored price development and discussed proposals for price changes, referring them up to the Czech Bureau. Under the supervision of their ministries, production trusts collected data necessary for price setting calculations (for instance, on the costs of production) from the enterprises below them. They also maintained lists of prices for goods whose production was under their administration and submitted proposals for price changes to their ministries. The price bureaus edited, printed, and distributed the price lists compiled by production trusts, while the trade trusts edited consumer price lists according to their commodity specialization. Finally, the Czech Trade Inspection Agency was responsible for price and quality control.

Neither retail trade nor production enterprises had any direct influence over prices, though they did negotiate and lobby with their trusts for price changes. As discussed in section II, production enterprises were able to employ indirect methods of effecting price increases. For instance, they might over-estimate the cost (and the benefit) of introducing some minor innovation in one of their products, and appeal for a larger price increase than would have been warranted based on the true cost. They could also lower the quality of the goods they had been producing, without adjusting the prices charged for them. Enterprises often resorted to methods of this kind because Price Bureaus were generally reluctant to adjust prices and seldom considered market clearing as a criterion when setting prices.[40] When prices were adjusted, the motivation was frequently macroeconomic not microeconomic.

The fixed-price policy dated to the 1950s, when communist leaders actually promised a general decline in prices, in sharp contrast to the supposedly typical inflation of the capitalist world. But despite the fact that it was politically troublesome, the Bureaus did at times increase the prices of some commodities, for instance gasoline, beer, cigarettes, liquor, and meat. Table I.A.14 traces the prices of some commodities since 1977.

Retail trade enterprises also had some ways of influencing price changes, though they were quite cumbersome. A Decree of the Ministry

[40] See subsection 4.4 for a discussion of other, more common, adjustment methods.

Table I.A.14 Prices of selected goods in the Czech Republic (Csk)*

Year	Pork (1 kg)	Beef (1 kg)	Wheat Flour (1 kg)	Gasoline (1 liter)	Bicycle (per unit)
1977	30	29	3.2	4.3	820
1978	30	29	3.2	4.3	820
1979	30	29	3.2	6.5	820
1980	30	29	3.2	6.5	1,100
1981	30	29	3.2	8.0	1,100
1982	46	46	3.2	8.0	1,100
1983	46	46	3.2	8.0	1,100
1984	46	46	3.2	8.0	1,100
1985	46	46	3.2	8.0	1,100
1986	46	46	3.2	8.0	1,100
1987	46	46	3.2	8.0	1,100
1988	46	46	4.2	8.0	1,530
1989	46	46	4.2	8.0	1,530
1990	50	60	4.8	16.0	2,058
1991	74	64	6.2	16.0	3,712
1992				16.0	

Sources: *Statistical Yearbook of CSFR 1992*, SNTL-ALFA (Prague), pp. 267, 269; *Statistical Yearbook of CSSR 1988*, SNTL-ALFA (Prague), pp. 260, 262; *Historical Yearbook of CSSR*, SNTL-ALFA (Prague), pp. 204, 208, 1985.

* The data for 1977–90 pertain also to Czechoslovakia as a whole, because prices varied geographically and therefore differed between the Czech and Slovak Republics only after the price liberalization of January 1, 1991. Until then, there was no geographic variation in prices.

of Internal Trade from March 10, 1986, for instance, established a complicated procedure by which the prices of goods in surplus could be lowered. No price reductions were permitted until at least one year after the commodity had been delivered to the shop, and two years if it had been imported for hard currency. Before receiving permission for the decrease, the retail trade enterprise in charge of selling the goods was required to prove that the following measures had been taken to try to sell the goods at prevailing prices:[41]

[41] The Decree spells these measures out in no more detail than provided here.

- take measures to increase sales;
- introduce special incentives (bonuses) for the sales staff to stimulate sales;
- try to sell the commodity to a "socialist organization" for the original price;[42]
- concentrate the commodity into a limited number of shops;
- export the commodity (to COMECON countries);
- other, unspecified measures.

Only when all of these measures had failed was it possible to obtain permission to decrease the price of the commodity.

Prices could also be implicitly adjusted through credit policy. Credit was rarely provided in cash, carried a very high interest rate (several times that for non-cash), and was given only for some narrowly defined purposes. The Czech Savings Bank maintained a frequently-changing list of commodities available on credit: imported and shortage commodities were not included. The list defined, for instance, the precise makes, models, and years of cars for which credits were available.[43]

4.4. Adjustment to shortages and shocks

Even if under stable conditions the retail trade sector in the socialist Czech Republic had been able to function relatively well in meeting most of the citizenry's basic needs, how the system adapted to exogenous changes – in tastes, technology, and foreign trade prices, for instance – is worth further consideration. Claims of "global equilibrium" notwithstanding, there were shortages of many individual consumer goods in the Czech socialist economy. These shortages became particularly pronounced following shocks, because of the system's inability to process information about problems and respond to malfunctions accurately and quickly. There existed no automatic feedback or adjustment mechanisms of the kinds present in market economies to eliminate short-run shortages or to prompt the system to adapt to long-run trends. There was very little entry into and essentially no exit from the trade

[42] This was an example of an explicit order to exploit the soft budget constraint and "suction principle" of socialist organizations.

[43] At the end of 1987, it was possible to obtain 100 percent credit for the Skoda 1987 model 105L, all 1986 Skoda models, and Dacia models 105L and 120L. However, only 60 percent credit was available for the latest Skoda model produced in 1987.

sector, perhaps the most important adjustment mechanisms in trade in a market economy. The business units in socialist trade generally constituted a stagnant pool with neither the ability nor the incentives to improve themselves.

Indeed, "central planning" was able to solve smaller and shorter-term problems largely only insofar as the planning itself was incomplete; agents at lower levels of the hierarchy retained some limited flexibility to adapt to changes.[44] And the feasibility of responses to larger and longer-term malfunctions depended solely on the ability and incentives of planners to perceive the problems and alter their plans. As discussed briefly in section 2, planners did have some political motivations to ameliorate shortage problems. This section provides evidence on shortages, and discusses the adjustments made by consumers and the techniques available to policymakers to respond to these shortages.

More important than the paltry contribution to adjustment made by central planners and the inadequacies of adjustment by the retail trade sector were adaptations by consumers. In Kornai's terminology, "shortage phenomena" refer to a wide variety of consumer responses to the lack of goods at given prices. These adjustments include queuing, search, "forced substitution," and "forced saving." To these may be added self-production, travel abroad, shopping at special "Tuzex" stores,[45] and the use of shadow economy, or black market channels to obtain goods in shortage. The evidence on "global equilibrium" examined in section 2.3 above indicates only that forced saving appears to have been relatively insignificant in the Czech economy. On the other hand, it says nothing about the prevalence of other shortage phenomena.

Various indicators may be employed to measure degrees of relative shortage. For instance, input inventories in manufacturing are likely to be inversely related to the reliability of supplies. By this measure, the Czechoslovak economy ranked first among five East European countries,[46] but still performed much worse than capitalist economies.

[44] For instance, supplier–distributor contracts (as most others) were often determined as a simple proportionate increase over the contract of the previous period. But in case of some external shock to supplies, the contract negotiations could have a different outcome.

[45] Tuzex stores carried imported and luxury goods; consumers could make purchases using either hard currency or "Tuzex crowns," in which the salaries of people working abroad or receiving official payments from the West were partially paid.

[46] The others were Bulgaria, Hungary, Poland, and the Soviet Union. Kornai, *The Socialist System*, p. 250, contains the figures for these five, plus eleven capitalist countries.

Table I.A.15 Shortage indicators for some goods in the Czech Republic

Year	Tea	Cigarettes	Gasoline	Bicycles	Textiles	Food	Non-food
1976	+1	–4	+50	–86	–13	–3	–6
1977	–9	–9	+50	–82	–25	–9	–17
1978	–11	–18	+38	–73	–34	–5	–25
1979	–4	–11	+38	–37	–32	–4	–25
1980	–12	–3	+50	–86	–29	–6	–16
1981	–2	0	+50	–73	–21	–8	–12
1982	+18	+16	+75	–72	–21	–11	–10
1983	+25	+9	+50	–63	–21	+4	–8
1984	+14	+8	+50	–56	–20	+10	–8
1985	–20	+18	+50	–54	–23	+10	–7
1986	–24	+9					

Sources: J. Šlechtová, "Odvětvová sumarizace vyésledku konjunkturních testů za 4. čtvrtletí 1984", VÚO (Prague), 1985; J. Šlechtová, "Roční odvětvová sumarizace výsledků konjunkturních testů za rok 1987", VÚO (Prague), 1988.

Comparisons of waiting time for particular consumer durables can also indicate relative shortages. The waiting time for cars and telephones was relatively short in Czechoslovakia, while it was necessary to wait roughly the same amount of time for housing, as in other East European countries.[47]

Table I.A.15 presents disaggregated "Indices of Demand Satisfaction," based on the subjective evaluation of shopkeepers on the degree of the shortage of goods in their establishments according to a five-level scale.[48]

Consumption of alcohol in communist countries may be a classic case of forced substitution. It is sometimes speculated that a kind of ratchet effect was at work here: after a year or two of forced substitution, alcohol consumption became voluntary. As shown in Table I.A.16,

[47] See Kornai, *The Socialist System*.

[48] As described in subsection 2.3, "very unsatisfied demand" was assigned the value –100, "partly unsatisfied" the value –50, "partly satisfied" the value 0, "quite satisfied" the value 50, "quite satisfied, difficult to sell" the value 100. The optimum was considered to be a range of 0 to 50; and down to –25 was thought "bearable." The fact that such surveys were conducted in an effort to evaluate the performance of consumer goods supply is in itself interesting.

Table I.A.16 Shortage indicators for alcoholic beverages in CSFR

Year	Alcohol	Beer	Wine	Spirits
1976	0	+8	−18	0
1977	−5	+13	−17	−17
1978	0	+21	−17	−11
1979	+9	−6	+13	+23
1980	+3	−16	−6	+20
1981	−1	−9	−10	+9
1982	−23	−23	−5	+13
1983	+17	+6	+40	+30
1984	+19	+7	+13	+23
1985	+15	+26	+9	+14
1986	+18	+15	+27	+18

Sources: J. Šlechtová, "Odvětvová sumarizace výsledků konjunkturních testů za 4. čtvrtletí 1984", VÚO (Prague), 1985; J. Šlechtová, "Roční sumarizace výsledků konjunkturních testů za rok 1987", VÚO (Prague), 1988.

however, this hypothesis is not supported by the time series evidence on the shortage of various types of alcoholic beverages. Aside from wine in the late 1970s and beer at the beginning of the 1980s, there seem to have been consistent surpluses of alcoholic beverages.

It is difficult to evaluate how responsive Czech planners were to the presence of shortages in specific commodities. Analysis of indices of demand satisfaction at a very detailed commodity group level[49] indicates that some goods remained in shortage over periods of up to five years. Among them, tropical and dried fruit, underwear and stockings, furs, refrigerators and freezers, sewing machines, china and cooking utensils, consumer electronics, color televisions, paper products, cosmetics, motorcycles, and bicycles were in persistent, "unbearable" shortage over the five year period from 1983 to 1987. Other goods were consistently oversupplied. Still others moved in and out of shortage.

What tools did planners have to respond to shortages? The most obvious answer is price adjustment, but, as noted above, prices were not systematically adjusted to clear markets in communist Czechoslovakia. However, the planners did have some "power in shortage

[49] The classification is roughly equivalent to the four-digit commodity codes in the West. These unpublished data are from the VUO (Retail Trade Institute), now EKOMA.

redistribution."[50] They recognized that the domestic consumer market was only one of several possible sources for demand of consumer goods. The planners' priorities for the distribution of consumer goods were, first, to export to hard currency markets and/or to supply the population; next, to export to CMEA countries; and only as a last resort to supply the "socialist organizations" (including state companies, budgetary organizations, and cooperatives). But there was a continual struggle between central planners and enterprises engaged in the production and sale of consumer goods, because enterprises preferred most of all to supply large quantities of goods to "soft" markets.[51] The consumers with the "softest" budget constraints were socialist organizations, which also cared least about quality, while the hardest markets were those which bought for hard currency, with domestic consumers somewhere in the middle. CMEA demand for Czech goods was also fairly easy to satisfy, and offered an opportunity to get rid of substandard products which could have been sold only with difficulty on the domestic consumer market.

In this context, planners could partially redirect goods from exports into the domestic market and also among agents within the domestic market. This was accomplished by limiting the access of socialist organizations to consumer goods, through tough administrative regulations. This part of demand accounted for between 5 and 10 percent of trade turnover, and was gradually rising from the 1960s to the 1980s. Officially, they were permitted to buy up to only Csk 500 worth of goods per day on the consumer market, and purchases valued at more than Csk 500 could be made only by invoice. Moreover, there was a long list of consumer items which socialist organizations were altogether restricted from buying.

Planners also used this list of restricted items to regulate the supply of goods on the consumer market. If a given commodity was in short supply, it was added to the list, technically preventing socialist organizations from buying it. However, if there was excess supply of a

[50] Kornai, *The Socialist System*. More details of the following discussion may be found in Mládek, "Global Equilibrium on the Internal Market."

[51] It would be possible to say more about the motivations of enterprise managers in this regard. Perhaps the effort minimization model is the most persuasive: given that production, profit, and costs were planned, and that any overfulfillment of the plan was rewarded primarily by an increase in the plan target for the next plan period (the so-called "ratchet effect"), managers were most interested in selling to customers who would not complain about quality and would be soft in bargaining over the terms of supply.

Table I.A.17 Socialist organizations' share in trade turnover (yearly average, calculated from current prices)

Period	Socialist organizations' share in trade
1956–60	7.1%
1961–65	5.8%
1966–70	7.3%
1971–75	8.3%
1976–80	8.7%
1981–85	9.5%
1986	10.2%

Source: J. Mládek, "Selected Problems of Modelling Consumption in a CPE: The Case of Czechoslovakia 1955–1986," *Jahrbuch der Wirtschaft Osteuropas*, Vol. 13, No. 2, p. 196.

given good, socialist organizations were granted permission to buy it, a policy it was hoped would eliminate the excess supply.

4.5. Labor and wages

The plan goals of ever-higher production, coupled with soft budget constraints and uncertainty, created excess demand for all resources, including labor. In negotiations, subordinate levels typically overestimated their labor and wage bill needs, knowing in advance that their requests would probably not be fully satisfied. The plan therefore set labor and wage "quotas," limiting the number of employees and the size of the wage bill, that were disaggregated to subordinate levels of the administrative hierarchy. These quotas were strictly enforced, and could not be manipulated once they had been set in place. Concerning employment, managers of enterprises and shops thus had essentially no power to determine the number of workers, and were left only the authority to decide which applicants to hire and which employees to dismiss.

The determination of individual wage levels was quite complex, and for the most part also prescribed from above in the form of a Labor Codex. The Codex defined the basic structure of tariff wages according to the branch, occupation, responsibilities, and educational requirements of the job. The trade sector was one of the lowest paid. Enterprises had some flexibility within this tariff structure, however, in rewarding performance with 20 to 50 percent higher wages. It was also possible for the enterprise to award an additional 33 percent of the tariff wage (the so-called "personal wage") for outstanding performance during some particular time period. An additional payment, usually of the order of a few hundred Csk, could be received on the basis of a positive monthly "personal" evaluation. Overtime, late shift, night, weekend, and language skills premia were paid. Finally, the Codex allowed bonuses to be paid quarterly for meeting the turnover or other targets. Incentive pay thus existed, but it was outside the managers' power to manipulate this structure. Perhaps none of these various forms of pay, however, were as incentive intensive as the "fringe benefits" connected with shadow market activities.

4.6. Investment

Resources for investment were also strictly rationed in the socialist Czech Republic, due to the widespread "investment hunger" under central planning and soft budget constraints. Investment planning was highly centralized, and large projects (over Csk 100 mln) required ministry and government approval. Only some large department stores and wholesale stores were in this category, the trade sector was relatively disfavored in terms of investment resources, but smaller projects (over Csk 1.5 mln) required approval of the trust, and only very small ones were left to the enterprise.

In the case of newly developed housing (which was common in the Czech Republic, as it was throughout Eastern Europe), shops were often constructed together with the housing and then transferred to the appropriate retail trade enterprise. Municipalities also organized the construction of new shops, again transferring them thereafter to the retail trade enterprise.

Only small renovation projects (less than Csk 2 mln) could be determined by the enterprise.

5. LEGAL PRIVATE ACTIVITY AND PERESTROIKA IN RETAIL TRADE AND CONSUMER SERVICES

What remained of the sphere of legitimate private economic activity in communist Czechoslovakia was very small, tightly regulated, and limited exclusively to handicrafts, services, and retail trade in agricultural products. Although no legislation explicitly forbidding private enterprise was ever passed, virtually all private businesses were either nationalized or in other ways absorbed into the state and cooperative network during the late 1940s. In particular, small business owners were "encouraged" to donate their establishments to consumer cooperatives and municipal companies. Those who refused saw their businesses strangled by exorbitant tax rates and supply discrimination. Only in the 1980s did conditions for private enterprise begin to relax.

Before 1981, only cooperative farms (and a few other "socialist organizations") were permitted to sell their goods privately, directly to the public. "Private" farmers were compelled to sell their produce to cooperatives and state stores, at fixed prices. However, the passage of the Law on Internal Trade in 1981 (No. 127/1981 Coll.) established the right of private farmers to sell their produce to the public as well, for prices which, though not fixed, could not exceed prices for foodstuffs found in state and cooperative retail trade. Although difficult to enforce, it was strictly forbidden to sell goods produced by other farmers. Furthermore, these farmers were required to sell only "class A" goods, while in state and cooperative stores goods of several classes of quality could be sold.

The Law on Internal Trade also entitled craftsmen to sell their goods to the public. It stipulated somewhat more liberal regulations of their activities and prescribed no price limits for handicrafts. In fact, this is one of the very few examples of free pricing that existed in communist Czechoslovakia.[52] Nonetheless, other regulations limited their entrepreneurial freedoms: craftsmen could sell only goods made entirely by their own hands, and could employ no-one but themselves.

In July of 1987, under the pressure of Soviet *perestroika*, the Central Committee of the Czechoslovak Communist Party articulated its intention to encourage the development of small, private, service establishments. Thus, in January 1988, a decree of the Czech government No.1/1988 granted private citizens the right to provide services to the population under strictly defined conditions. A person engaging in such activity was required to obtain a license, could not employ people outside of his or her immediate family, and was obliged to set prices for services according to very cumbersome rules designed to align them

[52] Other examples include prices for souvenirs and for second-hand goods, though the latter could not exceed the price for which the good was bought originally.

Table I.A.18 Units providing services in the Czech Republic, 1989

	Number of units	Employment
State	2,612 (3.83%)	257,634 (58%)
Cooperatives	290 (0.43%)	123,625 (28%)
Private	65,202 (95.74%)	65,202 (14%)
Total	68,104	446,461

Source: *Statistical Yearbook of CSFR 1990*, SNTL-ALFA (Prague), pp. 517, 530, 577.

with those for services provided in the state and cooperative sectors. In addition to these regulations, prohibitive taxation further hindered the development of private service business. Incomes of entrepreneurs in the services sector which exceeded Csk 80,000 per year were taxed at rates that ranged between 70 percent and 80 percent.[53]

As shown in Table I.A.18, by 1989, 65,202 people in the Czech Republic were registered as providing services privately.[54] However, this figure includes part-time entrepreneurs, working in their spare time or holding multiple jobs, a point which supports the claim that legitimate private business was only a marginal phenomenon. It should be emphasized that "shadow" activities not included in official statistics represented the bulk of private entrepreneurial activity.[55]

The passage of Decree No. 1/1988 was by far the most progressive of all of the economic reforms initiated in Czechoslovakia under the influence of *perestroika*. The only other reform measure worth mentioning, established by Government Decree No. 176/1988, was the introduction of a new management system for the trade and services sector. The decree abolished the system of "trusts," placing the entire state retail trade network under the direct control of the Ministry of Trade and Tourism. Consequently, company headquarters were granted greater freedom to choose their suppliers, determine areas of specialization, and

[53] Taken from I. Ryglova and J. Schultz, "Souhlas Mam – A Co Dal?" ("I Agree – What Next?"), *Hospodarske Noviny*, No. 47, p. 7, 1988.
[54] *Statistical Yearbook of the CSFR 1990*, SNTL-ALFA (Prague), 1990, p. 577.
[55] Though employment in the second economy is not reflected in official figures, some part of its production is. For example, construction of private homes and estimates of consumption of home-grown produce is included in NMP as imputed numbers.

decide for themselves their regional spheres of activity. Finally, obligatory plan targets for these companies were reduced from fifty in 1987 to five in 1989.

Although these initiatives nominally represented a move toward decentralization and self-management, in fact they had little effect. Since prices remained strictly controlled and budgets remained "soft," managers had little incentive to improve the efficiency, profitability, or responsiveness of their distribution system, even under the new order of management. Not until the revolutionary changes of November 1989 did the Czech trade and service sector experience any significant reform.

B. PRIVATIZATION OF RETAIL TRADE AND CONSUMER SERVICES

1. INTRODUCTION

This section analyzes the various routes for the privatization of retail trade and service assets in the Czech Republic. Although the distinction is generally unappreciated, the privatization of this sector should by no means be identified exclusively with so-called "small privatization," a program of competitive auctions of individual establishments completed by the end of 1993. Not only did the small privatization program include some assets that cannot be classified as part of retail trade and consumer services, but much of the sector has and continues to be privatized through other programs and methods.

"Reprivatization," the restitution of expropriated property to former owners, has been quite important quantitatively. A significant segment of the sector is also included in the "large privatization" program, which applies voucher, direct sale, and other methods to privatize generally larger entities. Other state-owned capital in trade, largely wholesale assets and the remaining shells of former trade enterprises, is being liquidated. As discussed in Part A above, consumer cooperatives constituted a quite significant proportion of the sector before 1990; since then, they have been gradually divesting themselves of control over these assets, while the remaining cooperative establishments are experiencing a partial "transformation" of their governance and decision-making structures. Finally, the future of some of the state-owned assets, particularly in wholesale distribution, is not yet decided, but probably also destined for either the large privatization program or liquidation.[1]

The eventual division of state assets among the variety of methods may be understood as the outcome of the competition among three competing arguments, each put forward by a different interest group beginning in 1990. First, popular antipathy towards the former regime led to a movement to compensate victims of nationalization and

[1] In the Czech Republic, as in other post-socialist countries, there was no doubt also some amount of "spontaneous privatization," whereby enterprise managers sold or transferred assets to the private sector and/or out of state control. The most blatant transactions were forbidden after March 1991, but it is speculated that a large number of assets may have been sold until that date. Quantitative data are naturally lacking.

expropriation. Beginning with the return of some monasteries to the Catholic Church, the subsequent extension of the restitution program (to include any physical property formerly owned by any Czechoslovak citizen) had particular significance for the retail trade and service sector, inasmuch as most commercial premises in city centers existed and had been privately owned prior to their nationalization in the late 1940s and 1950s. Although restitution may appear simple in principle, there were many debates over which kinds of assets were to be covered and over which former owners would be eligible. Because reprivatization had legal precedence with respect to other methods, the difficulties in re-establishing ownership rights, which had often become muddled over time, affected privatization throughout the sector.

Second, the sector's "insiders," including Ministry of Trade officials and enterprise managers, favored gradual decentralization and privatization of the existing structures with little reorganization and disintegration of retail trade enterprises. They proposed leasing arrangements for some establishments and the re-organization of the rest into new companies along the lines of the former district divisions. These proposals can be regarded either as attempts by retail trade officials and enterprise insiders to maintain control of their valuable empires, or as "technocratic" arguments based on the experience and knowledge of "experts" and "specialists."

Third, reformers who had just come to power, for instance in the Ministry of Privatization, supported rapid privatization of individual retail trade units with few or no preferences for insiders. This policy was consistent with what became the predominant component of the Czechoslovak approach to privatization more generally: to break the monopoly of the *nomenklatura* and create a new class of small-scale entrepreneurs who would therefore support the reform program and the new government.

From an economic viewpoint, each of the three approaches had advantages and disadvantages, which were to some degree also reflected in the political debates over the appropriate priorities.[2] Restitution had

2 Of course, this description oversimplifies the political forces at work in 1990, as well as later. Naturally, attitudes concerning restitution could be independent of positions on the insider/outsider issue, and in practice the groups of proponents overlapped to a considerable degree. The emergence of distinct party programs really came only later, after the restitution program was firmly in place and widely accepted, and the power of the Ministry of Trade and enterprise insiders had already been broken. Our purpose is not to provide a complete history of the intellectual debates and political struggles over these policies (although this would be an interesting undertaking), but to relate the key outcomes of privatization in the sector to the prominent ideas of the early reform period.

the advantage of strong public support, which created an opportunity to effect quick transfers in those cases where ownership titles were transparent. But it also met objections, to which we have already alluded, concerning the problems associated with defining the boundaries of coverage and eligibility and with establishing clear property rights of former owners. These difficulties both delayed the introduction of other methods and altered the set of assets that could be privatized through other means. For instance, the possibility that a building would be reprivatized left only the business it housed, the equipment, and the inventory to be sold through the small privatization program, while only a lease would be granted on the premises.

The debate between the second and third lines of argument, what we may term the "insider/outsider debate," turns on much more than simple self-interest, concerning additionally the issues of whether shops should be privatized singly or in chains, whether retail should be separated from wholesale trade, and what should be done with accumulated financial liabilities and other obligations.[3] Ministry of Trade officials pointed out that chains and large stores account for a significant proportion of retail turnover in the West, employing the implicit argument that substantial scale economies exist in supply networks, and that vertical integration would be the best solution to the problem of many small shops confronting monopolistic wholesalers. On the other hand, it could be contended that retail trade in the West also began with independent, individual units, that horizontal and/or vertical integration would develop naturally if it were efficient, and that the political and economic monopolies of the *nomenklatura* could be broken only by granting each citizen an equal opportunity. The debt and obligations issue was still more complicated: legally they were the responsibility of the enterprise and could not easily be allocated among the enterprise sub-units, nor could they simply be written off.

The composition of methods eventually applied to privatize the sector can be understood as the outcome of a process in which these competing arguments and interests contended. In addition to enterprise managers, restituents, and Privatization and Trade Ministry officials, various interest groups attempting to influence asset transfers emerged during the process. Among them were a variety of potential new owners: entrepreneurs, foreigners, and shop managers and workers. The keenest

[3] Thus, a more appropriate characterization of the insider/outsider debate (certainly from the insider point of view) might rather be "technocratic/ideological."

competition for control over assets in the sector was between the new entrepreneurs and the sector insiders, each representing a distinct political constituency.

From the beginning, the insiders identified their interests in the retention of control over large supply networks and chains of stores, which they hoped to accomplish by transforming their enterprises in fact into joint stock companies that they could control. However, they were blocked by a series of four somewhat independent developments. First, the movement for restitution gathered great force over 1990, and the laws which were enacted made plain the possibility that any enterprise assets, particularly retail units, were vulnerable to reprivatization. For enterprise insiders, it thus became unclear which assets would remain to provide the basis for corporatization.

Second, public debate on the design of the small privatization program became heated in the summer of 1990. Backed by the new President, Václav Havel, insiders pressed both for special preferences and for preserving chains of shops, and they threatened strikes if their demands were not met. Fed by resentment over the poor performance of the consumer sectors in the past, however, the general public had little sympathy for the insiders' plight, and newspapers campaigned against insider preferences. Consequently, the Parliament enacted a program that allowed anyone to propose any asset for sale by auction and granted no preferences to insiders.[4] Coming in the Fall 1990, early in the overall privatization process, this precedent-setting decision was portentous for the complete absence of insider preferences enacted in the subsequent large privatization program, thereby distinguishing the "equal-opportunity" path of privatization in Czechoslovakia from the substantial preferences and advantages received by insiders in all the other post-socialist countries of Eastern Europe.

The third development was the actual beginning of the small privatization program in January 1991. It quickly became apparent that the Privatization Ministry, which had the ultimate authority on decisions concerning inclusion of assets in the program, supported privatizing as much property as rapidly as possible. The policy of "privatization for its

[4] Insiders, of course, were not prohibited from participating in the small privatization program. The results of our establishment survey, discussed in Part IV below, indicate that about half the small privatization auctions were, in fact, won by former shop employees. Although we have no data on the extent to which former Ministry of Trade officials or enterprise managers became new owners, it seems that insiders may have been able to use their informational advantages to retain some of their former control.

own sake" paid little heed to "technocratic" arguments and tended to favor quick approval of the small privatization proposals.[5] This once again placed enterprise assets in jeopardy from the standpoint of insiders, and they responded by attempting to manipulate the outcome of the program as much as possible in order to salvage the best shops within the enterprise for themselves and only allow the less profitable ones to be included in the small privatization program.

Finally, some of the enterprise remnants that survived the onslaughts of restitution and small privatization were corporatized, for inclusion in the large privatization program. Enterprise managers anticipated that they could none the less maintain control of their companies if the predominant method of transfer was to be voucher privatization.[6] They hoped that this "mass privatization" method would produce a large number of small shareholders unable to exercise effective governance. But the situation was drastically altered by the greater opportunity given to outsiders in late 1991 to submit "competing projects" to the "basic projects" that had been submitted by the managers and by the outsiders' alacritous response. As a result, direct sales of smaller enterprises and of assets to entrepreneurs became more important and vouchers became less important than originally envisaged, implying a correspondingly higher ownership concentration. Furthermore, the astonishing success of Investment Privatization Funds in early 1992, which in total attracted 72 percent of all voucher points, promised to create a less dispersed share ownership structure and therefore increased possibilities for effective control, even through voucher privatization.

It was according to these processes that state-owned trade and service assets have been allocated among the principal methods of privatization restitution, small privatization, and large privatization, while most remaining state-owned assets are undergoing liquidation. In addition, cooperative establishments have undergone transformation and divestment. Data on the results of some of these processes are incomplete, but we attempt here to estimate the number of establishments involved in each.

[5] Any asset was fair game to be proposed for small privatization until the Ministry of Privatization gave final approval to a large privatization project containing that asset. In 1992, the Ministry partially reversed its priorities to increase the supply of assets to the voucher program. See section 4 below, for a detailed discussion of this process.

[6] They may also have attempted to arrange sweetheart deals with outside investors, or even to acquire the assets directly themselves, but such possibilities were constrained by the requirement for approval from the Ministry of Privatization.

Table I.B.1 Trade and service establishments in the Czech Republic at December 31, 1989

Type of establishment	State	Coop.	Total
Retail trade	26,905	16,876	43,781
Food	10,580	4,290	14,870
Mixed	400	8,029	8,429
Non-food	12,220	2,525	14,745
Department stores	53	762	815
Kiosks	3,216	307	3,523
Others	436	963	1,399
Restaurants and bars	10,105	9,374	19,479
Lodging	–	–	2,863
Boarding houses	–	–	1,353
Hotels and motels	–	–	860
Camps	–	–	650
Municipal service units	2,088	–	2,088
Total	39,038*	26,250	68,211†

Sources: "Ukazatele v maloobchode", ECOMA (Prague), mimeo, 1993; *Statistical Yearbook of CSFR 1990*, SNTL-ALFA (Prague), pp. 515, 517 and 534.

* This figure and the total for cooperatives do not include hotels, motels, pensions, and camps, since the available data allow no breakdown of this category by ownership.
† Unlike the totals for state and cooperatives separately, this total includes hotels, motels, boarding houses and camps.

Table I.B.1 shows the composition of the sector at the end of 1989, as described in section 3 of Part A. A total of 43,781 retail trade establishments and 19,479 catering units existed in the Czech Republic on December 31, 1989. There were 2,088 services units under municipalities and 2,863 included in the category of "hotels, motels, boarding houses, and camps." The data for this latter category do not permit the classification of these units by ownership. Moreover, it is impossible to count the total number of services units existing at the time, due to the integration of services into larger enterprises conducting other activities.

Leaving aside the cooperatives, it is also not possible to obtain a complete and precise breakdown of the methods applied to the total 39,038 to 41,961 countable establishments under state control. Assuming an approximate total of 40,000, Table I.B.2 displays quantitative estimates of the relative importance of different methods. Between

Table I.B.2 Estimated division of state-owned trade and service establishments according to method of privatization

Method	Number of establishments
Restitution	13,500–16,500
Small privatization	23,500
Large privatization	2,000
Liquidation	0–3,000
Total	41,000

Note: Estimates are authors'. Liquidation is calculated as a residual.

13,500 and 16,500 retail trade and services properties were reprivatized, as described in section 2 below, but complete data are not available. The small privatization program, analyzed in section 3, included about 23,500 establishments from this sector, while we estimate roughly 2,300 in the large privatization program, described in section 4. Again there are no complete records. An indeterminate number of remaining units is likely to be liquidated or will be privatized later in the large privatization program. It bears emphasis that each of these privatization methods/programs also included a variety of other assets (outside the trade and services sectors), which we will explain further below.

Regarding cooperatives, there were approximately 26,250 establishments in trade and catering in 1989, plus some hotels and motels, but the exact number of cooperatives in the latter category is not known. Of the total number, about 3,500 were reprivatized, 4,000 were leased, and about 12,000 have either been sold or lost to municipalities.[7] Only about 7,000 remaining cooperative establishments are thus subject to the new regulations intended to transform their decision-making structures, discussed in section 5.

[7] Many of the premises used by cooperatives in rural areas were actually owned by local governments, which have in numerous cases recently reclaimed their ownership rights. See section 5 below.

2. RESTITUTION

2.1. History of restitution debates

Immediately following the "Velvet Revolution," when reformers began to discuss in earnest which methods of property transformation they might employ in their reform programs, they did not include restitution on their agenda. They feared that processing restitution claims would be both time consuming and enormously expensive. Furthermore, they anticipated that disputes over restitution claims, which could keep the status of property units in question for long periods of time, would jeopardize the speed and perhaps the success of other privatization programs.

Increasingly strong pressure from public opinion in 1990 concerning the rehabilitation of political prisoners and other victims of the communist regime,[8] however, softened the completely antirestitution position. Czechoslovakia subsequently developed one of the most extensive programs of restitution among postsocialist countries. A distinguishing characteristic of Czechoslovak restitution is its emphasis on return of specific assets to their former owners, as opposed to providing them with monetary or other compensation; thus, the program is frequently termed "reprivatization."[9]

Because nationalization of property had begun in Czechoslovakia even before the communist takeover, the scope of restitution was, and to some degree still is, a matter of debate. Among the most politically sensitive issues were the questions of what to do with property which formerly belonged to Jews who had fallen victim to the Nazis, and with property of Sudeten Germans who had been expelled from Czechoslovakia immediately after the close of World War II. Various groups, including Czechoslovak nobility, former Czechoslovak citizens living abroad, and members of "real cooperatives", whose property though nominally transferred to other cooperative structures had actually been

[8] Punishment for "enemies of the state" invariably included the confiscation of their property. Among these was the Catholic Church, a part of whose property has been returned to them under Law No. 298/1990 on the Regulation of Property Relations of Religious Orders and Congregations and the Olomouc Archdiocese. Lately, the question of further restitutions to the Catholic Church has again become a focus of public debates.

[9] By avoiding the need to determine the value of formerly confiscated property, reprivatization may be much simpler than compensation. The problems of reprivatization in determining legal ownership, on the other hand, are avoided with compensation. The Czech program does use compensation in some situations, for instance for destroyed property.

nationalized, also lobbied for the creation of a reprivatization program that would include the properties they had formerly owned.

2.2. Restitution laws

Two principal laws and amendments to these laws now regulate the restitution of former property owners in the retail trade, catering, and services sector of the Czech economy: Law No. 403/1990 on Relieving the Consequences of Some Property Injustices (Small Restitution) and its amendments, and Law No. 87/1991 on Out-of-Court Rehabilitation (Large Restitution).[10]

- Law No. 298/1990 on Regulation of Property Relations of Religious Orders and Congregations and the Olomouc Archdiocese.
- Law No. 403/1990 on Relieving the Consequences of Some Property Injustices (Small Reprivatization).
- Law No. 458/1990 Amendment to Law 403/1990.
- Law No. 528/1990 Amendment to Law No. 403/1990.
- Law No. 87/1991 on Out-of-Court Rehabilitations (Large Restitution).
- Law No. 137/1991 Amendment of Law No. 403/1990.
- Decree No. 174/1991 (executing Law No. 87/1991).
- Law No. 229/1991 on the Regulation of the Relations of Ownership of Land and Other Agricultural Property.

2.3. Assets in reprivatization

According to the reprivatization laws, restitution applies only to property which was nationalized after February 25, 1948, the date on which the communists assumed full control of the Czechoslovak parliament. By 1948, 82.3 percent of capital assets in the "productive" sectors of the Czechoslovak economy had already been nationalized and private sector business accounted for only 33.4 percent of total NMP, 13.7 percent of industrial production, and 15.3 per cent of construction.[11] Thus, although most industrial assets were effectively excluded from the

[10] In addition to restitution, the Large Restitution Law provided many other forms of "rehabilitation" of political prisoners and victims of communism.

[11] However, private activity still accounted for 95 percent of agricultural production in 1948. Figures taken from the *Historical Statistical Yearbook of CSSR*, SNTL-ALFA (Prague), 1985, p. 55.

restitution program, many shops,[12] workshops, restaurants, hotels, as well as small factories, houses, and plots of land were eligible for reprivatization. As noted in section 1 above, most commercial premises in central cities existed and had been privately owned prior to their nationalization in the late 1940s and 1950s. Thus, the restitution program includes many of the most valuable premises in the Czech Republic.

After 1948, ownership of nationalized assets was scattered among state, legal, and sometimes physical persons. Of the state and legal persons, most were state enterprises under the jurisdiction of the Ministry of Internal Trade and Tourism, enterprises which fell under the category of "other state trade," cooperatives under the jurisdiction of the Union of Consumer Cooperatives, and restaurants and services under the authority of local governments. Property transferred to physical persons after 1948, which would otherwise have been eligible for restitution, could not be returned to its original owners unless the transfer had involved a violation of the laws valid at the time of transfer.

Two additional exceptions to the general category of "property nationalized after 1948" are stipulated in the laws. The first of these are financial assets and shares of companies which were eventually nationalized. It was decided that compensation for financial losses of this sort would be too complicated to administer.[13] The second exception was made on moral grounds: subsequently nationalized property that had been given as reward for aiding the Nazis is not eligible for reprivatization.

In the event that property which had been nationalized after 1948 had later been destroyed, claimants have been entitled to receive monetary compensation. However, the amount of compensation is calculated according to a relevant decree dating back to 1964, and would adjust for the increase in value since the 1964 valuation by simply adding 3 percent for each year. Thus, compensation typically has been valued at far below what would have been the present market value of the property. A further restriction on restitution was imposed if the property to be returned housed social, medical, or cultural organizations. In this event, the former owners would be required to rent the premises of their property to the current users for no less than ten years.

[12] Among these shops were many nationalized family businesses, attached to the living quarters of the previous owners. They were perhaps the easiest to privatize through restitution. In many cases not only was there a single, undisputed, previous owner, but quite often that previous owner was still living on the premises and still operating the shop.

[13] Intellectual property was also excluded from the program.

2.4. Restituents

Eligibility for participation in the program was limited to physical persons who are resident Czechoslovak citizens, and whose property was nationalized between February 25, 1948 and January 1, 1990. Legal persons (excluding religious organizations), foreigners, and Czechoslovak emigrants could not participate. However, although emigrants are generally ineligible, any emigrant could have become eligible by renewing their Czechoslovak citizenship and establishing permanent residence on Czechoslovak territory.

2.5. The process of privatization

Since the legislation on restitution was passed in two stages, in October 1990 ("Small") and March 1991 ("Large"), so the administration of the program followed two distinct phases. It was required that claims for restitution property which had been nationalized after 1955 (the last wave of nationalization) be submitted between November 1, 1990 and April 30, 1991, while it was necessary to submit claims for property which had been nationalized after 1948 but before 1955 between April 1, 1991 and September 30, 1991. Potential applicants lost all potential rights to property which formerly belonged to them if they failed to submit claims before the expiration of these deadlines.

Applicants submitted their claims for restitution in the form of a petition directly to the state or cooperative organization using the property in question. If the claim was clearly valid (for example, if only one claimant held proof of previous ownership), the current user was obliged to either return the property to its former owner within 30 days, or within 30 days sign an agreement with the former owner which stated precisely when the property would be returned. The Laws also stipulated that if the current user was responsible for any delay in the return of the property beyond 30 days, it would be fined Csk 3,000,[14] payable to the Ministry of Privatization, for each day of delay.

[14] In Fall 1991, Csk 3,000 was the equivalent of approximately US$ 100; we use the exchange rate of US$ 1 = Csk 28, which was roughly constant over the 1991–1993 period. On February 8, 1993, the Czechoslovak crown was split into two separate Czech and Slovak currencies. The Czech crown (Csk) maintains roughly the same exchange rate as its predecessor, and is also pegged to a basket of hard currencies.

Disputed restitution claims were referred to district courts. District level governments were entirely responsible for the administration of restitution, and provided both court and notary services to claimants free of charge. In addition to disputes arising from competing claims, disputes between former owners and current users also were brought to the attention of the courts. In one instance, a former owner might demand compensation for neglect which resulted in decay or disrepair of the property. In another, a current user might demand compensation for repairs, renovations, and additions to the property.

2.6. Results

Aside from the former GDR, Czechoslovakia has developed the most extensive restitution program of all postcommunist countries in Central and Eastern Europe. Although it is difficult to obtain data on the scope of restitution in the retail trade and services sector of the Czech economy, Table I.B.3 presents some rough estimates calculated from a variety of sources.

These figures, however, do not fully reflect the impact of restitution on the transformation of the retail trade and consumer service sector. First, the restitution of residential houses, not included in the table above, created much ground floor space potentially usable by private entrepreneurs.[15] Tomas Jezek, current chairman of the Czech National Property Fund, estimates that in total, over 100,000 items have been returned to their former owners, of which the majority are residential houses. Second, recipients of this property suddenly found themselves owning assets which could be used as collateral for obtaining bank credit, including for the purpose of establishing new businesses.

Even so, the Czechoslovak reprivatization program did cause complications in the other privatization programs. The six-month application terms may have somewhat delayed the implementation of both small

[15] As a qualifier, we should point out that although there are no restrictions on the use of returned property in particular, there exist rent controls and eviction regulations on property which has been used as residential space, which also affect the use of this property for business purposes. It seems that rent ceilings are so low, and the restrictions on tenant evictions so stringent, that rents for ground floor business space have come under great pressure.

Table I.B.3 Estimated number of outlets returned by various state bodies in the Czech Republic

	Number of units
Ministry of Internal Trade and Tourism	5,000
Union of Consumer Cooperatives	3,500
Other state retail trade	500
Local governments*	8,000–11,000
Total	17,000–20,000

Sources: Estimates from Ivan Rulf of the Czech Ministry of Industry and Trade; L. Sipek, "Problematika Transformace Druzstev" (The Issue of Cooperative Transformation), mimeo, Ministry of Internal Trade and Tourism (Prague), 1991; and authors' own estimates.

* These units are mainly restaurants and services.

and large-scale privatization,[16] since until the expiration of those periods it was unclear which state assets would be available for transfer into private ownership by means other than restitution. Furthermore, the restitution of property to more than one owner (which sometimes happened) led to disagreements over rights of control and even over how to use the property, again stalling the efficient utilization of assets in the economy. Some of these sorts of disputes have persisted even into 1993.

Unfortunately, there exist no data on how many businesses in the retail trade and consumer services sector which were returned to their former owners are currently operating in the Czech economy, rendering it difficult to gauge the program's direct effects with any precision. Nevertheless, it seems clear that restitution was a successful political strategy and economic policy. Through its reprivatization program, the Czechoslovak government maintained public interest in privatization and popular support for reform, even during the painful periods of

16 Although the argument that restitution would stall other "quick" privatization (small and large privatization) schemes was one of the most important objections to introducing a restitution program, neither small nor large privatization have proceeded as quickly as originally had been hoped. In retrospect, we may consider that restitution was implemented in a relatively short time at the very beginning of a lengthy privatization process. See sections 3 and 4 on small and large privatization, below.

macroeconomic stabilization between 1990 and 1991. At the same time, it may have also created a first "critical mass" of private businesses.

3. THE SMALL PRIVATIZATION PROGRAM

3.1. Objectives

As described in section 1 above, the small privatization program developed in an atmosphere of political battles mingled with economic arguments, in the year 1990. After the first free elections in forty-two years were held in the summer, popular impatience grew in reaction to the "slow" pace economic transformation was perceived to have taken. The new government, dominated by "radical," free-market reformers, was eager to demonstrate its ability to carry out reforms and selected trade and services as the first target for privatization.[17] As discussed in section 1, this sector was in many ways the "easiest" to privatize: there could be little controversy that private ownership of retail trade and consumer services would be more efficient, the comparative absence of economies of scale and indivisible capital implied that relatively few corporate governance problems would arise, and the under-representation of trade and services in the economy as a whole suggested that there were tremendous possibilities for growth, certainly relative to the antiquated, inefficient, and over-sized industrial sector. There was also little political resistance to privatization of the sector, save that from insiders, who, as described in section 1 above, mostly lost their struggle to preserve large chains of stores.[18] Although other methods have also been significant, the small privatization program has been the main policy vehicle for the direct transformation of trade and services in the Czech Republic. It was implemented from the beginning of 1991 and concluded at the end of 1993.

3.2. Legal and organizational framework

The Law No. 427/1990, Coll., "on the Transfer of State Ownership of Certain Properties to Other Legal or Natural Persons," created the small

[17] In retrospect, it seems that Czechoslovak reformers were always very attentive to maintaining the political momentum of the economic transformation.
[18] Section 4 discusses the privatization of remaining chains in the large privatization program.

privatization program. The Law established basic principles for the program: the conditions for the selection of assets, the use of auctions as the sole method of privatization to be employed, and the collection of the revenues in a central fund to be used to pay the debts of parent enterprises. The corresponding implementation law was Law No. 500/1990 Coll., "on Competencies of Czech Republic Governmental Bodies in the Matter of Transfer of State Property of Some Things to Other Legal or Physical Persons," approved by the Czech National Council for the regulation of small privatization on the territory of the Czech Republic.[19] The rules governing the execution of public auctions are stipulated in the Decree of the Ministry of Privatization No. 535, and the tax-free status of auction purchases was announced by Federal Ministry of Finance Announcement No. 90/1990/1 Coll.

The laws on small privatization were amended through Czechoslovak and Czech parliamentary acts and by specific decrees of the federal and republican governments. The following is a complete list of the relevant legal acts:

— Law No. 427/1990 Coll., on "the Transfer of State Property and Some Goods to Other Legal or Natural Persons."
— Law No. 500/1990 Coll., on "Competencies of Czech Republic Governmental Bodies in the Matter of Transfer of State Property of Some Things to Other Legal or Physical Persons."
— Law No. 528/1990 Coll., Amendment of Law No. 427/1990 Coll.
— Decree No. 535/1990 Coll., Ministry of Privatization Decree on the Logistics of Auctions.
— Law No. 541/1990 Coll., Amendment of Law No. 427/1990 Coll.
— Announcement 90/1990/1 Coll., "on the Tax-Free Status of Auction Purchases."
— Law No. 429/1991 Coll., Amendment of Law No. 427/1990 Coll.
— Law No. 438/1991 Coll., Amendment of Law No. 500/1990 Coll.
— Law No. 561/1991 Coll., Amendment of Law No. 427/1990 Coll.
— Law No. 573/1991 Coll., Amendment of Law No. 568/1990 Coll.
— Law No. 282/1992 Coll., Amendment of Law No. 500/1990 Coll.
— Law No. 307/1992 Coll., Amendment of Law No. 427/1990 Coll.

[19] The Slovak National Council also enacted such an implementation law with respect to property in Slovakia. After 1989, most laws applying to both Republics in the Federation had to be approved at the Republican as well as the Federal level.

Three sets of state institutions were involved in the program. First, the Government and Ministry of Privatization set the broad outlines of the policy and were responsible for the final decision about the sale of each property. Second, the founding ministries (usually the Ministry of Internal Trade and Tourism) and state enterprise managements played a role in the selection of assets. Formally, they negotiated over the desirability of including certain assets in the program, discussing the "technological necessity" of the assets for the parent enterprise. In practice, however, they may have often attempted to prevent the loss of their best shops, as described in section 1. Finally, District (*okres*) Privatization Committees were established to recommend assets for the program, to publish information about assets and sales, and to administer the auctions. The Committee members, of which there were 20–25 in most districts and 70–100 for the city of Prague, were appointed by the Minister of Privatization and include professional employees and representatives of the Ministry of Privatization and the local union of entrepreneurs. The relationship between the Committees and the Ministry of Privatization was not completely clear, and occasionally the Ministry actively interfered in Committee activities.[20]

3.3. Assets in small privatization

The small privatization "program" was by no means a detailed plan enumerating precisely which assets would be privatized in the Czech Republic according to a predetermined timetable. The Law specified only that "the subjects of the ownership transfer . . . are movable and immovable assets, as a property basis of enterprises that act in the spheres of services, trade, and other areas, excluding agricultural production" (Article 2). The Law also excluded properties subject to reprivatization and those owned or used by persons with foreign residency. Two final exclusion criteria played significant roles in the

[20] Having completed their work in small privatization, these powerful Committees took on additional responsibilities and roles in connection with liquidation and the large privatization program. In January 1994, the Minister of Privatization declared that the Committees will be funded for only one employee per district, and only until June 1994, after which the Committees should finally be dissolved. The final outcome is still uncertain.

struggles over assets in the program. First, the program excluded those considered "technologically necessary" to the operation of the parent enterprise. Second, all obligations were excluded: the assets were sold "unencumbered."[21]

Otherwise there were no quantitative or qualitative restrictions on the inclusion of assets. Whether the land and building were sold or merely leased varied from case to case. Only if the lot of land on which the asset was located were held by a state organization, did the law require that the land and building be sold with the unit, a provision that was not applied in the case of multi-unit structures. On the other hand, inventory was necessarily included in the sale of shops.[22] Both the determination of the length of the lease for premises and the value of inventories later became sources of problems and disputes, as described below.

Unlike the privatization of trade in many other countries, the Czech program carried few restrictions on the operation of a privatized business after the new owner has assumed control. The Small Privatization Law required only that shops selling groceries must continue such sales for a period of at least one year, and the local government was given the discretionary right to shorten this period. The right of alienation was attenuated to the degree that sales to foreigners were forbidden for a period of two years.[23]

Given the openness of the law, the determination of the assets to be included in the program was decentralized, relying primarily on local decision-making and initiative. Though District Privatization Committees selected many assets on their own, any person, presumably motivated by the possibility of becoming the new owner, could also propose any eligible asset by submitting a proposal to the Committee. If the Committee approved the proposal, the state enterprise could still attempt to block the privatization by claiming that the unit was "technologically necessary" for the continued operation of the enterprise

[21] The provision that units with liabilities could be privatized only in the large privatization program may be considered the most important legal distinction between the kinds of assets covered by the two programs.

[22] The revenue was received by the parent enterprise rather than the Fund of National Property.

[23] This held true only if the auction was completed in one round, which implies that the purchaser had to be a Czechoslovak citizen. If the auction required multiple rounds, which allowed the possibility of a foreign purchaser, then the resale restriction no longer applied.

as a whole.[24] Disputes were resolved in negotiation with the enterprise's founding organ and with the Ministry of Privatization, which made the final decision.

Enterprise managers could also redistribute obligations within the enterprise, for instance by moving apprentices (whose training constituted a legal obligation) to the most desirable units in order to prevent those assets from being "lost" to small privatization. There is only anecdotal evidence of this sort of manipulation, however, and it is therefore difficult to assess the degree to which enterprises succeeded in such endeavors. One disincentive to blocking an asset from small privatization was the possibility of fines levied on both the enterprise (up to Csk 200,000 or about US$ 7,100) and the manager (up to Csk 20,000), which were enacted in an Amendment to the Small Privatization Law.

Out of a total of approximately 68,000 trade and service establishments in the Czech Republic in 1989, we estimate that 18,910 had been sold in the small privatization program as of the end of 1993, when the program was officially concluded. Although this is the sector with which we are concerned in this report, the Law also allowed many other types of assets to be sold in the program, and the composition was quite heterogeneous: factories, shops, small kiosks, large hotels, warehouses, cars, and trucks. We estimate the number of those items at 3,435, making altogether a total of some 22,345 assets sold in Czech "small privatization."

Table I.B.4 shows that most of the assets sold in small privatization were shops (58 percent), restaurants (8 percent), or service facilities (18 percent): the assets which the small privatization program was designed to target. Among other items, the share of "means of transport" is surprisingly large (7 percent). Although not strictly speaking part of the privatization of the retail trade sector, these "means of transport" may represent a significant addition to the available supply of delivery vehicles, thus contributing to the development of retail trade, which is of course heavily dependent on the transport of goods.[25] Some whole

[24] Although such claims seem to have been common, we may speculate that they were probably relatively difficult to justify for retail outlets, while for business services it may have been easier. According to the Prague Privatization Committee, sectors of particularly keen dispute were restaurants, greengrocers, and services.

[25] Our survey of 100 establishments in the small privatization program, on which we provide a full report below, found that 36 percent use their own vehicles for the delivery of supplies, perhaps a surprisingly large proportion given the cost of new vehicles in the Czech Republic. It may be that the sale of used vehicles in the small privatization program significantly reduced the cost of this complementary investment for new owners of retail trade outlets.

Table I.B.4 Items sold in small privatization by December 31, 1993

Type of item	Number of items	Average starting price (Csk '000)	Average final price (Csk '000)	Average final price as percent of average starting price
Retail Shops	13,042	684	1,194	175%
Kiosks	464	253	320	126%
Confectioners	278	526	1,075	205%
Household goods	2,031	444	1,000	225%
Newspaper and tobacco	2,242	26	189	725%
Shoes and leather	184	333	540	162%
Department stores	55	14,982	21,239	142%
Food	3,446	1,233	1,820	148%
Books	264	112	551	493%
Furniture	85	1,373	2,763	201%
Florists	345	142	665	467%
Textiles and clothing	1,144	366	983	268%
Butchers	776	403	846	210%
Vegetables and fruit	1,092	405	734	181%
Bakeries	103	4,249	5,494	129%
Gasoline stations	129	1,165	4,003	344%
Other shops	404	1,482	2,106	142%
Restaurants	1,861	1,166	1,790	154%
Service establishments	4,007	1,136	1,491	131%
Hotels	430	3,629	5,944	164%
Other services	3,577	837	956	114%
Other items	3,435	1,788	2,185	122%
Transport	41	4,121	4,138	100%
Cars and trucks	1,611	171	153	90%
Warehouses	455	2,428	2,773	114%
Production units	482	3,515	3,399	97%
Factories	142	11,091	15,772	142%
Houses and offices	200	1,095	1,739	159%
Cultural centers	18	1,132	885	78%
Computer centers	3	969	822	85%
Other	483	2,240	3,283	147%
Total	22,345	975	1,449	149%

Source: Ministry of Privatization.

Table I.B.5 Items sold in small privatization according to former controlling body (at December 31, 1993)

	Former controlling body			
	Local government	Czech MITT	Other ministries	Total
Units sold with real estate				
Number	2,093	3,119	756	5,968
Distribution	35%	52%	13%	100%
Average starting price	2,903	2,574	5,035	3,002
Average final price	3,228	3,410	7,751	3,896
Average final starting price	111	132	154	130
Units sold without real estate				
Number	4,471	8,753	1,295	14,519
Distribution	31%	60%	9%	100%
Average starting price	199	128	142	144
Average final price	495	536	372	502
Average final starting price	249	419	262	349
Total units sold:				
Number	6,615	11,872	2,000	20,487
Distribution	32%	58%	10%	100%
Average starting price	1,053	762	1,996	978
Average final price	1,369	1,300	3,171	1,495
Average final starting price	130	171	159	154

Source: Ministry of Privatization.

enterprises and productive units were also included in the program, but their number is relatively insignificant: 624 units, or 2.8 percent of all items. Because in small privatization assets may only be sold without liabilities, most factories, productive units, and large department stores are being privatized in the large privatization program. To the extent that these and other items, such as buildings and offices, essentially constitute business premises, their privatization could also have contributed to the development of the trade and service sector.

The attempts of Ministry of Trade and enterprise insiders to prevent their best shops from being sold in the small privatization program were mentioned in section 1. Table I.B.5 compares the numbers and average prices according to the former controlling body of the unit's enterprise. Out of 22,345 items sold in the small privatization program, only 20,487 (92 percent) have provided information about the former controlling body. The main source was the Ministry of Internal Trade and Tourism, representing 58 percent of all items. Second were local authorities, supplying 32 percent of all items, while the rest (10 percent) came from other branch ministries.[26]

Both starting and final prices were lower for state retail trade assets than for other state and local assets, which may appear to suggest that the retail trade insiders were successful. But this conclusion is not necessarily warranted. As described in Part A above, the composition of state retail trade was systematically different from other state trade and from units under local control. It is thoroughly possible that other state trade simply involved larger, more valuable properties.

Table I.B.5 also shows the number of units where premises were sold and the number where the premises were merely leased; 5,968 units, 29 percent of the total, were sold with premises, while 14,519 items were sold without (71 percent of the total). From the total 18,910 trade and service establishments in the program, only about 28 percent are "full privatizations," that is, they were or are to be sold with the building and land.

In the remaining 72 percent, the auction winner purchases equipment and inventories and receives the right only to rent the premises for a fixed term. Although an issue of considerable controversy, this proportion is roughly the same as in other East European countries and, based on casual observation, may not be very different from the situation in the West.[27] On the other hand, the Small Privatization Law fixed the initial rental term for auction winners at two years. Although rather too short a time horizon to encourage investment and restructuring, concern over the rights of owners to determine the use of their property seems to have motivated this provision.[28] A later amendment increased the term to five years for subsequent auction winners.

[26] It is probable that the estimate of the number of units under local authorities is downwardly biased, since it is more difficult to get information about these units.

[27] Among the establishments in our survey, 77 percent in Hungary and 79 percent in Poland are leased. In the Czech Republic sample, 71 percent are leased.

[28] Among these owners are restituents, to whom many business premises were returned and who have now become lessors, and municipalities, to which many premises have been transferred. The transfers to municipalities take place under Law 172/1991, according to which municipalities have restitution rights to property they owned prior to 1949. This Law also allows municipalities to apply to the Ministry of Finance to receive any state-owned property; often the Ministry of Privatization and the District Privatization Committees are consulted on these requests. Municipalities have become important landlords, although as business operators they have become much less important than they were formerly.

The fact that the contract with the lessor is signed only after the auction has potentially cast still greater uncertainty on the object of the bidding. Eventually winning the auction, the new business "owners" who have won leasing rights must still negotiate with the premises owner or administrator over the size of rental payments, and the District Privatization Committees play no role in these negotiations. Because rather stringent rent controls apply to business premises as well as housing,[29] in most cases the maximum amount of rent could be foreseen in advance of the auction. But the regulations also contained the provision that local governments could choose to increase the ceilings or even allow completely free negotiation. It seems that only three large cities, Prague, Brno, and Carlsbad, chose this route. The City of Prague, for instance, set new ceilings for particular locations at 200, 300, and 400 percent of the nation-wide regulations; in other locations, free negotiations were permitted. In these cases, bidders sometimes tried to ascertain the intentions of the lessor in advance, but it may have been difficult to obtain an absolute commitment. On the other hand, the Small Privatization Law essentially gives the auction winner an absolute right to occupy the premises. It is, thus, difficult to evict such a tenant even for non-payment of rent.[30]

Considering the asset selection process retrospectively, it seems remarkable that it was accomplished in a decentralized fashion and primarily through private initiative. The Small Privatization Law only established a basic legal framework, and it allowed individual incentives and seemingly well-functioning institutions to do the rest: 22,345 objects were auctioned, with remarkably few problems.

3.4. New owners

The equal opportunity of all citizens to participate is a unique feature of the privatization process in the Czech and Slovak Republics, and

[29] Business premises are regulated by Ministry of Finance Decree No. 585/1990, setting maximum rents for four categories. The highest-rent category, which includes trade, restaurants, and offices, has an annual ceiling of Csk 190 (about US$ 7) per square meter. This provision applies neither to foreign natural persons, nor to legal persons with over 50 percent foreign ownership. Housing rents are regulated separately.

[30] Law No. 116/1990, Coll., on "Lease and Sublease of Non-Flat Premises," permits termination of any rental agreement concerning business premises with three months' advance notice. The courts, however, seem to be interpreting the rights of auction winners under the Small Privatization Law as taking precedence.

applied particularly to the small privatization program. Once assets were selected for inclusion in the program, the auctions were open to everyone, with essentially no special preferences for anyone, including insiders. Of course, insiders may have had an informational advantage in both the small and large privatization programs in Czechoslovakia, but the absence of lower prices, special credits, and pre-emptive rights for them forms a striking contrast with most privatization programs in other countries of the region.

This openness was not achieved without a struggle, however. In early 1990, worker groups demanded closed rounds of auctions, restricted to employees only in both large and small privatization. Trade unions in retail trade threatened industrial action and strikes. Government (Czech, Slovak, and Federal) debates on this subject flared in the summer of 1990; the compromise proposal to Parliament permitted all Czechoslovak citizens to participate in the first round and anyone in the second, but gave employees special access to loans for up to 50 percent of the starting price, at very low interest. It therefore came as something of a surprise when Parliament rejected the government's proposals for special loans, together with any other preferences for insiders.

Only one exception was granted, for about 2,000 units which had been leased between January and October 1990. The lessees of such units received the pre-emptive right to purchase the property they were leasing if they applied at least five days before the public auction was scheduled. The price in this case was the auction starting price (estimated land value plus book value for all other assets).

In the first round, foreigners were excluded from participating: technically, only people who had been Czechoslovak citizens for at least some time since February 25, 1948, or legal persons consisting entirely of Czechoslovak citizens, were permitted to participate.[31] Speculation was rife, however, that foreigners may have participated as silent partners. The rationale for the citizenship restriction was that foreign participation in small businesses was thought to be desirable only if Czechoslovak citizens were not interested or did not have enough money to start a business, since the program was meant to be a vehicle for the creation of an indigenous business class. Legal persons founded under communism

[31] In order to acquire real estate, a foreigner had first to establish a company in the Czech Republic. This seems not to have been an important obstacle.

were precluded, because their participation could lead to the transfer of the privatized property back into state or cooperative hands. Only legal persons completely owned by natural persons were permitted, and cooperatives of all types were excluded.

3.5. The allocation process

The exclusive method of allocation of ownership rights used in Czechoslovak small privatization was public auction. Information about the unit to be sold had to be announced thirty days in advance of the auction. Prospective buyers were allowed two visits to the unit for sale, for a fee of Csk 50 (approximately US$ 1.8) per visit. Auction participants were required to pay a nonrefundable entrance fee of Csk 1,000 (US$ 36) as well as a refundable deposit of either 10 percent of the starting price or Csk 10,000 (US$ 360), whichever was higher.

The starting price was determined as the sum of the values of land, buildings, machinery, equipment, and inventories. Land was appraised on the basis of simplified valuation methods from which the Czech Ministry of Finance drew administrative price maps. Book value was used for other assets. Although included in the starting price, for some reason the cost of the inventories was not part of the purchase price, but instead paid separately to the state enterprise.

If no participant was willing to pay the starting price and there were at least five participants, a "Dutch" auction could be employed in which the price was progressively decreased by amounts of 10 percent. If a bid was made during this process, the standard auction procedure, with increasing bids, could be resumed.[32] In the first round, the price could fall to as low as 50 percent of the starting value. For items remaining unsold even after their price was decreased, a second round could be held in which the price could decrease to 20 percent of the starting price. If there was a foreign participant (which was permitted in the second round), the price could fall to only 50 percent.[33]

[32] In a standard Dutch auction, the price is usually progressively lowered until the object is claimed by the first bidder willing to pay the offered price.

[33] Because of suspected collusion among bidders, the procedure was amended in 1992 to permit the price to fall only in the second round and only to 50 percent of the starting price, in the case of sales of premises.

3.6. Results

The development of small privatization sales over the last three years is shown in Figure I.B.1. The program quickly blossomed after it began in early 1991 and about 18,000 units were sold between April 1991 and April 1992. Only about 4,000 more were sold until the program was concluded at the end of 1993. Remaining unsold items will be transferred to the large privatization program, potentially to be auctioned under somewhat different rules (see section 4), or they will be placed under liquidation, again possibly to be auctioned.

The average starting price for all units was Csk 943,000 (US$ 33,700), while the average final price reached Csk 1,353,000 (US$ 48,300), or 51 percent higher than the average starting price. Table I.B.6 shows the distribution of final prices.

Dutch auctions were used to sell 3,720 items, 16.6 percent of the total. Average starting price for those units was Csk 2,250,000 (US$ 90,000) and average final price was Csk 1,377,000 (US$ 47,700), on average 53 percent of the starting price. The composition of items sold using Dutch auctions is shown in Table I.B.7.

Little information is available concerning the identity of the new owners. It is interesting to note, however, that the lack of special preferences for employees does not imply that few former employees acquired the units in which they worked. Our random sample of 100 establishments, from the total 15,231 retail trade, catering, and service establishments already sold as of December 31, 1991, yielded fifty-three establishments whose owners had worked in the units prior to privatization. Former employees may have inside information about the value of the assets, and thus it may not be surprising that they win about half of the auctions.

The primary problems that developed during the execution of the program involved some aspects of the ownership rights over the assets being transferred. The first of these concerned the length of rental agreements for premises in the transfers in which real estate was not sold. According to the Small Privatization Law, the winner of an auction which did not include premises acquired only the right to a two year rental agreement. As mentioned above, this clearly raised incentive problems for shopkeepers by shortening their time horizons. Beginning in October 1991, new leases were signed for an obligatory five year period. As the earlier two year leases began to expire in Spring 1993, the Union of Entrepreneurs pushed for an extension for at least five years and for rights of purchase of premises thereafter. The counter-argument

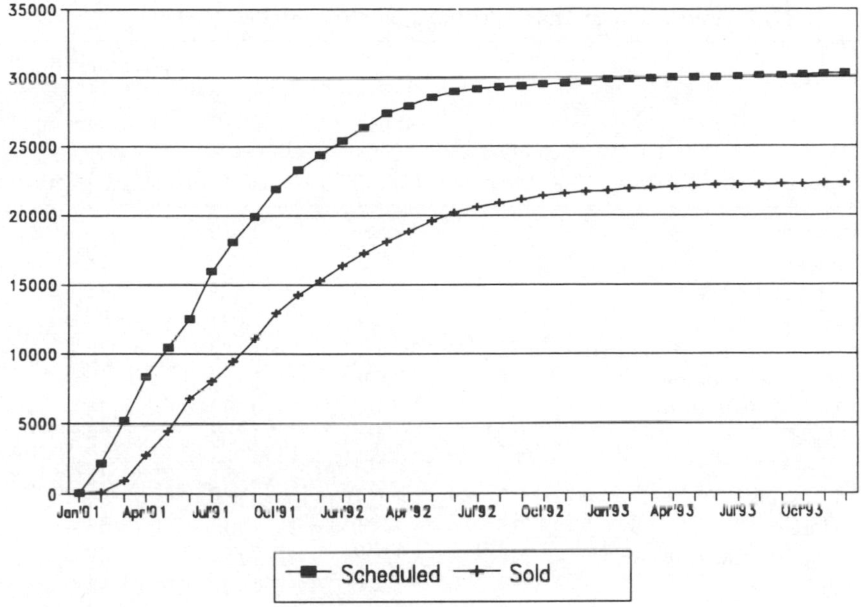

Figure I.B.1 Number of items scheduled and sold in small privatization (all items, cumul.)

Source: Ministry of Privatization.

Table I.B.6 Cumulative distribution of sales according to final price at December 31, 1993

Amount of sale	Number of sales
up to Csk 0.1 mln	7,005
from Csk 0.1 mln to 0.5 mln	6,641
from Csk 0.5 mln to 1 mln	3,133
from Csk 1 mln to 5 mln	4,374
from Csk 5 mln to 10 mln	757
from Csk 10 mln to 20 mln	295
from Csk 20 mln to 50 mln	139
above Csk 50 mln	37
Total	22,345

Source: Ministry of Privatization.

Table I.B.7 Items sold in Dutch auctions as at December 31, 1993

Type of item	Number of items	Average starting price (Csk '000)	Average final price (Csk '000)	Average final price as percent of average starting price
Retail shops	1,315	2,516	1,315	52%
Kiosks	62	819	393	48%
Confectioners	25	2,029	923	45%
Household goods	179	2,049	1,041	51%
Newspaper and tobacco	53	213	83	39%
Shoes and leather	16	2,538	1,279	50%
Department stores	12	20,967	9,143	44%
Food	560	2,897	1,604	55%
Books	20	197	82	42%
Furniture	5	1,112	565	51%
Florists	15	1,350	717	53%
Textiles and clothing	113	1,213	599	49%
Butchers	53	1,950	793	41%
Vegetables and fruit	105	1,409	695	49%
Bakeries	24	7,477	4,117	55%
Gasoline stations	25	1,420	693	49%
Other shops	48	5,857	3,098	53%
Restaurants	374	2,869	1,465	51%
Service establishments	855	2,321	1,201	52%
Hotels	106	5,322	2,676	50%
Other services	749	1,896	993	52%
Other items	1,176	2,558	1,419	55%
Transport	575	238	111	47%
Cars and trucks	163	3,022	1,906	63%
Warehouses	160	6,890	4,049	59%
Production units	41	15,867	8,065	51%
Factories	36	1,849	1,029	56%
Houses and offices	54	1,726	1,003	58%
Cultural centers	7	1,940	976	50%
Computer centers	1	2,201	1,650	75%
Other	139	3,242	1,558	48%
Total	3,720	2,520	1,337	53%

Source: Ministry of Privatization.

from the Minister of Privatization was that it would be unfair to auction losers to change the lease terms, because they might have bid higher if they had known the term would have been longer. Moreover, most of the lessor parties to these agreements are either municipalities or private persons (restituents), and the state legally cannot interfere in their contracts.[34]

A second problem arose from the liabilities left behind in the parent enterprise by the auctioning of unencumbered single units. The Law stipulates that for two years the proceeds of small privatization auctions can be used for the satisfaction of claims arising as a result of the Law. It often took a long time, however, for those debts to be satisfied.

Thirdly, the sale of inventories together with other assets created the possibility for manipulation of the inventory value in the period between the auction and the moment when the new owner took possession. The Law stipulated that the inventory levels and prices cannot differ significantly from the date of sale, but this was difficult to enforce in practice. Anecdotes abound of new owners finding useless, damaged, or low quality inventories, for which they were expected to pay.

On the other hand, an opposite problem was created through the legal requirement that the cost of the inventories be paid to the parent enterprise, rather than with the rest of the price into the Fund of National Property. If the payment to the Fund was not complete in thirty days, the auction winner lost the property and his/her deposit. But there was no such penalty prescribed for nonpayment for inventories to the enterprise. Apparently many have not paid, and at the end of 1992 this debt amounted to a total of about Csk 1.5 bln (US$ 54 mln) in the Czech Republic.

A fourth problem arose from the scarcity of capital and the poor availability of credit. Credit conditions for the privatization auctions were quite restrictive. Bidders with good collateral were usually offered credits equal at most to the amount of the starting auction price of an asset. If the final price was bid up much higher than the original starting price, such credit quickly became insufficient. There was great competition for less valuable assets from liquidity-constrained investors interested in creating a family business. Compared to a situation with well-functioning capital markets, the resultant demand pattern may have raised the relative price of smaller, less valuable items, because few

[34] "Minister of Privatization Skalicky: Mr. Baranek was not telling the truth," *Mlada Fronta Dnes*, May 24, 1993, pp. 1–2.

citizens were able to participate in the purchase of larger, more valuable ones. It may have also, paradoxically, brought the final auction prices closer in line with the arbitrary starting values.

Finally, although auctions in general seemed to offer the best chance for equal participation of all interested parties, and the least opportunities for corruption, there seems to have been collusion among bidders in a fair number of cases. Collusion arose due to the requirement that at least five participants be present for a Dutch auction to be held. But side payments among participants seem to have been fairly easy. As evidence for the existence of side-contracting, we may cite the fact that there were some second round auctions with five participants where the price fell to 20 percent; but, even at that price, only one bidder was willing to make the purchase. Since it was known in advance that 20 percent was the lowest possible price, anyone participating should have been willing to pay at least that amount. This suggests that the other participants could not have been serious bidders.

It was also simple to avoid the restrictions on foreign capital in the first round of auctions merely by signing a registered agreement, for instance in Austria or Germany, to resell an item as quickly as possible. It is, of course, difficult to estimate the incidence of such agreements or the size of foreign capital inflows through this so-called "dirty money" technique, but they are generally believed to have been high in particularly attractive locations such as Prague and Carlsbad. Other irregularities include the purposeful overbidding by a participant with insufficient capital, who would then forfeit the deposit, in order to have more time to raise more capital to win the auction in the second round.

Nonetheless, the Czech Small Privatization Program seems to have been remarkably successful in avoiding major scandals that could have slowed down the whole process, and to have been extremely efficient in reallocating control over a large number of shop premises in a short period of time.

4. LARGE PRIVATIZATION

4.1. Introduction

The foundations for the "large privatization" program were established by the passage of Law No. 92/1991 "on Conditions and Terms Governing the Transfer of State Property to Other Persons." The program employs a wide variety of methods of property transfer, including "standard methods" of auctions, tenders, and direct sales, as well as free transfer through the "non-standard" voucher program. By contrast with the restitution and small privatization programs, large privatization embraces going concerns and shares in corporatized enterprises, in addition to unencumbered assets. The organization of the program is quite complex, and of considerable independent interest. However, in this report we limit our discussion chiefly to those aspects of large privatization which directly concern the trade and service sector of the economy, describing the types of trade and service assets included in the program, the methods of privatization applied to these assets, and the results of the process as of late Spring 1993.

4.2. Assets

The determination of the supply of assets to the large privatization program began in mid-1991 with the Government's division of all state enterprises into those to be retained by the state, those to be liquidated, and those to be privatized in the first and the second "waves" of large privatization. This allocation covered all state-owned enterprises in the Czech Republic, although later splitting of companies altered the numbers in each category. Table I.B.8 shows the allocation for all enterprises in the Czech Republic, and for those subordinated to the Ministry of Internal Trade and Tourism.

Yet not all of the assets belonging to the enterprises designated for large privatization were to be included in the program. As discussed in detail in preceding sections, trade enterprises in particular lost large numbers of assets both to reprivatization and to the small privatization program. While the allocation of assets between restitution and large privatization was, at least in principle, only a legal matter of establishing the identity of former owners, the allocation between the small and the large privatization programs has been a major source of conflict in the struggle for control over assets in the sector.

Because in principle any asset could be proposed for small privatization, the inclusion of an asset in large privatization implied one of two conditions. First, no one may have proposed its inclusion in small privatization. Since the hope of obtaining an attractive asset was presumably the primary motivation of those making such a proposal, such assets were probably not considered valuable. On the other hand, capital requirements for large assets were usually excessive relative to individual savings, thus reducing the probability that such assets would

Table I.B.8 Allocation of enterprises to large privatization in the Czech Republic, mid-1991

	First wave	Second wave	State	Liquidation	Total
All enterprises	1,630	1,248	584	41	3,503
MITT*	126	57	34†	15	227

Source: *Ekonom*, No. 43, 1991.

* Enterprises subordinated to the Ministry for Internal Trade and Tourism.
† Thirty-two of these are training centers for apprentices.

be proposed for small privatization. Second, the Ministry of Privatization sometimes ruled against small privatization proposals when they did occur, usually in response to active lobbying by trade enterprise insiders on behalf of particularly valuable assets. In either case, the enterprise retained the asset for the large privatization program. Thus, although small privatization mostly included "smaller" assets and large privatization included "larger" ones, it is difficult to assess whether the types of trade and service assets differed systematically across the two programs.

Three features significantly distinguish large privatization from small privatization. The first is that large privatization can involve the transfer of whole enterprises or groups of assets, including those joined together in a single joint stock company. The second distinguishing feature is that assets can be privatized with obligations and as going concerns within large privatization. The third involves the variety of methods of transfer employed in the program, including the possibilities both of the voucher method and of direct sales.

Each of these features played a role in the negotiations between insiders and privatization officials over the division of assets between the small privatization and large privatization programs. Perhaps the most common argument employed by insiders in favor of large privatization was the claim that a certain unit (or group of units) made an essential contribution to the operation of the enterprise, without which the entire network would lose viability.[35] A similar

[35] The legal basis for this argument is a clause in the Small Privatization Law which states that any unit "technically necessary" to the operation of an enterprise may be excluded from small privatization. See section 3, above.

argument, sometimes enunciated by Ministry of Trade officials, reasoned that the sale of individual units through small privatization auctions would destroy economies of scale in chains of shops and vertically integrated retail trade networks. Thus, they lobbied that trade and service networks should be included in the large privatization program and sold or transferred in one piece, perhaps through the distribution of shares of a new joint stock company, perhaps through a direct sale.

Concerning the second feature, it is plausible that managers were able to exclude assets from small privatization by manipulating the profiles of their units. In particular, the Small Privatization Law states that only "movable and non-movable property" qualifies for sale in the program, effectively eliminating obligations such as contracts, leases, debts, and apprenticeship responsibilities. On the other hand, since large privatization can transfer going concerns as well as individual assets, it could be argued that units tied to obligations or unusually heavy financial responsibilities might be transferred more easily in large privatization. Thus, there is speculation that managers intentionally reorganized the allocation of obligations among their shops, possibly concentrating them in the most valuable ones, in order to increase the chances that these units would be privatized as going concerns in large privatization.

Third, the struggle between managers, attempting to preserve the network of shops under their direction, and new entrepreneurs, trying to gain entry into the most dynamic sector of the economy, had implications for both the kind of assets included in the large privatization program and the division of these assets among alternative methods within the program. By diverting units away from small into large privatization, managers could increase the probability that the assets would be privatized through a method which preserved their control. As discussed in section 4.3 below, managers may have been particularly predisposed towards voucher privatization, believing that widely dispersed ownership would result in ineffective corporate governance.

Data on the principal assets of trade and service sector projects approved for large privatization as at the end of 1992 appear in Table I.B.9. Some groups of retail shops are subsumed in the trade categories, included together with wholesale assets; some are in the form of joint stock companies. Measured in terms of employment, the largest categories are hotels, department stores, and wholesale trade stores.

Table I.B.9 Privatization projects of trade and services assets approved for large privatization* as at December 31, 1992

Principle assets	Number	Basic capital† (Csk mln)	Fixed capital (Csk mln)	Employment in 1991
Warehouses	14	94	65	0
Supermarkets	58	2,259	2,233	1,019
Department stores	30	2,562	2,260	4,161
Wholesale trade stores	48	3,040	3,281	11,882
Restaurants	17	364	472	300
Travel agencies	2	499	556	2,344
Hotels	50	4,245	4,888	6,154
Other services	55	864	947	3,368
Production units	19	730	757	1,801
Buildings	39	92	83	0
Land	21	0	14	0
Miscellaneous and n.e.c.	31	6,949	869	518
Total	348	21,698	16,425	31,547

Source: Czech Ministry of Privatization.

Notes: These categories are from the large privatization data set, and thus do not correspond to those in the discussion of small privatization in section 3 above. "N.e.c." represents "not elsewhere classified."

* This table includes projects involving enterprises from four branches of the Czech economy: internal trade, accommodation services, tourist services, and municipal services.

† "Basic capital" includes inventories, financial assets and liabilities, as well as fixed capital.

4.3. The choice of method: privatization projects

As noted above, the large privatization program allows the employment of a variety of privatization methods. "Standard" techniques of auction, tender, and direct sale, conforming closely to Western practice, may be applied to assets, with or without attached obligations. Whole state enterprises or their sub-units may be converted into corporate entities, and their shares sold to foreign and domestic investors. Some shares are reserved for compensation (restitution),[36] and both assets and shares may be transferred to various funds and to municipalities. Finally and most prominently, "non-standard" voucher privatization involves the exchange of shares in incorporated enterprises for artificially created capital, with which citizens and private funds place bids in a multi-round allocation process. In addition to these methods of privatization, shares may be retained permanently or temporarily in the Fund of National Property (FNP).

The determination of the particular method or combination of methods applied to a given enterprise involves the selection of a "privatization project" from proposals submitted by enterprise managers or any other interested parties.[37] The management of any enterprise subject to large privatization was required to submit a "basic project" first to the controlling body and then to the Ministry of Privatization. Basic projects included a business plan and a proposal specifying which parts of the enterprise should be privatized through which method. In addition, any other interested parties could submit "competing projects", which did not necessarily contain privatization plans for the entire enterprise but could focus on the privatization of individual units or groups of assets.

Although the Ministry of Privatization was officially responsible for making the final choice of which project or combination of projects to apply to each enterprise in the program, the District Privatization Commissions (see section 3.3 above) often play a significant role as well.[38] The Ministry typically sends projects to the local commissions for review and, according to some estimates, accepts between 70 and 80 percent of their recommendations. It also seems that the founding

[36] These shares are distributed as compensation to those entitled to reprivatization under the restitution laws (described in section 2 above), but whose expropriated property was destroyed during the period of state control.

[37] The details of this procedure are discussed at length in R. Frydman, A. Rapaczynski, J. Earle, *et al.*, *The Privatization Process in Central Europe*, CEU Press, 1993, and in M. Mejstrik and J. Burger, "The Czechoslovak Large Privatization," CERGE Working Paper, No. 10, 1992.

[38] During the first wave of large privatization, the District Commissions were occupied with the administration of small privatization auctions, the purpose for which they were created. Since the volume of small privatization sales began to dwindle in late 1992, they have begun to assume a larger role in large privatization, often executing large privatization auctions and participating in the evaluation of tenders. The addition of these functions may be construed as a useful further exploitation of their acquired expertise or, alternatively, as illustrative of the inherent problem of new institutions created to implement privatization policies: their *raison d'être* is to destroy their *raison d'être*.

organs (typically branch ministries, but sometimes local governments) became more influential in project evaluation in late 1992 compared to 1991 and early 1992.

The voucher method has been extensively described elsewhere,[39] but the standard methods merit some additional words. Although auctions in this program generally follow the same procedures as those conducted in small privatization, the Fund of National Property occasionally limits access to participation. In auctions of optician shops and pharmacies, for instance, bids were accepted only from registered opticians and pharmacists, respectively.[40] The FNP also occasionally attaches restrictions on changes in the line of business for assets auctioned in large privatization; in the example of pharmacies again, the activity must be maintained for at least ten years.

Tenders are usually evaluated according to three criteria: willingness to assume liabilities, commitment to maintaining the same line of activity, and price. Since virtually all tender bids include the first two of these criteria (bids without them are refused almost automatically), it seems that price is by and large the decisive factor. Although investment promises and employment guarantees have been important in some widely publicized directly negotiated sales, they are not standard criteria in most tenders. Tenders are thus essentially sealed bid first-price auctions. The evaluating committee is appointed by the FNP, with a representative from the District Privatization Commission. Employing arguments about non-price criteria, FNP officials have occasionally interfered directly in the tender outcome. The ensuing allegations of corruption illustrate the pitfalls in the nontransparency of the tender method.

4.4. Submitted privatization projects

Insiders and outsiders had various motives in submitting projects. Many of the same insider interests responsible for the inclusion of retail trade

[39] In addition to *The Privatization Process in Central Europe*, the reader may consult J.S. Earle, R. Frydman, and A. Rapaczynski, "Notes on Voucher Privatization in Eastern Europe," in *The New Europe: Evolving Economic and Financial Systems in East and West*, Fair and Raymond (eds), Kluwer Academic Publishers, (New York, 1993), and in Mejstrik and Burger, "The Czechoslovak Large Privatization."

[40] In another case, the Fund of National Property limited participation in the auction of a milk factory to those with certification in milk production and processing.

and service assets in large privatization could have also influenced the methods of privatization proposed for those assets. Powerless to prevent the privatization of their enterprises, managers may have hoped to influence the process to their advantage by proposing methods of privatization which would allow them to maintain some measure of control. Where it was possible to devise a plausible business plan, managers were likely to favor direct sales (particularly to new companies formed by a group of insiders, although only anecdotal evidence exists of such arrangements), management buyouts, and sweetheart deals with foreign buyers. Although many enterprises sought foreign and domestic partners, constraints imposed by the deadlines of the program made it very difficult to secure serious interest in time. The managers may, therefore, have viewed voucher privatization as attractive, insofar as it could be expected to result in dispersed ownership across large numbers of shareholders, who would be unable to exercise effective corporate governance. Distributing small numbers of shares to a wide variety of new owners, such as municipalities and the various social insurance and restitution funds, may have been attractive for the same reason.

"Outsiders" were on the other side of the struggle to acquire assets through large privatization, proposing alternative methods of privatization in their competing projects. The government commitment to the involvement of entrepreneurs in the program by encouraging the submission of competing projects was particularly significant in the case of the retail trade and consumer service sector assets, due to the prospects for growth and relatively low capital requirements in this sector. Potential investors in these assets would have been likely to favor direct sales and other standard methods.

We may investigate the empirical validity of these hypotheses by examining the composition of basic and competing projects according to the methods proposed in both waves of large privatization.[41] Table I.B.10 shows the proportion of the book value of property in the trade and services branches proposed for different methods in all submitted projects. The ratio of the number of competing to the number of basic projects is 3.88, higher than the average of 2.84 for all projects in all

[41] There is, of course, an identification problem in that those who were advancing projects naturally took into account both their own interests and their expectation of what the Ministry of Privatization was likely to approve.

Table I.B.10 Privatization methods proposed in basic and competing projects for enterprises by sector (percent of book value)

	Sector							
	Domestic trade*		Accommodation and tourist services†		Municipal services‡		All sectors	
Method of privatization	Basic	Competing	Basic	Competing	Basic	Competing	Basic	Competing
Auction	6.56	11.68	10.04	2.14	15.85	7.79	3.7	6.4
Tender	3.50	7.26	6.53	18.35	15.64	17.63	10.2	5.8
Direct sale	6.01	34.44	2.58	22.85	5.20	53.84	5.8	35.4
Asset transfer	0.64	2.59	1.67	0.93	3.09	1.00	2.8	4.9
Vouchers	45.25	23.75	42.14	16.15	56.35	18.50	32.9	26.5
Share sales and transfers	38.04	20.28	37.04	39.58	3.87	1.24	44.6	21.0
Number of submitted projects	113	476	23	80	24	65	2,906	8,257

Source: Czech Ministry of Privatization.

* Includes wholesale and retail trade, restaurants and associated services, and offices.
† Includes accommodation and tourism services such as hotels, restaurants, and travel agencies.
‡ Includes auto services, laundries, electrical services, car hire, blocks of flats, small textile and furniture production, street cleaning, printing services, gardening, and swimming pools.

sectors.[42] This result supports the supposition that the retail trade and consumer service assets were particularly attractive targets for potential entrepreneurs, as discussed above.

The table also demonstrates that voucher privatization is clearly favored among basic projects in the retail trade and consumer service sector, while it is equally clearly disfavored among competing projects. The overwhelming preference of outsiders for auctions and direct sales contrasts sharply with the preference of insiders for voucher privatization. Unfortunately, no further breakdown of the "share sales and transfer" is available for submitted projects, so we cannot determine the precise division of this category between share sales to foreign and direct and share transfers to municipalities and the restitution and various other funds.[43] The high proportion of share sale and transfer proposals in domestic trade may provide some further evidence for the view that managers were interested in a dispersed ownership structure, as discussed above.

4.5. Results: approved projects

Although nowhere precisely defined, the preferences of the Ministry of Privatization concerning alternative methods of privatization were partially revealed over time. The Ministry favored small over large privatization in 1991, a preference that diminished in 1992. In the first period, the large privatization program was still in its early organizational stages, and the Government started small privatization quickly, in an effort to maintain a steady, palpable pace of reform. This choice also reflected the preference for relatively transparent, competitive methods over direct sales, a predilection that also became apparent within the large privatization program.

In choosing among alternative methods within large privatization, the Ministry's priorities regarding vouchers versus other methods are more difficult to assess. On the one hand, the extension of the deadline for the submission of competing projects in the fall of 1991 resulted in a larger number of proposals for the use of standard methods, which were favored by outsiders. On the other hand, the rather stringent deadlines

[42] There were 2,906 basic and 8,257 competing projects in total.
[43] These funds include the so-called Foundation Fund (for which 1 percent is obligatory in the second wave), Pension Fund, and Health Care Fund.

for the completion of voucher privatization in the first wave[44] meant that a greater priority was given to the approval process for assets for which projects including vouchers had been proposed, compared to those for which there were no voucher proposals. A huge and largely unexpected increase in demand for participation in the voucher program in early 1992 decreased the average value of property that each voucher-holder could expect to receive.[45] The Ministry, therefore, began to place higher priority on voucher privatization relative to other methods, and on large privatization relative to small privatization, in order to increase the value of assets backing the vouchers.[46] At the same time, the possibility of generating significant revenues from auctions and direct sales may also have influenced the Ministry of Privatization's preferences for sales versus transfers and voucher privatization.

While the demand for trade and services assets varied according to the method of privatization, demand may have conversely influenced the choice of privatization method applied to a particular asset. For instance, an especially valuable asset might be privatized either through corporatization leading to voucher privatization, the result of the political need to include some "family jewels" in the voucher program.[47] On the other hand, direct sales to foreign investors were probably attractive for assets requiring substantial investment or restructuring.

Table I.B.11 displays the division of the book value of property in approved projects according to the methods of transfer employed. The first four types of method apply to asset sales and transfers, the last five

[44] Although these deadlines were postponed several times, they seemed to function to push the process forward. The original schedule for the Large Privatization Program indicated that the first wave would be completed by May 1992. However, the distribution of shares, the final stage of the process, began only in late May 1993.

[45] Although less than half a million voucher holders were registered at the end of 1992, participation soared in January 1992, with 8.57 million registered by the end of February, the final deadline. This unexpected swelling of participation (in November 1991, forecasts of 2 million were considered optimistic) is usually attributed to the spectacular offers by Harvard Capital and Consulting and other investment privatization funds to offer guaranteed 900 percent rates of return. See J.S. Earle, R. Frydman, and A. Rapaczynski, *The Privatization Process in Central Europe* or "Notes on Voucher Privatization" for more details.

[46] The property backing the vouchers was also strengthened by including the partial privatization of some state companies, including the Electric Company, in the voucher program. Since the state retains a majority stake, it may even be doubted whether these transactions strictly speaking constitute privatization.

[47] The company controlling the world-renowned Pilsner Urquell Brewery is such an example, with two-thirds of its shares distributed to voucher holders, including almost 20 percent to Harvard Capital and Consulting.

Table I.B.11 Composition of the large privatization program by method of transfer, January and August 1993

		Method of transferring assets				Method of transferring shares					
							Sales				
Through January 1993	Number	Auction	Tender	Direct sale	Free transfer	Vouchers	Foreign investor	Domestic investor	FNP	Free transfer	Book value (Csk mln)
Warehouses	14	63.41	0.00	34.98	1.61	0.00	0.00	0.00	0.00	0.00	65.1
Supermarkets	58	8.55	1.76	69.49	0.45	14.59	0.00	0.98	0.01	4.18	2,233.2
Department stores	30	11.75	2.06	34.66	0.00	30.04	8.41	0.73	1.34	11.02	2,260.5
Wholesale trade stores	48	6.69	0.12	5.00	0.24	70.63	0.00	0.00	0.00	17.33	3,280.4
Restaurants	17	11.40	0.00	2.57	21.77	54.33	0.00	0.00	1.03	8.90	472.1
Travel agencies	2	0.00	0.00	1.50	0.00	52.90	0.00	0.00	8.82	36.78	555.9
Hotels	50	0.42	4.72	5.56	0.06	40.70	4.57	0.54	3.28	40.15	4,887.6
Other services	55	5.06	16.60	12.63	2.84	52.76	0.00	1.45	0.00	8.66	946.6
Production units	19	2.82	1.85	6.25	0.05	63.28	5.41	0.00	3.47	16.87	756.9
Buildings	39	19.70	5.35	8.85	66.11	0.00	0.00	0.00	0.00	0.00	83.0
Land	21	0.00	0.00	0.21	99.79	0.00	0.00	0.00	0.00	0.00	14.3
Miscellaneous and n.e.c.	31	24.73	1.37	54.85	2.14	12.16	0.00	2.35	0.00	2.40	868.8
Total (retail)	384	6.65	3.09	21.10	1.46	42.29	2.76	0.60	1.65	20.40	16,424.5
Through August 1993											
Total (retail)	509	6.94	2.82	42.12	1.51	34.46	1.77	0.40	1.83	8.15	25,661.4
Total (all sectors)	2,318	2.37	1.73	35.22	1.73	35.95	0.98	0.95	9.79	11.28	718,006.3

Source: Czech Ministry of Privatization.

Notes: "n.e.c." represents "not elsewhere classified." "Number" denotes the number of new entities in each category. The detailed structure was not available for data after December 31, 1992. The methods of privatization add up horizontally to 100 percent.

to share sales and transfers. Therefore, the columns labeled "foreign investor" and "domestic investor" refer only to the sales of shares; separate data on foreign purchases of assets are unfortunately unavailable. It should also be emphasized that the table shows the number of new entities and the value of projects approved, not the number of individual establishments privatized by those projects; unfortunately, such information is unavailable. However, it seems likely that auctions and direct sales are likely to involve fewer units than public tenders and corporatizations.

By far the most important privatization method applied in the distributive trade and consumer service sector is voucher privatization, with 42 percent of the total book value. Direct sales account for 21 percent, share transfers 20 percent, and auctions an additional 7 percent. Vouchers are particularly important in wholesale trade stores, restaurants, travel agencies, and other services; auctions predominate in warehouses; direct sales are important in warehouses, supermarkets (see the discussion concerning foreign investors below), and department stores; and share transfers are most significant in travel agencies and hotels.

Information about the privatization of Czech wholesale trade is particularly scarce. Although some wholesale units (primarily warehouses) were auctioned under the small privatization program, it seems that the newest and most valuable wholesale trade assets were included in large privatization, accounting for approximately 50 percent of all storage capacity in the Czech Republic.[48] However, from the available statistics it is difficult to determine, even roughly, how many of these units are included in the program. Official records usually reflect the number of approved privatization projects, which can involve a whole range of possible groups of enterprise assets, and which are classified only according to primary line of business. While this complicates the task of quantifying any of the different types of assets transferred in the program, it is particularly cumbersome in the case of wholesale trade. Typically, wholesale units are privatized as parts of larger retail networks and rarely constitute the primary business of a privatization project. Published statistics may therefore often fail to capture wholesale trade.

[48] Based on evidence collected during an interview with Josef Riha of the Czech Ministry of Industry and Trade, May 1993.

4.6. Results: new owners

Although no general restrictions exist on who may purchase shares of corporatized companies, nor on who may participate in direct sales, auctions, or tenders, participation in voucher privatization is limited to resident Czechoslovak citizens over the age of 18, who purchased and registered voucher booklets. They could choose to bid their voucher points as individual investors or to place them with privately created investment privatization funds, which would then use them to bid for the shares of companies in the program. The funds attracted over 72 percent of all points, and the largest thirteen control 40 percent of the total. This concentration implies that the insiders' hopes for dispersed ownership and ineffective control resulting from voucher privatization may have remained largely unrealized. Otherwise, only scattered information is available concerning the new ownership structure resulting from the voucher program.[49]

Though it may have played only a modest role in the privatization of the sector as a whole, foreign investment has been responsible for several well-publicized direct sales. Through five direct purchases and one majority stake acquisition in the large privatization program and of one cooperatively-owned establishment (in an excellent location on the Wenceslaus Square in downtown Prague), the American company K-Mart has created a chain of large department stores in all of the largest cities in the Czech Republic. Other major investors in Czech trade and services include Tchibo of Germany, Sara Lee and Dougwe Egberts of Holland, and Delhaize Le Lion of Belgium. The most important cases of foreign participation in privatization are shown in Table I.B.12.

4.7. Conclusion

As we have shown, some of the retail trade and consumer service sector, including about 2,000 establishments according to our estimates, is

[49] Vouchers were distributed between October 1991 and February 1992, before the split of the Czech and Slovak Republics. The two governments agreed to carry out the first wave of voucher privatization after the split as originally planned. However, complications arising from disputes over federal property stalled the distribution of Czech company shares until May 24, 1993. Subsequent privatization will be carried out independently by the two countries.

Table I.B.12 Major cases of foreign privatization in the trade and service sector, as of 1993

Czech company	Foreign investor	Type of participation	Book value of stake (Csk mln)	Purchase price of stake (Csk mln)
Maj a.s. Praha (Department store)	K-Mart (USA)	76.04% of shares	245	330
Brno, Hradec Karlove, Paradubice, Plzen, Liberec (Department stores)	K-Mart (USA)	direct sale	663	930
Balirny Jihlava	Tchibo (Germany)	32% of shares	36	94
Prazirny a balirny Praha	Sara Lee (Holland)	100% of shares	163	100
Darex-Praha (Department store)	Zane May (USA)	75% of shares	3	3
Potraviny Praha 4,8,9 (partial)	Delhaize Le Lion (Belgium)	direct sale	68	106
Interhotel Jalta Praha	Fukuoka Jisho and Miki Tourist (Japan)	36% and 4% of shares	324	688

Source: Czech Ministry of Industry and Trade.

undergoing privatization in groups, thereby preserving to some degree the chains of their progenitor state enterprises. In this respect, the Czech Republic stands somewhere in the middle between Poland and Hungary: in Poland, nearly all establishments in the sector were privatized singly, while there was a much stronger tendency in Hungary to privatize joint stock companies comprised of chains of shops. The retail trade and consumer service sector is unlike heavy industry, in which scale economies and indivisibility of capital practically compelled multiplicity of owners and complex organizational forms. But if scale economies play some role in retail trade and services as well, and if reconsolidation of the shops privatized singly is a slow and costly process, then the firms established through the large privatization program may be advantageously situated in the overall market.

5. CONSUMER COOPERATIVE TRANSFORMATION

5.1. Introduction

Cooperatives have played a special role in the transformation of Czech trade and services, both because of their numerical importance and because of the particular ambiguities in assessing the extent to which genuine transformation has taken place. Under the communist regime, cooperatives were at least nominally owned by their individual members rather than by the state, and their transformation fundamentally differs from the privatization of state property. While some elements of such a transformation seem to be taking place, a perhaps more important phenomenon is the relative and absolute decline in the numbers of shops and service establishments operated by cooperatives. This section discusses both of these processes: the internal reorganization and changes in the governance of cooperatives and the ways in which the numbers of cooperative establishments have declined.

5.2. Cooperatives under socialism

Since the middle of the nineteenth century, cooperatives have played a significant role in the Czech food industry, commerce, and services.[50] The origins of consumer cooperatives in particular, the type of cooperative most active in trade and service activity,[51] are associated with the social democratic movement of the early twentieth century. They gained popularity in the Czech lands throughout the first half of the 1900s, and by the 1940s, sixty-seven consumer cooperatives claimed 608,000 members and operated 4,672 shops on Czech territory.

The socialist regime which assumed power in 1948 chose not to nationalize the cooperative sector of the economy. Rather, consumer cooperatives became a vehicle for "socializing" private commercial property: shopkeepers were "encouraged" to contribute their shops to cooperative organizations, and they did so, although not always

[50] The first cooperative in continental Europe was founded in Slovakia, in 1847, and the first laws governing cooperatives were passed in 1873.

[51] Within the cooperative sector of the economy, consumer cooperatives account for the largest share of trade and services activity. Although producer cooperatives also engage in some service activity, data and information concerning their contribution to the sector is not available. See subsections 3.1 and 3.3 of Part A for a discussion of this issue.

voluntarily. The number of consumer cooperative establishments grew to 30,000 by 1951 and their share of retail trade turnover reached 25 percent, from 11 percent in 1945. As a result, the average number of shops per cooperative rose from roughly 70 to 450.[52]

Consumer cooperatives also underwent significant reorganization during the socialist period. Management of cooperative shops quickly was brought under the authority of the Communist Party planning apparatus. As described in Part A, cooperatives of all kinds came to be organized under the Party-directed Union of Cooperatives, to which plan targets were "suggested" by the Central Planning Committee. The Union, in turn, parceled out directions to individual cooperatives. In addition, much of the existing cooperative wholesale network was absorbed into the state trade system. Finally, in the mid-1950s, consumer cooperatives were shouldered with the responsibility of supplying rural areas with goods and services. They subsequently forfeited 15,000 of their city shops in exchange for 6,000 shops in the countryside.

Thus, consumer cooperatives lost many of the unique characteristics associated with member ownership and governance. Significant numbers of original members (particularly those in urban areas) were no longer able to participate in the cooperatives they had helped to establish, while those who remained members saw drastic changes in the purposes and assets of their cooperatives. Unlike the earlier cooperative practice, new members contributed only nominal sums and received token dividends which had only an indirect correspondence to profits. And although members retained the right to exit, such action no longer carried weight in the governance of the organization, since most decisions were subject to the general economic plan. Cooperatives came to resemble state enterprises closely.

Still, the resulting organization of "pseudo-cooperatives" became important economic and social institutions of rural communities. They served not only as the single suppliers of essential foodstuffs and consumer goods, they also built many new enterprises in the countryside, including shops, pubs, cultural centers, and recreation facilities. Communist Party ideologues exploited this social network, using cooperatives to monitor and safeguard the "political integrity" of the rural population.

[52] Figures come from L. Sipek, "Problematika Transformace Druzstev" ("The Issue of Cooperative Transformation"), mimeo, Ministry of Internal Trade and Tourism (Prague), 1991.

Table I.B.13 Consumer cooperatives in the Czech Republic in 1989

Number of consumer cooperatives	73
Number of members (in thousands)	1,420
Number of employees (in thousands)	111
Number of shops	16,014
Number of catering units	9,374
Retail trade turnover (Csk bln)	52.2
of which catering (Csk bln)	6.8
Wholesale trade turnover (Csl bln)*	19.3
Purchase of agricultural products (Csk bln)	0.7
Volume of foodstuff production (Csk bln)	0.9

Sources: L. Sipek, "Problematika Transformace Druzstev" ("The Issue of Cooperative Transformation"), mimeo, Ministry of Internal Trade and Tourism (Prague), 1991; *Statistical Yearbook of CSFR 1991*, SNTL-ALFA (Prague), pp. 498, 499.

* Data on wholesale trade turnover, purchase of agricultural products, and volume of foodstuff production are for 1990.

The number of consumer cooperatives grew only slightly between the 1960s and 1980s.[53] In 1988, the *perestroika* movement inspired the government to pass Law No. 94 "Collection on Housing, Consumer, and Production Cooperatives," allowing the establishment of new co-operatives. However, the restrictive environment of the time precluded any significant number of new entrants.

As discussed in section 3 of Part A above, by 1989 consumer cooperatives accounted for 40.3 percent of all shops in Czechoslovakia, though because cooperative establishments were smaller, their share of trade turnover and employment reached only 22 percent and 21.5 percent, respectively.[54] Table I.B.13 shows other indicators of the consumer cooperative sector in 1989.

[53] See Table I.A.7 in section 3 of Part A, above.

[54] See section 3 of Part A above, for more details on the composition of Czech trade in 1989.

5.3. Cooperative transformation: after 1990

After the Velvet Revolution of 1989, the question of how to "denationalize" cooperatives became one of the most fractious disputes in the Czech Republic. The form into which cooperatives had evolved under socialism was neither fully private nor fully state. Nominally members owned their cooperatives, by having originally made significant contributions. However, over time consumer cooperatives acquired much property which had not been voluntarily contributed. In addition, they had been managed and, it was felt, exploited by socialist planners.

The debate followed lines which may or may not have represented the self-interest of cooperative outsiders and insiders. Though recognizing that cooperatives constituted a kind of intermediate form of ownership, some argued that because they had lost their voluntary nature and in many ways had become just another arm of the party apparatus, cooperatives should simply be liquidated, and their assets sold through auction. Others claimed that cooperatives had served many useful commercial and social functions, that they had a long tradition in the Czech lands, and thus should be given the opportunity to transform themselves back to their original form of voluntary association.[55] Other proposals suggested that cooperative members should have a choice: either to participate in the transformation of their cooperative, or to partake in the voucher privatization program.

As in other postsocialist countries, most attention was focused on the fate of agricultural cooperatives, which in Czechoslovakia had exclusive rights to the use of land formally belonging to nearly 2 million people. However, the resulting legislation, designed first of all to address the question of agricultural cooperatives, also includes provisions relevant for cooperatives of all types and consumer cooperatives in particular. Since 1989, three laws have been passed affecting the organization and governance of cooperatives:

— Law No. 176/1990 Collection of Laws and Decrees on Housing, Consumer, Production, and other Cooperatives of Czechoslovakia, ("Cooperative Law");

[55] For a persuasive presentation of this position, see, "The Mission of the Cooperative and Legislation," by Deputy Prime Minister Rychecky, in *Druzstevni noviny*, 46, February 5, 1991, p. 1.

— Law No. 513/1991 Commercial Code;
— Law No. 42/1992 Law on the Regulation of Property Relations in Cooperatives, ("Transformation Law").

Passed by the first postcommunist government, the Cooperative Law of 1990 attempted to resolve the conflicting arguments surrounding the fate of cooperatives. According to this policy, cooperatives would not be privatized like state enterprises, but instead should undergo "transformation" into a more genuine form of cooperative association. However, soon after the first elections, the legitimacy of this policy was brought into question, since it had been enacted by a non-elected government. Thus, in 1992 the Transformation Law superseded the previous legislation. Any cooperatives which had already undergone transformation were required to repeat the process as prescribed by the new law.

The Transformation Law established three fundamental changes in the organization of consumer cooperatives. First, individual cooperatives were granted independence from the Union of Consumer Cooperatives and the freedom to operate under whatever grouping they chose. Second, cooperatives had to "transform" themselves by January 1993, by passing new bylaws, deciding whether to split into separate, smaller cooperatives, proposing a plan to satisfy all debts to the state, and reorganizing the equity structure of the cooperative's capital assets. Third, once transformation is complete, consumer cooperatives are regulated according to the provisions of the Commercial Code, which apply to all commercial enterprises. In other words, after transformation is complete, they may sell any assets belonging to them, liquidate themselves, and in general, operate in the economy as any other legal entity.

Of these three changes, the transformation process is by far the most complex, although its influence on the operation of cooperatives is unclear. Primarily at issue is the distribution between the consumer cooperative's two basic capital funds, the membership fund and the indivisible fund. In principle, the membership fund is accumulated through member contributions, and it is from this fund that members are reimbursed if they withdraw from the cooperative. On the other hand, the indivisible fund is accumulated from retained earnings and investments, and can be distributed to members only if the cooperative is liquidated.

Each cooperative established a Transformation Council responsible for formulating a "transformation project." Execution of the transformation project was supervised by the Ministry of Finance, and involved satisfying all of the cooperative's liabilities to the state, redistributing the cooperative's capital assets between the membership and indivisible capital funds, and revaluing each member's share in the membership fund.[56]

Originally, the Cooperative Law set no restrictions on the redistribution of cooperative funds or on the revaluation of member shares. The Transformation Law, however, included a clause stipulating two significant restrictions on the transformation of consumer cooperatives. First, the membership fund of a consumer cooperative cannot comprise more than 25 percent of the cooperative's assets, thus limiting the revaluation of member shares. Second, the law states that if a consumer cooperative is liquidated any time in the next ten years, the whole of its indivisible fund (75 percent of its capital assets) will be allocated to the Fund of National Property.

At the time of the Transformation Law's passage, all discussion centered on the fate of agricultural cooperatives, as mentioned above. Thus, it is possible only to speculate why such a restrictive clause was included in the regulations governing consumer cooperatives. A highly capitalized membership fund would maximize the value of member shares, increase the effect of membership exit on the cooperative, and thus contribute to members' ability to exercise voice in the governance of their cooperatives. Of course, it is possible that policy makers intended to limit the windfall gains which cooperative members might have received, had all cooperative assets been redistributed to the membership funds. However, it seems that the primary beneficiaries of the restrictions limiting members' ownership rights will be the managers of consumer cooperatives. Their decision-making autonomy has been secured for the next ten years, since it is unlikely that any cooperative would choose to liquidate if the largest share of the proceeds will be allocated to the government.

And indeed, there has been no case of consumer cooperative liquidation since the passage of the Transformation Law. Moreover, transformation seems to have had little effect on the governance of cooperatives. Although most cooperatives have reallocated between 15 and 25 percent of their capital assets into their membership fund, members remain mostly passive and managers have retained their independence, in part because membership remains large and dispersed,

[56] Liabilities to the state included unpaid taxes, social insurance, and health care costs.

and in part because member voice in governance is substantially limited.[57] One interesting development can be observed, however, in the decline of membership, from 1.42 million in 1989 to 840,000 by the end of 1992, perhaps indicating that many former members were quite eager to "cash in" on their shares.

Although transformation seems to have had little perceptible impact on the internal operations of consumer cooperatives, other provisions in the laws regulating their activities have had pronounced effects. The consumer cooperative union changed its name to the Union of Czech and Moravian Consumer Cooperatives, and has taken dramatic steps to benefit its members more effectively. It now functions as a source of technical support and reportedly hopes to become the central purchasing agent for cooperative stores. Recently, the Union also established the Coop Bank, a commercial bank designed specifically to serve the needs of cooperatives.[58]

The most significant effect of the cooperative legislation, however, is the massive reorganization of assets in the sector, discussed below.

5.4. Divestment of assets and operations

Consumer cooperatives have sold or leased nearly three quarters of their establishments in the last four years. Of the 26,250 shops and restaurants which consumer cooperatives operated in 1989, only 7,089 remain under their direct control. Roughly 3,500 of these were returned to their previous owners under the restitution program, while some 11,700 units have been either sold or returned to the control of municipal bodies that originally funded their construction.[59] Most dramatically, cooperatives no longer operate 95 percent of the restaurants they maintained in 1989.

Leasing is also common, and accounts for as many as 3,972 of the units formerly operated by cooperatives.[60] As of March 1993, consumer cooperatives were leasing out 2,768 shops and 1,204 restaurants to

[57] According to some accounts, most consumer cooperative members are rural housewives who joined by making very small contributions and remain members for the sake of discounts on shop purchases.

[58] This evaluation is derived from interviews with Milan Sulc, former chairman of the Czech and Moravian Union of Consumer Cooperatives. Mr Sulc is currently managing the Coop Bank.

[59] These estimates were provided by Ladislav Sipek, former Deputy Minister of Internal Trade and Tourism. See section 2 for an account of restitution.

[60] Unpublished statistics, Union of Czech and Moravian Consumer Cooperatives.

Table I.B.14 Shops and restaurants operated by consumer cooperatives

	1989	1990	1991*	1992	1993
Number of shops (units)	16,876	16,075	12,702	7,114†	6,755
Number of restaurants (units)	9,374	7,770	2,990	465†	334
Employment ('000)	113.2	108.8	83.7	41.9†	–
Profit (Csk mln)	–	1,253	–515	–406†	–
Turnover (Csk bln)	51.8	57.7	40.6	28.0	–
Total turnover of Czech trade and services (Csk bln)	232.6	260.9	252.6	329.8	–
Cooperative share in total trade turnover	22.3%	22.1%	16.1%	8.5%†	–

Sources: *Statistical Yearbook of CSFR 1992*, SNTL-ALFA (Prague), pp. 501, 502; *Statistical Yearbook of CSFR 1990*, SNTL-ALFA (Prague), pp. 517, 530; *Ukazatele maloobchodni site*, ECOMA (Prague), 1993; Sipek, "Problematika Transformace Druzstev"; V. Chudlarsky, "Analyza vyvoje ekonomiky CR a organizaci MPO CR" ("Analysis of economic development in CR and in the organizations of MPO CR"), Ministry of Industry and Trade (Prague), 1993.

* Shops and restaurants as of June 30, 1991.
† These are official figures from the Union of Czech and Moravian Consumer Cooperatives. Shops, restaurants, and employment are end-of-year figures, others are flows over the year.

private parties. Typically, one of two types of leasing arrangements exists. Less profitable establishments tend to be rented for defined periods with few lease conditions. More profitable units, especially those supplied by cooperative wholesale distribution systems, are required to maintain the business name and purchase many goods from a particular supplier. Table I.B.14 presents a summary of the decreasing significance of consumer cooperatives in trade and catering since 1989.

It seems that market reforms, competition from new private entrants, and, in particular, the withdrawal of state subsidies have forced consumer cooperatives to restructure and reorganize their operations. Many cooperative shops in the countryside are unprofitable, and have been either closed or rented out. Debt accumulated over decades of subsidized lending has constituted a heavy burden for cooperatives.

In addition to liquidating or leasing the overgrown parts of their retail networks, many consumer cooperatives have begun restructuring their operations in other ways as well. In some cooperatives there is discussion of what we may call "returning to their roots;" to provide their members with cheaper food and other products by marking up prices less than private outlets. There were sixty-three cooperative "discount shops" for consumers in February 1993 in the Czech Republic. But other cooperatives, in particular those in districts close to the German and Austrian borders, are more concerned with maximizing profits by selling to foreign day-trippers.

Some cooperatives make an effort to support each other by coordinating their activities through the Union, establishing joint wholesale operations, and uniting with other cooperatives in negotiating with suppliers. Officials from cooperative organizations estimate that cooperative stores now purchase 50 percent of their supplies from other cooperatives, representing a significant increase from earlier years.[61]

Still, the importance of cooperative activity in trade has declined dramatically, possibly leaving many rural communities without easy access to shops and restaurants. And with managers firmly in control of consumer cooperative assets, this trend seems likely to continue.

[61] Before 1989, it is estimated that cooperatives received between 30 percent and 40 percent of their supplies from other cooperatives (source: interviews with Milan Sulc).

PART II: HUNGARY

1. INTRODUCTION

The Hungarian approach to the privatization of the retail trade and consumer service sector has been very different from those adopted in Poland or the Czech Republic. While those two countries attempted, above all, to remove the state as fast as possible from the running of their shops and restaurants, the primary objectives of the Hungarian authorities were much more complex and less unambiguous. In addition to the goal of eliminating the role of the state, Hungary's approach might be characterized as focused around three important objectives: 1) to create a market structure similar to that found in advanced Western economies; 2) to raise revenues to finance the state budget deficit; and 3) to assert effective governmental control over the process of privatization itself.

In their efforts to realize their policy goals, Hungarian officials have applied a number of privatization strategies, and the emphasis on privatizing individual shops separately from large state retail trade organizations has been considered appropriate only for a portion of the sector. The majority of state assets in retail trade and consumer services have been, or are poised to be, privatized in ways that emphasize the transfer of many units together, grouped to form integrated commercial entities. "Small privatization," in the usual sense of this term, is thus in no way synonymous in the Hungarian context with the privatization of the whole trade and service sector.

Why have the Hungarian officials elected to pursue privatization strategies so markedly different from neighboring Poland and the Czech Republic? To be able to answer this question, events following the demise of the communist system must be placed in a much broader historical context. In essence, the situation in Hungary was very different from that in Poland and the Czech Republic because of the legacy of many years of reforms which had preceded the change of the regime. The Hungarian retail and service sector, in particular, was an object of a series of reforms dating back to the late 1960s, when the so-called New Economic Mechanism (NEM) changed the relations between enterprise managers and government officials, as well as between enterprise managers and the managers of individual stores and restaurants.

Under NEM, the locus of most economic decision-making shifted from the ministries to individual enterprise managers. Enterprise managers were gradually given decisive control over such decisions as the line of business in which individual stores were engaged, their supply arrangements, the internal organization of the enterprise, and ultimately the pricing of the goods sold in state shops. The devolution of real authority onto enterprise management culminated, in 1988, with the "Company Law," which allowed managers to divide their enterprises and spin off diverse subsidiaries without obtaining a ministerial nod of approval. Retail trade enterprise managers quickly moved to augment their control over valuable state assets by the creation of new commercial companies which shielded them from state oversight. Exploiting notoriously lax controls over the movement of state property, some managers arranged a transfer of prime state assets to themselves personally or to their foreign and domestic business partners. These improvised privatizations in the retail trade sector incited some of the largest scandals of the last years of the socialist regime.

Other reforms begun in 1968 affected the relations between enterprises and managers of individual state stores. The first step was the introduction of profit incentives into the pay packages of shop managers. These profit-sharing arrangements were then gradually expanded during the next two decades as many shops were leased to employees and other parties, and as shop managers acquired ever greater autonomy in running their units. As a result, an increasing number of decisions concerning the operation of the sector were made not in accordance with the dictates of remote planners, but by store and enterprise managers, based on profitability and consumer demand.

Consumer cooperatives, the other half of the socialized trade sector, were also affected by the general movement away from centralized controls. Between 1969 and 1971, a series of laws freed consumer cooperatives from many restrictions that had previously prevented them from operating stores in urban areas and interfered with their business decisions. The role of the National Federation of Cooperatives in running the daily operations of cooperative stores was reduced and, as in the state sector, profit-sharing and other contractual arrangements became common.

Perhaps most importantly, the reforms of the last two decades of the communist regime also ended the socialized sector's monopoly in trade and catering. Although private entrepreneurs were restricted by all kinds of limitations on the size of their businesses, access to foreign markets, and the opportunity to limit personal liability for losses, the state permitted, and even encouraged, a variety of private economic entities. Legislation concerning private economic activity became ever more liberal, and resulted in a very rapid growth of the new private sector. By the late 1980s, all segments of Hungarian retail trade and services included a sizeable private component.

To be sure, the degree of the advancement of the Hungarian reform, described in more detail in section 2 below, should not be overstated. The state still retained its monopoly on wholesale trade, severely restricting the range of products offered to consumers. Regional enterprises still operated extensive networks of shops and dominated the market in urban areas, while rural trade was the all but exclusive domain of large consumer cooperatives. The maze of regulations and restrictions was responsible for a very odd ownership and control structure of the sector, with state enterprises being able to derive substantial profits through subleasing their state stores to private parties. But combined with macroeconomic changes, such as price liberalization and the growth of foreign trade, the new system introduced a measure of competition and efficiency into the provision of consumer goods and services, unknown in the other countries of the "socialist camp." Hungary's communist reforms bequeathed to the new democratic government, elected in 1990, a trade sector that bore scant resemblance to those in Poland and Czechoslovakia.

It was precisely this superior performance of the Hungarian trade sector that explains the very different Hungarian approach to privatization after the fall of the old regime. To begin with, the importance of the immediate privatization of most shops and restaurants was less evident than in, say, Poland, since the population was tolerably well served by the existing system. In fact, privatization had been given a bit of a bad name by its "spontaneous" version under the old regime, and calls to curtail its abuses initially drowned out the demand, heard so loudly in Czechoslovakia and Poland, for pursuing further ownership reforms. The government's pressing need for money to service Hungary's large foreign debt only deepened its resolve to exert control over privatization. Since the trade sector was identified as a particularly attractive area for foreign investment, halting its spontaneous privatization was of special interest to the new government.

The government thus proceeded with rather deliberate speed in elaborating its privatization programs. While the reassertion of control over state property certainly slowed down its progress, the desire to assure that the proceeds from privatization were available for the state budget acted as an incentive to get the program off the ground. In addition, the need to act quickly, at least with respect to the trade sector, was also underscored by the numerous calls, heard during the first postcommunist election campaign, for the restitution of private property nationalized during the communist period. Since the government was afraid that restitution might interfere with its objective of raising revenues from privatization, the formation of a privatization strategy for the retail trade sector was given a heightened degree of priority.

The core of the government's emerging privatization program was quite threatening to the managers of state enterprises. They had succeeded over the years in solidifying their control over state assets, creating a complicated governance structure that made it very difficult for the government to assert its control. The predictable opposition of the sectoral insiders to any centralized program and the desire of the state to circumvent this opposition without causing a major confrontation are the main factors accounting for the further course of events.

In September 1990, six months after coming to power, the Antall government announced its "Preprivatization" program, described in section 3 below, designed to fulfill the dual political need to assert governmental control over the privatization process and to spawn a stream of revenues for the state. Preprivatization was a centralized program to be run by the newly established State Property Agency (SPA), aimed at selling, at public auctions, the state's rights to a part of its shops, restaurants, and service outlets. But Preprivatization was also designed to avoid excessive confrontation with the managers of the sectoral state enterprises, and for this reason the program did not apply to all state assets in the sector. Instead, the primary targets were those shops and restaurants which had been leased to private entrepreneurs and were thus the least integrated into the functioning of state enterprises. In all, the program applied to no more than 20 percent of the state establishments, and even the most optimistic assessments of the scope of Preprivatization predicted that the program would involve no more than 10,000–15,000 units.

Strategies by the SPA for dealing with the portion of the commercial sector not affected by Preprivatization were slow to develop and even slower to be implemented. The programs that followed included the

First Privatization Program (reviewed in section 4), and Self-Privatization (described in section 5), both of which had a broader scope and included a range of enterprises outside the trade and service sector. Both of these programs have been plagued by problems and have succeeded in privatizing only a small number of enterprises. In addition to these major efforts, the SPA has either announced, or is in the process of preparing, other, more limited privatization schemes designed specifically for certain portions of the commercial sector, such as pharmacies, or new chains carved out from units now belonging to various state enterprises. (These alternative approaches to the privatization of the remainder of the state commercial sector are examined in section 6.) The government has had only a limited involvement in the changes which have altered the role played by the consumer cooperatives, a process that has occurred with only minimal property transfers. (The transformation of the cooperative sector is reviewed in section 7.)

The variety of privatization techniques is not necessarily synonymous with a genuinely diverse set of approaches to the problem of ownership transformation. Indeed, despite the large number of privatization programs in Hungary, one can clearly discern a consistent and persisting strategy of the SPA. In every program since Preprivatization, the SPA has been active in selecting the enterprises and units to be included, and it has been integrally involved in the elaboration of detailed privatization and postprivatization plans for the new firms. While its activist, "engineering" role was most visible in the First Privatization Program, the SPA's influence in Self-Privatization has also been pervasive; it has retained control over the entry into the program and all essential decisions along the way. Plans for the privatization of the new chains in the retail sector are similarly based on the SPA's choice of the subsectors and enterprises involved, as well as of the detailed mechanics of the process.

In all of its programs after Preprivatization, the SPA has focused on the privatization of entire enterprises rather than individual shops and restaurants. This move away from the usual model of "small privatization" has been predicated on the desire to shape the postprivatization trade sector in Hungary in the image of the commercial sector in the West, with its emphasis on companies that integrate wholesale activities with large chains of retail or service outlets. This approach, which we have previously labeled (in our earlier discussion of Czech privatization) as "insider" or "technocratic," gained much greater acceptance in Hungary than in the Czech Republic or Poland.

We have explained earlier in this volume[1] the factors that led to the defeat of the proposals for keeping intact the organizational structure of state enterprises in the Czech Republic: the widespread antipathy to sectoral insiders; the enactment of restitution legislation; and an ideological opposition by the controlling Ministry of Privatization. In Poland, the technocratic approach to the privatization of the trade sector was even more decisively rejected from the very beginning: since the endemic shortages of most goods were taken as irrefutable proof of the bankruptcy of the old system, the idea of preserving the structure of the old state enterprises did not have even superficial appeal. In Hungary, by contrast, the situation was quite different. As we have explained, the old system, while far from perfect, did manage to deliver a substantial improvement in the availability of consumer goods and services, and the managers in control of state retail trade enterprises could claim a measure of social approval. The hostility to sectoral insiders was also lessened by the more pragmatic nature of the communist regime, perceived to have been much less oppressive or confrontational than in Czechoslovakia or Poland. Finally, the financial needs of the state further spurred the adoption of a technocratic strategy since government officials assumed that sales of retail trade enterprises with large networks of shops would be more lucrative and, unlike individual stores, would attract wealthy foreign investors.

A certain degree of conviction that Hungary was "different" and more "advanced" than the other postcommunist countries may have also contributed to the feeling that Western models were more appropriate for Hungary than the strong antistatist bias of the Czechs or the Poles. A large proportion of the SPA staff was in fact drawn from the former branch ministries and selected for their expertise in restructuring state enterprises. They were thus naturally predisposed to support technocratic privatization strategies that called for the utilization of their particular skills.

The continued reliance on technocratic programs is remarkable, given the disappointing record of these efforts. The near complete failure of the First Privatization Program provided seemingly ample warning against further "over-engineered" solutions. Nevertheless, the SPA has not fundamentally changed its approach. Its Self-Privatization program has been more successful in privatizing a number of small service firms, but has not achieved notable success with respect to larger retail trade

[1] See section 1 of Part I.B.

enterprises. SPA's efforts to privatize the remaining parts of the state sector have also been stalled so far by debates over which technocratic model to follow.

Interestingly, the SPA's failure to devise smoothly functioning privatization mechanisms has given rise to a peculiar internal dynamic common to many Hungarian privatization programs. Faced with the hopelessly clogged central mechanisms for privatization, enterprise insiders, anxious to move ahead with the privatization process as *they* understand it, as well as outside investors eager to purchase the remaining state units, have naturally attempted to find alternative avenues of ownership transformation. This pressure, combined with the considerable ingenuity of the interested players, has led to a situation in which each program has ended up with its own unintended privatization mechanisms, many of which allow the interested parties to detach individual units from their enterprises. It appears likely, for example, that – despite the SPA's intentions – fewer than one-half of the units ultimately privatized under the Self-Privatization program will be privatized as part of entire enterprises, and that ways have also been found to get around the rigorously competitive procedures designated as "exclusive" in the program. The majority of units appears destined to be transferred individually, through liquidation sales or other unpredicted transfer procedures. While, on the surface, therefore, Hungarian privatization programs have followed the technocratic models, their actual outcomes have often differed significantly from the planned ones, and many fewer enterprises have been sold as a whole than may have been originally expected.

Assorted goals, a myriad of programs, and the problems encountered in their implementation have combined together to produce a privatization process that, overall, has moved at a halting gait. While the Czech Republic and Poland have all but completed the privatization of their trade sectors, a significant portion of Hungarian stores still remains under state ownership. Since the speed of the process has never been considered as important in Hungary as it was in the Czech Republic or Poland, the lagging of Hungarian trade privatization is not surprising. The incomplete status of small privatization in Hungary does not absolutely force the conclusion that Hungary was less successful than the other countries in reforming the trade and service sector of its economy. Success in this area must ultimately be evaluated by the final test of consumer satisfaction, and the Hungarian consumer sector is not markedly inferior to that in Poland or the Czech Republic. Only time will tell whether their long-term interests have been equally well served by the slower Hungarian efforts to divest the state of its assets and the attempts to engineer the future development of the whole consumer sector.

1.1. Quantitative evidence on the transformation of the retail, catering, and service sectors in Hungary

A comparison of two snapshot pictures of the Hungarian retail trade and catering sector taken in 1988 and 1992 would reveal both how much the sector has changed and how different its development has been from those in Poland or the Czech Republic (see Table II.1). The contrast is most dramatic with the Czech Republic, which has roughly the same population as Hungary and which had a much more orthodox communist regime. Although the total number of shops and catering establishments in the Czech Republic, was barely three-quarters of Hungary's total in 1988,[2] the state sector in the Czech Republic was 1.6 times as large as in Hungary. By 1989, the Hungarian state sector was only half as large as the Czech one.

Overall, since 1988, the total number of active establishments in the Hungarian retail trade sector has grown by over 90 percent. This growth has been spearheaded by the almost 300 percent increase in the number of new private units. The entry of new private stores and restaurants into the sector has accelerated in the years since the end of the communist regime, with their number almost doubling between 1990 to 1992.

Doubtless the increase in the number of units has improved the lot of Hungarian consumers and was a factor in the development of a truly competitive sector. Still, the numerical significance of the private units is not matched by their market share, at least as measured by the official statistics (see Table II.2). Although the market share of the new private sector has been expanding, according to official statistics, units operated by private dealers and incorporated companies in 1992 captured no more than 50 percent of total retail trade turnover, even though they accounted for almost 80 percent of the stores and restaurants.[3] Moreover, since the state-owned joint stock companies are included in

[2] For data on the size of the Czech commercial sector see section 1 of Part I.B.
[3] *Economic Trends in Eastern Europe*, p. 51.

Table II.1 Change in the affiliation of units in the retail and catering sector from 1988 to 1992*

Year	1988	1990	1992
State enterprises	26,366	17,410	14,000
Incorporated companies†	671	6,240	30,000
Cooperatives	27,349	22,323	18,000
Private entrepreneurs	34,541	60,141	102,755
Total	88,927	106,114	164,755

Source: *Hungarian Statistical Yearbooks*; E. Gem, "Private Enterprises in Retail Trade", mimeo, 1993; unpublished data from the Central Statistical Office. Data on service units are not included because the Hungarian Statistical Office has ceased to provide them after 1990.

* There is some disagreement concerning the number of private shops and catering establishments at the end of 1992, with estimates ranging as high as 200,000. (*Economic Trends in Eastern Europe*, Kopint-Datorg, Vol. 2, No. 1, 1993, p. 51.) Difficulties encountered with relating the number of registered entrepreneurs to the number of operating establishments account for a good deal of the variance of estimates. Koping-Datorg also lists a slightly higher number of cooperative and state units, estimating a combined end of 1992 total of between 38,000 and 39,000.

† Incorporated companies include limited partnerships, limited liability companies, and joint stock companies. They may be either privately or state owned.

Table II.2 The increase in private entrepreneurial units in retail trade and catering (1988–90)

Year	Number of private entrepreneurial units	Share of entrepreneurial units in the total number of units	Share of entrepreneurial turnover in total turnover
1988	34,541	38.6%	11.5%
1989	39,612	42.5%	12.9%
1990	60,141	56.4%	18.1%

Sources: E. Gem,"Private Enterprises in Retail Trade" and Central Statistical Office data.

this 50 percent total, the state sector in Hungary still predominates over the private firms.

Official turnover figures, however, nearly certainly underestimate the importance of the private sector. The reasons for this are the same as they are around the world: turnover figures are used to calculate taxes, and shop owners everywhere take great pains to hide at least a portion of their income. As the size of the establishment increases or the degree of state involvement rises, it becomes ever more difficult to tinker with income figures. Determining an appropriate scaling coefficient to control for the differential turnover distortions may not be possible, but it is estimated by many analysts that up to 70 percent of retail trade turnover in Hungary is actually captured by the private sector.

But even if one accepts the higher estimates of the size of the private sector, clearly both the remaining state stores and those that have been privatized form a large and important segment of all the retail trade and consumer service establishments. These stores tend to occupy the more attractive locations and account for a disproportionately large share of the sectoral turnover. For this reason, the unfinished nature of the Hungarian small privatization remains significant. Moreover, in contrast to Poland and the Czech Republic, a large state sector is likely to continue to exist in Hungary; in fact the pace of privatization has sharply declined in the postcommunist period. The number of establishments exiting the state sector between 1990 and 1992 was scarcely one-third of the number of the transfers occurring in the 1988–90 period. The cooperative sector also shrank at a much faster rate at the end of the communist regime than in the first two years under the Antall government.

It is, however, very difficult to determine the precise magnitude of the contraction of the state sector since 1988, and a cursory glance at the figures in Table II.1 is apt to give the reader a false picture of the extent of privatization which has taken place. The reason for this is that the Hungarian Central Statistical Office has ceased to record ownership data concerning the newly registered commercial companies, making it impossible to say with full confidence which of the new joint stock and limited liability companies are genuinely private, and which are, in fact, state entities in a new organizational guise. And since the decrease in the number of units owned by state enterprises during the period of 1988–90 was in large measure caused by their transfer to the rapidly rising number of new joint stock and limited liability companies, the extent of actual privatization cannot be properly estimated without gaining some insight into the ownership structure of these "incorporated companies" (as they are called in the Hungarian statistics).

One may be sure that a transfer of state stores into a commercial company did not always mean its effective privatization. State enterprises have, in fact, remained the majority shareholders of many of these new companies, and the whole transaction was often designed to insulate a portion of assets from state control without actual privatization.

Probably the best (perhaps the only) way of estimating the rough ownership structure of the new companies is to look at their size, which happens to parallel rather faithfully the division between the organizational forms. Thus, it may be observed that joint stock companies usually operate as chains comprised of more than ten units and most of them were carved out of state companies between 1988 and 1990. Large capital requirements and the organizational complexity of these companies make it unlikely that they were fully appropriated during the process of spontaneous privatization. It thus appears safe to assume that most of these joint stock companies are either partially or totally owned by state entities. In 1990, joint stock companies operated slightly more than 3,000 shops and restaurants.[4] A large proportion of this figure should therefore be added to the 17,410 establishments listed in Table II.1 as state-owned in 1990, and most of them are probably still state-owned today. Interestingly enough, the change of legal form continues effectively to insulate the units shielded in this way from state interference, and the establishments owned by commercial companies have been successfully excluded from all the SPA-controlled privatization programs.

Limited liability companies, in contrast to the joint stock companies, are simple structures, usually consisting of one to three units. They are likely to have been created by enterprise insiders in order to gain complete ownership rights over individual stores, as well as by private persons starting genuinely new commercial establishments. Unlike joint stock companies, they thus appear to be genuinely private entities.

While adjustments in the calculations of the size of the state sector are necessary to account for the incomplete privatizations before 1990, we are on firmer ground estimating the extent of privatization since the demise of the communist regime. A brief summary of the numerical importance of the three major Hungarian privatization programs in the retail trade and consumer service sector is provided in Table II.3. It illustrates the overwhelming importance of the Preprivatization program

[4] *1990 Hungarian Statistical Yearbook*, Central Statistical Office, p. 169.

Table II.3 Estimated division of state-owned trade and service enterprises according to method of privatization

	Year of initiation	Number of affected enterprises	Number of privatized assets
Preprivatization	1990	419	ca. 7,016
First Privatization	1990	6	Portions of 6 enterprises
Self-Privatization	1991	200	73 enterprises

Note: Authors' estimates.

for the post-1990 privatization. So far, enterprises privatized in the Self-Privatization program have been concentrated in the service sector, and have had only a negligible impact on retail shops and restaurants. Other privatization programs have been excluded from Table II.3, since in most cases they still exist more as future plans than as realized programs. They have, therefore, yielded a negligible number of completed privatization transactions.

2. REFORMS UNDER SOCIALISM

2.1. History of reforms under socialism

Hungarian economic reforms instituted prior to 1990 introduced important structural and functional changes in the retail trade and consumer service sector. Deregulation, distribution of decision-making authority among sectoral participants, and the encouragement of small establishments were the hallmark of these policy changes. Although socialist reforms progressed along a continuum, it is useful to divide them into two periods: 1) those undertaken prior to 1988; and 2) those initiated between 1988 and 1990. The 1988 demarcation line is drawn due to the enactment in that year of the Law on Business Societies, Associations, Companies, and Ventures ("Company Law"), which represented the first effective catalyst in breaking up state enterprises. Free elections in 1990 announced the end of this first period of Hungarian retail trade transformation.

Despite our focus on property reforms, evolution in the Hungarian retail trade sector was not prompted exclusively or even primarily by modifications in property relations. In addition to ownership transfers, decentralization played a prominent role, and changes in macro-economic conditions and general economic policy also shaped the Hungarian retail trade sector. Government price setting by government policy and the structure of foreign and wholesale trade were of particular significance.

Experiments in freeing prices began in the 1960s, at the same time as the early microeconomic reforms of the state sector. By the middle of the 1980s, the budgetary burden of extensive subsidies, the need to service the foreign debt, and the desire to build a competitive, export-oriented economy led the Hungarian government to abandon the traditional price setting for most commodities.[5] By 1988, between 60 and 70 percent of retail prices were freely set and price adjustments were often linked to the convertible currency prices for goods traded on foreign markets. Reliance on market mechanisms decreased arbitrage opportunities for private individuals seeking to exploit the difference between official and black market prices. At the same time, legitimate private enterprise was encouraged by the freedom to price goods according to market responses rather than in compliance with centralized dictates.

Although price liberalization encouraged the creation of private commercial establishments, unwillingness of governmental authorities to allow private entrepreneurs into wholesale and foreign trade had a crippling impact on the development of private retail trade establishments. A state monopoly on wholesale trade was retained until 1989, and the communist state relaxed its monopoly on foreign trade only in January 1990.

2.2. Pre-1988 reforms

The overall structure in the Hungarian retail, catering, and service sector as of 1988 is provided by Table II.4.

Although the numbers in Table II.4 reflect the impressive growth of the private sector in the late 1980s, they are still unable to convey the full depth and variety of arrangements existing within businesses classified as belonging to the state sector and the degree of reforms which had already changed the face of the sector as a whole. Two

[5] Council of Ministers Decree XXXVIII of 1984 established a tiered structure of pricing, with prices of some commodities being fixed, others subject to price floors or ceilings, and others set by market conditions. The Decree was modified by a series of orders issued during the following years.

Table II.4 The 1988 Hungarian retail, catering, and service sector by ownership form

	Retail shops	Catering units	Service units
State	17,680	8,533	17,398
Cooperatives	20,496	8,336	13,652
Private	25,563	8,978	54,516
Total	63,739	25,847	85,566

Source: Compiled from publications of the Central Statistical Office.

distinct categories mark these reforms: the reform of state enterprises; and the creation of private business opportunities.

2.2.1. *Reform of state enterprises*

By 1988, Hungarian state enterprises had experienced twenty years of reform. State enterprises were centrally controlled by branch ministries until 1968. The Ministry of Domestic Trade[6] oversaw the activity of state enterprises organized by product line and by region. In each of the twenty regions in Hungary, one state enterprise held a monopoly position concerning a particular line of activity.[7] Even more severe concentration marked some lines of activity, such as food, where only fifteen large enterprises operated throughout the whole country. Each enterprise in turn supervised a number of retail units, setting plan targets for sales and wages and the allocation of inputs. Wholesale supply was organized along a parallel structure, with enterprises purchasing supplies from designated regional suppliers. Interregional or *ad hoc* supply relationships were forbidden.

In contrast to retail trade and catering, services were organized in a less rigidly hierarchical fashion. Locally founded non-material service enterprises, for example, competed with cooperative and private establishments. But capital intensive services, such as car repairs, were

[6] In 1990, the Ministry was re-organized as the Ministry of Industry and Trade.

[7] The state enterprise monopoly did not extend to rural areas, which were also served by local consumer cooperatives. See section 7 for further discussion of cooperatives. State enterprises were also supplemented by a limited number of small enterprises founded by local government entities to carry out local trade activities.

organized along lines similar to retail trade enterprises, and were inevitably dominated by state enterprises.[8]

Flexibility (up to a point) was introduced in 1968 with the "New Economic Mechanism" program. Fundamental regional structures of organization were left unchanged, but decision-making authority was shifted over time from branch ministries to the enterprise level. Obligatory input and output quotas were abolished in 1968, and scope for genuine profit and loss calculations in state enterprises was expanded. Wholesale enterprises were permitted to engage in cross-regional trading, and retail trade enterprises were allowed to buy directly from producing enterprises.

Further reforms dealing with the governance of the state enterprises themselves were enacted with Law No. VI on State Enterprises of 1977, subsequently amended by Law No. XXXIII on Enterprise Councils of 1984 ("Law on Enterprise Councils"). In accordance with the 1984 amendments, two-thirds of state enterprises came to be administered by an "Enterprise Council," a majority of whose members were elected by workers and employees, although, by all reports, the Councils were under the thumb of enterprise managers. The responsibilities of the Council included the election of the enterprise director, determining changes in the line of the firm's activities, and organizational changes in the enterprise. Direct state oversight of enterprise activities was retained in only roughly one-third of the enterprises which were classified as of strategic importance.[9]

The Law on Enterprise Councils tipped the distribution of power among the sectoral parties. State managers were given a wider degree of freedom from bureaucrats to operate and restructure self-managed enterprises. Devolution of authority and the decentralization of decision-making in the economy resulted in a far-reaching separation of the ownership of state assets from their day-to-day control.

8 In addition to car repair services, state enterprises were of particular importance in operating laundries, electric and electronic repair shops, and maintenance services for gas, refrigeration, and heating equipment.

9 Surprisingly, directly-supervised enterprises continued to play a substantial role in the operation of commercial stores. In 1988, directly-supervised enterprises operated 30 percent of state retail stores and 7 percent of the catering units. It is not possible to provide subsector disaggregation of directly-supervised stores but anecdotal evidence indicates that such enterprises maintained stores throughout the retail trade sector. See Table II.10 for a detailed breakdown of the ownership structure of the commercial sector in 1988.

Reforms of the state sector taking place extended not only to enterprises but also to the level of individual units, such as stores or service outlets. By 1988, a substantial number of these units operated under managerial arrangements allowing varying degrees of entrepreneurial innovation. Changes on the level of individual units resulted in three different arrangements: so called independent-accounting arrangements; contractual agreements; and rental (or "lease") agreements. These agreements were permitted by the Law on Domestic Trade (Law No I/1978) as interpreted by the implementing regulations found in Government Decrees No. XXXVIII of 1980 and No. XXIX–XXX of 1981.

Independent-accounting arrangements created performance-based compensation for individual commercial units, which maintained their own accounts and were allowed to retain some portion of the unit's residual profits. These units were still required to maintain their profile, pricing, and supply deals and were of lesser importance for the development of the sector. *Contractual arrangements* called for greater unit independence, since they gave shop managers the right to make product line, supply, and pricing decisions. In return, the units had to pay a set fee to the parent enterprise, along with an agreement to purchase certain specified goods from the parent. Finally, *rental agreements* removed the contractual supply conditions on managers and were essentially indistinguishable from familiar subleases.[10]

Contract and rental unit workers retained the status of state employees, but by the mid-1980s, shop managers had acquired the right to hire and fire workers. Rental and contractual agreements were, however, limited to units of relatively small size; retail units were initially limited to five employees, and catering units covered by some form of agreement could employ a maximum of twelve employees.[11] Typically auctioned to the highest bidder, contract and rental agreements had a term of between four and five years.[12] Restrictions on bidder eligibility were gradually relaxed during the 1980s. Among those permitted to be a party to a contract or rental agreement were

[10] Rental agreements between enterprises and private managers were subleases since the enterprise usually did not own the premises on which its stores were located. Instead, the enterprise leased them from the local municipality.

[11] Size constraints were made less restrictive in 1988, when the maximum number of permissible employees in both retail and catering units was raised to thirty.

[12] See Éva Palócz, "The Emergence and Implementation of the Small-Scale Privatization Program in Eastern European Countries: the Case of Hungary," mimeo, Kopint Datorg, June 1992.

Table II.5 Contractual and rental arrangements in state enterprises, 1988

	Number of units under arrangements	Percent of state units
Retail	2,027	11.5
Catering	3,239	37.9
Total	5,266	20.0

Sources: *1988 Hungarian Statistical Yearbook*, Central Statistical Office, pp. 243, 258; *Statistical Data of Consumer Cooperatives for 1990*, AFEOSZ, p. 35.

employees, individuals willing to be employed by the parent enterprise, and Civil Law partnerships. In most cases, individuals were limited to operating one business, although this restriction was also modified to allow for a simultaneous operation of two businesses in certain circumstances.[13]

Contracted and rented units quickly became a core component of the state sector.[14] In 1988, 20 percent of state enterprise units operated in a semi-independent fashion, with the proportion reaching nearly 40 percent in the state catering sector (see Table II.5).

Contractual and rental shops, while numerous, were usually small, less efficient establishments. Their share of total employment in the sector was nearly twice as large as their share of turnover, and per unit employment (similar to the mostly rural cooperatives) was less than half of the overall 1988 average of 6.8 workers in state-enterprise units (see Table II.6). Still, the new arrangements were credited with improving the performance of the least profitable portion of the state retail trade sector and injecting some market elements into retail and catering enterprises. Also, statistics may perhaps underestimate the performance of contracted units, since small shops may have been concealing some of their transactions for the purpose of tax avoidance.

An important effect of the introduction of contractual and rental arrangements, however, was also their rather perverse impact on the

[13] Dual businesses were permitted in cases where the second business was open for less than six months a year (due to a seasonal market) or if both businesses were in settlements of fewer than 1,500 residents.

[14] Contract and rental arrangements, in slightly modified form, also existed in the cooperative sector. See section 7.

Table II.6 Employment and turnover in contractual and rental establishments, 1988*

	1988
Total employment ('000)	35.4
As % of total enterprise and coop employment	12.8%
Employment per unit	3.1
Cumulative turnover (Ft bln)	52.1
As % of total enterprise and coop turnover	7.7%
Turnover per unit (Ft mln)	4.58

Source: *1989 Hungarian Statistical Yearbook*, Central Statistical Office, p. 239.

* Data on state enterprise units subject to contractual and rental agreements is aggregated with data on the roughly equal number of consumer cooperative units operating under similar conditions. The Hungarian Central Statistical Office did not distinguish between enterprise and cooperative rented and contracted units when reporting turnover data. In 1988, 6,119 consumer cooperative units operated under contractual or rental agreement. This number is equal to 26 percent of the trade and catering units controlled by cooperatives. See section 7 for additional information on contractual arrangements in the cooperative sector.

role of state enterprises in the provision of consumer goods and services. Allocating rental and contractual rights, in fact, became an animating factor in the economic activity of many state enterprises, with some analysts estimating that a number of state enterprises received as much as 40 to 50 percent of their revenues from contractual and rental payments.[15] The oddity of state enterprises functioning as a fusion of real-estate agencies and franchising agents was a short-lived response to the strange brew of freedom and constraint that marked the pre-1990 Hungarian economy. No state interest was served by this two-tier renting structure, but state enterprise managers and the managers of individual shops had reasons to maintain the *status quo*.

Semi-independent arrangements may have represented the optimal economic structure for enterprise managers. Empowered by the Enterprise Council Law, they had wide control over distribution of rental and contract payments. Moreover, ample opportunity for private benefit was afforded by their control of rental allocations. Contractual

[15] See Palócz, "The Emergence and Implementation of the Small-Scale Privatization Program in Eastern European Countries," p. 3.

and rental agreements thus allowed managers to keep their enterprises intact, to milk profits derived from the system, all the while being insulated from personal responsibility for any and all losses.

Shop managers holding contractual or rental rights had a more ambiguous relation to the *status quo*. They had ready access to state suppliers and, being formally a part of the state system of wage controls, were immune to rising labor costs. After making their rental payments, shop managers were able to retain profits derived from their economic activity at the same time as their state status offered a measure of protection from personal liability for losses. Uncertainty over the long-term retention of their rental rights, on the other hand, was a significant negative feature for the shop managers, and pointed to the inchoate nature of their property rights. Benefits derived from their status were purchased at the price of insecure control over economic decision-making, a cost which may have been judged too high.

2.2.2. *Creation of private businesses*

Liberating private initiative, independent from the developments affecting state enterprises and cooperatives in the retail trade and service sector, began in the late 1970s, with the passage of Law No. IV of 1977 which allowed for the creation of Civil Law partnerships, and the enactment of the Law on Domestic Trade (Law No. I/1978).[15] These regulations provided a legal framework for operating private businesses, and nudged open the commercial sector to private initiative. Private activity was constrained, however, by the need to obtain official approval prior to operating a business and also by strict size limitations.[16]

Additional legislation to promote private development was enacted in

[15] This law was subsequently amended by Law Decree No. XXVIII of 1986. Unlike laws, which were passed by the Parliament, "law decrees" were enacted by the Presidential Council, a body composed of high party and governmental officials. Governmental or ministerial decrees, a third type of legal enactment, contained implementing regulations for laws and law decrees.

[16] Private business associations, for example, were initially limited to thirty participants. This represented the largest permissible private entity. Private retail traders, by contrast, could employ a maximum of only five people. These limits were steadily loosened throughout the 1980s, and by 1988, associations could have thirty members and thirty employees, and retail traders could employ up to thirty people.

the early 1980s. In 1981, the Law Decree on Small Cooperatives, Special Work Teams, Contractual Arrangements, and Work Partnerships (Law Decree No. XIV of 1981) increased the array of accepted legal forms of business organization. By the middle 1980s, private business activity in the trade sector could take a myriad of forms: artisan, private retail trader, private caterer, small cooperative, and a form roughly analogous to general partnerships.[17]

Growth of private economic activity in the sector was concentrated primarily in the simplest permissible forms: "private trader," "private caterer," and "artisan". Tables II.7 and II.8 chart the development of these forms between 1983 and 1988. At a higher level of organizational complexity, there existed 1,300 Civil Law partnerships by 1985.[18]

The steady increase in the number of private traders did not, however, translate into a corresponding growth in the volume of sales; although private retail and catering establishments comprised close to 40 percent of the total businesses in the sector in 1988, they controlled only slightly more than 10 percent of the market.[19]

2.3. Transformation in the period 1988 to 1990

Further reforms of the structurally inefficient state retail trade and catering sector could have proceeded according to two separate strategies: 1) the state retail trade enterprises could have been administratively forced to relinquish control over the individual stores and to give up their role as real-estate intermediaries; or 2) incentives

[17] An extensive body of literature exists on the political, economic and social importance of these alternative economic forms. For instance, see D. Stark, "Coexisting Organizational Forms in Hungary's Emerging Mixed Economy," in V. Nee and D. Stark, eds, *Remaking the Economic Institutions of Socialism: China and Eastern Europe* (Stanford), 1989; D. Stark, "Work, Worth, and Justice in the Hungarian Mixed Economy," *Working Papers on Central and Eastern Europe*, No. 5, Center for European Studies, Harvard University, 1990; and A. Seleny, "Hidden Enterprise, Property Rights Reform and Political Transformation in Hungary," *Working Papers on Central and Eastern Europe*, No. 11, Center for European Studies, Harvard University, 1991.

[18] *Small Business Development Through Privatization*, Foundation for Market Economy (Budapest), 1992, p. 43.

[19] These statistics probably underestimate the size of the private sector, however, since they do not include the significant "black market" activity that was long a feature of the Hungarian economy. Estimates of the size of the informal economy range as high as 10–15 percent of GDP. See *Small Business Development Through Privatization*, p. 51.

Table II.7 Increase in the number of private traders in the retail and catering business

Year	Number of shops and catering units	Share of private entrepreneurs in the total number of retail trade units	Share of private turnover in total retail trade turnover
1983	19,293	–	6.2%
1984	22,360	–	7.5%
1985	25,455	31.5%	8.3%
1986	28,965	34.3%	9.4%
1987	31,827	36.6%	10.0%
1988	34,541	38.8%	11.5%

Source: Compiled from publications of the Hungarian Central Statistical Office.

Table II.8 Number of (full-time and part-time) private artisans

Year	Number of artisans
1970	86,303
1980	103,412
1985	145,583
1986	150,664
1987	154,611

Source: *1989 Hungarian Statistical Yearbook*, Hungarian Central Statistical Office (Budapest), pp. 396–7, 1990; and *A Nemzetgazdaság Szervezeti Struktúrája*, Central Statistical Office (Budapest), p. 21, April 1992.

could have been created for state enterprise insiders to change and restructure their institutions on their own. In the period between 1988 and 1990, the Grosz and Nemeth governments chose to rely solely on the second reform strategy. Three legal regulations, Law. No. VI of 1988 (as amended) on Business Societies, Associations, Companies and Ventures ("Company Law"), Law No. XXIV of 1988 on Foreign Investment in Hungary ("Foreign Investment Law"), and Law No. XIII of 1989 on the Transformation of Economic Organizations and Business Associations ("Transformation Law"), played a crucial role in this process and gave the enterprises the freedom to subdivide into smaller entities organized as commercial companies, such as limited liability and joint stock companies.[20]

These laws were not designed specifically for the retail trade sector. A substantial degree of the activity engendered by the reforms, however, occurred in this sector, with retail and service enterprises becoming the parents of a significant portion of the smaller companies created in this period. Many scandals associated with the transformation of state enterprises also concerned retail trade and consumer service enterprises.[21] The ease with which discrete portions of retail trade networks could be organized into separate commercial companies, and the special concern of trade enterprise managers that their enterprises were being considered for dismemberment and sale, explain the high level of the sector's activity.

Legislative enactments of this period were primarily targeted at modifications in the structure and size of state enterprises, not transfer of ownership to private parties. Government declined to enact the one proposed reform that focused on the sale of state property.[22] Also, reforms of this period affected primarily the rights of sectoral insiders to particular assets; outsiders played at most a subsidiary role.

Taken as a whole, the pre-1990 reforms magnified the already considerable powers of enterprise insiders, especially in relation to government officials. Managers dominated the transformation process, and by using a variety of techniques, solidified their control over valuable assets.[23] Ministry officials progressively lost the ability to coordinate the

[20] The 1984 Law on Enterprise Councils allowed for the subdivision of enterprises, but made such spin-offs procedurally difficult by requiring a large number of initial founders for any commercial company. The Company Law removed these barriers.

[21] For a more extensive discussion of company formation and enterprise transformation see M. Móra, "The (Pseudo)-Privatization of State-Owned Enterprises (Changes in Organizational and Proprietary Forms, 1987–1990)," *Acta Oeconomica*, Vol. 43, pp. 37–58, 1991; É. Voszka, "Spontaneous Privatization", in J. Earle, R. Frydman and A. Rapaczynski, *Privatization in the Transition to a Market Economy*, Pinter Publishers (London), 1993; É. Voszka, "Rope-Walking: Ganz Danubius Ship and Crane Factory Transformed into Company," *Acta Oeconomica*, Vol. 42, pp. 285–302, 1990; É. Voszka, "From Twilight into Twilight: Transformation of the Ownership Structure in the Big Industries," *Acta Oeconomica*, Vol. 43, pp. 281–96, 1991; É. Voszka, "Not Even the Contrary is True: the Transfigurations of Centralization and Decentralization," *Acta Oeconomica*, Vol. 44, pp. 74–94, 1992.

[22] Draft versions of a law concerning the transfer of ownership of the smallest retail trade and catering units to private parties were circulated within the Ministry of Trade starting in 1988. The existence of this proposed legislation was widely known in the sector. See Móra, "The (Pseudo)-Privatization of State-Owned Enterprises," p. 7.

[23] For a detailed explanation of the methods by which enterprise transformation led to increased managerial authority, see Frydman, Rapaczynski, and Earle, *et al.*, *The Privatization Process in Central Europe*, CEU Press (Budapest and London), 1993.

workings of the state sector, and were often unable even to record accurately the convoluted property transactions taking place among an expanded and ever growing group of entities organized to lay claim to state-owned assets.

2.3.1. The transformation process

Initiation of enterprise restructuring predated the enactment of the Company Law, for prior to 1988 a handful of state enterprise managers began creating commercial companies based on some unrevoked provisions of the 1875 Commercial Code and Law No. V of 1930. But it was the Company Law, which came into force in January 1989, that gave most enterprises the right to establish such subsidiaries as partnerships, limited liability and joint stock companies, or economic associations.[24] Because subsidiaries were not deemed the legal successors of their parent enterprises (which continued to exist) they were usually not saddled with inherited debts.

Establishment of new companies was encouraged by granting tax abatements; starting in 1988, all new businesses, including those created on the basis of state assets, were given three-year graduated reductions in their taxes on profit.[25] Capital formation was also assisted by Law No. XXIV of 1988 on Foreign Investment in Hungary ("Foreign Investment Law"). In addition to allowing for 100 percent repatriation of profits, the frequently amended law permitted any Hungarian legal entity to enter, without government supervision, into a joint venture with one or more foreign investors. State enterprise managers were thus freed to clinch deals with foreign investors, creating new companies that mixed state-owned assets and foreign capital. The resulting joint ventures were also supported by generous tax reductions.[26]

Decisions regarding the formation of subsidiary commercial businesses and the determination of the composition of the new companies

[24] Economic associations under the Company Law are entities composed of legal persons, created to coordinate commercial activity; they are not independent profit-producing entities.

[25] Profit taxes were reduced by 55 percent in the first year of operation, 35 percent in the second year, and 25 percent in the third year. These tax preferences were withdrawn in 1992.

[26] Thus, for example, a joint venture hotel in which the foreign contribution was above 30 percent received a tax reduction of 60 percent for the first five years, and up to 40 percent for the next five years. Rumors abounded of companies using a foreign "front" to set up a joint venture and qualify for tax subsides.

were made by the manager-controlled Enterprise Councils; other than in very narrowly defined circumstances, the state sought no formal role in supervising this process in self-managed enterprises. Shares in the newly established commercial companies were also held at the parent enterprise level and the government had no formal role in the exercise of ownership rights. Although the state enterprise managers sheltered in the new companies did not necessarily gain the right to dispose of the assets, the creation of commercial companies hindered the government officials' ability to transfer these assets. New companies were required to be registered, but denial of registration could be based only on a limited number of defined infractions.

Unlike the Company Law, which allowed only partial transformations, the Transformation Law sanctioned transformations of entire enterprises into joint stock or limited liability companies. In the case of self-managed enterprises, the change was initiated by a two-thirds vote of the Enterprise Council, and, until 1990, decisions to transform an enterprise, and the transformation plan itself, were not subject to ministerial supervision.[27] Enterprises which had more than 50 percent of their assets invested in other companies were required to transform themselves within two years.

Complete transformation was less appealing for enterprise managers than partial transformation, since it required the new company to assume the debt obligations of its state enterprise predecessor. Still, transformation held out potential benefits to enterprise employees, since the Transformation Law permitted the distribution of special "worker shares," with a value of up to 20 percent of the capitalization of the newly created joint stock companies, at discounts of up to 90 percent. Overall, there were ultimately very few total transformations, and most of the new company formation involved spin-offs under the Company Law.[28]

[27] Registration was a judicial process, with the courts receiving the plan of transformation, the profit and loss statement, the minutes of the meetings concerning the approval of the plan, and the auditor's report on the profit and loss statement.

[28] Only twenty-seven enterprises had been transformed in the entire Hungarian economy by the end of 1990. However, eleven out of these twenty-seven transformations involved enterprises in the domestic trade and food industry. See *National Bank of Hungary Monthly Report*, November 1992, p. 63.

Table II.9 Affiliation of retail and catering units, 1988–90

	1988	1989	1990
State enterprises	26,366	23,414	17,410
Commercial companies	671	2,510	6,248
Cooperatives	27,394	26,977	22,323
Private entrepreneurs	34,541	39,612	60,141
Sectoral total	88,972	92,514	106,122

Source: 1990 Hungarian Statistical Yearbook, Central Statistical Office, p. 169.

2.3.2. The results of the transformation process

The consequences of the last reforms of the socialist period can be assessed along two separate but connected lines: 1) the changes in the organizational composition of the sector; and 2) the alterations in the distribution of property rights among the sectoral participants.

The extent of organizational change in the sector from 1988 to 1990 is broadly revealed in Table II.9.[29] Table II.10 details with more precision developments within state enterprises and commercial companies.

As Table II.10 demonstrates, the number of state retail trade enterprises remained relatively constant, confirming the fact that complete transformations played only a marginal role in the developments of this period. On the other hand, the impact of partial transformations was pervasive, as more than one-third of state shops changed their organizational form. Over 65 percent of the decrease in state shops occurred in the last year of communist rule, perhaps indicating the lack of institutional constraints during the 1989 Round Table negotiations and the subsequent run-up to the first elections, as well as heightened anxiety over the reassertion of control over state assets. Exit from enterprises was distributed relatively evenly, with 31 percent of retail stores and 41 percent of catering units leaving their enterprises. The shift of shops and catering establishments occurred exclusively in self-administered enterprises or those founded by local governments. An

[29] While the first postcommunist government took office on May 24, 1990, its first privatization program was operative only at the beginning of 1991. Therefore, we assume that organizational developments through the end of 1990 reflect changes associated with the Company and Transformation Laws.

Table II.10 Hungarian enterprise and commercial company development in retail trade and catering, 1988–90

	Number of organizations			Number of retail stores			Number of catering units		
Organizational form	1988	1989	1990	1988	1989	1990	1988	1989	1990
State supervised enterprise	270	277	274	5,575	5,511	5,610	599	595	839
Locally founded or self-admin.	667	675	660	11,165	9,536	5,996	7,337	6,261	3,738
Other enterprise	143	138	143	1,412	1,212	977	278	300	250
Total enterprise	1,080	1,090	1,077	18,152	16,259	12,583	8,214	7,156	4,827
Joint ventures	53	60	93	388	336	215	48	44	34
Limited liability companies	12	264	1,168	10	531	2,009	7	149	714
Joint stock companies	13	66	244	137	923	2,210	58	512	1,051
Other business organizations	4	3	3	22	14	15	1	1	0
Total commercial companies	82	393	1,508	557	1,804	4,449	114	706	1,799

Source: Central Statistical Office.

average self-administered or locally-founded enterprise lost ten shops between 1988 and 1990, as the number of shops per enterprise fell from 27.7 in 1988 to 14.7 at the end of 1990. The number of shops operated by state-supervised enterprises actually increased over the period, suggesting active efforts on the part of government officials to enlarge the number of assets under their control. In 1990, state-supervised enterprises operated an average of 23.5 shops per enterprise.

As the state enterprise sector shrank, dramatic increases were registered in both the number of commercial companies, and the number of establishments they operated. The number of limited liability companies almost doubled, with a corresponding increase in the number of shops. Growth in joint stock companies was only slightly less robust. Almost two-thirds of the 5,577 new commercial company units were added between 1989 and 1990. Foreign investors were of marginal numerical significance in the sector throughout the period; their importance was due not to the number of stores they controlled but to the prominence of their investments.

Partial or complete transformation of state enterprises was often accompanied by a significant transfer of property entitlements. The degree to which property rights shifted from state organs to individual parties during this process has, in fact, occasioned a great deal of debate and has been the source of heated controversy.

The Hungarian Central Statistical Office did not keep records of company ownership data, and thus no precise information on the extent of privatization in the years 1988–90 is available. However, it is possible to form some estimates of the resulting ownership structure on the basis of an assumption relating ownership structure to organizational size.

As can be seen from Table II.10, limited liability companies were, on average, much smaller than joint stock companies, and most of them controlled no more than a couple of stores (2.3, to be exact). There is little doubt that these small limited liability companies had been, in fact, privatized. Transformations of a small group of stores was predominantly a way for insiders, perhaps with some foreign or domestic partners, to gain nearly complete ownership rights over particular stores. Therefore, we can assume that nearly all limited liability companies were genuinely private establishments. Joint stock companies, on the other hand, with their extensive networks of units, and much higher capital needs, were likely to remain, in large part, state-owned, so that most units operated by joint stock companies should be counted within the state sector.

Table II.11 Employment per unit in retail trade and catering establishments, 1988–90

	1988	1989	1990
Enterprises	6.8	6.8	7.1
Locally-founded and self-administered enterprises	7.3	7.4	8.4
Limited liability companies	41.2	6.6	6.6
Joint stock companies	10.3	7.6	7.6
Private entrepreneurs	1.7	1.7	na

Source: Calculations based on data in *1990 Hungarian Statistical Yearbook*, Central Statistical Office.

Using these assumptions, we can estimate that, at the end of 1990, an ownership transfer had occurred with respect to approximately 2,700 stores controlled by limited liability companies, which constituted 8.0 percent of the retail trade and catering market (based on turnover data). Firmly in the saddle of the transformation process, enterprise managers may be assumed to have been the main beneficiaries of these transfers.

Less frequently formed, joint stock companies nevertheless affected a slightly larger portion of the sector. The 3,261 units operated by 244 joint stock companies in retail trade and catering in 1990 (i.e. 13.4 units per company) represented 8.8 percent of the sectoral turnover. In the case of these companies, enterprise managers strengthened their control, but probably did not acquire more than a fraction of ownership.

Stores and catering shops operated by each of the organizational forms show distinct characteristics. The increase in average employment registered in self-administered enterprises in 1990 indicates that the shops which had been spun off had fewer employees than those which were retained in the old structures (see Table II.11). While joint stock company and limited liability company shops had employment profiles comparable to each other and to state enterprise shops,[30] private entrepreneur establishments had significantly fewer employees per shop.

[30] The extraordinarily high average employment figures for 1988 limited liability companies was presumably a consequence of a few very large establishments among the seventeen limited liability trade and catering stores.

Table II.12 Turnover per unit in Hungarian retail trade and catering, 1988–90 (Ft mln)

	1988	1989	1990
Enterprises	16.98	19.67	25.49
Locally-founded or self-administered enterprises	16.23	19.01	25.60
Limited liability companies	64.71	42.50	31.51
Joint stock companies	9.23	28.92	29.14
Private entrepreneurs	2.55	2.93	3.25

Source: Calculations based on data in *1990 Hungarian Statistical Yearbook*, Hungarian Statistical Office.

Table II.13 Productivity of labor (ratio of turnover to employment) in retail trade and catering establishments, 1988–90

	1988	1989	1990
Enterprises	2.50	2.89	3.59
Locally-founded and self-administered enterprises	2.22	2.57	3.05
Limited liability companies	1.57	6.44	4.77
Joint stock companies	0.90	3.81	3.83
Private entrepreneurs	1.50	1.72	na

It should be noted, however, that statistics probably underestimate the number of employees in entrepreneurial shops, since they often employed family members and other persons who were not officially registered in order to avoid the payment of benefits.

Combining the data concerning employment with those concerning turnover per unit (presented in Table II.12), we may arrive at a reasonable measure of labor productivity in the different types of shops and catering establishments (see Table II.13). Superficially, the most surprising aspect is perhaps the low productivity of the private entrepreneurial units, but the explanation is quite clear: the stores owned by these entrepreneurs were not only the smallest (witness their low average employment), but also the least attractive ones. Many of them were in remote locations, and the independent private owners had much more restricted access to most domestic and imported supply channels (which remained fully state-owned). Private entrepreneurs probably also under-reported their turnover figures even more than they under-reported their employment, and this may have further affected the available statistics.

Generally speaking, the main factor affecting productivity in the shops and catering establishments operated under the different legal forms was probably the attractiveness of the unit's location, although levels of investment, overstaffing, and other factors may also have played a role. In this context, it is interesting to note that at the other extreme with respect to productivity figures stand the shops owned by limited liability companies which, from the moment when the Company Law began to operate in earnest, outperformed all the other types of units by a very significant margin. The explanation is, again, rather obvious: these were also mostly privately-owned units, but their owners were not small entrepreneurs starting up their own businesses. Instead, the units involved were probably the most attractive ones in the former state sector, spun off during the heyday of spontaneous privatization.

As opposed to limited liability companies, joint stock companies, which were much larger, were probably mostly state-owned, and the productivity figures of their shops, at least by 1990, were in line with those of the other types of state-owned units. Indeed, the state-owned units, flanked by the two extremes of private businesses – those of the independent and the *nomenklatura* entrepreneurs – show an impressive consistency in their productivity figures.

3. PREPRIVATIZATION

3.1 Objectives

By the time the Antall government took office in May 1990, ownership and organizational transfers had both diminished the size of the state sector and created a unique set of power configurations in the remaining state-owned enterprises. Public attention, sensing a grand rip-off, focused not on the satisfaction of consumer demand, but on the need to halt the uncontrolled, "spontaneous" privatization of state assets. Thus, ironically, Hungary's first postsocialist government assumed power with a popular mandate to slow the pace of privatization in the trade sector, not to spur it on.

Preprivatization,[31] the only Hungarian privatization program designed specifically for the retail trade, catering, and service sectors of the economy, was originally conceived during the last years of the communist rule. Driven by a need to generate income for the state budget, and by a desire to establish its reform credentials, the Nemeth government prepared a draft law for a privatization program that envisioned the sale of a discrete portion of the state retail trade and consumer service units.

Shops operating under contractual or rental arrangements were the primary targets of the program. As described in section 2, relations between these units and their parent enterprises made real-estate operations into a core activity of some state enterprises in this sector. By selling the rented and contracted shops to independent entrepreneurs, the program would eliminate this particular manifestation of managerial parasitism.

The Preprivatization Law was not, however, enacted until after the change of government in 1990, and the scope of the program was reduced dramatically as a consequence of this delay. Aware of the government's plans to privatize their shops, enterprise managers sought to protect their interests by reintegrating the rented and leased units into their enterprises, reasoning (quite rightly) that this would increase the complexity of privatization for the new authorities. The 27 percent reduction in the number of units which operated under contractual or rental agreements between 1989 and 1990 indicates the extent to which managers resorted to this type of antiprivatization measures.[32]

When the first postcommunist government was elected, in early 1990, it immediately confronted calls to end the abuses associated with the so-called "spontaneous privatization." Some well-publicized examples of these abuses concerned enterprises in the trade and service sector. The new government proposed Preprivatization as a partial solution to uncontrolled privatization and transformation, and as a means for raising revenues to finance the growing budget deficit.

[31] The Preprivatization program owes its name to the belief that the sale of small stores was just the beginning of the privatization process, the most significant part of which was to be the privatization of large enterprises.

[32] The number of state enterprise and cooperative units operating under contractual and rental agreements fell from 11,570 in 1989 to 8,397 in 1990. See *1989 Hungarian Statistical Yearbook*, Central Statistical Office, p. 254, and *1990 Hungarian Statistical Yearbook*, Central Statistical Office, p. 170.

3.2. Legal framework

Legislation establishing and regulating Preprivatization consists of the following enactments:

— Law No. VII/1990 on the State Property Agency and on the Management of State Property in State Enterprises;
— Law No. LXXIV/1990 on the Privatization, Alienation, and Utilization of Assets of State Enterprises Involved in Retail Trade, Catering, and Consumer Services ("The Preprivatization Law");
— 1990 Guidelines for the Sale of Assets of State-Owned Units Engaged in Retail Trade, Catering, and Consumer Service Activities, SPA Preprivatization Program Directorate;
— 1991 Circular Letter to State-Owned firms conducting Retail Trading, Catering, and Consumer Service activities, SPA Preprivatization Program Directorate;
— 1991 Auction Regulations, SPA Preprivatization Program Directorate.

Coming into effect on September 25, 1990, the Preprivatization Law outlined the role of the SPA and identified which types of assets would be included in the program. Auctions were established as the sole mechanism for SPA-initiated sales.[33] The law also mandated that privatization of all units included in the program be commenced by September 25, 1992. The types of assets to be included in the Preprivatization program were clarified by the Circular Letter. The Guidelines for the Sale of Assets regulated the valuation of assets in the program. Detailed instructions on auction procedures were provided in the Auction Regulations.

At first, all proceeds from Preprivatization auctions were to be contributed to the central state budget. Later, however, 20 percent of the proceeds from the sale of units belonging to regional institutions were given to regional governments and 50 percent of the proceeds from the sale of units founded by local governments were channeled to the local government.[34]

[33] Direct negotiations with the SPA were permitted for sales initiated by an enterprise or an outside investor.
[34] The modified distribution of proceeds from Preprivatization sales was governed by Law CIV/1990.

3.3. Assets in the Preprivatization Program

Sale of several types of units involved in retail trade, catering, and services was mandated by the Preprivatization Law. All units which operated under a contractual or leasing arrangement at any time since December 31, 1988 were to be included in the program.[35] The second category comprised all retail trade units which employed fewer than ten people, and all catering and service establishments and hotels employing fewer than fifteen people. Units involved in the sale of gas, heating oil, gasoline, and diesel fuels comprised the third type of the affected establishments. Given that the average employment in a state trade or catering unit in 1990 was only a fraction over seven, Preprivatization had the potential to affect the majority of state enterprise units in the sector.[36] Preprivatization did not, however, apply to units operated by commercial companies, even if those companies were entirely state-owned.

A number of exclusions removed large categories of units from the purview of Preprivatization. Among the units excluded were travel agencies, pharmacies, pawn shops, factory outlets, shops operating on the premises of hotels, and shops selling goods for foreign currency. Also excluded were chains of stores, defined as "shops which offer . . . a specific assortment of commodities or services, apply identical sales methods and uniform prices, and [in which] the determinant characteristics of their business activity . . . are also uniform."[37] In addition, Law VII/1990 allowed state enterprises to sell their units directly if the selling enterprise was bankrupt and intended to use the proceeds of the sale to finance its debt repayment.

No later than thirty days after the effective date of the Preprivatization Law, state enterprises were required to present to the SPA a list of all their units falling within the boundaries of the program. Little incentive existed for enterprise managers to comply fully with this requirement, and many enterprises delayed reporting, while others, it seems, never reported at all. Moreover, the criteria for inclusion were vague, and a majority of large retail trade enterprises with potentially eligible units could have argued that their shops were part of a chain of stores, and should thus be excluded from the program. Certainly,

[35] During the 1980's it became possible for state enterprises to lease their units to private entrepreneurs. See section 2 above.
[36] See Table II.11 in section 2 above, for data on employment per unit in the trade sector.
[37] Law No. LXXIV/1990, section 2, clause 4.

enterprise managers had incentives to keep their most valuable units together, and release, only if necessary, their least valuable stores.

It is also not clear whether the SPA had strong enough incentives to insist on the inclusion of a large number of units in the program. Forcing state enterprises into full compliance with the law would have demanded an aggressive action on the part of the SPA, confronting enterprise managers for limited gains. Case studies performed by the CEU Privatization Project suggest that enterprises typically engaged in dilatory haggling, which often resulted in the inclusion of only the least valuable, often loss-making units. In its October 1992 Testimony for the Trade Commission of the Parliament, the SPA confirmed that "many of the units [in the program] are situated in less developed districts, [and] poorer areas." Doubtlessly, the SPA's incentives were also affected by the fact that Preprivatization sales generated little revenue, but involved a costly valuation of each individual unit, thus straining the SPA's limited resources.

As of August 1993, 421 enterprises had reported 10,674 units to the SPA.[38] This represents approximately one-third of the trade, catering, and service units operated by state enterprises in 1990.[39] Nearly 30 percent of the reported units had previously functioned under contractual arrangements and 17 percent under rental agreements.[40] Roughly 50 percent of the units in the program were retail shops, 30 percent restaurants, and 20 percent service establishments.

Typically, shops in the program were owned by enterprises founded by either local or regional governments. But usually neither the shops nor their parent enterprises owned the premises on which they operated. Instead, they rented them from local governments on very favorable terms.[41] In over 70 percent of the sales in the program, the buyer of the business did not acquire the title to the premises, but only the right to rent the premises for a period of ten years.

[38] SPA, Department of Preprivatization. Despite the October 1990 deadline, some units were still being reported in the Spring of 1993.

[39] The Statistical Office ceased compiling data on consumer services after 1988. The absence of data on commercial services prevents precise calculation of the total number of state enterprise units in 1990. Assuming that, between 1988 and 1990, service enterprises experienced a rate of transformation equal to that in retail trade enterprises, we estimate that state enterprises operated between 29,000 and 30,000 retail trade, catering, and service outlets at the close of 1990.

[40] SPA, Department of Preprivatization.

[41] After several unsuccessful attempts to centralize authority and property rights over commercial real estate, the SPA finally ceded control over most state-owned property to local governments.

Table II.14 Size distribution of units in Preprivatization*

Size (sq. m)	No. of units	% of units
0–30	144	10.1
31–60	306	21.5
61–90	272	19.1
91–120	194	13.6
121–180	226	15.9
181-over	286	19.8
Total	1,424	100.0

Source: I. Toth, "Characteristics and Supply Effects of Pre-Privatization in Hungarian Retail Trade," Kopint-Datorg Discussion Paper, No. 13, August 1993.

* The data is derived from responses to a questionnaire answered by 1,473 Preprivatization owners of units auctioned as of the end of 1991.

Units in the program are sold as going concerns, and include equipment, brand names, existing contracts, and obligations of the business. Identification of debt obligations of individual stores was made possible by the pre-1990 accounting practice of noting on all enterprise credit and loan disbursements the units receiving the funds. Inventories were not included in sales.

As in the Czech Small Privatization Program, restrictions on the operation of privatized shops are permissible for certain categories of units. Four types of shops are subject to restrictions on the change of the line of business: book stores, food shops, stores selling children's goods, and workplace catering establishments. While the number of restricted operations is small, the number of restricted units is likely to be significant, due to the large proportion of food stores in Hungarian retail trade.[42] In contrast to the Czech Small Privatization Program, restrictions can be maintained for a long period of time, up to five years. In this limbo, a business may change its line of activity only with the approval from local authorities.

Only Hungarian citizens or private legal entities have been eligible to

[42] One survey of shops sold in Preprivatization found more than 50 percent of the surveyed units functioning under some form of operating restrictions. See Toth, "Characteristics and Supply Effects of Pre-Privatization in Hungarian Retail Trade," Kopint-Datorg Discussion Paper, No. 13, August 1993.

purchase the assets in the Preprivatization program. Nonetheless, there is speculation that foreigners may have participated in auctions as silent, invisible partners.

3.4. The allocation process

The SPA immediately assumed ownership of all units included in the program, forbidding asset alienation, and depriving the enterprise of all the unit's inventories. If a unit was to be sold through an auction, the SPA commissioned a private consulting firm to examine the unit's assets and provide a valuation. In its report to the SPA, the consulting firm would include the value of inventories, premises, machinery, equipment, goodwill, and the discounted future income streams, as well as calculations of comparative value, replacement value, and yield calculations. Based on this information, the SPA would then determine the starting price at the auction.

Auctions are conducted by independent agents designated by the SPA. These agents are responsible for placing announcements in at least two daily newspapers and on the premises of the unit being sold at least thirty days in advance of the proceedings. If no bids are offered at the initial asking price, the auction is suspended, and resumed only after the seller has again advertised the sale and the SPA has determined a lower starting price. If a second auction leaves the unit unsold, it may be sold through other means determined by the SPA.

The Preprivatization laws stipulate that certain groups and interests should be given priority if an auction yields equal bids for the same property. First among these are the insiders: shop managers, employees, business associations formed by the employees of the shop, and employees or business associations of the enterprise to which the shop formerly belonged (in that order). Similar preferences were also granted to purchasers offering to pay in cash. After June 1992, individuals who are parties to contractual or rental agreements involving the units in the program could avoid the auctions altogether, purchasing their shops at the starting price determined by the SPA.[43]

Auction winners conclude a transfer of title agreement with the SPA within fifteen days of the auction. Buyers may pay in cash or

[43] This modification was implemented by the Law "On the Sale, Utilization and Protection of Assets Temporarily Owned by the State" (Law LIV/1992).

Compensation Bonds awarded to Hungarian citizens whose property had been expropriated during the years of communist rule.[44] Also, buyers may obtain preferential credit under the special "E credit" program, designed specifically to finance purchases of state assets, although this comes with rather burdensome collateral requirements.[45]

3.5. The results

A comprehensive overview of the progress of Preprivatization to date is provided by Table II.15. After a slow start, the number of units privatized rose steeply in the fourth quarter of 1991. The pace of privatization remained relatively rapid throughout 1992, but dropped sharply in the first half of 1993. By the end of August 1993, Preprivatization proceedings had been completed with respect to 8,723 of the 10,674 reported units, but this figure does not represent the number of units actually privatized, since in 1,707 cases, ownership rights were transferred to state-owned organizations.[46] So far, subtracting intrastate transfers, 7,016 units have left the state sector through the program. Preprivatization has thus been responsible for the

[44] Although Hungary has no in-kind reprivatization or restitution program, the government has awarded approximately Ft 87 bln worth of Compensation Bonds. These interest-bearing bonds may be used to purchase any state property privatized by the SPA, land from local cooperatives, and houses from local governments. The bonds may also be exchanged for shares in the Social Security Fund. They are freely tradeable on the Budapest Stock Market. It is an interesting fact about the SPA's pricing practices that, in the Fall of 1993, compensation bonds could be purchased on the market for 65 percent of their face value, but they were accepted as payment for state property at about 141 percent. For more details see Frydman, Rapaczynski, Earle, *et al.*, *The Privatization Process in Central Europe.*

[45] E-credit is available to Hungarian natural persons and companies owned by them, for all state property purchases. Loans are refinanced by the Hungarian Central Bank and distributed by commercial banks, which typically require 150 percent collateral from any borrower. The interest rate for these loans is set at 60 percent of the Central Bank's refinancing rate. When corrected for inflation, E-credit loans have always had negative interest rates, even more so since March 1993, when following the pronouncement of Government Decree No. XXXVI/1993, the total cost to borrowers, including the commercial bank margin, has been lowered to approximately 7 percent.

[46] Normally, only private parties can acquire units in the program. But transfer of units to state bodies occurred in some cases where the unit functioned as a component of a larger organization. For example, in instances where a food canteen operated within a state hospital, the right to rent out the canteen was transferred to the hospital. Given the precarious financial condition of these organizations, it is assumed that many of these units have been since sold or rented to private parties.

Table II.15 Cumulative data on Preprivatization (as of June 31, 1993)

	1991			1992				1993	
	2nd Qtr	3rd Qtr	4th Qtr	1st Qtr	2nd Qtr	3rd Qtr	4th Qtr	1st Qtr	2nd Qtr
State enterprises reported (cumulative)	367	377	372*	373*	381	409	417	419	419
Units reported (cumulative)	9,992	10,081	10,065†	10,047†	10,080†	10,153	10,529	10,617	10,642
Terminated proceedings‡	770	2,118	4,066	4,689	5,807	6,864	7,637	8,134	8,583
Total units privatized (cumulative)	523	1,390	3,133	3,667	4,481	5,214	5,931	6,391	6,857
Units sold at auction (cumulative)§	272	645	1,729	2,216	2,892	3,379	3,713	4,205	4,573
Average quarterly starting price (Ft '000)	334.56	229.85	182.75	177.41	228.55	181.39	183.31	0.51	0.77
Average quarterly selling price (Ft '000)	406.02	297.27	261.84	253.98	329.37	288.14	345.72	0.92	1.73
Average quarterly selling price as % of starting price	121.37	129.50	143.77	143.99	144.12	162.13	188.63	106.3	202.19

Source: SPA Preprivatization Database.

* Decrease due to liquidation of state enterprises;
† Decrease due to the removal of units determined to be excluded from the program;
‡ "Terminated proceedings" includes completed privatization transactions and intra-enterprise transfers.
§ A sharp-eyed reader will note that in the first quarter of 1993, the number of units sold at auction increased by 491, while the total number of units privatized increased by only 460. This apparent confusion is a result of the nullification of 97 nonauction transfers previously concluded within Preprivatization. Properly classified, auction sales accounted for 89 percent of the 557 privatization transactions in the first quarter of 1993.

privatization of more than 23 percent of the state trade and service units existing in 1990.[47]

The number of privatization transactions does not imply that all units were sold at auction by the SPA. By the end of August 1993, the SPA had auctioned only 4,731 units.[48] The remaining 2,285 shops were either restored to private individuals or nonstate organizations, such as cooperatives, judged to be the true owners, or sold by the enterprises to which they belonged in order to satisfy enterprise debts. The number of auctioned units is also misleading, since the SPA classifies as auctions cases in which the existing contract or rental holders exercise their pre-emptive option to purchase their units. Adjusted for these transactions, we estimate that fewer than 4,000 shops have been sold through competitive proceedings.

To give the reader a better picture, the ratios of the number of units privatized in Preprivatization and the number of units sold through SPA proceedings are graphed in Figure II.1. The proportion of units auctioned has gradually risen from its low point of 46 percent of the cumulative number of units privatized as of the third quarter of 1991, to its current level of 67 percent of cumulative transactions. The first quarter of 1992 was the period when auctions comprised the largest share of Preprivatization transactions, with over 91 percent of ownership transfers involving such proceedings.

Some of the rise in the proportion of auctions to privatizations is due to the unclogging of procedural dams which stalled the start of the program. Passage of the Budget Law for 1991, which diverted sale proceeds to local and regional governments, for example, contradicted the laws concerning Preprivatization, and the confusion surrounding this issue in the first half of 1991 retarded the scheduling of auctions. A recent surge of auctions is probably also, in part, an artifact of the SPA's classification of purchases by existing contract and rental holders as

[47] A comparison of the Preprivatization program with other programs examined in this study shows the limited nature of its success. In the Czech Republic's Small Privatization Program, for example, 18,542 retail trade, catering, and service units were successfully auctioned between January 1991 and December 1992.

[48] The precise proportion of sales of premises to sales of rental rights could not be determined. According to one analysis, in April 1992, 680 outlets had been sold outright, and rental rights had been sold in 1,980 cases. See J. Gacs, I. Karimov and C. Schneider, "Small Scale Privatization in Eastern Europe and Russia from a Historical and Comparative Perspective," IISA Working Paper 92-067, 1992. The total of 2,660 total SPA sales recorded by Gacs, *et al.* diverges slightly from the 2,216 sales listed at the end of the first quarter of 1992 in Table II.15.

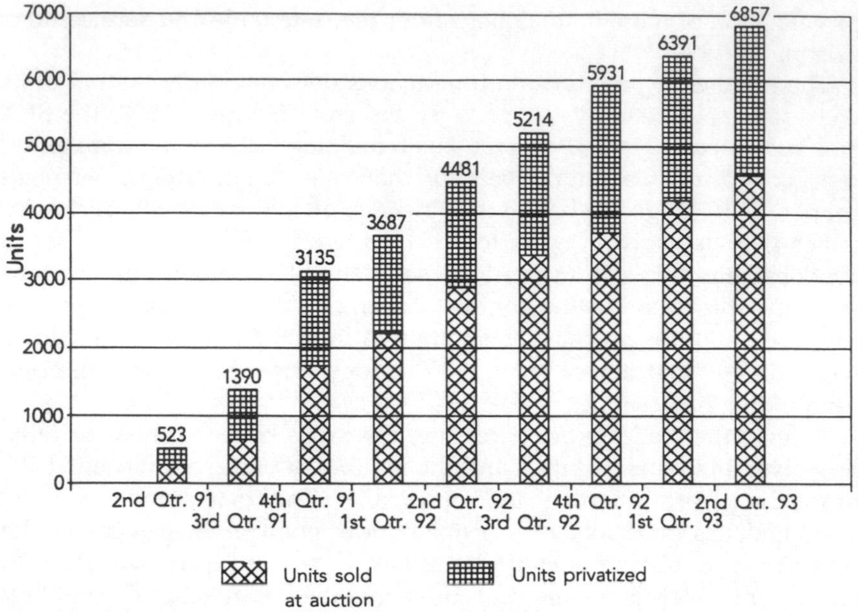

Figure II.1 Cumulative units sold at auction as a proportion of units privatized (as of March 31, 1993).

Source: SPA Preprivatization database.

auctions. Of the units which remained unsold at the end of 1992, a large proportion, estimated at up to 90 percent, were still functioning under valid contractual agreements, and most of the post-1992 Preprivatization transactions have involved preferential purchases rather than auctions.[49]

Overall, the data indicate that Preprivatization, properly understood, is less an auction mechanism than a mechanism of privatization with a possible auction component. Although nonauction transfers, occurring without SPA involvement, decreased the revenues the state obtained

[49] According to a CEU Privatization Project interview with SPA officials, by December 31, 1992, more than 2,500 Preprivatization units continued to operate under contractual agreements. As of this date, slightly more than 2,800 reported units remained unsold. Over 70 percent of contract holders have indicated their intention to utilize their buy-out option.

from the program, the large-scale use of nonauction mechanisms may have positive long-term consequences for the ownership structure and performance of the business units involved. In general, auctions are very important avenues of entry for dynamic new participants, and resort to nonauction methods may be expected to decrease the entry of outsiders into the privatization process. There is good reason, however, to believe that this observation does not apply fully to the Preprivatization program. Indeed, nonauction Preprivatization transfers often operated as expedited mechanisms for the resolution of pre-existing property disputes which the Hungarian legal system was otherwise incapable of quickly processing, and which resulted in a transfer of ownership to enterprise outsiders. Thus, in over 1,000 cases, the resolution of property disputes led to a transfer of all property rights to individuals judged to be the true owners, and only an insignificant number of these new owners were probably sectoral insiders.[50] Moreover, since insiders acquired many of the units sold at auctions, the largest number of new owners may, ironically, have entered the sector through the 33 percent of Preprivatization transfers which occurred outside of the auction proceedings. Furthermore, although most Preprivatization auctions transferred the right to rent the premise for a set period, nonauction transactions involved a complete transfer of ownership rights. On the other hand, it should be noted that the units transferred through nonauction proceedings were among the smallest shops in the Preprivatization program.

It is also likely that the SPA, fearful of accusations of abuse, was overly cautious in setting the starting price in most auctions, since the success rate of auctions in the first round has fluctuated between 50 to 60 percent.[51] As of December 1992, over 11 percent of the units in the program remained unsold after two auctions.[52] Approximately 50

[50] It is, unfortunately, not possible to determine the ultimate ownership disposition of the 1,707 units that devolved to non-state organizations or were sold directly by state enterprises.

[51] As of May 1992, 43 percent of initial auctions were unsuccessful. See Gacs, *et al.*, "Small Scale Privatization in Eastern Europe and Russia from a Historical and Comparative Perspective." For overall estimates of the percentage of successful auctions, see "Testimony for the Trade Commission of the Parliament about the Implementation of Preprivatization Law," submitted by the SPA and the Ministry of Industry and Trade, October 1992; and E. Palocz, "The Emergence and Implementation of the Small Scale Privatization Program in Eastern European Countries: The Case of Hungary," Kopint-Datorg (Budapest), June 1992.

[52] SPA Preprivatization database.

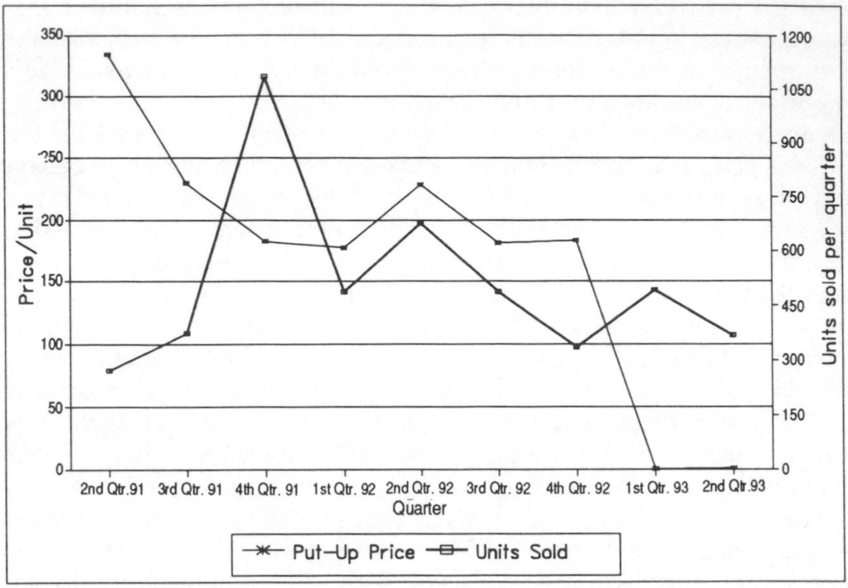

Figure II.2 Average starting price per unit (in Ft '000) and the number of units sold.

Source: SPA Preprivatization Database.

percent of all auctioned units are sold at the starting price, a clear indication that only one person bid for the unit,[53] and a handful of units have been transferred free of charge to municipalities after several unsuccessful sale attempts.

Figure II.2 illustrates the tenuous relationship between the auction starting price and the number of units privatized in each quarter. It also highlights the dramatic slashing of prices in the first half of 1993, with prices reduced to less than 0.2 percent of the first quarter of 1991 level. Managers of individual shops appear to have been the prime beneficiaries of these price cuts, because the discounts came at a time

[53] See Toth, "Characteristics and Supply Effects of Pre-Privatization in Hungarian Retail Trade."

when contractual buy-outs dominated Preprivatization transactions. Price reductions, in the later stages of the program, also may indicate the poor quality of the remaining units and the SPA's growing impatience with the slow progress of Preprivatization.

Overall, sales appear to be only moderately price sensitive, and they clearly depend also on the number of units available for sale. Unfortunately, it is not possible to correlate the levels of starting prices with the number of unsuccessful auctions, since the SPA has failed to keep precise records concerning the number and timing of failed proceedings.

The demand for units was also limited by several other non-price factors. Paramount among these was the uncertainty surrounding the transfer of property rights to the real estate involved. No legal provisions seem to have governed the process by which leases were negotiated after the units were auctioned, except for the length of the term, which was set at ten years. This fact, coupled with the fifteen-day deadline by which an auction winner had to secure his lease from the real estate owner, created a dramatic imbalance in the bargaining position between the local governments (which owned the premises) and their prospective tenants. Many new owners were forced to accept unconditionally the local government's rent demands because otherwise they risked a denial of access to their newly purchased businesses. Refusal to accept the terms offered by the local government, followed by a withdrawal of the intent to purchase the auctioned business, forced the auction winner to forfeit automatically his auction deposit.

Uncertainty concerning the terms of the lease was very significant, given the nature of the assets being sold. The postcommunist shops have little of value in terms of equipment and furniture, and the location of a shop is frequently critical to its success. Indeed, if the rental agreement involved no premium for the tenant (i.e. if the rents were not lower than their market value) it is not clear why any person would be ready to bid anything but a pittance at the SPA's auctions for the 70 percent of the shops sold without premises. But even if rents are below market, the fact that the negotiations for the premises only followed a successful bid, meant that an auction bidder, without local connections, had no way of knowing the real value of the property for sale. Although past rents may have been some indication of the future, concern over potential rental increases was well founded. While only slightly less than half of the units in Preprivatization experienced any increase in the wake of the auction, the rent increases in the other cases were frequently very significant: 80.5 percent of increases were above 20 percent, and 23 percent above 100 percent.[54]

Demand for Preprivatization units was also dampened by the lack of financing. Although the "E-credit" program of government-assisted loans was specifically targeted to aid small domestic investors in the purchase of state assets, the commercial banks that distributed the loans supported by E-credits proved to be very cautious lenders, demanding collateral far in excess of most loan applicants' ability to provide.

The results of an extensive study of Preprivatization allow us to draw a detailed picture of the purchasers in Preprivatization auctions.[55] Slightly over half of auction buyers, 54.7 percent, previously worked in the units they purchased. Managers of the units made up the single largest group of buyers, comprising 48.4 percent of the total population, while 12.1 percent were former employees.[56] Artisans and private traders made up 19.7 percent of the remaining purchasers, while members of the intelligentsia (a broad group of white-collar workers and professionals) bought 9.3 percent of the units. A large portion of successful buyers had already been active in the private sector. Over 40 percent of buyers owned another outlet, with 26.8 percent owning another store in the sector. E-credit financing was received by 53.1 percent of purchasers.

The population of Preprivatization purchasers also seems to fall into two distinct groups: the individuals buying smaller units are markedly different from those buying the larger ones.[57] Managers and employees are disproportionately represented among the large purchasers, along with members of the intelligentsia. Large purchasers financed a greater percentage of their acquisitions with loans; in fact, small purchasers frequently had to put up more cash in absolute terms than the large purchasers.

Large and small buyers are also differentiated by their post-privatization behavior. A greater proportion of the larger units operate

[54] See Toth, "Characteristics and Supply Effects of Pre-Privatization in Hungarian Retail Trade," p. 13.

[55] Toth, "Characteristics and Supply Effects of Pre-Privatization in Hungarian Retail Trade.". Toth's analysis is based on two studies of Privatization purchasers as of April 1992. A total of 1,473 individuals, randomly selected, were interviewed.

[56] Managers and employees did not necessarily purchase the units in which they had previously been employed, explaining the slight discrepancy between the percentage of purchasers who bought their former units and the aggregate total of managerial and employee buyers.

[57] The size of the unit is defined by number of employees, with units having fewer than three employees classified as "small."

under locally imposed line-of-business restrictions, and a higher proportion of the larger units experience rental increases. Larger units tend to sell a higher percentage of foreign goods, and they secure more of their products from state suppliers. Small unit operators, on the other hand, judged their financial position to be more precarious, with 32.3 percent of owners of stores employing one individual saying that they were in a "bad" economic situation. As a response to the worsening economic conditions, owners of small units have been actively expanding the range of products offered in their shops. Finally, large purchasers have a different set of future business plans: they plan to spend less money on the restructuring of their units and they intend to form companies which operate chains of stores.

It appears, therefore, that Preprivatization auctions have served to distribute the state retail trade units that most resemble the private start-up units to outside investors while keeping the larger units, for the most part, in the hands of the insiders. The outside investors are, therefore, much like the other small investors who own most of the new start-up businesses in Hungary and they act like their fellow small store owners in trying to diversify their sources of supply and product mix. The owners of the large, insider-dominated units, on the other hand, continue to use their old state contacts and remain integrated in the state wholesale network, even as they deal more in high-profit foreign products. The future business plans of these owners also reveal their roots: they do not focus on restructuring, seeking instead to create extensive chains of joined commercial establishments.

4. THE FIRST PRIVATIZATION PROGRAM

In September 1990, the SPA launched, under the name of the "First Privatization Program" ("FPP"), its first attempt to privatize entire state-owned enterprises ("SOEs"). The FPP was to be both a testing ground for future programs and, like the simultaneously initiated Preprivatization Program, also a source of revenue for the state budget. With FPP, it was the SPA's intent to assert its control over the Hungarian privatization process, until then dominated by enterprise managers. In light of the all too predictable resistance of these managers, the inexperience of the consulting firms used by the SPA, and the rapid collapse of the COMECON market, the program proved to be almost a complete failure; not one of the enterprises in the program has been sold as planned.[58]

Despite this record, the FPP has served an important role in subsequent Hungarian privatization efforts. On the one hand, the SPA has never again tried to impose a centrally-managed program to privatize entire enterprises. On the other hand, certain key ingredients in the design of the FPP (such as the focus on privatizing on-going enterprises, the restructuring of enterprises prior to privatization, and the use of non-SPA personnel) can be discerned in subsequent attempts to privatize many enterprises in the trade sector.

4.1. The objectives of the First Privatization Program

In order to ensure the program's success, the SPA carefully selected twenty enterprises deemed attractive to both domestic and foreign investors, six of which were in the retail trade sector[59] (see Table II.16).

The SPA envisaged the FPP as much more than just a sale of the companies involved. Instead, each consultant employed in the program had to comply with detailed terms of reference aiming at three main objectives: 1) the maximization of sale proceeds; 2) the design of postprivatization ownership and business structure of the company; and 3) the bolstering of Hungary's capital markets.

Officially, the maximization of sale proceeds was not supposed to play a dominant role.[60] It is clear, however, that the SPA had high financial expectations from the FPP, and the valuation of the companies in the program assumed a very high price/earnings[61] (P/E) ratio of eight to twelve, or one and a half to two times the book value of the assets (estimated at Ft 73 bln).[62] The privatization proceeds were intended to help pay off the state debt, and thus no proceeds were to be used to restructure the companies themselves: in only one of the six

58 For a general discussion of the First Privatization Program, see Frydman, Rapaczynski, Earle *et al.*, *The Privatization Process in Central Europe*.

59 It was not possible to identify accurately the retail trade portion of some of the manufacturing SOEs in the FPP. The decision was thus made to include here only those companies which were primarily active in retail trade, catering and services (including the hotel industry).

60 The bid price accounted for only 25 percent of the total in the evaluation of the consultants' bids, with 75 percent assigned to the analysis of options and the qualifications of the advisory team.

61 Earnings are after-tax, assuming an effective corporate tax rate of 50 percent (which is very conservative).

62 Equivalent of US$ 1,123 mln in 1990.

Table II.16 FPP – Companies in retail trade, catering and services (in Ft mln, as of December 31, 1989)

	Activity	Total assets	Total equity	Annual sales	Profit margin*
Centrum	Retail trade	5,218.9	2,696.3	18,620.8	2.15%
Danubius	Hotels	6,640.0	2,453.0	3,900.0	14.56%
Hungexpo	Conference services	1,654.0	973.0	2,072.0	5.69%
HungarHotels	Hotels	10,935.6	3,304.1	7,537.0	12.37%
IBUSZ, plc	Tourism, trade, financial services	2,144.3	1,458.3	9,428.2	12.08%
Pannonia	Hotels, catering	6,201.0	2,862.0	5,213.0	11.30%
Sector total		32,793.8	13,746.7	46,771.0	8.01%
Total FPP		73,890.8	33,364.4	93,699.8	7.95%
Sector as a % of total FPP		44.38%	41.20%	49.92%	

Source: *First Privatization Program 1990*, SPA (Budapest), 1990.

* Profit margins have been calculated by the authors assuming 50 percent corporate tax rate.

enterprises did the terms of reference mandate an increase in the share capital as a component of privatization.

The second objective, that of shaping the postprivatization structure of the company, was reflected in the degree of detail with which the terms of reference specified the postprivatization ownership distribution, including the number of shares to be sold to foreign and domestic institutional investors, small investors, employees, foreign and Hungarian technical partners, etc. In the trade and service sector, for example, it was proposed to preserve the three chains of hotels and supermarkets included in the program in the hands of Hungarian institutional or technical investors, and to auction only minority stakes to other investors. The SPA's concerns extended not only to planning the initial ownership structure, but also to seeking ways to ensure the continued maintenance of the basic ownership pattern of domestic control.[63] Similarly, the SPA was concerned with a number of operative details of postprivatization

[63] Four of the six terms of references included a requirement that consultant bids include provisions for protecting against hostile takeovers. Concern with potential takeovers appears to have been focused on bids financed by foreign capital.

restructuring and required elaborate new business plans for each company.

Finally, the SPA also wanted to use the FPP as a way to aid the development of Hungary's capital markets and it consequently placed much emphasis on the public trading (on Budapest's stock market) of the privatized companies' securities.[64]

The three objectives of the SPA were not easily complementary to one another. Profit maximization, which would best be pursued through attracting foreign investment, ran afoul of desires to dictate the long-term ownership structure and business plans of the privatized entities. It also sharply conflicted with the urge to retain the "jewels" of the Hungarian economy in Hungarian hands. Similarly, the development of a smoothly functioning, liquid stock market, did not fit well with the desire to create a semipermanent ownership structure. By creating elaborate sectoral plans and extensive enterprise restructuring schemes, the cost of the proceedings was raised, thus also decreasing the total proceeds to be earned.

4.2. The results of the First Privatization Program

In the final analysis, the mutually competing objectives proved to be disastrous for the success of the FPP. Enterprise valuation and restructuring wrought countless delays,[65] at a time when the economic situation continually worsened due to the rapid collapse of the COMECON market. When the National Bank of Hungary mandated an adjustment in the interest rates of existing loans, profitability of the companies in the FPP vanished. Debt restructuring became a necessity, and the SPA had either to repay the debt outright (using state treasury funds in the case of Centrum) or to earmark all or a portion of the sale proceeds for debt repayment (as in the case of HungarHotels).

In attempting to juggle this mix of objectives, the SPA was also forced to make a number of compromises. Ultimately it decided on privatization plans for Pannonia, HungarHotels, and Centrum that called for the division of the enterprises into two parts: one, comprised of one-half to

[64] All terms of reference documents contain the following phrase: "The privatization technique selected is intended to help the evolution of the Budapest Stock Exchange."

[65] The privatization of Danubius provides an indication of the extent of these delays. A quarter of Danubius shares were offered for sale in December 1992, which represented the first opportunity to purchase the company's shares.

two-thirds of the former enterprise assets, to be privatized as an integrated company and; the second part, consisting of the remaining assets, to be sold individually. The privatization plans for the remaining trade enterprises envisioned less restructuring prior to sale. The companies are to be privatized through a mixture of negotiated sales to core investors and the sale of shares on the Budapest Stock Exchange.

The SPA has had some success in selling off individual assets. Six of the nine Centrum stores offered to buyers separately had been sold by March 1993, and individual purchases have been finalized for several former Pannonia and HungarHotels assets, including the high profile sale of the Duna Hotel in Budapest. Many of these sales appear to have been to domestic groups organized by enterprise officials. On the other hand, efforts to sell entire enterprises have generally failed. Some of this failure is due to factors other than the program design and linked to the poor performance of the trade enterprises in the years since 1990, when the value of most of the companies plummeted.[66] On the other hand, decisions regarding the proportion of shares to be sold to core investors and the timing of such sales have been the source of many problems. At the urging of enterprise managers, who wanted to control the process, the privatization plans for trade enterprises, with the exception of IBUSZ, call for a sale through a tender procedure of a significant (though far less than 100 percent) stake in the company to one or several strategic investors, to be followed later by a sale of shares to the public.[67] However, as of March 1993, the SPA has been unable to finalize sale contracts with core investors for any of the enterprises involved. The lack of strategic sales has delayed the public offerings of shares and forced the SPA to rethink its original strategy.

Perhaps ironically, enterprise insiders appear to be the only Hungarian group to have benefited from the FPP. Proceeds from the sales of assets, originally slated to be used to decrease the federal budget deficit, were devoted to paying off former enterprise debts. Able to locate only a small number of interested foreign investors, the SPA's domestic sales (when they occur) have repeatedly been to enterprise managers and employees, with financing through government programs designed to promote domestic investment. A program founded, in part,

[66] IBUSZ shares, for example, were first offered at Ft 4,900 in June 1990. In July 1993, the shares were trading at Ft 1,250.

[67] The size of the stake to be sold to strategic investors varies. A 51 percent share of Pannonia was offered to investors, the same percentage originally was set aside in Centrum. The current Centrum plans propose a sale of 40 percent of the company. No plan has proposed the sale of an entire company to core investors.

on a desire to dislodge recalcitrant enterprise insiders has ultimately been turned to their advantage.

5. SELF-PRIVATIZATION

5.1. Objectives

In mid-1991, the SPA announced the start of the Self-Privatization Program, designed to privatize a large number of state enterprises in a short time. It had long been clear that individual privatization programs for each state enterprise were beyond the staffing capabilities and expertise of the SPA. Moreover, the experience of the First Privatization Program showed that even for a limited number of enterprises such a strategy was riddled with problems that could derail the privatization process. Faced with criticism of the First Privatization Program and Preprivatization from both inside and outside the governing coalition, the SPA embarked on a privatization program that promised better results by involving a wide range of parties and outside expertise, as well as provided a measure of bureaucratic immunity for possible failures. The program was, again, not created especially for trade enterprises, but trade and service enterprises have played a pronounced role.

Self-Privatization's core feature is a shift of responsibility for transforming and privatizing (primarily small) enterprises from the SPA to private intermediaries. Within the framework of a general contract defining the responsibilities of each party, the SPA transfers the right to privatize selected state enterprises to a group of independent consulting firms. In order to assure the proper alignment of incentives, the SPA ties the remuneration of the participating consulting firms to proceeds generated through privatization. Additional bonus payments are linked to the speed with which the sales are completed and for sales above the offering price determined by independent accountants.[68]

[68] The SPA created an additional layer of separation between itself and the conduct of Self-Privatization through the establishment of the subsidiary company, "PriMan" (short for "Privatization Management"). PriMan's responsibilities include the dissemination of information to enterprises and consulting firms, the preparation of recommendations on transformation proposals, and the evaluation of the performance of consulting firms. PriMan also documents the progress of Self-Privatization transformations and sales. The decision to establish a separate subsidiary was, in part, related to the peculiarities of SPA financing: while the laws governing the SPA's finances limited its payroll, its budget did have room for outside consulting fees.

Self-Privatization was also designed to secure the cooperation of enterprise managers, who had been instrumental in the failure of the First Privatization Program. Enterprises participating in Self-Privatization would themselves enter into contracts with the consulting firms of their choice, although they would be limited to firms pre-approved by the SPA. The consulting firms would then conduct the valuation of the enterprise and create a transformation and privatization plan. The insiders were further encouraged to participate by a system of important preferences included for their benefit in the Property Policy Guidelines drawn up by Parliament.[69]

Not all enterprises were eligible to take part. In the first phase of the program, employment and turnover ceilings restricted Self-Privatization to generally small enterprises. Although trade enterprises comprised only a small portion of the program, service enterprises were prominent. Roughly one year after Self-Privatization began, the program was extended to somewhat larger firms, and the proportion of trade and service enterprises diminished in this phase.

Although Self-Privatization was hailed as "privatizing privatization" and decentralizing the privatization process, the actual workings of the program cast doubt on the accuracy of these claims. Private parties do participate as agents of Self-Privatization, but in many cases, their participation has more to do with the distorted structure of the Hungarian market for consulting services than with real profit incentives. Although some firms (especially smaller ones) believed that Self-Privatization offered profitable business opportunities, the exclusive focus on small enterprises in the program drastically limited the revenues from sales and, thus, restricted the returns expected by most consulting firms.[70] Indeed, the SPA's readiness to rid itself of the responsibility for the privatization of small enterprises was in part due to the limited revenue streams associated with this process, especially when measured against the amount of work required to value and create satisfactory business plans for these companies. The Self-Privatization contracts signed by the SPA also contained a variety of

[69] "Property Policy Guidelines" are enacted by Parliament, to guide SPA behavior and decision-making.

[70] The average basic revenue derived from the sale of service enterprises in the first phase of Self-Privatization was less than US$ 13,000. The privatization of two trade enterprises in the second phase of the program did generate a few cases of more substantial revenues (over US$ 100,000) for the consultants, but these were far in excess of the average.

potentially disadvantageous conditions for the consulting firms, such as the obligation to indemnify the SPA for any liability arising from the sale and the responsibility to act as company owners during the frequently long period between transformation and privatization.[71] Enterprises in the program were supposed to pay for the services of the consulting firms, but their limited financial resources precluded the payment of sufficiently large fees to allow many consulting firms to make a profit.[72]

Although economic calculations thus argued against participation, consulting firms were not in a position to decline to take part. A surplus of consulting firms exists in Hungary, and the SPA is by far the largest consumer of their services. By refusing to participate the firms risked being excluded from truly profitable contracts.[73]

The SPA's actions in the administration of Self-Privatization also casts doubt on the degree of actual decentralization. Although the SPA nominally transferred many responsibilities to the consulting firms, it retained control over the most essential decisions. Property transfers, enterprise valuation, and the determination of share prices all remain subject to SPA oversight. Long delays in the process occur, as consulting firms wait for the SPA to hand down its decisions. In some situations, the ability of the firm to satisfy its obligations is seriously endangered by the incomplete transfer of responsibilities. For example, while the consulting firms are entrusted with the governance of a company in the process of privatization, their efficacy in acting as owners is impaired by the need to obtain a written permission from the SPA before they are allowed to dismiss general managers.

Claims about the voluntary nature of enterprise participation in Self-

[71] As payment for their governance efforts consulting firms were entitled to receive 5 percent of any dividends distributed by Self-Privatization companies in phase I, and 10 percent of the dividends paid out during phase II. It is unlikely, however, that dividends, if distributed at all, are significant, since most companies in Self-Privatization are in a precarious financial condition.

[72] The limited pecuniary value of the payments enterprises could afford to pay induced some consulting firms to forgo any payment for their work. The most active consulting firm in Self-Privatization initially adopted this policy, but was later forced to renounce it as well as scale back its participation due to financial setbacks. See *Privinfo*, VI/2 1992, Vol. 2, No. 5, pp. 12–13 for further discussion of the consulting firm's behavior in Self-Privatization.

[73] The critical importance for consulting firms of creating enduring relations with the SPA has long been a feature of Hungarian privatization. See D. Stark, "Path Dependence and Privatization Strategies in East Central Europe," *East European Politics and Societies*, Vol. 6, No. 1, Winter 1992.

Privatization are also exaggerated. Over eighty enterprises did join the program, motivated by, among other reasons, a perception that Self-Privatization might provide the best chance for an infusion of new capital from outside investors. Trade and service enterprises, in addition, hoped through joining the program to recover some of the units they had lost to Preprivatization.[74] But the vast majority of the enterprises involved entered into the program as a consequence of being included in the lists of participants drawn up by the SPA. Although the firms are nominally free to exit from the program, such behavior is discouraged by the SPA's threat of "forced transformation," which may include the firing of enterprise managers and terms quite disadvantageous to the enterprise insiders. This threat was given added currency by the passage (in July 1992) of Law LIV "On the Utilization and Management of Temporary State Assets," which set June 30, 1993, as a deadline for the initiation of transformation in all state enterprises. Enterprises not meeting the deadline on their own are subject to SPA-directed privatization.

Overall, the actual practice of Self-Privatization seems rather far removed from the picture drawn by its official proponents: instead of eagerly embracing the program, the consulting firms mostly seek to earn the goodwill of the SPA as they try to limit their losses; the enterprises use the program as a safe harbor providing shelter from SPA meddling, and only partially as a mechanism for privatization.

5.2. Organizational framework

In the summer of 1991, the SPA invited all consulting firms registered in Hungary with either stock capital or bank guarantees of at least Ft 10 mln to apply for the right to participate in Self-Privatization. Eighty-three firms were chosen out of an applicant pool of 150. Upon acceptance, all the firms signed a "frame contract" with the SPA, which gave them exclusive rights to sell the shares of companies transformed

[74] Enterprise insiders used the postprivatization business plans drawn up and submitted to the SPA for all Self-Privatization enterprises to show that units which otherwise were to be privatized through the Preprivatization Program were integral to the future success of the company and, thus, should be returned to the enterprise. Therefore, Self-Privatization held out a potential avenue for the reacquisition of units removed from enterprises via the Preprivatization Program. See section 3 for additional information on units included in the Preprivatization Program.

through Self-Privatization. The contracts were originally scheduled to expire in March 1993, but they were later extended by a second frame contract until the end of December 1993.

Results of the first phase of Self-Privatization were considered so promising that in August 1992 the SPA announced the start of the program's second phase. The SPA called for a new tender for consulting firms and required the firms participating in the first phase to pass a SPA evaluation prior to being included in the second phase. Forty-three consulting firms signed the second phase frame contract, which was also due to expire in December 1993.

5.3. Assets in Self-Privatization

In September 1991, the SPA announced that state enterprises employing fewer than 300 employees, owning equity of less than Ft 300 mln, and maintaining a sales turnover of less than Ft 300 mln, could participate in the Self-Privatization program.[75] The SPA also published a list of 350 companies whose 1990 balance sheets indicated that they were eligible for participation. The number of companies included in the program grew to 433 within six months, as over eighty additional companies successfully petitioned to enter the program.[76] These enterprises, though nominally too large, argued that their poor post-1990 performance made them comparable to the enterprises automatically included in the program.

The petitioning enterprises appear to have been primarily motivated by the desire of the management to retain influence over the privatization of their enterprises. Hope that Self-Privatization would provide a mechanism for the recovery of units lost in Preprivatization also played a role for trade and service enterprises.[77] This may explain the unusually high percentage of trade enterprises which volunteered for Self-Privatization. Anecdotal evidence suggests that several additional trade enterprises unsuccessfully attempted to be included.

[75] Due to the economic upheavals that had occurred in the years since 1990, the SPA ultimately chose to rely on the book value of an enterprise as the sole criterion for inclusion in the program.

[76] The number of participating enterprises ultimately dropped to 421 as of the end of January 1993 as a result of the exit of twelve enterprises.

[77] Several of the trade enterprises participating in the first phase have more than twenty units involved in Preprivatization. See PriMan Self-Privatization database, July 1993.

Table II.17 Trade and service enterprises in Phase 1 of Self-privatization, as of June 1993*

	Trade	Consumer services
Number of enterprises	8	179
Average employment	223	112
Average turnover (Ft '000)	958,150	258,246

Source: PriMan Self-Privatization database, July 1993.

* The database used to construct this table is plagued by missing variables. While the data on trade enterprises are derived from a representative number of entries (six), the data on consumer service enterprises is considerably less reliable.

Table II.18 Trade and service enterprises in Phase II of Self-privatization, as of June 1993*

	Trade	Consumer services
Number of enterprises	21	12
Average employment	192	281
Average turnover (Ft 1,000)	224,427	414,102

Source: PriMan Self-Privatization database, July 1993.

* In contrast to the Phase I database, the data source used to compile this table has almost no missing values. All of the calculations listed in the table are derived from a representative number of entries.

Service enterprises, broadly defined, make up 62 percent of all participants in Phase I,[78] with consumer service enterprises comprising 43 percent. In contrast, trade enterprises constitute only 2 percent of the total, but when measured both by employment and turnover, they are significantly larger than service enterprises. In fact, the average trade enterprise's turnover exceeds by a factor of more than three the official ceiling for Phase I enterprises, which shows that some large trade enterprises were mixed in with the supposedly small Self-Privatization enterprises.

[78] In addition to consumer service enterprises, eighty-two other service enterprises are included in the first phase. Most of these enterprises are concentrated in the provision of professional services (accountants, lawyers, etc.) and have been excluded from our analysis.

The second phase of Self-Privatization involved somewhat larger firms. The SPA's list of 279 eligible enterprises, published in Fall 1992, included firms with under 1,000 employees, assets of under Ft 1 bln, and an annual turnover of under Ft 1 bln. As of June 1993, thirteen of these enterprises have declined to participate, leaving a total of 267 enterprises currently in Phase II of Self-Privatization. There have been no entries of additional enterprises into the second phase. It is worth noting that although the program's eligibility rules were changed to admit larger enterprises, the trade enterprises included in Phase II are significantly smaller than in Phase I.

5.4. The allocation process

Self-Privatization involves a two-step process of privatization. First, with the assistance of the consulting firms, the enterprises are supposed to be transformed into commercial companies ("corporatized"). Then, they are to be privatized through the sale of company shares.[79]

The transformation contract signed between a participating enterprise and a consulting firm commits the firm to help the enterprise decide how best to transform. As part of this effort, the firm conducts a valuation of the company,[80] determines which assets, if any, should be sold prior to corporatization,[81] appeals for the return of units taken from the enterprise in Preprivatization,[82] and sets the offering price for the company shares.

[79] For a full description of the transformation process see Frydman, Rapaczynski, Earle, *et al.*, *The Privatization Process in Central Europe.*

[80] The second frame contract altered the distribution of responsibilities between consulting firms and enterprises. Enterprises were assigned the task of arranging for an independent accountant to conduct the valuation. A special SPA department reviews all enterprise valuations, conducting separate valuations of enterprises it suspects are undervalued. Enterprises are required to pay for the SPA-initiated valuation procedures in all cases in which the SPA valuation is over 20 percent greater than the initial calculation.

[81] Asset sales appear to have been limited due to the requirement, imposed by the Law on the Protection of State Property, of gaining SPA approval for all sales above Ft 20 mln, a prohibitively time consuming process.

[82] According to a PriMan report, sixty-one trade and service enterprises had applied for the release of 246 Preprivatization units as early as October 1991; 145 of these units have been returned to their original enterprises. See E. Voszka, "Ket ur szolgaja Ksz" ("Serving Two Masters"), *Kozgozdasagi Szemle,* May 1993.

A consulting firm may also determine that the enterprise is unable to satisfy its debt obligations, and recommend putting it into bankruptcy.[83] If the consulting firm determines that the company is solvent, it will suggest a business plan for the new company which often includes the firm's conception of the most desirable ownership structure.[84] All these tasks entail extensive and time consuming negotiations between enterprise insiders, consulting firms, and the SPA.[85] As a general rule, enterprise insiders push for low valuations and low starting prices, the SPA argues for high valuations and prices, and the consulting firms are caught between their clients' rival desires. Enterprise insiders also argue for plans that involve majority employee ownership,[86] but this generates resistance from the SPA, which is interested in revenue maximization. The consulting firms are forced to balance these interests, while they simultaneously weigh the need to raise additional capital for the company and to resolve quickly the issues of future ownership.[87] Disputes between consulting firms and enterprises over business plans have at times led to the cancellation of the firm–enterprise contract.[88]

In addition to the responsibilities related to enterprise transformation, the basic frame contracts give the consulting firms exclusive rights, until their contracts expire, to sell the shares of new companies. All sales of controlling stakes must be conducted by tender, the procedures for which are defined in SPA regulations and Law LIV of 1992.[89] The

[83] For a more detailed description of Hungarian bankruptcy and liquidation proceedings, see Frydman, Rapaczynski, Earle, *et al.*, *The Privatization Process in Central Europe*.

[84] Firms were required to elaborate ownership structure plans whenever their privatization plans included the distribution of preferential shares to employees or any other mechanism (such as an ESOP) which decreased the revenue obtained from the sale.

[85] Decisions on appeals for the return of Preprivatization units, for example, frequently have taken up to six months.

[86] The following is an example of a provision inserted by the management into its enterprise contract with the consulting firm: "Privatization should be carried out with the direct participation of managers and employees. Mid-level managerial proficiency is instrumental in the success of the privatized company due to the need for their skills in financial matters and investment decisions." Such attempts to dictate the conditions of privatization are apparently common. *Privinfo*, I/16, pp. 46–7, December 1992.

[87] Revenue raising needs often argue for the sale of a majority stake to outside investors. However, such sales normally take a considerable period of time to develop, thereby delaying the resolution of the questions surrounding the ownership structure of the new company. Company performance frequently declines drastically at the height of the ownership uncertainty, with skilled employees exiting the establishment.

[88] See *Privinfo*, I/16, pp. 46–7, December 1992, for revealing interviews with the parties in one such dispute.

[89] Law LIV/1992 on the Sale, Utilization and Protection of Assets Temporarily Owned by the State, sections 76 through 80.

consultants receive a commission from the sale proceeds,[90] plus a premium for sales completed by certain dates.[91] In the second phase, a consulting firm also receives a bonus for sales above the initial share price determined by the accountants hired by the enterprise and approved by the SPA.[92]

All Self-Privatization sales include preferences for the enterprise insiders and the general framework of these is spelled out in the privatization legislation in effect at the time of the signing of the frame contracts. Employee preferences for Phase I sales completed before March 1993 were defined by the Company Law of 1988 and the Property Policy Guidelines of 1990 (extended for 1991 and 1992). Under the Guidelines, the employees had a right to match the winning tender bid for the majority stake in their enterprise. In addition, the consulting firms were obliged to elaborate special plans for the employees to purchase the common shares, as well as the opportunity to purchase, at a 90 percent discount, a relatively small number of special shares (with the combined value of preferential shares not to exceed 10 percent of the share capital) with limited voting rights.[93] A variety of financing mechanisms, including E-credit and compensation bonds[94] were also available to the employees for their acquisitions.

The scope of insider preferences in the second frame contract of Phase I (which extended the deadline for sales until December 1993), as well as in the second phase, changed somewhat as a result of the passage, in 1992, of three laws: Law XLIX "On the Employees' Stock-Ownership

[90] In the first phase, the selling commission is 5 percent of the selling price. The second phase introduced a graduated payment schedule with 5 percent commission for sales under Ft 300 mln, 4 percent for sales between Ft 300–600 mln, and 3 percent for sales above Ft 600 mln. The selling price is calculated as 80 percent of the cash, credit, and compensation bonds received for the sale (the remaining 20 percent is re-invested in the company). While these rates potentially yield significant commissions, the majority of sales, to date, have generally been for amounts far less than Ft 300 mln. For example, the average value of sales of service enterprises has been slightly over Ft 20 mln.

[91] In Phase I, firms received a bonus equal to 7.5 percent of the sale price for sales completed before December 31, 1991, a 5 percent bonus for sales completed before March 31, 1992. After March 1992, the amount of the bonus decreased by 0.5 percent each succeeding month. For Phase II, firms gained a 5 percent bonus for sales completed before September 30, 1992, and 3 percent bonuses for sales before December 31, 1992.

[92] Bonuses of 5 percent are distributed for sales concluded at between 125–135 percent of the initial price, 10 percent bonuses for sales between 135–150 percent of the asking price, and 15 percent bonuses for sales over 150 percent of the initial price.

[93] See Frydman, Rapaczynski, Earle, *et al.*, *The Privatization Process in Central Europe*, pp. 137–8, for a description of the shares.

[94] For information on E-credits and compensation bonds, see section 3, [footnote 45].

Program" (ESOP),[95] Law LIV "On the Sale, Utilization, and Protection of Assets Temporarily Owned by the State," and the new Property Policy Guidelines for 1993. Law XLIX allowed employees to purchase a limited number of shares at a 50 percent discount, if they established an ESOP organization representing at least 40 percent of the employees. Law LIV established a new financing technique through so-called "leasing" – in fact, a form of installment sale, in which if an enterprise cannot be sold through other means, it may be transferred to an entrepreneur, who at the conclusion of the lease becomes the owner of the company. Though open to outside investors as well, this technique was designed primarily for enterprise managers without sufficient resources to buy their companies outright. The new Property Policy Guidelines eliminated the employees' preemptive right to purchase the controlling stake in their enterprises, but because of the law's timing, it did not affect the frame contract for Phase II.[96] The preferences granted to the employees in the three frame contracts of Self-Privatization are charted in Table II.19.

5.5. The results

The results of the Self-Privatization program for enterprises in the trade and service sectors can be evaluated on the basis of the number of enterprises transformed and, more importantly, the number of enterprises privatized.

Table II.20 indicates the incidence of transformation of trade and consumer service enterprises in Self-Privatization. Overall, only 126 out of the 220 trade and service enterprises (57 percent) have been transformed successfully in the two years during which the program has operated. A low rate of transformations among consumer service enterprises in the first phase is particularly noticeable. This might be

[95] The value of shares which any employee may purchase at the 50 percent discount is limited to either the amount of that employee's yearly wage, or 10 percent of the company equity divided by the total number of employees, whichever value is smaller. ESOPs may employ E-credit and compensation bonds to finance their purchases. See sections 4 through 19 and section 26 of Law XLIV/1992 for additional information.

[96] Insider preferences in Self-Privatization present a classic example of the divergence of the Hungarian privatization process from any set of formal rules and provide a rich source for future research. An analysis of insider preference provisions included in each of the frame contracts reveals a number of inconsistencies, and the actual procedures seem to follow still another path, strongly influenced by informal pressure from the SPA, which apparently discouraged the use of the full component of insider preferences allowed by the law.

Table II.19 Preferential terms for sales to insiders in Self-Privatization

	Insider preference	Implementing law or regulation
First frame contract of First Phase (9/91–3/93)	90% discount on employee shares	Company Law – 1988
	Preemptive rights for majority stake purchases	Property Policy Guidelines – 1990 (extended through 1992)
Second frame contract of First Phase (3/93–12/93)	90% discount on employee shares	Company Law – 1988
	No preemptive purchase rights	Property Policy Guidelines – 1993
	ESOP financing and 50% discount	Law XLIX – 1992
	Lease financing	Law LIV – 1992
Frame contract of Second Phase (8/92–12/93)	90% discount on employee shares	Company Law – 1988
	Preemptive rights for majority stake purchases	Property Policy Guidelines – 1990 (extended through 1992)
	ESOP financing and 50% discount	Law XLIX – 1992
	Lease financing	Law LIV – 1992

Table II.20 Transformation of trade and service enterprises in Self-Privatization, as of June 1993

	Trade		Consumer services	
	Phase 1	Phase 2	Phase 1	Phase 2
Total number of enterprises	8	21	179	12
Number of transformed enterprises	6	14	98	8
Average share capital (Ft '000)	119,177	250,619	41,658	115,409

Source: PriMan Self-Privatization database, July 1993.

Table II.21 Privatization of trade and service enterprises in Self-Privatization, as of June 1993

	Trade enterprises		Consumer service enterprises	
	Phase 1	Phase 2	Phase 1	Phase 2
Transformed enterprises	6	14	98	8
Completely sold	4	2	67	0
Partially sold	0	1	9	1
Mean value of sale (Ft '000)	81,518	332,407	20,716	–
% of starting price	63.7%	88.8%	84.4%	–
Incidence of majority stakes	4	2	54	–
Mean size of majority stake	83.7%	75.5%	85.9%	–

Source: PriMan Self-Privatization database, July 1993.

explained, in part, by the high proportion of consumer service enterprises which had lost their economic viability as a result of having their units being stripped away in the course of Preprivatization. Although the transformation of trade enterprises has been more successful, more than 30 percent of these enterprises also have yet to be transformed.

While transformation is simply a change of corporate form, privatization is the real objective of the program. But, as may be seen from Table II.21, the number of trade and consumer service enterprises which have been sold in Self-Privatization, despite the praise lavished on the program, is rather modest: a total of seventy-three, or 33 percent, out of the 220 trade and service enterprises included in the program have been fully sold. Slightly over 60 percent of the enterprises that have been transformed have been later privatized. As of June 1993, a total of only two trade and service privatizations in the trade and service sector have taken place in Phase II of the program. With the exception of ESOP purchases, all sales which have taken place have been through competitive tender procedures.

Sales have also been slow and, presumably, labor intensive, since the initial sales of trade enterprises did not take place until the end of January 1993,[97] and over 80 percent of the trade and service enterprise

[97] The first sales of service enterprises occurred over a year earlier, in December 1991.

sales have been concluded since October 1992. At least in the retail trade and service sector, few firms received any bonuses for quick sales.

A comparison of successfully privatized enterprises with those which have been transformed but not sold reveals no statistically significant differences in employment or share capital.

Who are the buyers of the trade and service enterprises in Self-Privatization? As may be seen from Table II.22, there are no foreign investors, and ESOPs have so far played only a minor role. Self-Privatization sales have been dominated by domestic and enterprise insider investors.

It is hazardous to draw fine distinctions regarding the buying behavior of these two dominant groups, given the very limited set of available data. Outside investors are not readily distinguishable from insider purchasers in either the value of their purchases or the size of their ownership position. Outside investors regularly purchased either minority stakes, or majority stakes of significantly less than 100 percent, resulting in companies with ownership composed of a mixture of insider and outsider interests. The dominant model in Self-Privatization thus appears to be for domestic investors and enterprise managers to combine their financial resources in order to purchase the viable privatized companies, rather than compete with each other for control.

Indeed, the readiness of both insiders and outsider investors to acquire minority stakes in Self-Privatization enterprises is somewhat surprising, especially given the small size of most companies involved. As a matter of fact, thirteen privatized consumer service companies have no majority shareholders, and some fifteen others have minority shareholders. Outside domestic investors took eleven of the twenty-eight service company minority positions, and three of the four minority stakes in the trade companies.[98] The willingness of outside investors to acquire minority stakes strongly suggests that they are brought in by the management in whom they have confidence.

It is rather striking that almost half of the 147 as yet not privatized trade and service enterprises in Self-Privatization are currently under (or have concluded) some form of bankruptcy or liquidation proceedings (see Table II.23). The large number of enterprise terminations[99] in the trade and service sector may indicate that many enterprises lost their

[98] See PriMan Self-Privatization database, July 1993.

[99] "Terminations" include cases of enterprises put into bankruptcy or under judicially-supervised liquidation, as well as those of enterprises liquidated by a decision of the founder or by an agreement between the creditors and the enterprise.

Table II.22 Distribution of Self-Privatization majority-stake purchasers, as of June 1993

Sector	Phase	Buyer	Number of majority purchases	Average value of purchase	Average stake in ownership (%)	Average discount (%)*
Trade	1	Domestic	2	76,010	67.7	44
	1	Insider	1	75,000	99.4	–3
	1	ESOP	1	48,720	100	40
	2	Domestic	1	135,800	51	0
	2	Insider	0	–	–	–
	2	ESOP	1	446,800	100	12
Consumer services	1	Domestic	25	25,477	85.2	15
	1	Insider	28	18,131	87.5	12
	1	ESOP	1	31,804	59.3	54

Source: PriMan Self-Privatization database, July 1993.

* Average discount is calculated by dividing the amount of the purchase by the original offering price.

Table II.23 Incidence of bankruptcy and liquidation in Self-Privatization trade and service enterprises, as of October 1993

	Trade	Consumer services
Bankruptcy	1	20
Liquidation	3	31
Other*	0	14
Total	4	65

Source: PriMan Self-Privatization database, October 1993.

* "other" includes enterprises terminated by decision of the founder and enterprises where proceedings have been concluded by an agreement among creditors.

economic viability due to the removal of their key shops and outlets in the course of Preprivatization. But termination proceedings may also have resulted from conscious decisions of both enterprise insiders and the consulting firms, since both groups had strong incentives to choose this option, instead of attempting to continue with the more standard mode of privatization. The start of termination proceedings usually signaled the end of the consulting firms' work, and thus an end to their mounting losses. Termination proceedings, which in the Hungarian context often amount to privatization without SPA supervision, also allowed the enterprise insiders a chance to purchase valuable assets on the cheap, unencumbered by debt and contractual obligations. Moreover, such procedures are usually concluded much faster than the one year it takes for most Self-Privatization transformations (to say nothing of privatizations).

Regardless of the reasons for their initiation, termination proceedings were involved in the privatization of approximately the same number of Self-Privatization enterprises as transformation-tender sales. The large number of enterprises in the program that remain untransformed and unsold suggests that Self-Privatization may in time become a program of privatization of individual assets through bankruptcy, rather than a sale of going concerns through competitive tenders.

6. SPA PLANS FOR THE REMAINING STATE UNITS

Over 10,000 shops and catering establishments will remain state-owned even after the end of the Preprivatization and Self-Privatization programs. The SPA is currently in the process of devising a number of strategies for the privatization of these remaining units. However, since the time frame for most of these plans is quite vague, it is impossible to predict when and how the remaining units will in fact be privatized.

The remaining state units are a rather varied assortment. Some are specialty stores that form a part of a state monopoly, such as the over 1,000 pharmacies still in the hands of the state. Other stores (the greatest portion of the remaining ones) serve as the retail outlets for enterprises involved in some form of manufacturing.

With respect to pharmacies, the SPA plans to privatize each store separately through sales to qualified individuals.[100] But with respect to the other remaining state stores, SPA plans usually envision the sale of many units grouped together in chains and integrated with wholesale and distribution facilities. The thinking behind this strategy is that such groupings will allow for economies of scale in purchasing and distribution.

The ambitious approach chosen by the SPA involves a very high degree of "engineering" of the postprivatization trade sector, and the tasks involved are very complex. In designing the new companies regrouping the existing units, the SPA is working in conjunction with officials from various ministries to produce an analysis of the particular subsectors of retail trade, attempting to determine the optimal number of firms that should be formed in light of the size of the respective markets and the concentration patterns found in similar subsectors in Western economies.[101]

The SPA's efforts to date have achieved only modest successes. The competing economic, social, and political interests involved have produced pressures in a number of directions, and the resulting privatization attempts are sometimes more notable for the speed with which they are modified than the speed of actual sales.

No comprehensive information is available concerning the proposed disposal of all the remaining state stores. An illustrative example,

[100] For information on the debate concerning the privatization of pharmacies and pharmaceutical wholesale companies, see *Privinfo*, Vol. 1, No. 4, p. 42, January 1992; *Privinfo*, Vol. 1, No. 16, pp. 27–8, December 1992.

[101] The Trade Privatization Committee coordinates the creation of subsector privatization plans. Formed in early 1993, the Committee is made up of officials from the SPA, the Ministries of Finance, Industry and Trade, Environmental Protection, and Labor, and the National Competition Agency, along with representatives from banks, and labor unions. Although the Committee only issues recommendations, its decisions are usually dispositive.

however, may be seen in the efforts to privatize the large "Kozert" food chain in Budapest.[102] In October 1992, the SPA sold at auctions 147 of the 330 stores in this chain; 102 stores grouped in ten chains were sold to domestic and foreign investors and thirty-two stores were sold separately. A further twenty stores were subsequently sold to a foreign buyer, leaving some 150 stores under state ownership. But even these numbers exaggerate somewhat the success of Kozert's privatization, since only sixty of the shops purchased in the October 1992 auction had been actually taken over by the auction winners as of May 1993. The domestic buyers, in particular, have for some reason chosen to delay or abandon taking possession of their stores. In order to force the hand of the auction winners, the SPA passed a resolution, in January 1993, mandating that the stores be taken over no later than April 30, 1993.

In the wake of the first Kozert sales, a considerable debate ensued among the SPA, the Ministry of Industry and Trade, and the shop owners whether to sell the remaining stores individually or in chains, and if in chains, how many. The Ministry of Industry and Trade argued for the creation of competing networks of chains, specializing in particular products. The management and workers argued against any transfer of ownership, and for the inclusion of employment and wage guarantees, if sales have to be made.

In April 1993, the SPA suddenly announced its decision to create a low-priced "discount" network of food stores, and it is now seeking to attract nonprofit companies to purchase the stores, with the agreement that they will sell low cost food items purchased directly from producers. Neither the exact number of stores to be included nor their identity have been announced (nor seem decided upon), and until the issue is resolved, no sales can be concluded. The fate of the units not included in the discount chain is similarly unclear: they may be offered individually, or as part of an alternative chain, or as part of a franchise system. In the meantime, a year since the first auction of Kozert stores, no further sales have been made.

The problems encountered in attempting to balance a variety of interests and objectives in the privatization of Kozert are not unique. In fact, they have appeared in different guises in many of the SPA's other efforts to engineer new retail trade subsectors. The household appliance sector provides another good example, with privatization of a large enterprise held up by the SPA's desire to privatize two "competitive

[102] For plans concerning Kozert privatization, see *Privinfo*, Vol. I, No. 14, November 1992, p. 46, and Vol. II, No. 9, May 1993, p. 39.

partners" simultaneously.[103] Indeed, given the number of parties involved, the diversity of their interests, and the fluctuations in their powers, it is unlikely that the SPA, unless it alters its fundamental approach, will be able to avoid extensive negotiations and countless delays. Committed to an ambitious technocratic model for privatizing the remainder of the state units, Hungary is likely to continue to feature a sizeable number of state-owned trade establishments for the next several years.

7. THE TRANSFORMATION OF HUNGARIAN CONSUMER COOPERATIVES[104]

The recent history of Hungarian consumer cooperatives parallels, to some extent, that of Hungarian state retail trade enterprises. Changes in the structure of the cooperatives have been occurring for several decades and, in the last few years, a great number of stores passed out of cooperative ownership. The period since the demise of the communist regime has seen only limited aggregate changes, but more significant structural transformations, as well as a large increase in the number of rental agreements through which the cooperatives have significantly decreased the number of stores under their direct operational control. The passage of a comprehensive cooperative transformation law, in 1992, has resulted in a more democratic structure of cooperative governance.

Overall, the number of retail and catering shops owned by consumer cooperatives has decreased in the period between 1988 and 1992 by approximately 30 percent, from 23,187 to 16,185.

7.1. The history of Hungarian consumer cooperatives

Like the Czech Republic and Poland, Hungary has a history of consumer cooperatives that dates to the middle of the nineteenth

[103] See *Privinfo*, Vol. 2, No. 6, March 1993, p. 39 and Vol. 2, No. 7, April 1993, p. 36.

[104] Although agricultural cooperatives also operated some retail shops, most of their activities were concentrated in food production, not in trade. Their contribution to the total volume of turnover in the sector is negligible, and they have been excluded from discussion in this section. Aggregate figures from statistical yearbooks, used in some of the tables below, do, however, include data on agricultural cooperatives.

century. The first consumer cooperatives were established in small villages neglected by conventional commercial trade establishments. Individual cooperatives operated as independent organizations, and their membership was usually small enough to allow for each member to exercise a relatively strong voice in the governance of the cooperative. Over time, the rural cooperatives grew substantially, both in number and in size, and in many cases became vertically integrated with other establishments engaged in agricultural and industrial production and wholesale trade. Starting with the late 1880s, rural cooperatives in Hungary came to be organized in a nationwide organization, with a centralized wholesale trade and food processing system structured as a joint stock company. While each local cooperative owned a portion of the shares, the organization was dominated by the state, which owned 70 percent of the shares.

In 1948, the communist government began to dismantle the existing cooperatives, forcing them to contribute their assets to an alternative cooperative system.[105] Virtually all consumer cooperatives in urban areas were disbanded. A single consumer cooperative was usually left in each village as rural retail trade became the exclusive responsibility of consumer cooperatives. The government nationalized the producer and wholesale operations of the cooperatives, and brought all the remaining consumer cooperatives, together with housing and credit cooperatives, under the authority of a National Federation of Cooperatives, or SZOVOSZ. Oversight of the everyday management of the cooperatives was handled by the twenty regional SZOVOSZ offices.

Consumer cooperatives retained only nominally their democratic governance structures. Representative organs within the individual cooperatives were dominated by the managers, who in turn answered to SZOVOSZ officials. SZOVOSZ was also responsible for determining delivery quotas for individual cooperatives and monitoring their performance. Membership in the federation was *de facto* obligatory, as were regular contributions to the investment fund it maintained.[106]

[105] Government resolution 8000/1948 required new cooperative elections for the board of directors, with the condition that four-fifths of the directors be poor peasants. Resolution 11,440/1948 mandated the merging of local cooperative assets with those held by the government-sponsored cooperatives, under the direction of the Party-controlled Hungarian National Cooperative Center.

[106] Universal membership in SZOVOSZ was ensured by making it impossible for the existing cooperatives to conclude contracts with state enterprises without the SZOVOSZ's assistance, and for the new chapters to register as legal entities without the bylaws incorporating a SZOVOSZ membership provision.

Consumer cooperatives underwent significant reforms in the last three decades of the communist regime. Beginning with the 1960s, cooperatives were substantially consolidated: the 3,356 individual consumer cooperatives which had existed in 1950 (most of which operated only one shop) were, by 1989, merged into 279 larger organizations, each with a small networks of stores. The average membership of a consumer cooperative grew from 460 to 5,541.[107]

Simultaneously, the administrative controls over the activities of cooperatives were relaxed. The required SZOVOSZ "assistance" in obtaining contracts with state suppliers was eliminated,[108] and special legislation gave the cooperatives the power to dispose of their assets without prior approval by SZOVOSZ or the government.[109] Consumer cooperatives were again permitted to maintain their own wholesale networks and to establish stores in urban areas. In the 1970s, the government even provided the cooperatives with special loans for the creation of an extensive network of department stores in larger cities. Together with the capital accumulated by the SZOVOSZ investment funds, and direct contributions from individual cooperatives, these loans financed the construction of several wholesale enterprises and ninety-five department stores in provincial cities.

Finally, the management of cooperative stores was transformed through the introduction of rental agreements into the cooperative sector. While these arrangements were in many ways similar to the contractual and rental practices of state enterprises, which we have discussed earlier,[110] cooperative agreements with private individuals were significantly more restrictive: they usually contained restrictions on changes in the line of business, as well as provisions mandating the distribution of end-of-year cooperative member rebates. Nevertheless, by 1988, 6,119 cooperative rental arrangements were in existence, covering 12 percent of cooperative retail stores and 59 percent of cooperative restaurants; in all, 26 percent of cooperative-owned establishments.[111]

[107] *1993 Official AFEOSZ Report*, prepared for the 1993 annual AFEOSZ conference.

[108] Government resolution No. 1003/1969 was the legal foundation of these changes.

[109] See the Cooperative Law of 1971 (III/1971) and Law XXXIV/1971. According to standard SZOVOSZ-prepared bylaws from this period, the Board of Directors could decide on the contribution of up to one-third of a cooperative's property to a new entity. A decision of the meeting of delegates was needed for a reassignment of up to two-thirds of the property, and a decision of the general assembly was necessary for a transfer of more than two-thirds of the property of an individual cooperative.

[110] See section 2 above.

[111] See *Fogyasztasi Szovetkezeti Statisztikai Zsebkonyv* (*Statistical Handbook on Consumer Cooperatives*), AFEOSZ pamphlet, Budapest, 1988, pp. 43, 44, 77, 80, and 105.

Table II.24 Basic indicators of the Hungarian trade and catering sector, 1988

Ownership	Number of units	Number of employees ('000)	Annual turnover (Ft 1000 mln)
Consumer cooperatives	23,187	91.1†	210.6
Other cooperatives*	5,645		32.2
State enterprises	26,213	177.7	435.9
Private	34,541	60.3	18.7
Total	89,586	329.1	697.4

Source: *1988 Hungarian Statistical Yearbook*, Central Statistical Office.

* "Other Cooperatives" includes agricultural, fishing, and an assortment of smaller cooperatives.

† Aggregate cooperative employment data.

At the end of 1988, consumer cooperatives still controlled over 25 percent of all the units in the retail trade and catering sector and accounted for approximately 30 percent of sectoral turnover. Table II.24 shows the position of consumer cooperatives relative to the other segments of the Hungarian retail trade and catering sector. Although formal government controls over cooperatives had by this time become relatively weak, the governance of consumer cooperatives was still not significantly influenced by the democratic organs originally designed to give the members a voice in decision-making. A general assembly of thousands of members could hardly supervise daily management. In fact, consumer cooperative members evidenced little desire to oversee the actual affairs of the cooperatives, although they did show some interest in their retail discounts, year-end rebates, and dividends.

7.2. Transfer of cooperative assets in the period 1988–90

The number of retail and catering units owned by consumer cooperatives dropped sharply between 1988 and 1990: the aggregate loss of 5,552 shops represented a decrease of 24 percent (see Table II.25). This dramatic change was a result of sales and other transfers of assets by the cooperative management in the last days of the communist regime. Two distinct incentives appear to have motivated these ownership changes. First, faced with a sharp reduction in governmental subsidies in the second half of the 1980s, cooperative officials attempted to streamline their operations by selling some of their least profitable

Table II.25 Retail trade and catering units owned directly by consumer cooperatives, 1988–90

	1988	1990
Retail trade	16,168	12,739
Catering	7,019	4,896
Total	23,187	17,635

Source: *Fogyasztasi Szovetkezeti Statistisztikai Zsebkonyv*, (Statistical Handbook of Consumer Cooperatives), 1988, pp. 43, 44, 73, 77, 80, and 105.

units. Simultaneously, some cooperative insiders appear to have taken advantage of the generally permissive environment of the period, characterized by the excesses of the "spontaneous privatization," in order to purchase some of the most valuable property for themselves.

While consumer cooperatives clearly participated in the rush of asset alienation from the "socialized" sector, their behavior differed somewhat from that of most state enterprises. Consumer cooperatives generally did not participate, for example, in the fashionable movement toward the formation of a maze of new commercial (joint stock and limited liability) companies which played such a prominent role in the efforts of state enterprise managers to shelter enterprise assets from state control. While no data exist concerning the exact number of previously cooperative units operated by incorporated companies during the period from 1988 to 1990, later figures strongly suggest that the creation of new commercial companies played only a peripheral role in the changes within the cooperative sector: by 1992, only 367 shops were operated by commercial companies owned by consumer cooperatives.[112] Thus, the exit of the large number of previously cooperative units during the period 1988–90 signified, for the most part, a genuine severing of all property relations with the former owners. The only important exception to this rule was the spin-off of nineteen previously cooperative department stores, most (if not all) of which appear to have been operated by incorporated companies owned, in part, by cooperatives.[113]

[112] *Report of the Consumer Cooperatives to the 2nd Congress*, December 10–11, 1992.

[113] Information concerning the ownership arrangements for the nineteen department stores which had exited the cooperative sector before the end of 1990 is not available. But deductions from data for 1992 allow for an inference that between fifteen and nineteen department stores functioned as part of cooperative-owned incorporated companies in 1990. See *Report of the Consumer Cooperatives to the 2nd Congress*.

Table II.26 Distribution of consumer cooperative units, 1988–92

	1988	1990	1992
Department stores	99	80	76
ABC (food and liquor stores)	778	695	962
Food shops	7,669	7,504	6,411
Clothing stores	872	602	461
Manufactured goods stores	5,125	2,443	2,474
Other stores	1,625	1,415	890
Restaurants	1,788	1,205	970
Confectioners and refreshment shops	4,909	3,504	3,896
Cafeterias	322	187	45
Total	23,187	17,635	16,185

Source: *Fogyasztasi Szovetkezeti Statisztikai Zsebkonyv* and *Report of the Consumer Cooperatives to the 2nd Congress.*

The composite image of the stores exiting the cooperative sector defies easy characterization (see Table II.26). The stores leaving the sector were smaller than the average, but do not appear to be concentrated solely at either the low end or the high end of the profitability spectrum or to be drawn disproportionately from the previously rented establishments.[114] In accordance with the dual motivation for the asset transfers, the profile of the units leaving the sector fits into two basic categories: the unprofitable small units in unattractive locations, often selling manufacturing goods of inferior quality, and the better stores, offering good prospects for "spontaneous privatization."

The overall impact of ownership transfers on the economic position of the cooperative sector during the period 1988–90 was mixed. In line with the transfer of a large number of small shops, turnover per unit in cooperative-owned establishments increased by over 40 percent, but this still left it at only 50 percent of the average for the state sector. At the same time, employment per unit more than tripled, leaving the cooperative stores with the highest level of employment per unit of any ownership group. The inflated employment figures may suggest that profit maximization was not the main objective of cooperative store

[114] At the end of 1990, 27 percent of cooperative units were subject to rental agreements, an almost identical proportion to the 26 percent rented in 1988. See *Fogyasztasi Szovetkezeti Statisztikai Zsebkonyv; Statistical Data of Consumer Cooperatives for 1990*, AFEOSZ, p. 35.

managers; the lower turnover figures are probably the result of a concentration of cooperative stores in rural areas.

7.3. Developments in the cooperative sector after 1990

Since the demise of the communist regime, the total number of units owned by consumer cooperatives has remained remarkably stable. This aggregate stability masks, however, a significant degree of restructuring which has been taking place. Important changes have occurred in the business management and composition of the cooperative stores, as well as in the overall governance of the cooperatives.

The institutional restructuring of the cooperative movement after 1990 has been quite impressive, although most of these changes have been too recent to have had a measurable impact on business operations. The reason for this was a significant delay in the enactment of the new cooperative legislation, as Parliament could not reach consensus over fundamental disagreements concerning the distribution of land owned by agricultural cooperatives. Only in 1992, did the Parliament pass Law I "On Cooperatives" as well as Law II "On the Entry into Force of Law I and the Rules of Transition," which required a transformation of all cooperatives in Hungary before June 31, 1992.

The 1992 legislation attempted to strengthen the ability of the members to influence the governance of the cooperatives: it mandated new democratic institutions, such as a more powerful supervisory board, and new elections for other representative organs. Each cooperative had a choice between reregistering under the new law or transforming itself into a limited liability or joint stock company. Groups of cooperative members could also elect to secede from a larger cooperative. In the event, only two consumer cooperatives elected to transform themselves into joint stock companies, and ten new cooperatives were formed as a result of secession from their parents.[115] The new elections resulted in the removal of 14 percent of all cooperative presidents, 29 percent of managers, and 36 percent of supervisory board members.[116]

The changes in the management and composition of the cooperative sector did not await, however, the passage of the new cooperative law.

[115] *Report on the Operation of Consumer Cooperatives in 1992*, National Federation of General Consumer Cooperatives, p. 2.

[116] *Report on the Operation of Consumer Cooperatives in 1992.*

As early as 1990, SZOVOSZ had been dismantled, to be replaced by entirely voluntary national associations for each type of cooperative. The new National Federation of General Consumer Cooperatives ("AFEOSZ") focused its attention on coordinating the economic activities of cooperatives and the management of its own considerable assets.[117]

Between 1990 and 1992, cooperatives also experienced an 8 percent net decline in the number of units. The actual movement of assets has been much greater, as cooperatives sold some units and acquired others, as well as restructured the operations of many remaining ones. These changes have been generally related to an increased attention paid by cooperative management to profitability and risk diversification. Specialty shops have been usually sold off or their line of business was changed, and the number of stores offering multiple types of goods or services expanded. Changes in the numbers of different categories of units may be seen from Table II.26.

Some cooperatives fared better than others in the recent restructuring. A number were left practically "empty" as a result of having sold most of their assets. According to data collected by the central consumer cooperative organization, forty-eight cooperatives owned fewer than five shops, and sixty-one did not own a single food store in 1992. It is not possible to determine how many of these sales were triggered by financial distress, but it is clear that a portion of the cooperative sector is in crisis. As of the end of 1992, seven consumer cooperatives had been liquidated due to bankruptcy.[118]

In line with the increased importance of economic factors in cooperative decision-making, the proportion of cooperative units rented out to private individuals grew rapidly since 1990, as managers did not want to be directly responsible for the running of cooperative stores. In two years since the change of the regime, the number of leased units went up from 4,612, or approximately 27 percent, to 7,242, or 45 percent. In some areas the proportion is still much greater, such as in catering, where it reached 84 percent.[119] The leases have generally been for terms no longer than five years and contain restrictions on changes in the line of business (but not on the selection of suppliers). A significant proportion of these leases are believed to have buy-out clauses and it is

[117] Many of the cooperative wholesale enterprises and department stores built in the 1970s were owned directly by the national organization and passed on to AFEOSZ.

[118] *Report on the Operation of Consumer Cooperatives in 1992.*

[119] *Statistical Data of Consumer Cooperatives for 1990; Report of the Consumer Cooperatives to the 2nd Congress.*

expected that many rented units will leave the cooperative sector in the near future.[120]

Overall, consumer cooperatives are currently in the process of diversifying their traditional focus on providing food and basic necessities to rural inhabitants. While still concentrated in nonurban settings, consumer cooperatives now own a mix of commercial establishments, offering a wide variety of products and services. They also increasingly function as real estate owners, preferring to parcel out the actual management of their stores to private parties. The designation of a store as a "cooperative" one now serves more to identify ownership rather than indicating a particular management structure or social function.

[120] Reliable data on the current operations of consumer cooperatives do not exist. Local cooperative officials are not inclined to divulge information about their organization to either central cooperative bodies or outside groups.

PART III: POLAND

1. INTRODUCTION

Small-scale privatization in Poland has brought about the most rapid transformation of retail, catering, and service sectors in Central and Eastern Europe. Official pronouncements state that over 97 percent of all shops and other consumer outlets in Poland are now private. Our research indicates that these claims are somewhat misleading, but there is no question that the magnitude of change in Poland's domestic trade has been the most prodigious in the Eastern bloc since the fall of communism.[1] Moreover, for the most part, the change has not been merely quantitative or limited to ownership transformations. Unlike Hungary or Czechoslovakia, where the disintegration of the consumer sector was never as pronounced, Poland, in 1989, reached a nadir of communist inefficiency and neglect of consumer needs. A simple task of buying necessary groceries consumed several hours of each day in the life of every Pole, with frustrating searches, endless standing in lines, barter, bribery, and ultimately very little to show for the effort. The stores were not only empty; they were also unappealing, lacking in modern equipment, and staffed by people who treated customers as a particularly noxious species of intruders. Barely a year later, the streets of Polish cities and towns were changed beyond recognition. Lines in front of the stores disappeared, premises had often been remodeled, the shelves were filled with all the domestic and imported goods expected in a civilized country, and the ubiquitous "Nie ma" ("We don't have it") was replaced by solicitous service and advice. By the end of 1992, the small privatization process was essentially complete.

Much as the ruination of the Czech economy under communism is sometimes cited as an example of the destructive force of Soviet domination, the transformation of the Polish consumer sector in the

[1] A summary of the quantitative nature of small-scale privatization in Poland is provided in section 1.1 below.

wake of the 1989 changes may be cited as a showcase of success of the market economy. It is especially important, therefore, to analyze the Polish case very carefully, since it may provide many lessons for other countries of the region, especially the newly emerging nations of the former Soviet Union. While many aspects of the dramatic transformation in Poland must be attributed to the effects of macroeconomic reforms introduced by the Mazowiecki government in January 1990, and many other aspects may have depended on unique local conditions, still the "case of Poland," probably more so than that of Hungary or the Czech Republic, may be used as a model of a successful restructuring of the vital consumer sector.

Perhaps the most interesting fact about small privatization in Poland is that the government never mandated or legislated its occurrence. There were, to be sure, several laws, ranging from housing administration to government decentralization and enterprise liquidation, that decisively influenced the process, and the government deserves much praise for the skillful way in which its limited interventions facilitated small privatization. But, unlike in any other country, there was no separate small privatization "program" in Poland, and the impact of the general privatization law was only minimal.[2] Instead, a series of governmental acts, unrelated to privatization *per se*, released a spontaneous and largely unregulated process in which the existing special interests were pitted against each other and were enlisted in the cause of the transformation. Indeed, only in such a decentralized fashion could change of this magnitude have been accomplished in such a short period of time.

The key to much of the success of small privatization in Poland has been a realization by the government that the transformation of retail trade, catering, and consumer services centered not around a privatization of the hopelessly substandard businesses run by the socialized domestic trade sector, but around a *transfer of real estate* on which these businesses had been operated. Thus, the salient features of small privatization in Poland had little to do with a transfer of ownership in business franchises or "going-concerns," or with ensuring the continuity of operation of old state-run stores and outlets. The implicit objective of governmental policy measures was to dissolve the state-run retail trade network; not to preserve it. Insofar as the retail units themselves were concerned, there was little of value in them beyond the premises that

[2] Law on Privatization of State-Owned Enterprises of July 1990.

could be used productively in the aftermath of the transfer. Given the impoverished state of the sector, the equipment of state and cooperative stores was not worth very much, and the inventory was either nonexistent or so substandard that even the chronic shortages of the communist period had not been enough to get rid of it. With the new influx of imported goods[3] and rapidly rising consumer expectations, the inventory was in fact likely to become a liability.

The essence of small privatization in Poland was thus a devolution of interests in commercial premises to private parties. While these interests were most often less than full ownership rights, all laws, regulations, and policy prescriptions created to govern the transfer of the use of real estate shared a common theme – the harnessing of private initiative for the purpose of creating market conditions of access to commercial property.

Two consequences followed from this focus on real estate utilization. First, since the old stores and outlets were essentially "stripped" to their real estate skeleton, and since new businesses as much as the old ones needed access to largely state-controlled commercial premises, the distinction between "startup" and "privatized" units became rather fluid. Indeed, while most businesses resulting from the transformation of the domestic trade sector were undoubtedly private, the state has often preserved its title to the premises on which both the new and the "privatized" units are operated, with the businesses usually acquiring only highly restricted, short-term use rights. Small privatization has thus been a rather elusive phenomenon, the main feature of which has not been a conferral of important property rights on private parties, but rather a destruction of the old system in which large socialized enterprises exercised control over the most valuable real estate necessary for the development of a genuinely private retail trade sector.[4]

The second consequence of the focus on real estate was the ability of policy-makers to bypass the old state domestic trade organizations. Unless suitable premises for their outlets were unavailable, these

[3] The liberal stance taken by the government concerning foreign trade was a major factor in the growth and expanded assortment of consumer goods. Between 1989 and 1992, consumer imports, as a percentage of total imports, grew from 12 to over 34 percent.

[4] Despite the fluid borders between privatized and startup businesses in Poland, this study largely concentrates on the privatized sector in the narrower sense of the term, i.e., stores and outlets operated on premises which had been previously used as a part of the socialized retail trade and consumer service sector.

organizations (consumer cooperatives and state enterprises) were never interested in the construction and ownership of premises on which their stores were located, relying instead on leasing them at low, administratively set prices from other state institutions and housing cooperatives. As a result, the ownership of real estate was in most cases separated from the ownership of retail businesses, but this fact was without significance as long as the allocation of commercial space was based on planning decisions, rather than market mechanisms. One of the early acts of the Mazowiecki government, however, was to restore genuine property rights to the previously merely titular owners of real estate, and to pit their interests against those of state enterprises and cooperatives in the consumer sector. The local governments and housing cooperatives – the main beneficiaries of this change – had no interest in preserving the old empires of state retail trade organizations, which had been run in a centralized fashion, and maintained no real ties to the local communities. The newly enfranchised owners of real estate had interests of their own, and the only potential obstacle to their takeover of state and cooperative stores, particularly in the case of local authorities, were the employees of the local units, who had local connections and the sympathy of their neighbors.

The result of this concatenation of interests was an alliance between local authorities and the insiders of the affected units who turned against their old employers and seized the opportunity to go into business for themselves. State enterprises were thus deprived of most of their stores, and consumer cooperatives suffered very significant losses as well. The near-mortal blow was delivered with astonishing speed, and the large retail trade organizations, which in all other countries (with the possible exception of former Czechoslovakia) have very effectively resisted a radical restructuring of their sector, were weakened beyond repair.

While the bleeding of the former socialized sector through a surgical removal of the premises owned by local authorities and housing cooperatives was accomplished with great efficiency, the privatization of the remaining retail and service units in the former socialized sector was a much more difficult and somewhat less successful operation. This process took different forms in the state and cooperative sectors.

The privatization of the rump state enterprises has been the only part of small privatization that took place according to the more general procedures specified by the Polish Privatization Law. The dominant form of transformation here has been the so-called "privatization through liquidation" which involves a sale or lease of enterprise assets to a company formed by the employees. Although it is the most decentralized of the Polish privatization programs, it is rather tightly controlled by the founding organ (most commonly the *voivoda* office)[5] and the Ministry of Privatization, and its progress in the domestic trade sector has been slow. A functional privatization of some of the units belonging to state enterprises has been accomplished, however, through a leasing of individual stores to employees.

The privatization of the consumer cooperative sector, which controlled the greatest number of stores in Poland, is the most complicated and the least studied part of Polish small privatization. It began immediately after the fall of the last communist government, even before the bleeding process resulting from the takeover of real estate by local authorities and housing cooperatives, with a law dissolving central and regional associations of cooperatives. While the associations usually did not run retail units themselves, they were the main tools of state control over the cooperative movement, and their domination of local cooperatives made the operation of the cooperative sector barely distinguishable from that of the state sector proper. The associations siphoned most of the resources and revenues from local cooperatives, ran the distribution system, and directly held very large amounts of property, including warehouses, means of transportation, food processing businesses, real estate, etc.

The dissolution of the associations had a twofold impact on the development of small privatization. First, the liquidators appointed to manage the dissolution process were charged with disposing of the property of the associations. This in turn led to a large-scale release of assets crucial for the formation of private wholesale and distribution systems, and contributed a very important element of "upstream" restructuring. Although the liquidation process has been messy and incomplete, it diminished the dependence of retail units on the monopolistic supply system, which, in many countries of the region, constitutes a barrier to the development of a properly functioning private retail economy.

Second, the dissolution of cooperative associations essentially decapitated the state-dominated cooperative system, and set local cooperatives adrift. Unfortunately, the early assault on cooperative associations was not followed by a new cooperative law, similar to that

5 Voivodships are the largest territorial units of the Polish government. There are forty-nine voivodships, each headed by a prefect, or *voivoda*.

enacted in many other postcommunist countries.[6] As a result, local cooperatives are still governed by the old rules, giving members much more limited rights than is common in more authentically cooperative movements. Still, elimination of the associations and the loss of units as a result of the termination of old leases opened the door for a decentralized process of transformation of local cooperatives. Large numbers of cooperative units were effectively privatized by being leased or franchised to private individuals, most often member-employees. Other units are still run by the cooperatives themselves, but they too have been "privatized" with a stroke of a bureaucrat's pen: they were simply reclassified as no longer belonging to the "socialized" sector. The extent to which changes in the mode of operation of these units have followed their statistical reclassification is not fully clear.

As is obvious from what has been said already, the process of small privatization in Poland has been dominated by the employees of the former state and cooperative units and local government insiders, with the central government skillfully manipulating the incentives of all parties. An overwhelming majority of the previously socialized units (or the premises on which they were located) have accordingly been allocated on the basis of a closed procedure and at prices that most often did not reflect their market value. In fact, in light of the very small number of premises that were made available to the general public, it is difficult to speak of a genuine real estate market in Poland, especially in the early period of reforms. The few properties that were sold at open auctions often brought astronomical prices, which all parties believed were well above their value; as a matter of fact, the unrealistically high prices at which properties were sold or leased at many auctions were used as one of the main arguments in favor of a more administrative allocation among the insiders.

The fact of insider domination in part explains the speed with which small privatization was achieved in Poland, and this may provide an important lesson for other countries. Unless the government is very strong and insiders are incapable of mounting effective resistance (which seems not to be true in most postcommunist countries), there is a clear trade-off between the speed of small privatization and an open, competitive method of allocation. But the problems raised by insider

[6] For a review of the cooperative laws in the region, see Frydman, Rapaczynski, Earle, *et al.*, *The Privatization Process in Central Europe*, CEU Press (Budapest and London), 1993, and *The Privatization Process in Russia, Ukraine, and the Baltic States*, CEU Press (Budapest and London), 1993.

domination are also serious, since insiders are less likely to restructure and invest in the newly privatized businesses.[7] Interestingly enough, however, while the results of our survey show that postprivatization investment levels in Poland are significantly lower than in Hungary or the Czech Republic, this did not seem to make a significant difference to the overall state of the domestic trade sector in the wake of the reforms. In fact, as we have said, the Polish consumer sector is booming and its performance appears to be second to none in the region.

The reasons for this are not fully clear. The effect of macroeconomic changes and the overall positive business climate in Poland is very likely to have been an important factor. The competition in the retail sector is very stiff, and all businesses, even those that remain state-run have been forced to either improve their performance or perish. Moreover, even though privatization of previously existing businesses has been dominated by insiders, the overall number of businesses increased dramatically since 1989, with an obvious impact on competition. In the beginning, many new businesses operated in makeshift conditions, sometimes selling from trucks or stands in the street.[8] Later new private businesses acquired access to real estate, including in many cases the premises previously operated by retail units of the socialized sector. Since acquisition by outsiders at the time of initial privatization of pre-existing units was not very common, some outsiders must have gained control on the secondary market. Information concerning the process by which such a market was created and the extent of its development would be of great value in assessing the process of small privatization in Poland. Unfortunately, no such information is available at this time.

1.1. Quantitative evidence on the transformation of the retail, catering, and service sectors in Poland

The extent of transformation in Poland's domestic consumer market is made evident by the statistics in Table III.1, which show changes in the

[7] See the Survey in Part IV. For further discussion, cf. R. Frydman and A. Rapaczynski, "Insiders and the State: Overview of Responses to Agency Problems in East European Privatizations", *The Economics of Transition*, 1 (January 1993), pp. 39–59; reprinted in R. Frydman and A. Rapaczynski, *Privatization in Eastern Europe: Is the State Withering Away?*, CEU Press (Budapest, London, New York), 1994.

[8] The government wisely suspended most regulations limiting street vendors in the first few months of the reform, and reintroduced them only when much of the initial restructuring had been accomplished.

Table III.1 Ownership transformation in retail trade, consumer, and service sectors ('000 units)

	1989	1992	Change
Total retail outlets*	249	750†	301%
Socialized‡	178	33	–82%
Private	72	717	996%
Total retail shops	151	353†	234%
Socialized‡	124	9	–93%
Private	27	344§	1,267%
Total catering outlets	31	53	171%
Socialized‡	16	1	–94%
Private	15	52	347%
Total service outlets	255	209	–18%
Socialized‡	42	8	–81%
Private	213	201	–6%
Total outlets in retail, catering, and service sectors	535	1,012	189%
Total socialized‡	236	42	–82%
Total private	300	970	323%

Sources: *GUS Statistical Yearbooks 1989–1992*; Institute of Internal Market; Pentor; Institute for Opinion and Market Research, Warsaw; and various interviews with representatives from the Domestic Market Department of the Main Statistical Office.

* Outlets include shops as well as kiosks, stands, booths, and other small points of sale.
† Estimated by GUS from a preliminary tally of year-end statistical reports.
‡ For 1989, socialized units include state-owned and cooperative units, as well as units owned by so-called "social organizations." For 1992, cooperative units have been reclassified as "private" by Polish statistics.
§ Includes approximately 46,000 stores run by cooperatives and other social organizations.

number of units and ownership structure within the retail, catering, and service sectors during the heyday of small privatization. In aggregate, between 1989 and 1992, the number of socialized retail, catering, and service outlets declined 82 percent, from 236,000 to 42,000, while the number of private units increased over 320 percent, from 300,000[9] to 970,000. The largest shift in the ownership structure occurred in the retail sector, where the number of private outlets increased by an extraordinary 996 percent, from 72,000 to 717,000. The number of privately owned retail stores, a subset of total retail outlets, increased by 1,267 percent, from 27,000 to 344,000.

The ownership structure of catering outlets has also shifted quite substantially. Private catering businesses grew 347 percent, from 15,000 to 52,000, and socialized catering units declined 94 percent, from 16,000 to approximately 1,000. It is also likely that the private catering sector did not achieve its full growth potential as of 1992. The reason for this is probably related to the depressed state of the market in the wake of the government's austerity program, which dampened the demand for restaurant services.

In the sphere of non-material services, where even prior to the fall of communism private outlets contributed over 43 percent of the total turnover and where there had been less pent-up demand, the number of units actually declined by 6 percent, from 213,000 to 201,000. This decline was also due to the general economic slowdown and lack of demand.

The numerical changes in the size of the private and socialized sectors may appear somewhat more dramatic than the underlying reality, since a large number of cooperative and other "socialized" units have been simply reclassified as "private" (some 46,000 shops alone were "privatized" in this way). But even if the extent of real changes in the cooperative sector is somewhat uncertain, its operation was, to a large degree, removed from state control. And even without counting the cooperative units, the growth of the private sector has been extremely impressive.

The overall increase in the number of units has improved dramatically the lot of the Polish consumers. As shown in Table III.2, the total

[9] The apparently very high number of private units in 1989 tends to exaggerate the private sector's share of trade at that time. Most private units were small stands, booths, and service workshops set up within months of the enactment of the Law on Economic Activity on January 1, 1989, liberalizing the rules governing establishment of small businesses. When looked at in terms of other measures, the size of the private sector appears much less impressive. Thus, for example, the average shop size in the state sector in 1989 was approximately 94.7 square meters – almost four times larger than that of shops in the private sector, which was 25.2 square meters. In terms of market share, private stores accounted for less than 3 percent of the total sector turnover in 1988 and 5 percent in 1989 (although this number is probably distorted by tax evasion). For more information on the private sector before 1989, see section 2 below.

Table III.2 Outlets and units per 1,000 inhabitants*

Year	1989	1992
Retail outlets	6.6	19.7
(retail shops)	(4.0)	(9.3)
Catering establishments	0.8	1.4
Service units	6.7	5.5

Source: *GUS Statistical Yearbooks 1989–1992*, Institute of Internal Market.

* Based on the population of approximately 38 million.

number of retail shops and catering outlets increased from 4 and .8 units per 1,000 people, respectively, in 1989, to over 9 and 1.4 units per 1,000 people, respectively, in 1992. The growth in the number of stores has in fact brought Polish shop density standards into line with those of the advanced Western economies. While the density of stores in Poland, in 1992, was 9.3 per 1,000 people, Austria, France, and the United States, had the average density of 7, 10, and 6 shops per 1,000 people, respectively. These measures cannot be taken quite at face value, since the average size of a store in the West is substantially larger than in Poland. In fact, the number of stores in the West has been decreasing for the last few years (the last decades in the United States), as small stores have been gradually replaced by large "superstores" and supermarkets.[10] Nevertheless, the density figures demonstrate a clear trend toward a level of services consistent with the organization of domestic trade in the more advanced market economies.

Changes in the ownership structure and the size of the domestic trade sector are also reflected in changes in the structure of employment, shown in Table III.3. Total employment in the sector grew 6 percent, from 1.4 million to 1.5 million, between 1989 to 1991. This increase may seem modest, especially in light of the tremendous magnitude of growth in the number of outlets and establishments. But the official numbers nearly certainly understate real employment in the private sector, since private owners commonly under-report the number of their employees

[10] Austria, for example, lost 12 percent of small stores between 1988 and 1992, France 11.8 percent, and Britain over 20 percent. In Italy, where large stores have not yet arrived, and where small stores have proliferated more than in any other country, the density of stores per 1,000 people is over 25. See C. Rohwedder, "Superstores Pose Threat to Europe's Small Retailers," *Wall Street Journal Europe*, April 21, 1993.

Table III.3 Employment structure changes in domestic trade ('000)

	1989	1991	Change
Total employment	1,424.8	1,505.7	6%
Employees	1,178.7	989.8	–16%
Self-employed or employer	93.9	477.2	508%
Independent agent	147.1	37.9	–74%
Other	5.1	0.8	–84%

Source: *GUS Statistical Yearbook.*

(often family members) in order to evade the extremely high social security and wage taxes. Also, the increase in employment in the trade sector should be considered in light of the overall growth of unemployment, which reached 12 percent of the labor force during the same period.

In addition to an overall increase in employment, there was a proportionally still much larger increase in the number of self-employed, reflecting the shift away from state dominance toward private ownership. The number of self-employed and persons employing others increased fivefold, from 93,900 in 1989 to over 470,000 in 1991, and amounted to over 30 percent of total employment (up from only 6.5 percent in 1989). Another sign of the disintegration of the state retail trade network is evident from a 74 percent decline in the number of "independent agents." These people, who, prior to 1990, operated approximately 30 percent of all retail units in the socialized sector, were essentially employees who managed their shops in exchange for compensation based on a fixed percentage of turnover. The agency arrangements were especially popular in the 1980s, when the authorities attempted to improve the performance of the retail sector by giving the employees a stake in the running of units in less desirable locations, in which the state-sector stores were particularly inefficient. In the course of privatization, many of the former "agents" became entrepreneurs in their own right and came to own the stores that they had once managed.

While the present study is mostly concerned with privatization in the narrower sense of the term, i.e. the process by which formerly socialized units were replaced by private businesses operating on the same premises, the transformation of the domestic trade sector in Poland, especially in the early period of the reforms, was also driven by the emergence of new businesses, operating on premises previously occupied by other types of state-run businesses, as well as in makeshift

Table III.4 Privatization vs. establishment of new firms, from 1989 through 1992 ('000)

Type of establishment	Privatized outlets	Net new private outlets*
Retail outlets	145	501
(retail stores)	(115)†	(202)
Catering outlets	15	22
Service outlets	34	46
Total	194	476

Source: GUS.

* Includes new outlets opened and closed on premises not originally part of the socialized domestic trade network.
† Includes about 46,000 cooperative and other stores which have been reclassified as "private."

locations, often on the streets or vacant lots. As shown in Table III.4, these new businesses, generally small kiosks and stands selling a limited and often changeable assortment of goods, account for over two-thirds of the growth in the number of units between 1989 and 1992. Much as they contributed to a change in the very look of Polish cities, their direct impact on national income statistics was much less impressive. According to a study by a reputable Warsaw-based public opinion research firm, Pentor, kiosks, stands and the like accounted for only 25 percent of total domestic trade turnover by 1992. In addition, official government statistics for 1991 indicate that the failure rate for these outlets ranged from 20 to 30 percent per year.[11]

Despite their small size and often transitional existence, the proliferation of small private outlets played an important role in creating a genuinely competitive environment in which both the remaining state stores and the newly privatized units had to operate. The more dynamic new small businesses quickly filled temporary gaps in supply, as well as forcing other units to modify their behavior, resulting in overall gains in the efficiency of the whole domestic trade sector. Indeed, the pressure of new small businesses may have been a decisive factor in moderating the potentially negative impact of the domination by former insiders of the

[11] Even these figures may underestimate the number of businesses that cease to operate in any one year. Research conducted by Pentor revealed that many private owners never officially report the closing of their businesses.

mainstream privatization process.[12] (The ability of the small private outlet owners to evade taxes may have also given them a competitive advantage with respect to the more established stores, and this gave rise to a significant number of complaints. More generally, the ability of private owners to evade taxes may have made the life of state owners more difficult and hastened the process of privatization.)

The mainstream privatization process, involving the establishment of private businesses on premises formerly occupied by socialized units, is the main object of the present study. Although less numerous than the rest of the new private businesses, the units formerly owned by the socialized sector constitute by far the most important segment of the domestic consumer trade sector, dominating from the point of view of their size and location, and their affiliation with wholesale establishments. The processes examined in the subsequent sections involve the privatization of approximately 69,000 retail stores and 76,000 smaller retail outlets, 15,000 catering units, and 34,000 service outlets – in total, approximately 82 percent of the former socialized sector trade network.

For reasons that will become clear, official data on the number of shops and other units privatized by the many "gminas," state enterprises, and consumer and housing cooperatives are largely unavailable. As a result, the present study is based on estimates obtained from a great variety of sources, including interviews with government officials, field studies, surveys, and data interpolations. Some of the specific calculations, including the ranges involved in many of the estimates, will be explained in the sections dealing with the particular aspects of the privatization process. At this point, the reader might find helpful a summary of the results arrived at by the CEU Privatization Project researchers concerning the proportions of the units privatized by various government authorities, state enterprises, and cooperatives. The estimates are presented in Table III.5.

2. HISTORICAL PERSPECTIVE

This section presents a brief overview of the historical development of the Polish retail trade sector and its organization on the eve of the dramatic changes in the postcommunist Poland. The overview is not

[12] Successful owners of kiosks, stands, etc. often expanded their businesses, moving into larger premises and often into other lines of business as well.

Table III.5 Estimates of retail stores, catering and service outlets privatized by various groups of owners ('000)

	Retail stores*	Catering outlets	Service outlets	Total
Gminas†	32 (47%)	7–9 (47–60%)	20 (59%)	59–61 (50–52%)
State-owned enterprises‡	3–5 (4–7%)	1–2 (7–13%)	1–3 (3–9%)	5–10 (4–8%)
Consumer cooperatives§	20–22 (12%)	2–5 (13–33%)	7–9 (21–26%)	29–36 (25–31%)
Housing cooperatives¶	12 (17%)	1–2 (7–13%)	4–5 (12–15%)	17–19 (14–16%)
Total	69 (100%)	15 (100%)	34 (100%)	118 (100%)

* Smaller nonshop retail outlets, in many instances small stands or kiosks, were omitted from the table above. Despite several attempts to compile information on the proportions of some 76,000 of these outlets privatized by various entities, the size and location of these outlets has prevented accurate estimates from being made. Even under communism, accurate records of these outlets were not maintained.

† Based on reports from the Central Planning Office, interpolations using official data on changes in the number of socialized sector shops, a survey conducted by the CEU Privatization Project, and data from the Ministry of Privatization.

‡ Based on proportions revealed in surveys conducted by the CEU Privatization Project and data from the Department of Domestic Market at the Main Statistical Office.

§ Based on information from the Main Statistical Office, proportions revealed in surveys conducted by the CEU Privatization Project, and interviews with various government officials. Includes only units actually conveyed to private hands, and not units which continue to be operated by cooperatives (which have also been reclassified as "private").

¶ Based on interviews with officials from the Housing Cooperative Institute, proportions revealed in surveys conducted by the CEU Privatization Project, and data interpolations.

designed to give the full picture of the communist retail trade and consumer service sector, but rather to point to a few distinguishing features of the Polish developments, as compared with the previously described situation in Hungary and the Czech Republic.

2.1. The ownership structure from 1945 to 1989

The ownership structure of the Polish retail trade sector crystallized within a few years after World War II, to undergo only relatively minor changes during the remainder of the communist regime. Still, the intensity of the nationalizing and centralizing tendencies of the government slackened somewhat in the wake of the political liberalization of 1956, allowing for a small number of new private shops to appear. A further decentralization and relaxation of limitations on private initiative followed the economic and political crisis in the 1980s. There have also been some changes inside the so-called "socialized sector," mainly the fluctuations in the relative growth of the slightly less rigid cooperative system and the typical state-owned trade organizations. All in all, the ownership structure of Poland's retail trade and service sector in the last few years of the communist regime was somewhere between that in Hungary and the Czech Republic. The private sector was much more developed and the public sector more decentralized than in the Czech Republic, but in both of these respects Poland was far behind Hungary on the way to a more market-oriented system. On the other hand, these distinctions are probably quite insignificant, as compared with the massive failure of the Polish regime to preserve even a semblance of an equilibrium between the supply and demand of consumer goods, which really differentiated Poland from the other two countries examined in this volume. Hungary's was a very special case of a communist economy, and the Czech Republic was able to control sufficiently its rigid system of consumer trade to prevent large-scale shortages. Poland's consumer sector, by contrast, was more like that of the countries of the former Soviet Union: riddled with endemic shortages, lines of customers, poor assortment, etc.

The postwar period and the installation of the new regime in the late 1940s brought a campaign commonly referred to as the "battle for trade." Until then, private, non-cooperative traders dominated the retail sector, accounting for over 89 percent of all shops and approximately 70 percent of all retail trade turnover. These predominantly small traders were a potentially growing, dynamic social stratum, generally unfriendly to the new regime. Their elimination became, therefore, one of the important planks in the communists' ideological platform, and the "battle for trade" was designed to thwart and ultimately eradicate them.

The upshot of the "battle" was an abrupt and comprehensive communist takeover of the trade sector, with the private traders becoming nearly extinct: between 1946 and 1953, privately-operated trade outlets declined from 157,000 to 17,000, or 89 percent (see Table III.6). In 1949 alone, when the communists finally consolidated their power, the number of private stores declined by nearly 40 percent.

Table III.6 Changes in the number of private trade businesses: 1946 to 1953

	1946	1947	1948	1949	1953
No. of private firms ('000)	157	131	112	70	17

Source: GUS.

Table III.7 Share in domestic retail trade (% of total turnover)

	Year			
Type of establishment	1946	1955	1978	1989
State-owned enterprises and other social organizations	9%	43%	29%	36%
Consumer cooperatives	21%	54%	69%	59%
Private firms	70%	3%	2%	5%

Source: GUS.

In part, the rapidity of the communist takeover simply meant a dramatic decrease in the number of shops and restaurants. This phenomenon was characteristic of all the communist countries, where small shops were displaced by a few large units that could be more easily managed by the state trade empires and supplied by the inefficient centralized system of distribution. But not all formerly private units disappeared altogether. Some of them, especially the larger ones, were taken over by the state, and the cooperative network, which the communist theory classified as "socialized," rather than private, was merely reorganized and subordinated much more tightly to the control of the central planners. Indeed, between 1945 and 1949, the cooperative sector expanded from 15,530 stores to over 41,151, and its share of the total retail turnover, which had been only 21 percent in 1946, expanded to 54 percent in 1955.

Apart from minor changes, the broad dominance of the "socialized sector," established in the first decade of communist rule, persisted until the end of the communist regime, at least insofar as its share of the total retail trade turnover was concerned (see Table III.7). By the middle 1950s, private traders were confined to small economic niches within the sphere of household services and handicrafts, while state enterprises

Table III.8 Ownership structure of retail shops in the 1980s (% of total number of units)

Type of establishment	Year				
	1984	1985	1986	1987	1988
State-owned enterprises	15%	15%	15%	16%	16%
Cooperatives	75%	68%	68%	66%	65%
Private	10%	17%	17%	18%	19%

Source: GUS.

dominated the sector by controlling most wholesale foodstuff trade and the retailing of all consumer goods manufactured by state-owned enterprises. Consumer cooperatives, while restrained by administrative links with the state planning mechanism, maintained a substantial (and growing) share of trade in foodstuffs and household services. With time (by the 1970s), the cooperatives acquired *de facto* monopolies in foodstuff trade, and broader responsibility in catering, household services, and basic consumer goods.[13]

The share of retail turnover, however, does not tell the whole story. Beginning with the 1980s, the private sector grew quite significantly in terms of the number of units, and while most of these units were very small, the figures concerning turnover nearly certainly under-estimate their importance. To begin with, the private firms were very likely to hide the magnitude of their operations, both for tax purposes and out of fear that the revelation of their genuine size might attract the attention of jealous and greedy bureaucrats. Also, the private stores dealt with a special assortment of goods (including much of the largely illicit imports) and provided better service. More will be said later about their increasingly important role in the last years of the communist regime.

The role of private businesses in the catering sector was becoming still more significant, as was the relative importance of the cooperative *vis à vis* the state sector. Thus, statistics on the ownership structure of the catering sector for 1987 show state enterprises as accounting for only 5 percent of the units, consumer cooperatives for 65 percent, and private

[13] See section 7 below, for more information on consumer cooperatives.

firms for 30 percent.[14] Finally, in the badly neglected household service sector, private firms gradually came to dominate the market: in 1988, they accounted for 86 percent of all registered units, while socialized sector firms (mostly consumer cooperatives) accounted for 12 percent.

2.2. Administrative organization of the socialized sector

The allocation of responsibilities for overseeing the various activities and services provided by the socialized sector of the Polish trade was made along classical lines, with the Ministry of Internal Trade maintaining its flagship post as a regulator of most state-owned retail trade entities, and various branch ministries and state organs responsible for smaller, specialized subsectors. The command system of distribution and allocation required a certain configuration of vertical links among the enterprises, which made the Polish system into a rather generic version of what existed in many other communist economies. Enterprises were subordinated to associations or unions, which were subordinated to ministerial organs, which were, in turn, subordinated to the Central Planning Committee. Moreover, unlike in the other areas, such as heavy industry, where the enterprises and branch ministries may have had significant bargaining power *vis à vis* the central planners (and were thus able to influence the plan to their advantage), the consumer sector was rarely considered a priority, and thus its formal hierarchical structure reflected more faithfully the actual distribution of power. The sector was often made to pay for costly mistakes in the other areas, having to make do with fewer goods, smaller allotments of imports, and other deficiencies in supply.

Figure III.1 shows the main organizational lines of the retail sector characterized by large, cooperative and state-owned trading conglomerates, excluding such minor players as the private traders, social organizations, socialized sector partnerships,[15] and the specialty areas of trade, such as bookstores, music shops, and the army PXs, governed by various state organs.

The state-owned portion of the sector was dominated by the

[14] Based on information provided by the Institute of Consumer Cooperatives.

[15] Social organizations and socialized partnerships were formed by the church, political parties, workers' unions, and tourist associations usually for the purpose of providing educational, cultural, or recreational benefits to their members. They also operated small retail trading outlets selling handicrafts or miscellaneous goods.

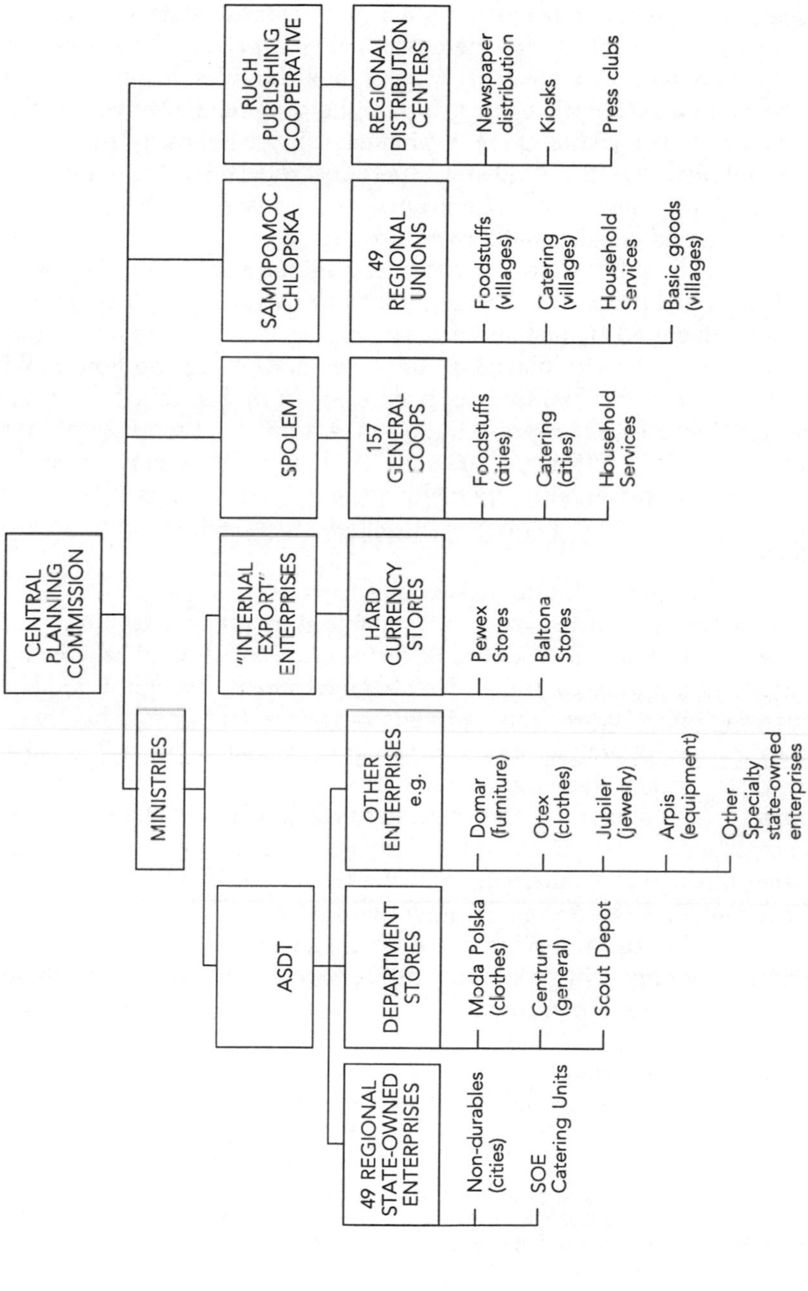

Figure III.1 Organizational structure of socialized retail trade in the 1980s

Association of State Domestic Trade (ASDT), which coordinated the activities of a large number of national and regional state enterprises. The association controlled forty-nine regional enterprises which operated over 12,000 outlets to provide consumer non-durables to residents of large cities and industrial regions. It was the dominant planner for the large national store chains such as Moda Polska, a relatively upmarket apparel retailer; the Scout Depot, specialty retailer of clothing and recreation equipment; and Centrum, an apparel, footwear, and household goods retailer with over fifty stores in major cities. Also subordinated to ASDT were a number of regional specialty enterprises, which functioned primarily as retail outlets for narrow lines of consumer goods manufactured by state-owned enterprises.[16]

The state-owned sector played a minor role in catering and household services. Through regional and local enterprises, it controlled approximately 2,800 small-scale catering outlets in factories and workshops and approximately 700 outlets in bars and on trains. On a very selective basis, state enterprises also operated ancillary service businesses, for example locksmith and photography shops, from within other trade establishments.

In addition to the traditional domestic trade outlets, Pewex and Baltona stores sold otherwise unavailable foreign goods for hard currency. Until 1988, the sale and distribution of foreign goods by enterprises was tightly controlled by the government through a number of licensing provisions and administrative restrictions. The hard currency stores, operating under strict government supervision were designed to attract the large "under the mattress" foreign currency holdings of the population, and their steady expansion in the last years of the regime are a testimony to the shortage of foreign currency due to the large indebtedness inherited from the Gierek policies of the 1970s.

The consumer cooperative movement was centralized under two large umbrellas: one, Spolem, serving mostly cities and the other, Samopomoc Chlopska, serving villages and rural townships. Both of these organizations were represented on, and accountable to, the Central Planning Committee.

Foodstuff trade throughout Poland and most household goods trade in the countryside were monopolized by Spolem and Samopomoc

[16] Domar (home furnishings), Otex (clothes), Arpis (small household equipment and some furniture) sold goods through a small number of regional enterprises. Jubiler manufactured and sold jewelry in over 100 stores operated by enterprises in four major cities.

Chlopska. In the 1980s, Spolem comprised 157 grocery cooperatives with over 30,000 retail outlets responsible for the foodstuff trade in all cities and townships. Samopomoc Chlopska, with over 69,000 retail outlets organized in thousands of small, rural cooperatives, dominated trade in all rural areas. The local cooperatives were subordinated to forty-nine regional associations, which were responsible for managing food purchasing and processing facilities, wholesale establishments, and intraregional distribution networks.

Samopomoc Chlopska and Spolem also jointly operated over 13,000 restaurants and bars – over 80 percent of the total for most of the communist period. They were also dominant in the provision of household services until the 1980s, when they were eclipsed by the new private sector, although the cooperatives' share in consumer services is partly concealed in official statistics by the inclusion of the social services, such as transportation, theater, museums, and education, which were provided by the state.

A separate cooperative, Ruch, subordinated directly to the Central Committee of the Communist party and providing its major source of income (as well as control over media), owned most newspapers and magazines, a large section of other publishing businesses, and a wide system of distribution. Ruch was in fact a huge conglomerate which sold magazines, newspapers, books, cigarettes, cosmetics, and other items. It controlled some 30,000 retail outlets, mostly kiosks present in almost every Polish city and village.

2.3. Between the socialized and the private sectors: the agency arrangements

We have noted already that until the 1980s, the private trade sector in the Polish consumer trade was largely suppressed or relegated to cover small gaps left by the socialized network (handicrafts, sundry consumer goods, and trivial household services). But for most of the 1980s, the conditions for private initiative were progressively changing, and the role of private traders in the formally socialized system took on greater importance. Except for services, the turnover of the fully private outlets remained quite small until the end of the 1980s, but the last decade of the communist regime, beginning with the Law on State Enterprises of 1982, saw some significant decentralizing reforms in the socialized sector. A prominent role in these reforms was played by the expansion on a large scale of so-called "agency" arrangements, which, without introducing genuine private property, lessened the level of rigid centralization in the socialized consumer trade.[17] The Polish reforms were much less successful than the already discussed Hungarian ones, partly because they were much less thorough, and partly because the general political and macroeconomic situation worsened to such an extent that the modest reforms were no longer able to lead to significant improvements. Still, the agency arrangements did represent a transitional step on the way to an expansion of private initiative in Polish retail trade.

The agency arrangement was essentially a lease with a number of restrictions reminiscent of something between a profit sharing and a franchise contract. Both state enterprises and consumer cooperatives used this device to lease a portion of their outlets and shops to employees and private traders, and both imposed on the agents the obligation to operate the stores in accordance with a set of prescribed conditions affecting the line of business, assortment, store design, employment, management, record keeping, maintenance requirements, hours of operation, etc. While specific provisions of the agency agreements differed somewhat from one enterprise or cooperative to another, the contractual term, the basis for calculating lease payments, and restrictions on employment were relatively standard. Contracts were usually for an indefinite term, terminable by either party upon a specified notice. Rents were based on a percentage of turnover, with a fixed minimum payment which limited the lessor's down-side risk if the entrepreneur failed to meet revenue targets. In order to control their growth, the state imposed restrictions on employment in the agency stores, but most agents were allowed – indeed expected – to use the help of their family members.

Leases with state enterprises included the most restrictive covenants, since they generally required agents to purchase a large portion (up to 70 percent) of their supplies from state-owned wholesalers. They rarely allowed any material modifications of the assortment of goods sold in their stores, but severe shortages in the late 1980s prompted some enterprises to allow private operators to sell complementary goods obtained from nonsocialized sector sources. Agreements with consumer cooperatives usually contained fewer restrictions on the supply of goods

[17] Agency arrangements existed in the 1970s as well, but they became much more widespread in the 1980s as a result of Decree 17 of the Council of Ministers (February 18, 1983).

Table III.9 Socialized sector units leased to agents ('000), as of December 1989

	Retail trade		Catering	
	Number ('000)	% of total	Number ('000)	% of total
State-owned enterprises and other social organizations	7	19%	1	42%
Cooperatives	51	36%	6	41%
Total	58	33%	7	41%

Source: GUS Domestic Market Department, Warsaw.

and the scope of the store's activities: in a standard agency contract, Spolem allowed the agents to obtain up to 95 percent of their supplies from private or alternative state-owned sources. But the cooperatives also had greater *de facto* control over their agents through the local, regional, and national auditing bureaus, and there may have existed an informal system of keeping the agents "in line."

Statistics on the annual growth of the number of agencies are not available, but in 1989, before small-scale privatization began, the agent-run units comprised a large portion of the formally "socialized" retail trade network: as shown in Table III.9, approximately 58,000 socialized-sector retail outlets (one-third of the total) and 7,000 (over 40 percent) restaurants and bars were operated by agents at that time. While statistical data are not available, unofficial estimates[18] indicate that these proportions might have even been greater for some types of household services.

As in Hungary, state enterprises and consumer cooperatives tended to spin off the smaller, less profitable outlets under agency arrangements, although in many cases the possibility of personal enrichment from illicit relationships among bureaucrats, party officials, enterprise managers, and potential agents created a powerful incentive for leasing out the more profitable units. And while official guidelines prescribed that agency contracts should be allocated through an auction, competitive proceedings were only rarely used, leaving much room for personal connections.

[18] Based on interviews with officials from the Ministry of Privatization.

On whole, the impact of the agency relationships on the changes in the trade sector was certainly significant. They allowed individuals to operate semi-independent businesses in a sphere which had been historically off-limits to private traders and provided opportunities for the agents to forge supply relationships outside of the socialized sector. Many of the future participants in the small privatization process had originally held their stores as agents, and the experience they acquired may have smoothed the process of transition.

2.4. The second economy

No picture of retail trade in communist Poland would be complete without a brief discussion of the second economy, which constituted an important complement to the regular allocation system in the 1980s.

The second economy developed as a result of imbalances in the supply and demand for a wide variety of goods and services, which intensified in the late 1970s and 1980s. Unlike in the Czech Republic, where indices of the availability and shortage of consumer goods were regularly compiled and used to attain a rough equilibrium between supply and demand, information on the consumer goods markets in Poland was nearly non-existent. What data did exist hardly provided the planners with the detail necessary to quantify production possibilities or the demand for specific goods, since the information was all geared toward aggregate measures. Also, the fixed price system was a supply-side accounting device, rather than a signal of potential disequilibrium in the product markets, and efforts to adjust prices to their market levels were met with the hostility of the workers, who were afraid of the inevitable increases. Even when the supply imbalances might have been observed, the planners' ability to correct them was thus largely hampered by the inflexibility of the price and allocation mechanisms.

The government had potentially greater control over the aggregate demand for consumer goods because of its theoretical ability to regulate wages. But the severe economic crisis developing since the mid-1970s helped spur a very powerful worker movement and forced the government to capitulate repeatedly to wage demands. Since the wage increases were not matched by a corresponding increase in supply, excess demand, with the resulting mixture of shortages, rationing, queuing, and accelerating inflation, was a permanent feature of the last years of the communist regime.

The "second economy" was the obvious effect of the government's inability to rationalize the price system or permit legal entrepreneurship. It permeated nearly every facet of the trade sector, with such activities as the "back door" sale of retail goods from state-owned outlets, resale of goods provided to special groups at subsidized prices, the hoarding of scarce goods for speculation, cheating on the apportionment of produced and processed food items or the quality of the manufactured goods, "phantom" deliveries of goods to stores, unlicensed provision of household services, and a large illegal cross-border trade.

By its very nature, the second economy is not adequately recorded in the official statistics. But there is no doubt that it was a major outlet for private individuals and enterprises for gaining access to most scarce goods and resources. Unofficial estimates of the extent of illicit private trade in Poland indicate that it was up to five times greater than the activities of the legal, registered private sector.[19] In 1986 alone, the government uncovered over 17,500 economic offenses involving illegal cross-border and domestic trade, with billions of zlotys in illegal revenues. According to official statistics, approximately 15–20 percent of the value of services provided, in the mid-1980s, to village residents and approximately 3–18 percent of services bought by city inhabitants were by unregistered businesses or individuals.[20] A non-government study done at the same time yielded estimates of much greater numbers: up to 40 percent of the money spent on household and repair services may have been paid to unregistered handymen.[21] The same study also estimated that the proportion of personal income received by the moonlighting technicians and handymen frequently exceeded 100 or even 200 percent of their official salaries.

The second economy was in many ways parasitic on the irrational system in which it was embedded. It survived in large part on pilfered and misdirected state resources, arbitraging the difference between a privileged access to the controlled official supply system and the much higher free market prices, or cashing in on large profits on shabby products made possible by the endemic shortages. The skills on which the second economy rested were in large part limited to the ability to

[19] Jacek Rostowski, "The Decay of Socialism and the Growth of Private Enterprise in Poland," *Soviet Studies*, 1989.

[20] M. Bendarski and D.R. Kokoszczynski, "The Unofficial Economy and Its Social Consequences," *The Economist*, Nos. 3–4, 1988.

[21] M. Bendarski and D.R. Kokoszczynski, "The Fourth Sector," *Survey of Organizations*, No. 1, 1988.

use illicit connections, stealing from a factory or the shop in which one was employed, bribing officials, exchanging favors with the security police in order to be able to travel abroad, etc. It is thus questionable whether these skills were easily transferable to the new situation in the wake of the regime's demise. In fact, the old black marketeers had been in many ways invested in the survival of the old system, and they may have been among the first victims of the introduction of more realistic exchange rates and foreign competition. Still, the second economy played, at the very least, a very important role of reallocating scarce consumer goods among the population on a more rational basis, and as such contributed to the general welfare. Moreover, even if the goods and services of the second economy were in many cases produced by using state-owned inputs, labor, and/or machinery, they were generally of better quality than the still more shoddy goods produced by the state. And despite its parasitism, some of the experiences acquired by the participants in the second economy were certainly useful in the more entrepreneurial environment of the postcommunist reforms.

2.5. The Law on Economic Activity

Prior to the fall of Communism, there was probably no event more consequential with respect to the growth of the private sector than the enactment, in December 1988, of the Law on Economic Activity (which took effect in 1989). This act nullified most regulations, directives, and restrictions adopted in the previous forty years which had established an unequal treatment of private economic activity *vis à vis* the socialized sector enterprises. The act also made liberal changes in the employment restrictions in trade outlets; equalized taxes for all business establishments; and mandated an end to all central associations previously erected to monitor and regulate the activities of the private sector.

In addition to the Law on Economic Activity, the last communist government also eliminated the remaining vestiges of the rationing of consumer goods and liberalized the prices of a large number of consumer products. Although the prices of basic foodstuffs continued to be subsidized, by the end of 1989, 35 percent of the volume of all sales of consumer goods were made at free-market prices.[22] Finally, the

[22] M. Iwanek and J. Ordover, "Transition to a Market Economy in Poland: Some Industrial Organization Issues," December 1991.

Table III.10 Growth in privately-owned outlets ('000)

Sector	Privately-owned outlets 1988	1989	Percent change
Retail trade	43	72	67%
Catering	9	15	66%

Source: P. Tamowicz, T. Aziewicz, and M. Stompór, *Small Privatization: Polish Experiences* (The Odansk Institute for Market Economics, June 1992), p. 32.

government announced a three-year tax holiday for all private enterprises registered in 1989.

As may be seen from Table III.10, the effect of these changes on the growth of the private sector was quite dramatic: the total number of private retail trade and catering units increased by 66 percent in 1989, as the sector stood poised at the edge of the new beginning.

3. THE CHANGES IN THE REAL ESTATE MARKET IN 1990 AND THEIR ROLE IN SMALL PRIVATIZATION

We have explained already that small privatization in Poland was less influenced by any formal programs of transferring title to the businesses run by the state and cooperative stores than by the changes in the real estate market, as a result of which these businesses lost their most valuable assets: the premises leased to them at highly preferential rates, unrelated to their potential value on the market. Perhaps the most interesting aspect of the sector's privatization was therefore the skillful manipulation of the real estate market by the central government, which led to a systematic "bleeding" process by which units in the state and cooperative sectors have been transferred to private hands.

One law, in particular, passed in the early days of the new regime, was of greater importance in this connection than many a privatization program: the revision of the Housing Act of 1974, which gave Polish real estate owners genuine rights to dispose of commercial premises. The law did not explicitly concern the privatization of existing retail and service outlets. Instead, its laconic provisions – the law contained only a few paragraphs – created a new set of incentives for real estate owners and released their spontaneous initiative toward better utilization of existing commercial space. Interestingly enough, the agents empowered by the Housing Act Amendments were not themselves for the most part private: the main beneficiaries of the new law were the many municipalities in Poland, which suddenly became genuine landlords with respect to most commercial premises in which state stores had been located.

Prior to 1990, the use and disposition of commercial premises by both private and state parties was strictly controlled by the Housing Act of 1974. Essentially, the Act gave the state a preemptive right to use any commercial property if a socialized (i.e. state or cooperative) enterprise needed the premises to conduct economic activities, or if the property was made part of a master plan for the allocation of retail or service outlets in a given area.[23] Rental arrangements with socialized enterprises were made on the basis of an administrative decision (with no negotiated, bilateral leases), and the property could be sold or leased only at prices set administratively by the Council of Ministers.

The "special renting mode," as the system came to be called, meant that a committee of local planning officials decided on the "best" use of each available unit, whether municipally or privately owned, and then chose an appropriate state enterprise or consumer cooperative to run the prescribed type of business. Although the Housing Act did not apply to housing cooperatives, which owned a significant portion of commercial real estate, the cooperatives operated under essentially the same regime as a result of a provision in the Law on Cooperatives of 1982, which obliged housing cooperatives to follow the "social economic plan," as implemented by the local planning council. When, for example, a housing cooperative constructed a new building, the council could decide that the obligatory commercial space would be used as a grocery store, and, say, the local branch of a large consumer cooperative would then be approached to equip and run the store, with the housing cooperative having no choice in the matter. Again, while the system of administratively set prices did not formally apply to housing cooperatives, they were not supposed to have been profit motivated and their pricing was supposed to have been strictly cost based.[24]

[23] The restrictions did not apply to privately-built shops and workshops, if they were used according to their designated purpose by the owner or his family, or to buildings owned by socialized enterprises.

[24] The rather strange formula used by the cooperatives amortized total capital investment over sixty years. The rents were notoriously low; in fact, usually lower than the administratively set rents for the premises owned by the municipalities.

The enforcement of the Housing Act and the related cooperative regime created strong disincentives for socialized enterprises to invest in their own premises, since the rents on premises they obtained from the state were set very low and lease terms were of indefinite duration.[25] Although socialized enterprises (especially consumer cooperatives which operated more often in rural areas) sometimes had to construct their own independent premises, their preferred mode of operation in larger cities was to rent from housing cooperatives and municipalities. Thus, for example, the Association of Domestic Trade (a large state retail empire) in Warsaw owned only 4 percent of its retail units; in Poznan, the same enterprise owned only 6 percent of its units.

A casual perusal of the 1990 Amendments to the Housing Act of 1974 would not reveal anything out of the ordinary. The new provisions simply stated that commercial premises hitherto rented on the basis of administrative decisions were, effective immediately, to be governed by the appropriate provisions of the Civil Code. The "trick" was that the Civil Code gave the owner of premises essentially unlimited freedom to terminate any lease of indefinite duration. The Amendments thus released municipalities and other parties from previous administrative controls, and conferred upon them the right to dispose essentially at will of the suddenly extremely valuable assets. The Amendments gave the existing tenants three months to renegotiate their rental agreements, after which the owners could simply evict them. The only right left to the old tenants was their ability to recover the expenses incurred for reconstruction, restoration, or modernization of the premises.[26]

The importance of the Amendments in terms of their impact on small privatization can hardly be over-estimated. At a time when demand for shop space was rising precipitously, state enterprises and consumer cooperatives found themselves, from one day to the next, competing with private entrepreneurs and other local parties for most of the premises in which their stores had been located. If the owners of the premises decided to dispose of them through open competition, rental prices for shop space usually rose to exorbitant levels which could no longer be afforded by the inefficient state enterprises and consumer cooperatives. If, on the other hand, commercial space was allocated

[25] Once assigned, the use of the premises was almost never changed.

[26] In the event, this right appears not to have been of great value either, and the socialized enterprises do not seem to have recovered much of their costs (which, given the seediness of most stores, had not been great anyway).

according to other criteria (as was most common in the case of municipal owners), state enterprises and consumer cooperatives, with few local connections, were rarely the favored parties. One way or the other, the old tenants had to relinquish control of thousands of shops and outlets. One of the consequences of this "mass exit," in addition to a massive transfer of premises to private parties, was a disintegration of old retail empires which, deprived of a large proportion of their units, were commonly pushed into bankruptcy or liquidation.

Although housing cooperatives, as we have seen, were not subject to the Housing Act, and thus were not affected by the 1990 Amendments, a parallel process of reform also released them from the old strictures and conferred on them genuine ownership rights to the commercial premises in their buildings. Formally, the housing cooperative leases had always had the form of bilateral agreements, rather than that of the "administrative leases" under the Housing Act, and the standard lease used by housing cooperatives allowed either party to terminate at any time, with only minimum notice requirements. In the old days, apparently none of the parties even considered the possibility that a housing cooperative might act independently, and probably for this reason they did not bother to negotiate the length of the term in advance. In the wake of the demise of the old regime, however, it was only a matter of time before the housing cooperatives would reclaim their rights. The precipitating event in the change of their renting behavior was the 1990 Law Governing Changes in the Organization and Activities of Cooperatives,[27] which abolished the old cooperative associations previously controlling the local cooperatives and also effected a certain amount of restructuring on the local level. Many local housing cooperatives split into smaller units, for example, and new authorities often took over from the old guard. As a result, local housing cooperatives acquired independence from the higher authorities, and their management became much more responsive to the needs of the cooperative residents (members). It is this series of events, more or less concurrent with the onset of the changes caused by the Housing Act Amendments, that initiated a parallel wave of terminations of the leases between housing cooperatives and state enterprises or consumer cooperatives, with the resulting process of privatization of a great number of shops, restaurants, and service

[27] For a more detailed discussion of this law, see below, the section on consumer cooperatives (section 7).

outlets. In fact, in a matter of a few months, a great majority of commercial premises in Poland were allocated to new users, and the realities of the real estate market changed beyond recognition.

4. GMINA PRIVATIZATION

Perhaps the main beneficiaries of the restoration of genuine ownership rights with respect to commercial real estate were the municipalities across Poland, which had owned a very large portion of commercial premises, especially in urban areas. The present section describes the processes by which municipal governments in Poland (known in Polish as "gminas") have carried out the privatization of a large number of retail, service, and catering outlets devolved on them through the operation of the 1990 Amendments to the Housing Act of 1974 and the new Law on Local Self-Government.

The passage of the Housing Law amendments coincided in time with a large-scale restructuring of municipal governments in Poland. As a result of the Law on Local Self-Government, enacted on March 8, 1990, and implemented in accordance with the Regulations Introducing the Law on Local Self-Government of May 10, 1990, municipal governments gained a large degree of independence from central authorities. Having been, over the years, mere transmission belts for centralized policies of the government in Warsaw, municipalities, headed by locally elected officials, acquired their own budgets and the ability to devise and implement their own policies. One aspect of the devolution of authority effected through the Law on Local Self-Government was a transfer to the newly created municipal governments of ownership rights to large amounts of commercial real estate, together with nearly complete autonomy to determine the purposes and uses of these properties. This transfer process, known as "communalization," became one of the major catalysts for the development of the private retail trade sector. As the gminas began to claim their newly acquired properties from the previous tenants and let them to private parties, the process of small privatization in Poland began in earnest. Indeed, even before the Law on the Privatization of State-Owned Enterprises was enacted in July 1990, the program of "gmina privatization" was already in full swing.

For reasons that will become obvious, gmina privatization is largely an undocumented process, and reliable, publicly available information concerning both the quantitative and qualitative aspects of this process is extremely scarce.[28] In addition to publicly available data, therefore, this section is based on a series of interviews with local officials and an empirical survey of a random sample of 100 gminas conducted by the CEU Privatization Project in March 1993. The principal aims of this survey were: i) to assess the importance of gminas as the agents of change in the broader context of small privatization; ii) to identify the various methods of ownership transfer used in gmina privatizations; and iii) to gain an insight into the policies and procedures devised by local officials for the administration of the privatization process.

4.1. The process of communalization

The Law on Local Self-Government conferred on the gminas the ownership and control over all divisible[29] property in the following three categories:

- movable and immovable state property which until the reform had been in the custody and control of the former basic territorial units of the central administration;
- movable and immovable property of state enterprises and other organizational units which until the reform had been answerable to the former territorial units of central administration;[30]
- state property which had been used to satisfy public needs and which was formerly controlled by the voivodships or its organizational units.[31]

The municipal departments responsible for the disposition of communalized property began their work by preparing claims to the

[28] An exception is a study by P. Tamowicz, T. Aziewicz, and M. Stompór, *Small Privatization: Polish Experiences*, The Gdansk Institute for Market Economics, June 1992. An earlier study by P. Tamowicz, entitled "Small Privatization in Poland: An Inside View," was published in J. Earle, R. Frydman, and A. Rapaczynski (eds), *Privatization in the Transition to A Market Economy: Studies of Preconditions and Policies in Eastern Europe*, Pinter Publishers, 1993.

[29] Indivisible property was not subject to communalization and was later transferred to voluntarily-formed intermunicipal unions or to a single municipality on the basis of an agreement between municipalities.

[30] State enterprises which had been answerable to the territorial units of the state administration became municipal enterprises and retained their own legal identity.

[31] The municipality had to show, however, that custody and control over this property was necessary for the fulfillment of its statutory responsibilities.

assets covered by the Law on Local Self-Government. In many cases, communalization was relatively straightforward, but the proportion of contested cases was also considerable, and uncertainty concerning title to a large number of units had significant influence on the subsequent privatization process.[32] The disputed cases could be brought before the appropriate *voivoda*, whose decisions could in turn be appealed to a special Property Devolution Commission, established by the Regulations Introducing the Law on Local Self-Government and appointed by the prime minister. Title disputes could also be brought before the courts. It appears, however, than many disputes are still unsettled.

4.2. The process of gmina privatization

There are some 2,700 gminas in Poland. In the absence of a centrally imposed, uniform procedure, "gmina privatization" has in fact been an amalgamation of 2,700 individual programs of ownership transformation. Indeed, the very idea of a "program" may overstate what was going on: in 87 percent of the gminas examined in the CEU Privatization Project's survey, the process took place without any formal privatization plan approved by the elected bodies of the gmina.[33] The degree of involvement of elected municipal councils apparently varied widely among the gminas: the councils and the municipal boards (chief executive bodies of the gminas) sometimes remained entirely passive, sometimes approved the privatization of certain types of assets and determined the method of their transfer, and sometimes intervened *ad hoc* in particular cases. In most cases, however, the responsibility for implementing most of the privatization of communalized assets was delegated to a poorly staffed department of the local administration, or, in the case of rural gminas, where the number of units was relatively small, often to a single individual.[34]

This does not mean, of course, that influential figures in gmina

[32] In the Mokotow gmina in Warsaw, for example, where a team from the CEU Privatization Project conducted a series of interviews, title disputes existed in approximately 10 percent of all units claimed by the gmina. Moreover, apparently the disputes often concerned the most valuable pieces of property.

[33] A rather large number of gminas in our study (34) did not obtain any units through communalization. When these are not taken into considerations, the percentage of gminas without a plan falls to 81 percent.

[34] In *Small Privatization: Polish Experiences,* Tamowicz *et al.* give a somewhat different picture of the role of municipal councils and boards. That study, however, was limited to very large municipalities, and its information on this subject came primarily from the municipal council resolutions themselves.

administration had no interest in the outcome of the process. On the contrary, the communalized units were some of the most valuable assets under the gminas' control, and they constituted important sources of patronage and other forms of political capital. But most of the interventions of the higher officials remained on an informal level, giving them more flexibility to use the communalized assets to their best political advantage. The process also freed a tremendous amount of spontaneous initiative that was responsible for a remarkable transformation of the *status quo* in the consumer sector.

In light of the informality of the process that followed the devolution of communalized property, it is especially important to understand who were the parties most interested in the disposition of the communalized property and what were their interests.

The parties most immediately and negatively affected were, of course, the state enterprises and consumer cooperatives which had previously enjoyed the use of the communalized premises at administratively set rents, usually bearing no relation to their true value on the emerging market. Since most stores in Poland had no valuable inventory, and since the general level of equipment (especially in the provinces) was quite low, the premium on the lease of the communalized premises constituted the main asset of the units involved. Moreover, cooperatives and state enterprises lost the allegiance of their own members and employees, who quickly understood that communalization provided them with an opportunity to convert their status into one of proprietors, if suitable arrangements could be made with the local authorities. These insiders were, of course, local people, with local ties and loyalties, and they argued that a transfer of their units to outsiders would unduly drive up rents and lead to a string of bankruptcies, social upheavals, and disruptions of supplies. In localities in which many stores belonged to the same enterprise, unions also constituted an important factor, defending the rights of the insiders to continue operating their units, sometimes backing their demands with a threat of strikes. Presumably, the insiders also used their informal connections with municipal authorities to defend their position.

The gmina officials themselves had a complex set of interests and motivations. Unlike the old functionaries, they were elected officials accountable to their constituencies. The provision of consumer goods and services had been the Achilles' heel of the old regime, and rapid improvement was considered politically very important. Fiscal considerations also played a role. The new Law on Local Self-Government gave the gminas considerable independence, but it did not give them significant fiscal powers, and the prospect of raising additional revenues from the rental or sale of the communalized units was an important consideration.

But there were also other, more personal factors that played an equally important role. Although the new officials had been elected, the speed of the process of governmental reform made it possible for a large proportion of former *nomenklatura* officials, especially in the smaller gminas, to preserve their positions. Despite this, their tenure was insecure and their old *nomenklatura* connections significantly influenced their behavior. The informality of the privatization process also offered the officials unique opportunities for patronage and, in some cases, personal enrichment: the possibility of passing titles to valuable properties to friends, family members, business associates, or colleagues was often an important factor in the decisions affecting the disposition of the communalized assets. Finally, local officials had a rather limited understanding of economic conditions, and were not predisposed to disturb too much the existing order of things: although they were willing to take the premises away from the distant state enterprises and consumer cooperatives, they were more sympathetic to the claims of the insiders employed in the local units.

Outsiders interested in acquiring newly communalized property represented a relatively minor political force in the gminas. Although the general political trend, strongly supported by the central government, was to foster market-type solutions, local entrepreneurs pushing for open, competitive allocation of the available properties were a new and still rather weak group, incapable of overcoming the standard popular resistance to radical changes that might exacerbate the already threatening levels of unemployment. Although outsiders often commanded substantial financial resources, this usually only contributed to the increase of the rental and sale prices on the open market, rather than increasing the number of units placed on the market by gmina officials.

A combination of these forces and factors was ultimately responsible for the predominance of insider-dominated arrangements, a host of restrictions on the changes that could be introduced in the wake of privatization, and the predominance of rentals over sales.

4.3. The extent of gmina privatization

Even prior to the change of the regime, local governments had controlled a large amount of real estate, and privatization of those assets had been moving forward for some time. While figures from individual interviews may not be entirely reliable, at the end of 1992, one gmina in the city of Warsaw had rented to private businesses, *in addition to the units reclaimed through the communalization process,* 1,079 units of real estate. Given that the total number of units controlled by that gmina, including those reclaimed through communalization, was only 1,500, the extent of local privatization preceding, or parallel to, the communalization process evidently had been very large. General statistics on the composition of the consumer sector in 1989, i.e. before the communalization process began, seem to confirm these numbers, since they show that slightly under 28,000 shops (out of slightly more than 151,000), 15,000 restaurants (out of 31,000), and 214,000 service establishments (out of the total of 256,000) were already private at that time. Nevertheless, the units of real estate involved in this early privatization were less desirable and very small (on average nearly four times smaller than the socialized units). Indeed, when data on the volume of trade are compared (even making a correction for the skewing due to tax evasion in the private sector), the size of the private sector looks much less impressive: in terms of volume, the proportion of private retail trade to the socialized sector in 1989 was still barely 5 percent. In the consumer service sector the proportion was 42.4 percent – still a rather small number compared to the number of units involved.

What is referred to here as "gmina privatization," i.e. the process of the privatization of real estate reclaimed by gminas through communalization, involved the larger and more desirable units which in the past constituted the core of the old socialized sector. In fact, out of the total of nearly 124,000 stores operated by state enterprises and cooperatives at the end of 1989, 31,662 were reclaimed by the municipalities and leased or sold to private individuals by 1992, when the process of gmina privatization was essentially completed, except for a handful of units the titles to which were still in dispute. During the same time, 19,690 out of 41,500 state service outlets were privatized by the gminas. The process was also extremely swift: by the end of 1991, 24,762 shops had already been privatized, a number which represents 40 percent of all shops lost to private persons by the state and cooperative sectors.

4.4. The nature of the privatized assets

One of the most interesting aspects of gmina privatization is that at no point in the process did the municipalities have any rights to the

Table III.11 Real estate controlled by municipal authorities sold or rented to individuals

Year	Method of disposal	Shops	Service and craft outlets	Total	Proportion
1990	Sale	778	428	1,206	5.59%
	Lease	13,101	7,252	20,353	94.40%
1991	Sale	296	271	567	3.16%
	Lease	10,587	6,777	17,364	96.84%
1992	Sale	824	852	1,676	14.13%
	Lease	6,076	4,110	10,186	85.87%
Total	Sale	1,898	1,551	3,449	6.72%
	Lease	29,764	18,139	47,903	93.28%

Sources: Tamowicz *et al.*, *Small Privatization: Polish Experiences*, pp. 28–31, and GUS.

businesses operated in the premises subject to communalization. The only rights acquired by them were those to the premises themselves, and the whole process, although leading to the privatization of the retail trade and services sector, was in fact driven by a conveyance of the rights to the real estate devolved on the gminas.

To make matters even more unique, the gminas have not really privatized the real estate under their control, at least not in the sense of conveying full-fledged property rights in the premises to the owners of the businesses operating on them. Instead, in a great majority of cases (over 94 percent in 1990 and nearly 97 percent in 1991), the gminas leased the communalized premises, and the leaseholds conveyed to the new owners, according to the civil law in force in Poland, have the status of contracts, rather than property rights valid against third parties.

Except for those cases in which the title to the communalized property is in dispute, the gminas' preference for leasing over sales (which tapered off only slightly in 1992, see Table III.11) is not easy to explain. The officials themselves justified their actions by a desire to maximize revenues. At the same time, however, only 20 percent of the officials interviewed in the 100 gminas covered in the CEU survey of gminas said that price was the only criterion in deciding on the method of disposal of the communalized units, and the rents charged in most gminas were set below market rates. But even apart from this, it is not clear why sales, which should bring the expected discounted present value of future rents, should be thought of as less advantageous from the fiscal point of view, especially at a time when the national system of taxation was very ineffective, and the central government, itself sorely strapped for funds, was not in a position to assure the gminas an appropriate stream of revenues. It is possible, of course, that the gminas feared that the same liquidity problem would also hamper private individuals from paying sufficiently high prices for the privatized municipal property, and that both rents and real estate prices would be moving upward in the future. This fear, if it was indeed a factor, was certainly unjustified, since the prices fetched by the few units that were actually sold were very high. A more rational economic explanation of the gminas' preference for rentals could be that the gminas did not want to divest themselves of their real estate holdings at a time of relatively high inflation and the absence of a proper opportunity to insure against it through other forms of investment. It is also possible that the gminas' desire to favor insiders, who did not have the means to purchase their stores, was an important factor in favor of leasing. Perhaps the most likely explanation is that gmina officials perceived an outright sale as diminishing their influence in their community, since their long-term control over real estate gave them a very powerful bargaining tool with a large number of potentially powerful outsiders.

Since gminas had no control over the businesses operated on communalized premises or any business assets other than the premises, in the overwhelming majority of cases it leased or sold those premises without the accompanying equipment or inventory.[35] For many stores, especially provincial food stores, inventory was probably an insignificant item. In other stores, especially those trading in more technical goods, much of the inventory may have become unsaleable in the wake of the influx of high quality imports during 1990 and 1991. But the question of what happened to the old equipment of state and cooperative units that fell victim to communalization is an interesting question. Presumably much of it was acquired in one way or another by the successor stores, especially since many of them were obliged to continue in the same line of business, but the exact way in which this was done has not been ascertained.

Finally, the assets were usually conveyed with additional limitations. Prohibition on changes of the line of business was added quite often,

[35] For reasons not entirely clear, 3.5 percent of the shops sold by the gminas surveyed included inventory and 4.0 percent included equipment. For the leased units, 0.2 percent included inventory and 0.5 per cent included equipment.

apparently reflecting the gminas' belief that sudden shifts in the composition of the sector would cause imbalances in supply.[36] It is hard to judge the degree to which such fears could have been justified, but there are good reasons to doubt that they were. First, restrictions of this kind were apparently added as often in large towns as in small villages (where the disappearance, even a temporary one, of the only grocery store could have caused great inconvenience). Second, the retail trade market has been an extremely dynamic area of development, and its ability to adapt to consumer demand should not have been doubted after the first few months of reforms (when restrictions continued to be inserted into new leases). Finally, the idea that the pre-existing distribution of shops, which resulted from the communist planning system, was anything approaching the requirements of satisfying the consumer demand is rather outlandish, so that the restrictions on changes of the line of business might have only retarded the needed readjustments.[37]

Among other common restrictions were those that prohibited sublets or resale. These restrictions may have been particularly unfortunate, given the fact that most of the units were leased to previous insiders, who, as shown in the survey in Part IV, were much less likely to invest in the business or restructure it in other ways. It has not been possible, in the studies conducted so far, to determine to what extent secondary markets for stores and other consumer outlets exist in Eastern Europe, and whether they are able to correct for mistakes in the initial allocation of the privatized units, but clearly the restrictions on transfer would very significantly impede this process. The reason why these restrictions were added have probably, again, more to do with politics than economics: given that the insiders were given preferential access to the privatized units, their ability to sell or sublet them would have allowed them to realize hefty windfalls, which would, in turn, quickly delegitimize the whole system of insider preferences.

4.5. The mode of transfer

The central government, with its preference for openness and market procedures, was very much in favor of privatizing retail units through

[36] These prohibitions often did not preclude a contraction of the existing line of business or its combination with a new one.

[37] The only saving grace of these restrictions was that they were apparently not impossible to circumvent. See the results of the survey in Part IV below.

Table III.12 Proportions of methods of transferring commercial premises to private individuals

Method of transfer	Percentage of units privatized by method
Direct negotiation	61%
Insider auction	2%
Auction with preferences for insiders	10%
Open auction	27%

Source: CEU Gmina Study.

auctions, and it evidently expected this mode of transfer to be followed after the gminas were given control over the premises which they had only nominally owned before. This wishful thinking still makes Polish officials sometimes talk as though a large part of gmina privatization indeed had proceeded through the use of auctions. In fact, however, both our general survey and the special gmina survey show that open auctions were used in Poland in only a small proportion of cases: in gmina privatization, the number was no greater than 27 percent (see Table III.12).[38]

In addition to open auctions, the gminas also used auctions in which only insiders (employees) could participate, or in which insiders were given special preferences, usually a rebate (sometimes as large as 70 percent) off the first year rental. But the most common mode of transfer was a negotiated rental or sale in which the price was most often administratively determined, with the insiders usually ending up as the main beneficiaries.

The choice of negotiated deals over auctions and competitive tenders resulted in marked, sometimes dramatic, losses of revenues from rents collected by the gminas. In one district of Warsaw, administratively set rents varied between Zl 5,000 and 25,000 per square meter, while competitive pricing brought them up to Zl 1,560,000. In other areas the differences were less dramatic, but still enormous: a spread between Zl 5,000 to 60,000 for administratively set rent and Zl 500,000 for

[38] In *Small Privatization: Polish Experiences* (p. 22), Tamowicz *et al.* give a still lower percentage (between 4 and 9 percent) of transfers by auction, and the sample used in that study comes from the largest Polish cities, in which many more units were sold.

auctions was registered, for example, in the provincial city of Opole.[39] Similar evidence is available for even very small towns from comparisons of rents obtained by gminas with those charged by housing cooperatives, which had fewer incentives to cater to insiders. Thus in a small town of Luków, rents set by the gmina varied between Zl 4,000 and 75,000, while those set by housing cooperatives or rented at an auction by state enterprises varied between Zl 59,000 and 600,000.[40]

In one sense, the low prices clearly reflected special terms offered to insiders, but evidence on a more economic justification of this practice is quite ambiguous. Auctions conducted in the absence of a reliable market for similar units were apt to produce relatively high rates of costly overbidding errors. During the prereform period, a shop of any kind produced absolutely extraordinary returns resulting from the simple phenomenon of shortage. Thus, at least in the early period of reforms, prospective buyers and tenants were apt to overestimate the value of the real estate for which they were bidding, especially in less desirable locations. There is some interesting evidence of that from an interview conducted by the CEU team in a large gmina in Warsaw (Mokotów),[41] which had auctioned 120 out of 421 reclaimed units: according to the local officials, most of the 120 auctioned stores went out of business within a year. In other areas, there is evidence that authorities were forced to renegotiate downward the rents established through auctions, since the prices were evidently too high and the new businesses could not pay the stipulated rentals.

The effect of overbidding at auctions also makes sense from a theoretical point of view. When a well-developed market for a given type of an auctioned asset exists, most auction participants will not bid above what is more or less known to be the market value of other comparable assets. In such a situation, the winner, who bids more than others, is likely to be the person who has some special skill that makes the asset more valuable to him, and it is this ability of the auction to pick the person with the highest use for the property that makes it such a valuable procedure. The situation is very different under conditions of high uncertainty concerning the real value of the property, such as exist in Eastern Europe, where some bidders are likely to overshoot by significant amounts. Now, the auction, under such conditions, is more

[39] Tamowicz *et al., Small Privatization: Polish Experiences*, p. 20.
[40] CEU Privatization Project case study.
[41] This is the same gmina in which a competitive tender produced rents as high as Zl 1,560,000.

likely to pick those persons who make the biggest upward miscalculation of the value of the auctioned asset than those who are its best users.

But after all is said and done, the number of units which had to be reclaimed by the gminas as a result of non-payment of rental fees was not very large: in the CEU survey of gminas it amounted to 5.8 percent of the privatized units. Moreover, although it is impossible to break down the failure figures according to the mode of transfer employed (auction or negotiated deals), there is substantial evidence that the greatest number of failures occurred among the insiders, most of whom obtained their property through negotiated rentals. Thus, for example, any time a unit was leased or sold to an insider with some preferences over outsiders, this very fact increased by 16 percent the probability that the unit would later be reclaimed by the gmina. Also, while the expected failure rate (the number of times the gmina had to reclaim the property) among the gminas in which negotiated rentals "typically" resulted in outsider-dominated establishments was 2.5 units, the same rate jumped to 5.4 units when the "typical" situation involved insider-dominated units.

An interesting aspect related to the mode of transfer is the degree of insecurity of the tenure enjoyed by the tenants and even the owners of the premises "privatized" by the gminas. While results of the CEU study of gminas are incomplete on this point, they show that 50 percent of the gminas which acquired any units through communalization had, by March 1993, renegotiated transactions involving 15 percent of all the privatized units. Although the nature of these renegotiations is not always clear, the number appears very high, given the short period of time since the program's initiation (in the second half of 1990). The first conclusion to be drawn from this fact is that the usual term of the leases entered into by the gminas was very short: assuming that the average lease was entered into no longer than two years prior to the study, a significant percentage of leases must be for a period shorter than two years.[42] The short term of the leases entered into by the gminas, especially when considered together with the gminas' tendency to treat rented premises as still under their "control" and to look to them as sources of higher revenues in the future, are likely to make the tenants quite insecure in their tenure and lead to adverse effects on investment

[42] For more data concerning the average lengths of leases in Poland, see the survey in Part IV.

and restructuring. Also, leases resulting from an auction were more than twice as likely (20 to 9 percent) to be renegotiated as the directly negotiated leases, which indicates that some of these may have been "hardship" renegotiations before the expiration of the term of the lease.

4.6. The beneficiaries of gmina privatization

While state enterprises and cooperatives were not excluded from the process through which the gminas have allocated the communalized real estate under their control, very few units subject to communalization were actually retained or reacquired by these institutions: consumer cooperatives managed to hold on to 1.8 percent of their units, and state enterprises to a bare 2 percent. As is evident from what has been said already, the primary beneficiaries of gmina privatization were the former employees of the consumer cooperatives and state enterprises who managed to convert their status into one of ownership. Although available information does not permit an estimation of the percentage of the communalized units that came to be controlled by their former employees, indirect data are in accord with the general belief in the insiders' dominance. The outsiders were excluded from 2 percent of all transfers, and had to contend with auctions which included insider preferences in another 10 percent. The ability of outsiders to compete in direct negotiations, through which the largest proportion of units (61 percent) were transferred, is not known, but the outcome was very heavily slanted toward the insiders: in 74 percent of gminas in which direct negotiations were used, insiders were said to be the "typical" negotiating partners.

5. PRIVATIZATION BY HOUSING COOPERATIVES

Next to the municipalities, housing cooperatives had been the main real estate owners before 1989, and they played a correspondingly important role in the transfer of the use of commercial real estate into private hands, which constituted the essence of Polish small privatization. As we have seen, housing cooperatives had not been formally subject to the Housing Act of 1974, and thus the effective causes of the change in their rental policies were not the Housing Act Amendments of 1990, but rather the dissolution of the cooperative associations and other changes related to the enactment of the 1990 Law Governing Changes in the

Organization and Activities of Cooperatives. Also, the structure of incentives for the housing cooperative officials was quite different from that of the representatives of the municipalities, and consequently the course of privatization controlled by the cooperatives was different from the already described dynamics of gmina privatization.

We have already explained,[43] that the abolition of the central cooperative associations conferred a new degree of independence on the local housing cooperatives and made their management much more responsive to the needs of their member-residents. The responsiveness of cooperative officials to their small constituencies in turn made their behavior quite different from that of municipal officials, who had to balance their desire to maximize revenues and satisfy their electorate with the political necessity of pleasing a number of powerful special interests. The housing cooperative officials thus often pursued a rental policy dictated by the rather simple interests of their membership, and these interests were twofold. First and foremost, the members wanted to maximize revenues from the rental of commercial space, so as to subsidize the residential tenants (especially in the wake of the withdrawal of state subsidies, which used to cover over 30 percent of the costs). Second, they were interested in maintaining certain types of stores in their housing complexes, especially when there were few other shopping areas in the vicinity.

The process of privatization by housing cooperatives was also somewhat more complicated than that of gmina privatization by the diversity of the rental and other arrangements between cooperative landlords and their commercial tenants. Thus, for example, it was not uncommon for housing cooperatives to lease only a plot of land in their projects, with the tenant state enterprises or consumer cooperatives financing the construction and maintenance of separate commercial premises in which their stores were located. Under the old regime, the effect of this kind of arrangement was not much different from the usual form of leasing commercial space, but the presence of a substantial tenant investment in the "land only" leases was the source of many disputes, as the old tenants claimed a right to recoup their investments. As a result, housing cooperatives and their "land only" tenants were often involved in protracted negotiations, with the landlords ultimately having to accept lower rents in order to avoid costly litigation and large indemnity payments.

[43] See section 3 above.

Another, much less common, arrangement was for state enterprises operating stores on the premises belonging to housing cooperatives to become members of the cooperatives. As a member, a state enterprise paid the same subsidized maintenance fees as the apartment dwellers, thus acquiring a quasi-ownership position. In such instances, the cooperative membership of state enterprises also often led to property disputes, with housing cooperatives seeking to recover control of the premises on the grounds that the equity held by state members was generated through involuntary subsidies by the housing cooperatives.

5.1. The extent of privatization by housing cooperatives

Even in the poorly documented retail sector, housing cooperatives are exceptional in the dearth of statistical information concerning their role in the privatization process. Reflecting the prereform lack of relevance of ownership rights, no data concerning the number of commercial premises owned by housing cooperatives seems to have been kept.[44] Moreover, like gmina privatization, small privatization by housing co-operatives was an amalgamation of many unregulated and unmonitored processes. Consequently, housing cooperative privatizations were largely unrecorded, and it is extremely difficult to come up with even approximate estimates of the number of units privatized in this process. The only, somewhat crude, estimates of the number of retail store premises[45] controlled by housing cooperatives could be derived by counting "backwards" from the number of privatized stores (the difference between the 1992 and 1989 number of units run by state enterprises and consumer cooperatives) and subtracting estimated numbers of units privatized by other institutions.[46] Using this method a residual number of some 12,000 stores was obtained as a likely number of units privatized by housing cooperatives.

[44] Efforts to find reliable statistics on floor space were also unsuccessful. Although it is known that there were some 6,500,000 square meters of nonresidential space belonging to housing cooperatives, this included premises such as warehouses and administrative buildings.

[45] No estimates are attempted here with respect to catering and service establishments, where the data are even more unreliable.

[46] Data from the survey discussed in Part IV were also used to estimate the proportion of privatized units rented from housing and consumer cooperatives.

5.2. The type of interest conveyed and the process of allocation

Housing cooperatives, like gminas, overwhelmingly favored rentals over sales of their commercial properties, but their preference seems more justified, in light of their need to ensure that certain types of services were provided to their tenants.

The strong incentive of housing cooperatives to maximize rental income from their commercial properties was responsible for the fact that auctions were apparently used more often by cooperatives than the gminas, but no precise data are available on the proportion of units sold or leased in this way. There is also evidence that cooperative rentals were, on the average, significantly higher than those entered into by the municipalities.

But direct negotiations also played an important role in the allocation of commercial premises by housing cooperatives, and the main reason for this was probably the desire to maintain certain types of stores in the cooperative housing complexes. The same reasoning also explains a rather peculiar pattern of rentals, with some cooperatives setting minimum rent levels based on the type of activity conducted by the tenant. Thus, in one Warsaw cooperative, for instance, tenants offering basic services, such as laundry or shoe repair, paid no less than Zl 15,000 per square meter; trade enterprises no less than Zl 50,000 per square meter; and providers of professional services, such as dentistry or medical care, were required to pay no less than Zl 65,000 per square meter. In other cooperatives, rental rates were not structured according to the type of activity, but adjustments were also made in negotiations with prospective tenants.

Another reason for negotiated rentals was to prevent over-bidding and reduce the chances that tenants would go bankrupt, with the ensuing disruptions in services and losses of rental income in the future. Indeed, once the original enthusiasm for small privatization began to fade and the overly optimistic estimates of rental income were replaced by a more realistic attitude, many cooperative managers became more risk-averse and tended to renew leases with more established tenants at rates that often fell below what the free market would fetch. There is also evidence that housing cooperatives began placing greater priority on their tenants' financial health, and offered the "safer" tenants better terms.

Housing cooperatives were also less likely than the gminas to impose burdensome restrictions on their tenants, but, for reasons related to their interest in preserving certain types of service for their residents, restrictions on changing the line of business during the lease terms were relatively common. In some cooperatives, such changes were simply forbidden, while in others tenants were required to obtain the landlord's approval. But, on the whole, the framework established by the housing cooperatives seems to have been oriented toward a market environment, balancing the need for basic services with the desire to maximize revenues.

6. PRIVATIZATION OF UNITS OWNED BY STATE ENTERPRISES

The preceding sections have described how a mortal blow was delivered to most state enterprises by the 1990 Housing Act Amendments and the changes in the laws governing housing cooperatives. In 1989, state enterprises in the trade sector had operated approximately 36,000 retail outlets (27,000 of which were stores), 2,800 catering establishments, and a portion of the 41,000 "socialized" service outlets.[47] It was impossible to obtain reliable figures for the number of lost catering and service establishments, and for small retail outlets other than stores. But of the 27,000 stores which had been operated by state enterprises, approximately 15,000–17,000 were lost to communalization and housing cooperatives. Even these numbers do not tell the whole story. The most valuable units belonging to state enterprises were in large cities,[48] and there the proportion of losses to gminas and housing cooperatives was still more devastating. Thus, for example, the largest state-owned retail empire, the Association of State Domestic Trade (ASDT), had owned approximately 1,500 stores in Warsaw in 1989, and employed over 9,000 people. As a result of the bleeding process initiated by the 1990 changes in the Cooperative Law and the Housing Act Amendments, ASDT lost 1,440, or 96 percent, of its units, and its employment fell to 360. Moreover, most of the remaining units were also subject to ownership disputes, so that ASDT was left with clear title to

[47] No breakdown of the number of these establishments between state enterprises and consumer cooperatives is available. While state enterprises were responsible for 73 percent of revenues from nonmaterial services provided by the socialized sector, this number includes such activities as transportation, theaters, and education, and may thus overstate the state sector's contribution to the provision of household services. See section 2 above.

[48] Generally, stores run by state enterprises were more concentrated in towns (96 percent of the total) than those run by the cooperatives (52 percent).

no more than fourteen shops. While the case of ASDT is extreme, losses of a great majority of stores were the rule in large cities rather than the exception. Another trade enterprise studied by the CEU Privatization Project, for example, a Poznan branch of the state jewelry chain Jubiler, lost thirty-three of its forty-seven stores to communalization alone.

But the hemorrhage of units did not lead to an immediate death of state retail trade enterprises. It had not been uncommon for these enterprises to construct and own stores in areas where commercial space in housing cooperatives or government-owned buildings was unavailable, and a certain number of their stores were located on the premises owned by the central government, which the state enterprises were able to hold on to in the wake of the onslaught by the other real estate owners. They were thus left with some 10–12,000 stores, and the reform of the old pseudo-cooperative system added some 2,300 new units to the state sector.[49] In addition, state enterprises were also left with a large amount of warehousing space, their old distribution systems, and an extensive and costly central bureaucracy of the former large corporate structures. It is the fate of these assets that is the subject of this section.

6.1. The liquidation process

The first thing to note is that, unlike that part of small privatization which was driven by the real estate transfer, the privatization of the remaining state-owned units has been a slow and tortuous process – in itself a lesson on the difficulty of dealing with existing organizations. A measure of this slowness is that, according to official statistics, state enterprises still operated 9,000 retail shops and 1,000 gastronomical units at the end of 1991, and they probably controlled the same number of stores at the end of 1992.[50] This means that state enterprises managed to privatize some 3,000–5,000 stores during this period – clearly not an impressive figure, even considering the fact that the stores lost to communalization and housing cooperatives were the more attractive ones, and the remaining units were more difficult to privatize. Also,

[49] The reform of the cooperative network of over 20,000 kiosks and some 2,300 stores, selling newspapers, cigarettes, and a variety of other goods, led to the establishment of a new state-owned joint stock company Ruch, which became a part of the state sector.

[50] They were likely not the same stores, however. State enterprises probably privatized some 2,000 stores in 1992, but over 2,000 units were added as a result of the transformation of Ruch.

since most state enterprises are in the process of liquidation, in which often their whole business is to be privatized in one fell swoop, a large number of the remaining units may be transferred to private hands in the near future.

Privatization of state enterprises in the retail trade sector occurs primarily through the so-called "liquidation" method, and secondarily through the leasing of individual units to third parties (often employees) by particular enterprises. In a few cases, such as that of large department stores or specialty shop chains, state enterprises are to be converted into joint stock companies, and privatization is scheduled to follow through a sale of shares to foreign or domestic investors.[51] Very little information is available on these "capital privatizations" (as they are known in Poland), but apparently, with the exception of a small number of partial acquisitions or joint ventures, not much has so far taken place. More information has been obtained about the process of liquidation.

"Liquidation" is a somewhat confusing name, which refers to two separate processes under Polish law.[52] First, enterprises that are insolvent may be liquidated under Article 19 of the 1981 Law on State Enterprises, which specifies a bankruptcy procedure for state firms. In the case of such liquidations, the assets of the bankrupt company are either sold or contributed by the state to a successor company, such as a joint venture or a similar arrangement. The most important fact about the insolvency liquidations is that they do not require the consent of the employee councils, which are a powerful force in many Polish state enterprises, and thus fewer concessions to the insiders are necessary. In practice, however, even though the sale of assets is supposed to be public, they are most often acquired by the enterprise insiders, who receive preferential terms and subsidized loans.

In addition to insolvency liquidations, state enterprises may also be subject to another form of liquidation, governed by Article 37 of the 1990 Law on Privatization of State-Owned Enterprises. In order to qualify for this process, enterprises must be solvent, and the "liquidation" is in fact a form of privatization, in which the assets of the enterprise are sold or

[51] The largest joint stock company of this type is the already mentioned Ruch chain, which has a near-monopoly on the distribution and sale of newspapers, periodicals, cigarettes, and a number of convenience items. The fate of other department store chains is discussed later in this section.

[52] For a more detailed description of both types of liquidation, see Frydman, Rapaczynski, Earle, *et al.*, *The Privatization Process in Central Europe.*

leased to a new company formed especially for this purpose by the employees, often with the participation of outside investors. In addition to requiring the consent of the employee council, Article 37 liquidations also permit a leasing of the enterprise assets (and not just their sale), which makes the whole process much more attractive to the employees.[53] A liquidation plan under Article 37 is worked out between the enterprise and the founding organ (usually, in the case of trade enterprises, the local *voivoda* or the mayor of a large city), with the Ministry of Privatization serving only a supervisory function. It is perhaps a measure of the spontaneity of the Polish small privatization that this most decentralized method of formal privatization under the Polish law is the most bureaucratic and cumbersome method of privatizing retail stores and catering and service establishments.

Table III.13 lists state enterprises subject to the process of liquidation as of mid-1992 (the last date for which data are available). Although the numbers of units operated by these enterprises refer to the state of affairs as of 1989 (before the "bleeding" process began), and thus bear no relation to the number of units actually in liquidation, they give some indication of how large these enterprises used to be.[54]

Prior to the beginning of any liquidation proceeding, most state enterprises had been broken up into a number of smaller organizations. In fact, even under the old regime, regional trade enterprises had their own legal identity, but they were held together in central associations, which coordinated and controlled their activities.[55] In the wake of the reform, the central enterprises or associations were most often dissolved by the Ministry of Trade (which was their "founding organ"), and the responsibility for the independent branches devolved on local officials (who took the role of the "founders"[56]). The assets of the old central enterprise might then be transferred to a separate joint stock company, with the regional enterprises becoming shareholders.

[53] The leasing involved is actually a form of installment sale, with the title passing at the end of the lease term. The terms are also advantageous because the interest rate on the sale is in practice negative.

[54] No statistics of units in liquidation are kept by any office in Poland. It should also be noted that only some branches of most enterprises were in liquidation as of 1992, while others may have still been in the preparatory stages described below.

[55] Some enterprises, such as ASDT, had branches in each voivodship. Others operated only in some parts of the country (Jubiler, for example, had only four branches).

[56] The founder organ, under the Law on State Enterprises, has a multitude of rights and responsibilities concerning the running of a state enterprise. As the formal representative of the state, it also plays an important role in enterprise privatization.

Table III.13 State-owned retail trade enterprises liquidated or in liquidation as of 1992

Enterprise	Description	Liquidation basis*	Retail shops in 1989†	Total shop floor space in 1989	Number of branches in liquidation‡
Jubiler	Jewelry	Art. 37	119	10,164	1
Eliza	General stores	Art. 37	2,098	237,071	1
Domar	Household durables	Art. 37	464	127,691	4
Polmozbyt	Auto repair	Art. 37	624	131,108	5
Otex	Clothes	Art. 37/19	1,700	205,451	6
Arpis	Stationery/sporting equipment	Art. 37/19	588	66,090	7
State Enterprise of Consumer Trade in Fuel and Construction Materials	Fuel and construction supplies	Art. 37	219	52,600	10
Assoc. of State Domestic Trade	General stores	Art. 37/19	12,165	1,840,248	31

Source: Ministry of Privatization and the Main Statistical Office.

* Article 37 of the Privatization Law; Article 19 of the Law on State Enterprises. Different branches of the same enterprise may be liquidated on a different basis.

† Includes units lost to communalization and housing cooperatives after May 1990.

‡ The enterprises listed here have been split and individual branches are being liquidated separately.

One of the first acts of the founders with respect to the regional enterprises was, usually, to appoint a new director[57] (or a liquidator, if the enterprise was insolvent), whose task was to restructure the firm and prepare it for privatization. The job of the director was very important from the point of view of the employees as well, because if the enterprise could be brought back into solvency, it would qualify for Article 37 privatization. The *voivoda*-founders also maintained an office supervising the liquidation process in enterprises under their jurisdiction, and some of these offices provided valuable assistance to the enterprises in transition.[58] Among other things, they might have organized courses for management and employees to explain the privatization process, as well as helped formulate restructuring and privatization plans, organized employee councils, and provided some financial expertise. The *voivoda* would also apply pressure on companies making slow progress, and change the management of those that lagged too far behind.

The first task of the new director would usually be to try to recover some of the enterprise assets taken over together with the real estate lost to communalization and housing cooperatives. During the "bleeding" process, employees of the stores subject to communalization, for example, would simply negotiate a new lease in their new name and continue operating the store, selling out the remaining inventory and even receiving new goods from the enterprise distribution system. (This also happened in the Jubiler chain, where the inventory was expensive jewelry.) The rump enterprises thus tried to claim payment for the inventory (sometimes receiving cash payments, but often only a recognition of indebtedness), and they formalized agreements with their former units to lease or sell to them the equipment left in the stores.

Another problem facing most of the rump enterprises was that of over-employment. In particular, the enterprises were usually left with much too large an administrative staff, too large even in the days when the number of units was much greater. Even after some attrition, a one-to-one ratio of shop to administrative employees would not be unusual. Layoffs, however, were not an easy matter in enterprises in which

[57] In enterprises run by the employee councils, the council often had a decisive role in the appointment of the director. But the rump enterprises in the domestic trade sector often had no employee councils, and in others the councils were weak.

[58] One of the better offices of this kind, in the city of Poznan, had a staff of twenty-nine officials.

employee councils were active, and the directors would have to exercise a considerable amount of tact and consultation before they were able to bring about significant staff reductions.

Finally, a privatization program would be prepared. A portion of the assets would usually be sold off to outsiders in order to improve liquidity and pay off the debts of the enterprise, while the remainder would be scheduled for an employee buyout or a leasing program. In some cases, all or most of the units would be kept together and the enterprise assets would be sold or leased as a whole to a successor employee-owned company. In other cases, individual shops would be privatized individually (usually sold or leased to the employees), with only a few assets remaining to be liquidated. The law requires that all sales of assets of liquidated enterprises be public but the property need not go to the highest bidder, and other criteria (including insider status) may be decisive. As a result, public participation is often minimal or nonexistent, and in most cases in which sales actually took place, they resulted from negotiations with the employees. The assets to be sold must usually be evaluated by a local consulting firm or the liquidator himself, but in the cases studied for this report, the actual sale price was no more than one-third of the original valuation.

6.2. The fate of state department stores

State enterprises under communism also controlled a number of department store chains.[59] While many of the stores involved were not very big and the problems involved in the privatization of the chains are no different from those in other retail trade enterprises, the case of Centrum stores merits a brief, separate discussion. Centrum employed over 12,000 people in the mid-1980s in a chain of fifty general department stores and three production enterprises, and its establishments were the biggest multi-unit retail establishments in Poland. It even ran its own foreign trade organization, which went bankrupt in 1992.

There are two ways in which Centrum may be said to privatize its assets: through leasing space in its stores to private traders, and attempting to lease or sell some large stores in their entirety. Interestingly enough, prior to 1990, Centrum had been more eager to lease its space (primarily to employees and other parties) than in the

[59] See Figure III.1 in subsection 2.2 above.

wake of the postcommunist reforms.[60] In fact, the chain has been curbing the leasing activity recently, leaving only very small units (less than 10 square meters) in the hands of private entrepreneurs. The exceptions have been rich foreign businesses in search of prestigious locations (a German artificial jewelry seller has been reportedly paying Zl 10 mln (US$500) per square meter per month (*sic!*)), and – things have not changed much, apparently, insofar as the bureaucrats' business acumen is concerned – tenants who have large rent arrears and would not pay if their leases were canceled.

The privatization of entire stores is in part hampered by disputes concerning the state- or municipally-owned real estate on which the Centrum stores are located. Five of the stores have so far been leased to employee companies for a three-year term, with the enterprise retaining between 15 and 40 percent of the shares, and the stores are reportedly doing badly: mismanagement and corporate governance problems were cited as the main reasons. Two stores were apparently sold, but no more precise information could be obtained. As of the summer of 1993, the rest were still fully owned by the enterprise, and the prospects for privatization were not clear.

Inquiries concerning the ownership status of the secretive Pewex and Baltona stores, which used to sell often upmarket goods for foreign currency, but have begun in recent years to cater to a less exclusive clientele, were not crowned with much success. Apparently, the chains have converted to joint stock companies with 51 percent Treasury ownership and the rest spread among other state-owned institutions and perhaps a few "lucky" individuals.

7. THE RESTRUCTURING AND PRIVATIZATION OF THE POLISH CONSUMER COOPERATIVES

Prior to 1989, consumer cooperatives were the largest owners and operators of retail and catering establishments in Poland. Cooperatives ran approximately 96,000 stores (65 percent of the total and 80 percent of the socialized sector) and 44,000 other outlets. They also operated over 13,000 restaurants and other catering establishments (42 percent of the

[60] Some 18 percent of Centrum's floor space had been leased between 1988 (when the store had trouble finding enough goods for their shelves) and 1990, with some stores leasing as much as 50 percent.

total and 81 percent of the socialized sector) and accounted for 13 percent of the sales of services.[61]

Consumer cooperatives were also organized in an extremely centralized fashion, making them into even more monopolistic structures than state enterprises. Although there existed a number of smaller specialized consumer cooperative organizations, two giants in the retail sector, Spolem and Samopomoc Chlopska, together controlled 57 percent of all retail shops and 71 percent of all catering establishments in the socialized sector. As if this were not enough, the two did not compete with one another: while Spolem operated mostly in cities and towns, Samopomoc Chlopska was nearly exclusively concentrated in rural areas. In addition to retail outlets, these organizations also owned their own distribution systems, processing plants, and other establishments. Samopomoc Chlopska alone held over 11,000 purchasing centers of cereals, potatoes, livestock, recycled materials, fruits, and vegetables, 1,052 meat packing houses, 1,100 bakeries, 750 mineral water plants, 225 feed mixing houses, and 3,000 manure warehouses.

The cooperative, or rather pseudo-cooperative, system (since the cooperatives were tightly controlled by central organizations dominated by the state) was thus clearly a fundamental impediment to the creation of an efficient consumer sector, and the termination of the monopolistic position of cooperatives was a necessary condition for the sector's transformation. Therefore, even prior to the Housing Act Amendments, which initiated the spontaneous process of small privatization in Poland, the first postcommunist government undertook to reform the cooperatives and destroy their monolithic organization. The outcome of this effort was the Law Governing Changes in the Organization and Activities of Cooperatives of January 1990 (the "Cooperative Restructuring Law"), which dissolved the central cooperative bodies and other cooperative associations and mandated a transfer of their assets to new owners.[62]

[61] For more information on the consumer cooperatives under socialism, see section 2 above.

[62] There were also other, more political, reasons for the speed with which the government acted to dissolve the central bodies of the cooperative movement. They were related to the fact that cooperatives, because of their formal independence from the state, had been used by the Communist Party and its allies to create special sources of income from commercial activities and to control the national system of information. The most dramatic example of the symbiotic relation between the Communist Party and the pseudocooperative movement was the party-owned Ruch cooperative, which held a virtual monopoly on newspaper and periodical publishing and distribution, and was a chief source of Party financing. The Peasant Party also had pseudocooperative connections.

Paradoxically, however, the Cooperative Restructuring Law was never followed by the planned more comprehensive reform of the cooperative movement, so that local cooperatives in Poland, unlike their Czech and Hungarian counterparts, are still governed by outdated communist legislation, dating back to 1982. All that the Cooperative Restructuring Law required of the local cooperatives was to run, before March 31, 1990, new elections for their governing bodies.

The restructuring and privatization of the consumer cooperative movement in Poland involved four different processes. First, the Cooperative Restructuring Law directly attacked the cooperative associations, privatized a significant portion of their property (which did not include many retail units, but had a very significant impact on the wholesale and distribution systems), and released individual cooperatives from centralized control. Second, the 1990 Housing Act Amendments and the restructuring of the housing cooperatives caused a hemorrhage of units from the consumer cooperative system, with similar effects to those described in the section on state enterprises. Third, local cooperatives, cut from the tutelage of the associations and the subsidies channeled through them by the state, as well as weakened by the loss of units through communalization and other claims to the premises on which many of their best units had been operating, started selling or leasing their stores and restaurants to private parties, most often their own members and employees, but sometimes also to small outside entrepreneurs. Finally, local cooperatives themselves were privatized, in part through a stroke of a bureaucrat's pen, since they were reclassified as "private" and ceased to be considered a part of the "socialized" sector, but in part also because they did cease to be state-controlled and, at least to some extent, restructured their operations.

7.1. The liquidation of cooperative associations

Under the old regime, cooperatives were organized in a hierarchical series of associations. All local consumer cooperatives of a particular organization (Spolem, Samopomoc Chlopska, etc.) were grouped together in regional associations, which were in turn linked together with other regional associations in nationwide unions. The upstream organizations also were instruments of the command system of distribution. They had control over purchasing centers, wholesale units, and transportation networks. They held financial assets, maintained relationships with the banking system, received obligatory payments to their "development funds" from local cooperatives, and decided upon the distribution of monies from that fund. The local cooperatives had no choice of suppliers, no control over their own expansion, and the overwhelming proportion of their revenues was siphoned off by the upstream organizations (disbursements to members was usually in the neighborhood of 3 percent of the profits). Not uncommonly, local cooperatives had been forced to transfer to the association a portion of their own assets, such as a plant or another enterprise that the association was interested in operating directly.

The Cooperative Restructuring Law placed all the associations into immediate receivership, to be followed by liquidation proceedings. A separate liquidator was appointed for each association by the Ministry of Finance or a local Treasury representative. The liquidators were responsible for developing plans for the disposition of all assets of the associations, and managing them in the transitional period. A liquidation plan would then be presented for the approval of the representatives of the local cooperative members of the association, with the Ministry of Finance and its representatives reserving the right to approve it if the membership failed to act within a thirty-day period.

The first point of a liquidation plan was to exclude from the assets of the association any plants or other assets which had been transferred to the association without payment from the local cooperatives during the preceding ten years. All assets of this kind were to be returned to their original owners. Financial assets of the association, such as working capital and reserves held in the development funds, were to be used to repay the liabilities of the association and defray the costs of the liquidation. With respect to the remaining assets, the Cooperative Restructuring Law provided for the following methods of disposition:

- Assets could be transferred to member cooperatives, with or without payment. Usually, no payment would be required if a local cooperative took over a business previously run by the association together with its liabilities. If the association paid the liabilities associated with the transferred business, the receiving cooperative would be required to make a partial or total payment.
- Another group of preferential recipients were the employees of the business associated with the transferred asset. For this purpose, at least half of the employees had to found their own cooperative and capitalize it at an appropriate level (at least three-months' salary

from each member), and the asset might then be transferred to them without payment.
- Assets not transferred to local member cooperatives or the employees could be sold at auctions open to the public.
- Subsequent amendments to the law allowed for assets to be transferred to joint stock or limited liability companies established by former workers or cooperative members.

The mechanics of the Cooperative Law ensured that the distribution of assets would be determined primarily by negotiations among the liquidators, employees, and local cooperative officials. Outside investors seem to have played a minor role, but they may have been involved behind the scenes in a number of cases. Cases of illicit transfers in fact appear to have been rather common, with the liquidators arranging for unpublicized and often undocumented sales, and in some cases becoming managers of commercial partnerships formed to buy the assets of dissolved associations. Despite the law's unambiguous mandate, few assets were sold through truly open auctions. (Apparently, despite their dubious legality, closed auctions, by invitation of the liquidator, were rather common.)

Partly as a result of the very decentralized nature of the process, comprehensive data on the liquidation of cooperative associations is unavailable. From a number of interviews conducted by the CEU Privatization Project with liquidators and cooperative officials, however, it appears that the process of liquidation is essentially completed at the regional level, with some work remaining to be done on the level of the central unions. It also appears that individual associations followed different patterns of asset disposition, partly as a result of the different economic realities, and partly because of variation in the relative strengths of the various participants.

From the point of view of small privatization, the most important assets of the associations were their vast networks of purchasing and distribution centers, including hundreds of warehouses, storage and shipping facilities, and sizeable inventories of (domestic and foreign) foodstuffs and other consumer goods. With respect to these assets, it was found that, generally speaking, member cooperatives of the Spolem system, which operated in urban areas and specialized in retail trade, acquired most of the wholesale and distribution related assets of their associations. Member cooperatives of Samopomoc Chlopska, on the other hand, which operated in the countryside and conducted much more diversified activities (thus being much less centered around retail trade[63]), were less interested, or less successful, in acquiring the supply systems of the old network. Consequently, a large number of assets related to the wholesale supply and distribution system found their way into private hands, decisively strengthening the private sector's role in this area.

The Cooperative Restructuring Law also created a new cooperative association, the Supreme Council of Cooperatives, to serve as the domestic and international representative of the cooperative sector, but membership in the Council is purely voluntary. The remaining cooperatives are also allowed to form other types of voluntary associations, and it is perhaps a measure of their difficulty in "going it alone" that the growth of such organizations has been very rapid. Thus, for example, shortly after the beginning of the liquidation process, some 200 local cooperatives from Samopomoc Chlopska formed an "economic chamber." As of the end of 1992, membership in the chamber had grown to 1,670 cooperatives.

7.2. Privatization of and by local cooperatives

The abolition of cooperative associations had two significant consequences for the Polish retail trade and consumer service sector. First, the sale of the property of the associations created a decentralized pattern of ownership over warehouses and other means of storage and product distribution. The resulting diversity of potential supply sources was essential to the genesis of competition and market behavior. Second, and perhaps more important, the breakup of the associations changed the cooperative sector from one characterized by hypercentralization into one where atomized cooperatives were forced to fend for themselves. Placed in the unfamiliar position of having to manage their own financial resources and make their own business decisions, cut off from their previous sources of ready credit and subsidization, individual cooperatives often found themselves forced to sell or lease their units in order to maintain even a semblance of stability. As a result, a large number of retail stores, restaurants, and service units were transferred to

[63] Many of the basic cooperative units of Samopomoc Chlopska were made up of food processing businesses, dairies, consumer goods manufacturers, and traders in fuel and building materials.

private hands, and the remaining cooperatives themselves were often transformed into more independent, business-oriented organizations.

We have said already that the Cooperative Restructuring Law did not seriously affect the governance system of the local cooperatives. All it did with respect to them was to require that they hold new elections within three months from the passage of the law. The cooperatives which failed to hold new elections were subject to liquidation. But the speed with which the democratization of the cooperatives was supposed to take place may have been too great, since it left no time for new forces to organize. Consequently, it is estimated that only 15 percent of those who won the early elections were new entrants, with the rest representing the old cooperative *nomenklatura.*

The Cooperative Restructuring Law also provided that each discrete organizational unit of an existing cooperative, or a unit that may become organizationally independent, had a right, by a vote of a majority of the members, to demand separation from the rest of the organization.[64] But there appears to have been only a minor movement toward separation among the consumer cooperatives, since, within the first two years after the enactment of the law, fewer than 100 new cooperatives were created.[65]

The only other legal change in the structure of the Polish cooperatives was brought about by the 1991 Law on Valorization of Members' Shares in Cooperatives, which allowed cooperatives to increase the value of each individual members' share, at the expense of the financial assets held in the indivisible common fund. While this change made the concept of cooperative membership somewhat more meaningful than before, the law also imposed a five-year restriction on cooperative asset alienation, which made exit more difficult and decreased the likelihood that cooperatives would be dissolved or transformed into other types of business entities.

In the period following the dissolution of cooperative associations, local cooperatives experienced three serious difficulties. First, most local cooperatives suffered from a lack of business experience and, faced with a radically new business climate and the unfamiliar phenomenon of competition, were unprepared to make essential business decisions.

[64] The membership of the "mother" organization could veto the separation only if such action was "dictated by important economic interests of the old cooperative or by the vital interests of its members."

[65] Separation was apparently much more common among the housing cooperatives, where it contributed significantly to a change in their *modus operandi.*

Second, many local cooperatives experienced a large drop in revenues caused by the abrupt cancellation of subsidies funneled through the cooperative associations and the loss of the most valuable units to municipalities and housing cooperatives. Third, they were often burdened with units and activities that had a social rather than economic *raison d'être* and could not be profitably operated.

In response to these developments, local cooperatives could select one of three alternatives. They could determine that their situation was so poor as to preclude success and elect to liquidate. They could attempt to continue operating their remaining units, building up the necessary capital and expertise as they went along. Finally, they could choose to sell or lease some of their assets in order to bring in alternative sources of revenue. Most of them chose the last of these alternatives, and this has been a sizeable source of newly privatized units.

7.3. The results of cooperative privatization

Again, privatization by local cooperatives, like most forms of small privatization in Poland, has been an extremely decentralized and diversified phenomenon, and it is extremely difficult to come up with reliable numbers concerning its results. In the absence of reliable statistics, no estimates can be ventured concerning the number of restaurants and service establishments transferred by consumer cooperatives into genuinely private hands. But some estimates of the involvement of these cooperatives in the privatization of shops can be made, based on a series of deductive calculations. Thus, we know that consumer cooperatives entered the reform period with some 96,000 stores. Extrapolating from the data provided by the Main Statistical Office, it appears that cooperatives were still running some 43,000 stores at the end of 1992. Of the units they lost, approximately 2,300 cooperative stores have been reclassified as belonging to the state sector as a result of the corporatization of the former cooperative Ruch.[66] This means that, through the end of 1992, the number of stores operated by consumer cooperatives had declined by approximately 51,000 units subject to some form of privatization. Of these, approximately 27,000 to 29,000, or 53 to 57 percent, were lost to communalization and housing

[66] See the section on state enterprises above.

cooperatives through the mechanisms described in sections 4 and 5.[67] We are thus left with a balance of 20,000 to 22,000 shops, which represents a fair estimate of the number of units privatized by consumer cooperatives themselves.

Unhampered by any legal regulations, cooperatives were free to privatize their units in any manner they selected, and attach any number of conditions on their subsequent operation. In general they have favored leases over sales, and offered the first choice of rental to the employees of the privatized unit. It appears, however, that the employees often did not believe in the ultimate viability of the offered business, and in such cases, attempts have been made (usually successfully) to rent the premises to an outsider. The opportunities of this kind have often been widely publicized, and auctions have been held.

The reason why consumer cooperatives favor leasing over sales (and the rentals are usually of rather short duration)[68] appear not to be related to revenue maximization and may be linked to a belief about the future development of the retail sector. Interviews with cooperative managers indicate the existence of a certain assurance among them that the financial conditions of the cooperatives will improve. Retention of ownership control over property might thus be viewed by them as an important factor for future growth and diversification.

Based on the available limited data, it appears that leases regularly contain restrictive provisions, mostly concerning changes in the line of business. These are more common in rural areas, where such restrictions may make sense (but may also be the result of lesser competition among the owners of real estate). There was also a detectable desire on the part of a number of cooperatives to ensure that lessors do not compete with stores retained by the cooperative or leased to other individuals. Protection of cooperative supply systems may also have played a role.

[67] The pattern of shop loss due to communalization was not uniform across the cooperative sector. Rural cooperatives, in particular, owned a far greater proportion of their shops than urban cooperatives. Thus, it has been estimated that the urban cooperative Spolem lost proportionally twice as many shops to communalization as the rural Samopomoc Chlopska.

[68] Case studies commissioned by the Privatization Project showed that leases with determinate time periods ranged from one to three years. Cooperatives also showed a propensity to conclude leases of indeterminate length, which, under the laws operative in Poland, allows for a termination of the lease by either party with thirty days' notice. Such behavior may prove to create significant disincentives for leaseholders to invest in their businesses. (Equipment and inventories were frequently included in the lease.)

The unwillingness of cooperatives to cede ownership or true operational control over their units, taken together with their attempts to recreate nationwide networks of cooperative associations, indicate that the transfer of the previously cooperative units to genuinely private hands may be a reversible phenomenon. It remains to be seen whether the cooperatives succeed in re-establishing themselves as a united force in the domestic trade sector, and what will be the effect of their new organization on the state of the competition in the retail market.

Part IV: The Survey

1. INTRODUCTION

The survey presented here has been designed to provide empirical evidence concerning the performance of the privatized trade and service establishments in the Czech Republic, Hungary, and Poland, and to identify the main driving forces of successful small privatization in the three countries. The survey was also designed to enable policymakers in the other countries of the region to draw some conclusions from the experiences of the most advanced postcommunist economies.

Many of the survey results attempt to capture the specific texture of local conditions, which may in fact be very hard to replicate in any other place. They should be read in light of the extensive background concerning each of the countries, contained in the earlier parts of this study, so that the quantitative results may be put in an appropriate context. Other conclusions of the survey, reinforced by the background information concerning privatization programs in the three countries, have potentially far-reaching implications that should be tested in the other countries of the region.

The presentation of the results of the survey will proceed in the following order:

Section 2 describes the way the sample was selected and states the various methodological assumptions of the study.

Sections 3 and 4 give a picture of the sample examined in the survey, including information concerning the type of units in the sample, the data concerning the interviewees, the types of assets transferred (premises, equipment, inventory), the nature of the rights conveyed (sale vs. lease, duration of leases, restrictions as to resale or sublet, change in the line of business, etc.), the mode of transfer (open vs. closed procedures, auctions vs. tenders, publicity about the transfer), prices, and ways in which the acquisition has been financed (savings, bank, or family loans, etc.).

Section 5 presents information concerning the environmental conditions in which the trade and service units operate following privatization. It examines changes in supply relations (including the degree of shift from state to private wholesalers, the quality of services provided by different types of suppliers, and the extent to which retailers serve as their own suppliers), the financing of business operations, employment patterns (including numbers of layoffs, changes in the ratio of managerial to other employees, wage policies, etc.), and the perceptions of the new owners concerning the impact of such factors as government interference, political stability, legal uncertainty, competition, and labor market conditions.

The next three sections examine behavioral implications of a number of factors related to the initial conditions of privatization and post-privatization experience. While other outcome variables are occasionally used, the survey relies heavily on the amount of postprivatization investment in the remodeling of premises as a proxy for the extent of postprivatization restructuring.

Section 6 looks into the effects of such features of the transfer contract as duration and the nature of the rights conveyed and examines their effect on the levels of postprivatization restructuring. Its primary result is that purchases lead to higher levels of investment than leases and that leases of long duration yield much greater postprivatization investment than those with shorter terms (under five years). More generally, the section shows that the security of property rights is of great importance for the level of postprivatization restructuring.

Section 7 examines the consequences of the mode of transfer, such as open and closed procedures, auctions, tenders, and noncompetitive transfers. It shows that tenders lead to the highest levels of postprivatization investment, and that auctions are not clearly superior to other modes of allocation.

Section 8 discusses the implications of postprivatization ownership structure, in particular the effect of insider and outsider domination of new firms on the levels of postprivatization investment and restructuring. Its shows that new entrepreneurs, not connected with the predecessor establishments, bring much needed capital, engage in significantly more restructuring, and generally serve as agents of change in the sector. This result and the significance of the impact of lease duration on postprivatization investment are further confirmed by a simple multivariate analysis.

Finally, Section 9 concludes by drawing some implications concerning the choice between open procedures and the overall effectiveness of small privatization policies, especially with respect to the size of the program and the entry of outside entrepreneurs.

2. POPULATION AND SAMPLE SELECTION

Decisions regarding the composition of the sample population were made with a view toward selecting categories of economic units that were both representative of the retail trade, catering, and service sector, and consistent across countries. The sampling methods used to identify the survey respondents were selected to fit the differing national characteristics of small privatization programs.

2.1. Population selection

2.1.1. Initial conditions

The study rationale dictated many of the initial conditions applied to population selection. The following set of conditions was established to create an initial screening mechanism:

1. Only economic units deriving the majority of their income from non-manufacturing, commercial activity in retail trade, catering, or the provision of services were included in the survey.
2. They had to operate a business (rather than solely own real estate).
3. They had to have acquired their business through some form of legal privatization.[1]
4. The owners of the business had to be its initial private purchasers.
5. The businesses had to have been in operation for at least one year.
6. They had to employ fifty or fewer individuals.

The importance attached by most small privatization programs to a speedy transformation of the consumer sector motivated the selection of retail trade, catering, and service units as the exclusive subjects of examination. The study's focus on postprivatization business behavior

[1] The meaning of privatization, for the purposes of this survey, is discussed in section 3.3. below.

guided the determination to interview only the operators of the privatized businesses,[2] and not the owners of shop premises. Since it was essential to interview people knowledgeable both about the privatization process and postprivatization modifications of business behavior, only the initial purchasers from the state were selected, and among them only those who had owned the business for more than one year. Finally, the desire to interview units with common organizational, managerial, supply, and distribution problems caused the exclusion of units with more than fifty employees or units involved in manufacturing.

Unavoidably, the initial set of conditions resulted in the exclusion of some groups of privatized units.[3] Also, differences in both the prereform sectoral composition and the subsequent methods of privatization affected the relative importance of the uniform conditions for the selection of the units to be included in the survey. For example, the exclusion of units employing over fifty individuals was constant, but the impact of this limiting condition was significantly greater in Hungary, where units of this size (or integrated chains of units employing a total of more than fifty employees) are more common than in the other two countries. In light of the delayed timing of cooperative transformation in Hungary and the Czech Republic, the requirement of at least one year of operation led to the exclusion of units privatized by Hungarian and Czech cooperatives.[4]

Potential sample bias was also introduced by the requirement that all surveyed units had to have gone through a legal privatization process. It can be assumed that legal processes, as opposed to spontaneous or shadow privatizations, were more open to outside investors, and may well have often dealt with assets that were less desirable than those that were illicitly transferred out of the state sector. This problem is most acute in Hungary where the requirement of legal privatization caused a significant over-representation of units in the Preprivatization Program.[5]

[2] Units rented or purchased directly from state enterprises or cooperatives were also considered to have been privatized.

[3] The intent to derive policy implications applicable to the former Soviet republics led to the exclusion of units privatized through the extensive Czech restitution program.

[4] For more information on cooperative privatization, see the respective sections describing each nation's privatization process.

[5] For the description of the Preprivatization Program, see Part II, section 3.

2.1.2. Conditions concerning the line of business

Concern over the potential impact of factors unique to particular types of businesses in one or more of the countries led to the adoption of a second set of selection criteria, designed to decrease the variety of the sampled businesses, while maintaining the representative character of the sample population. We settled on the following categories of units,[6] based on their representation in the economies of the Czech Republic, Hungary, and Poland: food stores;[7] household necessity stores;[8] clothing and textile stores; restaurants;[9] and service units.[10]

A large proportion of privatized businesses fall under one of these classifications. However, some degree of sample bias was introduced through the exclusion of other types of units. Thus, for example, the exclusion of bookstores and pharmacies, both of which were frequently prevented from changing their line of business, may well have decreased the percentage of units found to operate with such restrictions.

Further, in order to ensure the comparability of the sample across the countries, a quota was adopted for each category of units in the sample. In each country, the sample population was thus composed of the following ratio of businesses: 40 food stores; 20 household necessity or clothing and textile stores; 15 restaurants; and 25 service establishments. These proportions are roughly equivalent to those found in the database for the Czech Small Privatization Program, which was the most extensive compilation available. There was no reason to assume significant Hungarian or Polish divergence from these ratios.

2.1.3. Locational distribution

Attempts were made to ensure locational distribution along two separate dimensions: geographic distribution and population density. In order to adjust for regional differences in privatization patterns, the

[6] Classification was based on the activity from which the business derived more than 50 percent of its revenue.

[7] Food stores were defined to include stores selling both fresh and processed foods. A "store" was defined as a business unit with a window located in a permanent structure, and thus distinguishable from kiosks, street vendors, and other types of commercial outlets.

[8] A "household necessity store" is defined as a store selling non-durable household goods.

[9] "Restaurants" were defined to include all catering establishments serving food.

[10] Excluded from "service units" were all businesses providing professional services such as law or accountancy.

sample population was drawn from a selected set of geographically representative areas. In both the Czech Republic and Hungary, five regions were selected. Because of the greater degree of decentralization of the privatization process and the relatively larger size and population, twenty-five different sampling areas were selected in Poland.

In each geographic region, the sample population was drawn from a mixture of urban, suburban, and rural localities. Due to differences in numbers of units, rates of privatization, and the difficulty in locating rural units, relatively few rural units were ultimately included in the final sample.

2.2. Sample selection

The sample consisted of 300 privatized establishments (units) in the retail trade, catering, and consumer service sector in the Czech Republic, Hungary, and Poland. A hundred interviews were conducted in each country, but some respondents failed to provide adequate answers to some questions (so that the number of valid responses to any particular question may be smaller than 100 for each country).

Sample selection methods were country specific and tied to both the particular structure of each nation's small privatization process and the availability of population lists from which to assemble a sample. The degree of centralization of the sample selection technique paralleled the degree of centralization of the privatization process.[11]

The Czech sample was drawn exclusively from units privatized through the Small Privatization Program.[12] Regional lists of privatized units were randomly ordered and provided to a private Czech firm selected to conduct the survey.

The Hungarian sample was selected from two separate sources. Half of the sample was fashioned from randomized regional lists of businesses privatized through the Preprivatization program.[13] The remaining half of the survey was chosen through a randomized list of telephone numbers of units listed in the 1989 Hungarian telephone directories.

[11] A detailed algorithm guided the selection of survey respondents. The selection protocol ensured the maximum degree of randomness within the constraints imposed by the population selection criteria.

[12] For a description of the Small Privatization Program, see Part IB, section 3, above.

[13] For a description of this program, see Part II section 3, above.

The sample in Poland was constructed entirely from randomized 1989 lists of state sector units existing in twenty-five geographically distributed census regions.

3. PARTICIPANTS AND ASSETS

3.1. Type of units

As noted earlier, the establishments surveyed were divided into three categories: shops, catering units, and service outlets, and the proportions among the three categories were set in advance on the basis of the proportions in the Small Privatization Program database in the Czech Republic. Table IV.1 shows the proportions of the different types of units in each country.

The geographical distribution of units in the survey is also in part an artifact of the sample selection method (although the desired distribution was not ultimately achieved), and no conclusions concerning overall distribution of units in each country can be drawn from it.

3.2. Interviewees

Table IV.2 presents a breakdown of interviewees according to their present position in the business, while Table IV.3 shows the position of present owners in the predecessor (preprivatization) businesses (state enterprises or cooperatives). A separate question in the survey asked how many establishments had preprivatization employees or managers among their new owners, but the answers to this question, despite attempts to reinterview respondents with unreliable replies, have turned out to be too inconsistent to provide a dependable count of units in the sample dominated by previous insiders or outsiders. Thus, the previous status of the interviewee owners became very important in distinguishing clearly between insider- and outsider-dominated firms. *In the survey, whenever any features of insider-dominated units are compared with those of outsider-dominated units, the universe of all the units is narrowed to those in which the interviewee was an owner or co-owner of the business, and the previous status of this interviewee is taken as determining whether the unit was dominated by insiders or outsiders.* (In those cases in which the

Table IV.1 Type and location of surveyed units

	Czech Republic	Hungary	Poland
Type of unit (as % of number of responses)			
Number of responses[1]	100	100	100
Shop	60	58	61
Restaurant	15	16	15
Service outlet	25	26	24
Location (as % of number of responses)			
Number of responses[2]	100	100	100
Central, commercial area	39	64	41
Suburban area	59	34	40
Rural area	2	2	19
Average floor space used for display or service (m^2)			
Number of responses[3]	100	100	100
Shop	62	71	75

1 Number of interviewees who responded to the question about the type of their establishment.
2 Number of interviewees who responded to the question about the location of their establishment.
3 Number of interviewees who responded to the question about the floor space of their establishment.

Table IV.2 Interviewees and their present position

Current position in surveyed unit (as % of number of responses)	Czech Republic	Hungary	Poland
Number of responses[1]	96	96	98
Sole owner	89	57	61
Co-owner	11	22	36
General manager	0	21	3

1 Number of interviewees who responded to the question about their current position in the surveyed unit.

Table IV.3 Ownership structure

Current position in surveyed unit (as % of number of responses)	Pre-transfer position of current owner, co-owner, or manager								
	Czech Republic			Hungary			Poland		
	Manager	Employee	Outsider	Manager	Employee	Outsider	Manager	Employee	Outsider
Number of responses[1]		96			68			94	
Sole owner	39	5	45	11	9	52	32	6	26
Co-owner	5	2	4	–	4	24	20	4	12
Total %[2]	44	7	49	11	13	76	52	10	38

[1] Number of interviewees who responded to the questions about their current and pre-transfer positions in the surveyed unit.
[2] Totals of percentages in each of the columns.

interviewee was a co-owner, rather than a sole owner of the business, there arises a possibility of mixed insider–outsider partnerships. In practice, however, very strong internal evidence indicates that probably few such combinations existed in the sample.)

The survey provided information on two types of previous insiders among the new owners: those who had been employees in the preprivatized establishments and those who had a managerial position in the old business. It is often argued that privatization through worker ownership is significantly worse than managerial buyouts in terms of the effect on postprivatization restructuring. The number of former employees in the sample was too small to confirm or reject this hypothesis.[14] For this reason, in order not to lump together two potentially distinct groups, we have decided to *limit the study of the insider-dominated businesses to businesses dominated by former managers*. A comparison of the size of insider and outsider groups according to this definition is given in Figure IV.1 (the "others" represent interviewees who were managers rather than owners and former employees who became owners).

The breakdown of the numbers of insider and outsider-dominated businesses is a function of the selection process, and should not be taken as fully indicative of the proportions for the countries as a whole. Thus, for example, Hungarian privatization is generally dominated by insiders, but our sample was largely drawn from units in the Preprivatization program (see above Part II, section 3), which was supposed to use auctions as the primary mode of transfer. Since auctions, as a general rule, increase the proportion of outsider owners, the Hungarian sample is not representative of the wider universe of all privatized units.[15]

Table IV.4 shows the breakdown of owners by gender. It reveals an interestingly high frequency of cases in which women became owners or co-owners of newly privatized units. Even more surprising, in light of the relatively low levels of gender awareness in the region, is the number of cases in which women owners are outsiders not previously connected with the privatized units. Since access to external financing is

[14] The survey does show, however, that the performance of the managerial group among the new owners is still significantly weaker than that of the outsiders. See section 8, below.

[15] The proportions are probably more representative in Poland. In the Czech Republic, the exclusion of units subject to restitution significantly lowers the number of outside owners in the sample.

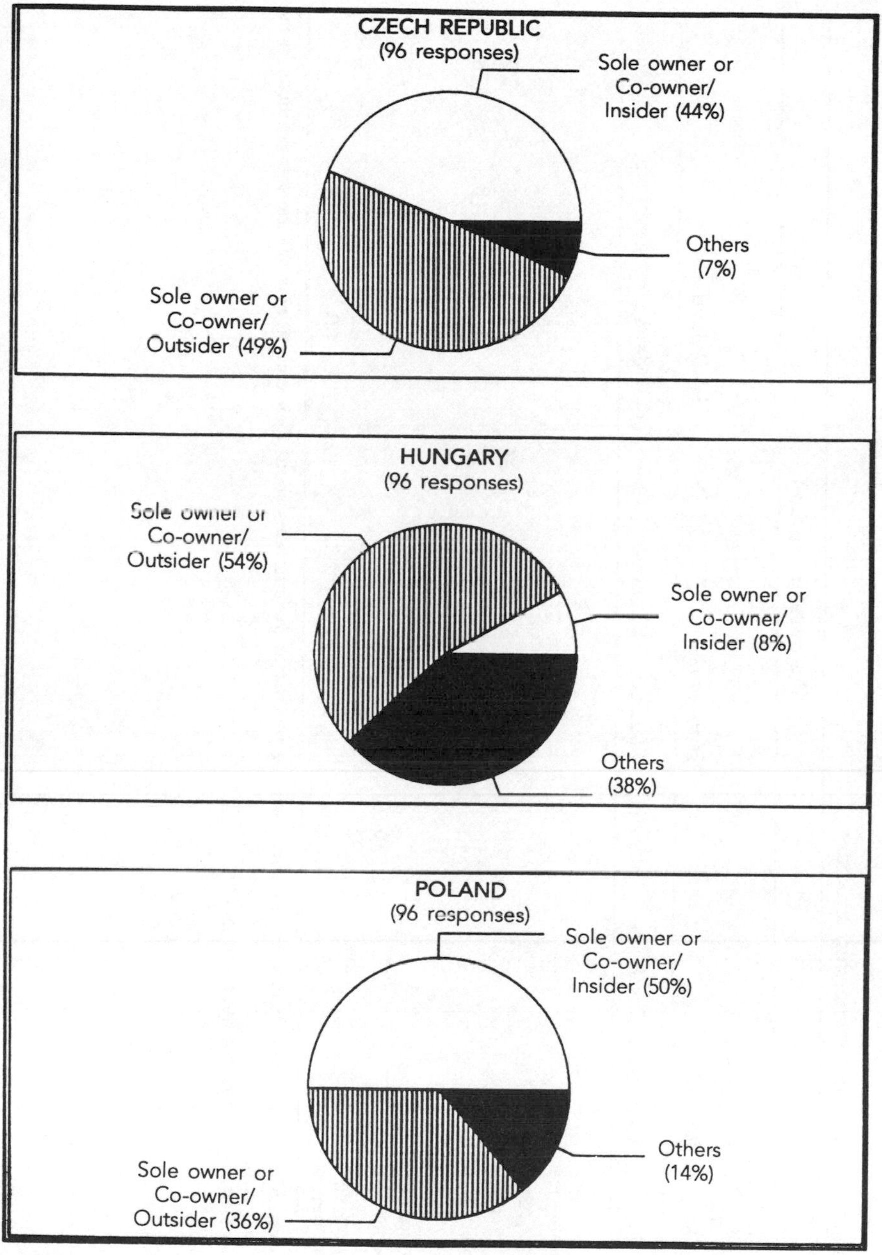

Figure IV.1 Participants in the transfer process

Table IV.4 Gender and ownership structure

Current position in surveyed unit (as % of number of responses)	Pre-transfer position								
	Czech Republic			Hungary			Poland		
	Manager	Employee	Outsider	Manager	Employee	Outsider	Manager	Employee	Outsider
Male									
Number of responses[1]	64			41			48		
Sole owner[2]	42	47	89	16	49	65	34	38	72
Co-owner	6	5	11	–	8	27	16	12	28
Female									
Number of responses	32	27	46						
Sole owner	47	45	92	28	55	83	42	14	56
Co-owner	5	3	8	–	17	17	30	14	44

[1] Number of male (or female, below) interviewees who responded to the questions about their current and pre-transfer positions in the surveyed unit.
[2] As % of all respondents of the same gender.

difficult (see section 4.7), the data seems to indicate that women have rather significant financial resources.[16]

3.3. Nature of the conveyed assets

As shown in Table IV.5, most of the privatized units were transferred to the new owners without equipment (and presumably without inventories). While the survey did not ask whether the privatized units had taken over a previously going concern or just the assets of the old establishments, Table IV.6 shows that most units did not assume any debts at the time of transfer. Moreover, even that number is probably overstated, since some respondents clearly confused the assumption of the debts of previous establishments with the assumption of debts to finance the transfer. Correcting as much as possible for this confusion, it appears that no more than 18 percent of the units in all three countries assumed any obligations of the pre-existing state or cooperative establishments.

The data from Tables IV.5 and IV.6 point to an often neglected feature of small privatization programs in all three countries, namely, that *small privatization is primarily not a transfer of businesses, but of assets, and more particularly, of real estate.* Indeed, the decoupling of premises from the business of the state enterprises and state-dominated cooperatives intent on defending their empires – the phenomenon particularly stark in Poland – may be one of the main factors responsible for the remarkable success of small privatization in the three countries. Given this paramount importance of the transfer of premises for the process of small privatization, our study concentrates on this aspect, around which we have anchored our presentation in the following pages.

The extent to which small privatization may be driven by actions concerning real estate becomes even more interesting when considered together with the fact that the premises themselves are most often not privatized in the strict sense of the word. Since 75 percent of the

[16] As an additional indication of this fact, no women owners said they financed their acquisitions with loans from their families. In order to correct for the fact that women interviewees may be co-owner wives in family-owned businesses, we have calculated the number of women co-owners in outsider-dominated businesses (since women co-owners in insider-dominated businesses are previous co-workers, rather than wives). This number is very small for each country (1 for the Czech Republic, 5 for Hungary, 6 for Poland), and does not significantly affect the picture.

Table IV.5 Parts of the business included in the transfer

Part of the business	Number of units for which a given part of the business was transferred: Czech Republic	Hungary	Poland
Number of responses[1]	100	83	90
Premises	100	83	90
Equipment	35	31	36
Land	20	9	14
Building	28	29	28

[1] Number of interviewees who responded to the question about the part of the business which was transferred.

Table IV.6 Financial obligations of transferred units

Units with obligations from:	Czech Republic	Hungary	Poland
Number of responses[1]	100	85	100
Suppliers for existing inventory[2]	2	6	17
State companies	21	5	10
Banks	0	2 (6)[3]	6 (12)

[1] Number of interviewees who responded to the questions about the pre-transfer obligations of their units, and, if any, specified the type of creditor.
[2] Number of units which assumed obligations from the indicated creditor.
[3] We present two sets of figures for the number of units which answered that they assumed obligations to the banks: the number of units reporting in the survey that they assumed bank loans (in parentheses) and the adjusted set of figures. The adjusted figures are based on the presumption that respondents who answered that they assumed obligations to the banks referred to the bank loans used to finance their transfer, rather than pre-existing (prior to transfer) obligations. Note, however, that unadjusted figures are used in the analysis of behavioral implications in section 6.2 of this part.

privatized units lease, rather than own, the premises on which their businesses are operated (see Table IV.8 below), the legal title to the most important asset controlled by the majority of the "privatized" businesses in the retail and service sector is never conveyed into private hands.

This fact also makes the distinction between a privatized and a newly founded business in the consumer trade and service sector rather fluid. As a definitional matter, *one may use the term "privatized" for those units which operate on the premises that had been previously occupied by consumer*

Table IV.7 Owner of rented (leased) premises

Category of owner (as % of number of responses)	Czech Republic	Hungary	Poland
Number of responses[1]	71	64	72
Municipality	58	61	21
Housing co-op	13	2	18
Trading/consumer co-op	0	9	32
State-owned enterprise	13	9	14
Private individual or company	10	17	10
Other	6	2	5

[1] Number of interviewees who responded to the question about the owner of the premises leased by their establishments.

trade and service units in the state sector, while "new" private businesses are those which operate on premises that had been either private all along or were previously state controlled but had not been used for the operation of establishments in the consumer sector.

While data on the institutions which conducted the privatization process or from which the premises were originally obtained is not available, Table IV.7 shows the present landlord of each privatized unit which is in rented premises. It is worth noting that only 12 percent of these premises are owned by private individuals or institutions (excluding cooperatives).[17]

4. THE TRANSFER PROCESS

The nature of the right in the transferred assets is of great importance for the level of security of the owner in the conduct of his or her business. The rights conveyed through the transfer of premises, which constitute the core of the newly privatized businesses, may be divided primarily along durational lines, distinguishing between sales (i.e. conveyances of rights of indefinite duration) and rentals (i.e. conveyances of

[17] Even some of the landlords counted as private may be incorporated businesses partially or wholly owned by the state. On the other hand, the sample does not include units privatized through restitutions in the Czech Republic, and in all those cases the ownership of the premises was transferred to private hands.

Table IV.8 Type of transfer of premises

	Czech Republic		Hungary		Poland	
	Rental (lease)	Purchase	Rental (lease)	Purchase	Rental (lease)	Purchase
Number of responses[1]	100		83		90	
% of number of responses	71	29	77	23	79	21

[1] Number of interviewees who responded to the question about the type of transfer of premises occupied by their units.

rights of limited duration). In addition, the rights conveyed may be limited at any particular moment of their duration through removing certain entitlements from the total bundle defining full ownership. Thus, for example, the right to the disposition of the premises occupied by a business may be restricted in various ways, such as by limitations on sublet or resale, change in the line of business, change in supply relationships, or laying off employees.

4.1. Lease vs. purchase

We noted already that most of the premises on which the privatized establishments are operating have been leased rather than sold. The more concrete breakdown is provided in Table IV.8, which shows that there are no very significant differences among the three countries in this respect. But the numbers may be somewhat misleading for the Czech Republic, since the sample does not include units privatized through restitution.

4.2. Features of the rental contract

Table IV.9 presents the breakdown of the durations of leases in the sample. A rather striking fact is the very high proportion (42 percent) of leases with terms of two years or less in Poland. Since short duration greatly reduces the security of tenure, it is important to note whether leases contain provisions concerning renewals.

Table IV.9 Duration of rental (lease) contracts for premises

	Czech Republic	Hungary	Poland
Number of responses[1]	69	34	40
Average duration (years)	4	7	4
Median duration (years)	5	10	3
One year[2]	0	1 (3%)	9 (22%)
Two years	23 (33%)	1 (3%)	8 (20%)
Three years	1 (2%)	2 (6%)	4 (10%)
Four years	1 (2%)	0	0
Five years	38 (55%)	11 (32%)	15 (37%)
Longer than five years	6 (8%)	20 (56%)	5 (11%)

[1] Number of interviewees who responded to the question about the duration of their lease contract.

[2] Number of interviewees (% of the number of interviewees) who responded that the duration of their lease contract is one year or less (more than one year, but less than or equal to two years, etc.).

While the number of valid responses in Figure IV.2 is too small to make confident generalizations, its seems that most leases have an option to renew, but without specifying the conditions of renewal (including price), and only a small proportion of leases contain purchase options. Except in Hungary, the latter usually also fail to specify the terms of the purchase.

4.3. Restrictions

In line with the fact that most transfers concern premises rather than going business concerns, very few transfer contracts, whether leases or sales, have restrictions on change of suppliers or layoffs of employees. A substantial proportion, however, have restrictions on the change of line of business or subletting and resale (see Table IV.10).

The reasons for the restriction on changes in the line of business are not difficult to fathom: they probably come from the fear of the

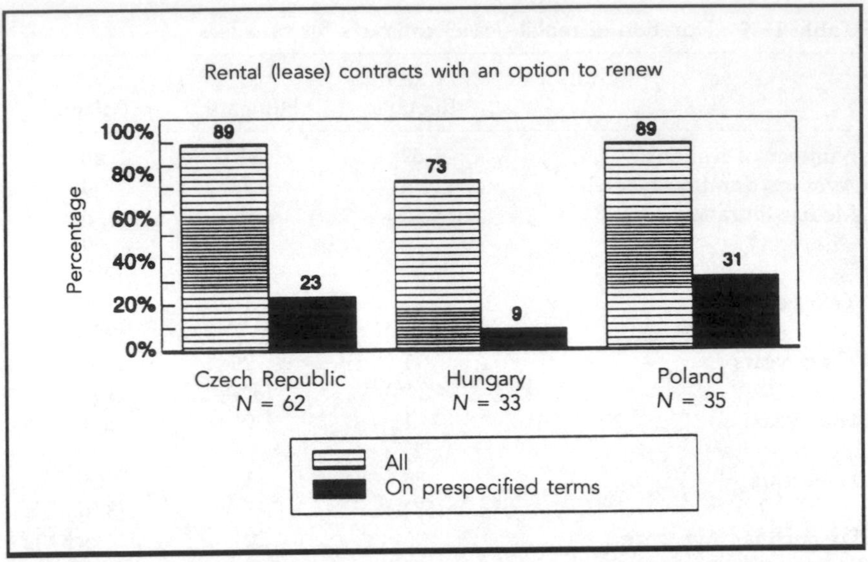

Note: "N" in this and all other figures denotes the number of valid responses to the relevant question.

Figure IV.2 Features of the rental (lease) contracts for premises

authorities that too rapid changes would lead to disruptions of supply. As noted before (see Part II, section 4), such fears are probably unjustified, except for rural districts (very under-represented in our sample), where frequently only one unit provides a particular, necessary service. The average length of these restrictions (49 months) is also much too long.

Even more puzzling is the case of restrictions on subletting and resale of the premises, which clearly impede the operation of secondary markets and, therefore, improvements in the original allocation. What makes the restrictions even more burdensome is that their length is approximately equal to the average length of the rental contracts in our sample, and in the case of the Czech Republic even exceeds it. A possible hypothesis explaining these restrictions is that they accompany transfers to insiders who were given preferential terms, thus preventing them from cashing in on the subsidies granted to them by the authorities. But our sample, while too small to disprove this hypothesis,

Table IV.10 Sample information on restrictions in the transfer contract

	Czech Republic	Hungary	Poland
Number of responses[1]	100	99	100
% of number of responses with any restrictions	28	52	41
Restrictions in transfer contract			
No closure for specified period (months)[2]	–	12	7
Number of units with this restriction[3]	–	2	5
Employees not to be laid off (months)	–	1	12
Number of units with this restriction	–	1	1
Business not to be closed or sublet (months)	60	66	47
Number of units with this restriction	15	9	14
Line of business not to be changed (months)	27	60	47
Number of units with this restriction	18	39	20
Supplier relationships not to be changed (months)	–	65	60
Number of units with this restriction	–	4	1

[1] Number of interviewees who responded to the question about restrictions in their transfer contract.

[2] Number of months recorded in the table are averages from those units reporting that they are subject to a given restriction.

does not support it either, since the restrictions are as common in the Czech Republic, where insiders received no preferences, as in the other countries, and generally appear to apply to insiders and outsiders alike.

The survey allows some gauging of the degree to which the restrictions contained in leases and sale contracts are in fact enforced by the authorities and complied with by the respondents. To begin with, a number of people who had some of the restrictions in their contracts (especially in the Czech Republic) stated that they were not enforced,

Table IV.11 Levels of noncompliance with restrictions on changes in the line of business (pooled data)

Type of change		Number of units subject to restrictions on changes in the line of business	
		Shorter than 50 months	At least 50 months
Number of responses[1]	286	32	41
Number of units reporting changes in the primary line of business	31	6	12
Number of units reporting adding a new line of business	43	9	27

1 Number of interviewees who responded to the questions about the changes in the line of business and restrictions in the transfer contracts of their units.

* Number of valid responses, defined as responses to at least one of the categories. The data from all three samples have been pooled.

although most said they were not easy to evade. More significantly, there is a striking difference in the behavior of people with restrictions of short and long duration: while those who are barred from changing the line of business for a period of less than 50 months usually comply with their contracts, the proportion of units with long-term restrictions (over 50 months) which change the line of business is the same as among the units with no restrictions at all (see Table IV.11). But clearly, those who have restrictions on the change in the line of business may also be the very ones who are more likely than the others to do so (which would show that the authorities do not impose these restrictions at random), since they also add new lines of business to the old one nearly twice as often as the others.

4.4. The competitiveness of the transfer process

Much discussion of small privatization focuses around the advisability of using open auctions or competitive tenders, as opposed to directly negotiated transfers which are likely to favor insiders and have a potential for breeding corruption and favoritism. On the other hand, open auctions may be very threatening to insiders in the units subject to privatization: these insiders often expect to lose their jobs when outsiders take over the business (see section 5.3 below) and put up stiff resistance to the whole process.

The proportions of auctions vs. directly negotiated sales and rentals in our sample are presented in Figure IV.3.

In fact, however, Figure IV.3 does not convey an adequate picture of the competitiveness of the process. One may ignore perhaps the fact that not all auctions generate more than one offer,[18] since once the process is *open* to all (insider and outsider) participants, one may consider it "competitive." But many of the negotiated transfers may be competitive as well, either because outsiders are involved in the negotiations or because more than one insider is bidding for the property. In order to capture these distinctions, we will adopt the following terminology in our subsequent discussions:

Open tender refers to directly negotiated transfers of premises in which outsiders (individuals not previously connected with the unit) were involved in the competition for the sale or rental.

Auction refers to an open bidding procedure in which both insiders and outsiders can participate.

Closed tender refers to directly negotiated transfers of premises in which outsiders are not involved and more than one insider is bidding for the property.

Closed non-competitive transfer refers to directly negotiated transfers of premises in which outsiders are not involved and only one insider is bidding for the property.

Open procedure refers to an auction or an open tender.

Closed procedure refers to a closed tender or a closed noncompetitive transfer.

Competitive transfer or procedure refers to all forms of transfer except closed non-competitive transfers.

[18] In fact 25.7 percent of auctions in our pooled sample did not generate more than one offer. It should be noted that the number of offers is dependent not only on the openness of the process, but also on how high is the starting price. Thus, for example, in the Hungarian sample, heavily skewed by the proportion of units in the Preprivatization program, in which starting prices were set relatively high, over 44 percent of transfers did not generate more than one offer, even though the process was quite open and resulted in the highest proportion of outsider-owners of all three countries.

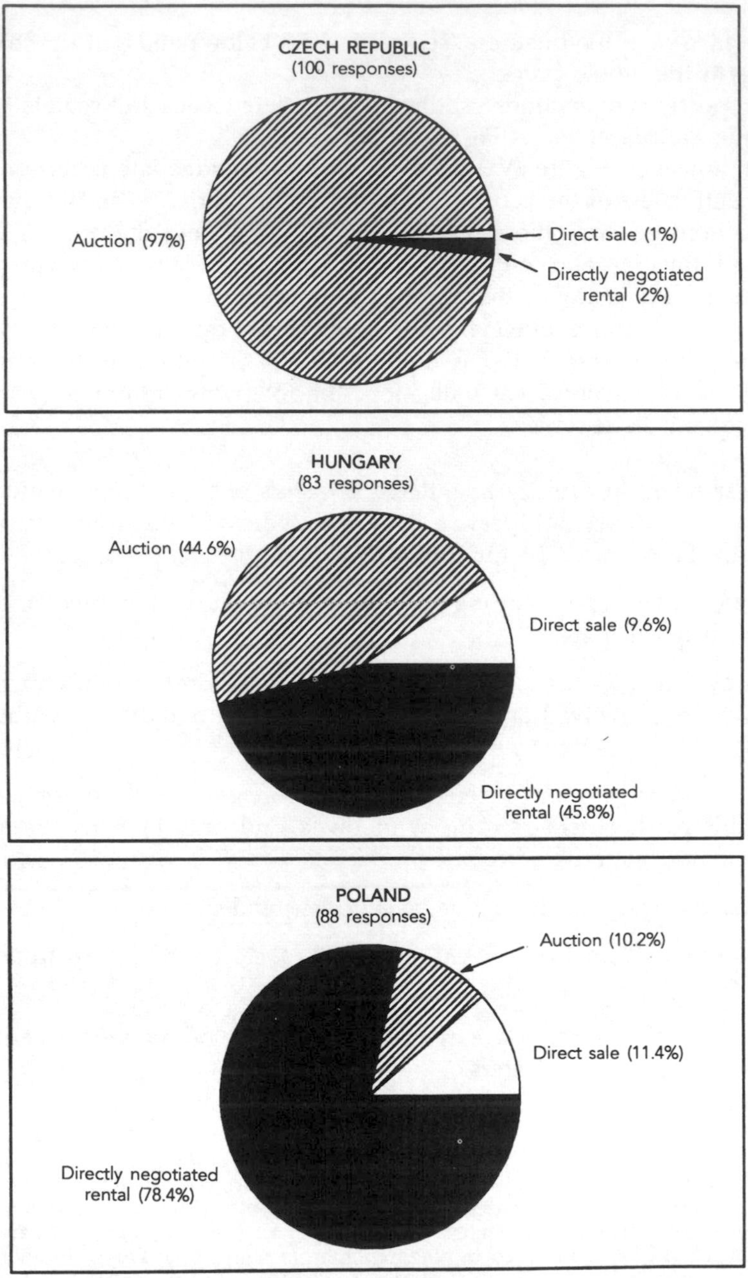

Figure IV.3 Mode of transfer of premises

The size of the sample in our survey does not permit conclusions to be drawn concerning the degree of competitiveness in all types of transactions. But the results presented in Figure IV.4 give a rather adequate picture for the transfer of those units that were leased (rather than sold).

4.5. Public knowledge of the transfer

Public knowledge of the transfer is a very important feature of small privatization, especially if participation of outsiders is considered essential. The survey asked how each respondent learned about the availability of the unit, and many responses indicated multiple sources of information (advertisement in the media, government announcement, acquaintances, and internal announcement). In order to assess the importance of the various modes of announcement, the following ranking was established: "advertisement in the media" was counted only if it was listed as the sole mode of announcement, "government announcement" was counted only if the respondent listed it and did not list "internal announcement" or "acquaintances" as his or her source of information, and "acquaintances" was counted only if "internal announcement" was not listed. The purpose of the ranking was to bring out the degree of publicity accompanying each particular transfer, with the most public form of announcement, presented in Figure IV.5, treated as characteristic for that transfer. In particular, this ranking focused on the marginal efficacy of the announcement in the media, and allowed us to estimate how many of the present owners would not have participated in the transfer process if no media advertisement had been made. When the results are broken down according to ownership structure, the result is rather striking: a full *26 percent of the outsider owners would not have participated but for the announcement in the media.*

4.6. Prices

While the survey asked for information concerning prices paid by respondent-owners for the premises on which their businesses were operated, the information concerning absolute levels of prices is difficult to interpret, since too many factors, such as location or attractiveness of individual properties, can influence the price paid for them. A more

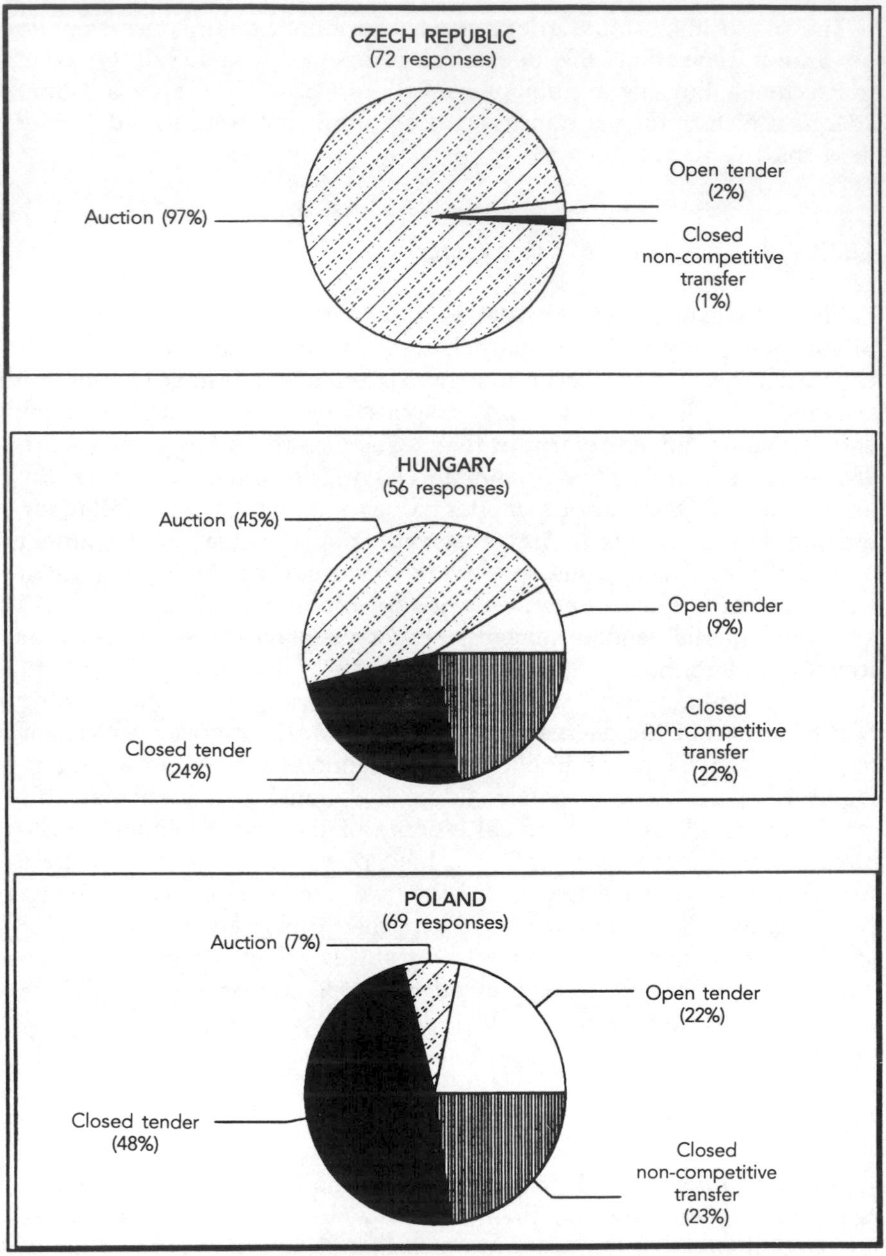

Figure IV.4 Mode of transfer of rental contracts for premises

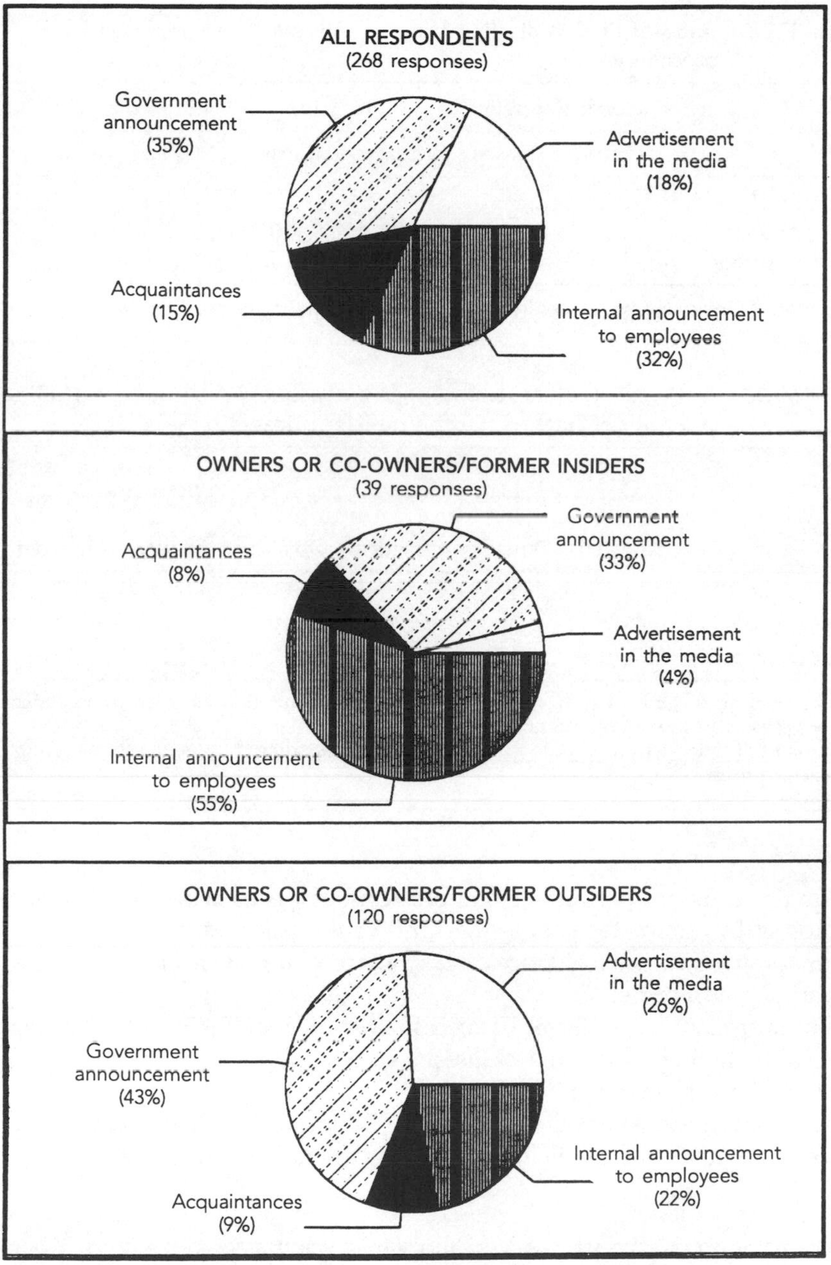

Figure IV.5 Sources of information about transfers (pooled data)

Table IV.12 Ratio of final to starting transfer prices in open or closed procedures

	Czech Republic		Hungary		Poland	
	Open	Closed	Open	Closed	Open	Closed
Number of responses[1]	82	1	24	10	17	34
Ratio of prices	5.2	.5	2.0	1.2	1.2	1.4

[1] Number of interviewees responding to the question about transfer prices.

Table IV.13 Participation of insiders in open competitions for transferred units and ratio of final to starting transfer prices

	Czech Republic		Hungary		Poland	
	Insider (adjusted)[1]	Outsider	Insider	Outsider	Insider	Outsider
Number of responses[2]	27 (22)	39	1	11	3	9
Ratio of prices	6.7 (6.4)	4.1	1.3	2.2	1.0	1.2

[1] Price ratio after elimination of apparently unusual opportunities. No such transactions were present in the Hungarian and Polish data.
[2] Number of interviewees (insiders or outsiders) responding to the questions about transfer prices.

adequate measure, permitting comparisons of prices paid by different groups of buyers or tenants, is the ratio of the price paid for the given premises to the starting price asked (or set up as a floor) by the privatizing authorities.[19]

Not surprisingly, the level of prices, as shown in Table IV.12, grows noticeably higher when the transfer is competitive and involves the participation of outsiders.

But quite unexpectedly, as shown in Table IV.13, when the transfer process involves the participation of outsiders, and insiders *win* the

[19] This conclusion presupposes, of course, that the starting prices, while perhaps widely inadequate (for example, because of being determined by unreliable book values), are set in a uniform manner in each individual country. (The starting prices need not, however, be set uniformly across different countries.)

bidding, insiders in the Czech Republic, but not in Hungary and Poland, pay, on the average, a significantly higher price for the premises than do outsiders in the same situation.

The explanation of this phenomenon may lie in the substantially greater propensity for new outside owners in the Czech Republic, as compared to Czech inside owners as well as the new Hungarian and Polish outside owners, to fire incumbent managers and employees. Due to their asset-specific investment in the privatized units and the high likelihood of being fired after the transfer,[20] Czech insiders might have been prone to over-bidding for the units in which they were employed.

An additional factor which might have contributed to higher price ratios for insider transactions is that some insiders may have had special information concerning certain units that was not available to outsiders. Under the Hungarian conditions, where the market was more likely to provide comparative information about property values, the informational advantages of insiders were likely to be smaller, and their inside information was likely to be divulged during the bidding process. But under the Czech conditions, insiders were much more likely to have special information, since no markets for real estate or stores had existed prior to the recent privatizations.

Some indication of the informational advantage enjoyed by insiders in the Czech Republic can be gleaned from the fact that insiders were prepared to pay high prices in a few (five) transactions in which they acquired what appears to have been particularly attractive properties.[21] It is worth noting, however, that when these cases are removed from the sample, as shown in Table IV.13, the price ratios remain essentially unaffected.

4.7. Financing of the acquisition

Owners of only approximately 59 percent of units in the sample had to make an initial payment for the purchase or rental of the premises. This low figure is still probably higher than the population mean, since the Hungarian sample was heavily biased in favor of units in the Pre-privatization program which probably required higher levels of payment than was usual in less supervised privatizations.

[20] See section 5.3 below.
[21] See section 6.1 below.

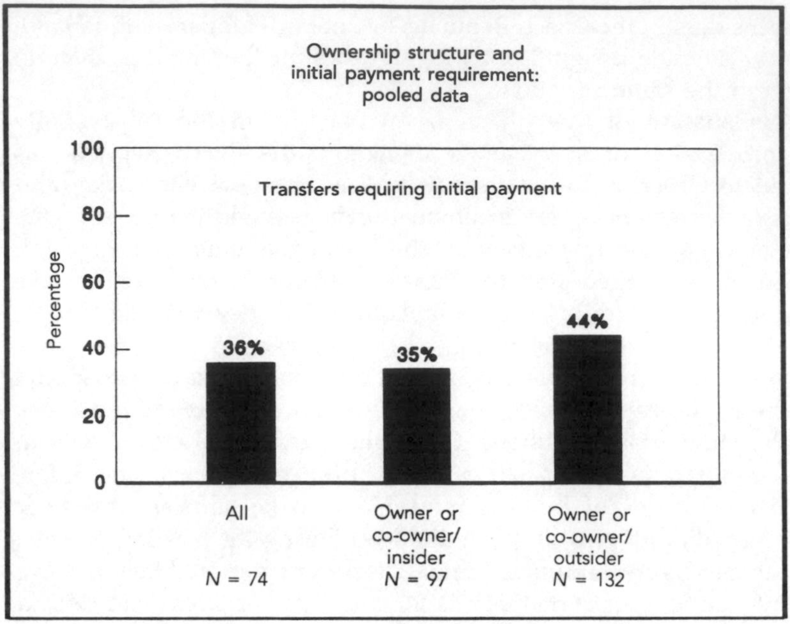

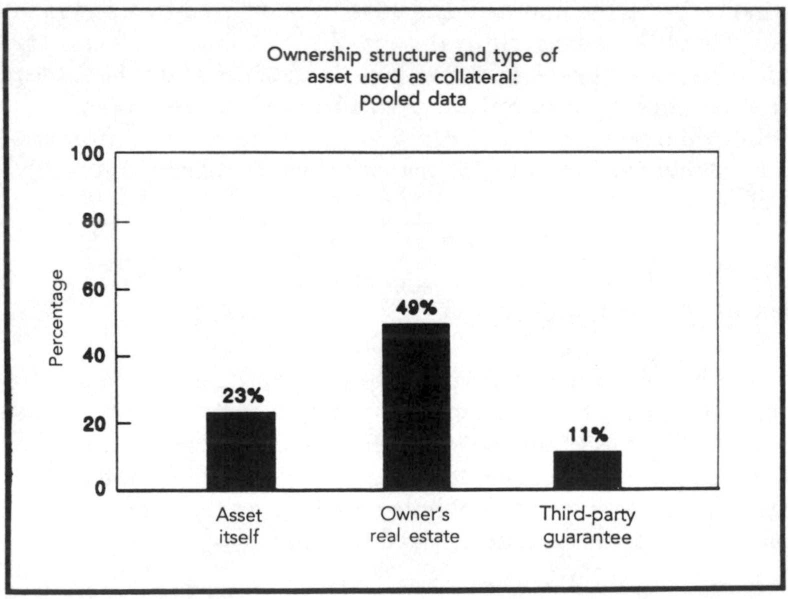

Figure IV.6 Collateral requirements for rentals (leases) for premises

As shown in Figure IV.6, in a significant proportion of cases in each country some form of collateral was required in the transfer contract. What is particularly worthy of note is that these proportions were also higher than the proportions of purchases in the sample, indicating that a significant proportion of *rental* contracts required collateral as well. The most commonly used form of collateral was the owner's real estate, followed by the asset itself, and third-party guarantees (used most often by insiders).

Figure IV.7 shows a surprising degree of availability of bank financing for the acquisition of the premises of the privatized units. While personal savings and loans from family and friends are the main sources of financing, bank financing is used in a very significant proportion of cases in all three countries, especially when purchases, rather than leases, are involved.

5. POSTTRANSFER BEHAVIOR AND ENVIRONMENT

The postprivatization behavior of the transferred units may be thought of as dependent on three basic factors: the environmental constraints faced by the units, the effects of the transfer process, and the post-transfer ownership structure. In this section, we will provide a picture of the environmental conditions in which the privatized units operate.

5.1. The quality and choice of suppliers

The relationship between a revitalization of the retail sector in consumer trade and the reform of the wholesale sector is an often debated "chicken-and-egg" problem. According to one point of view, rapid privatization of the retail sector is bound to produce dramatic changes in demand in the wholesale sector and induce necessary upstream restructuring. According to another point of view, however, the reform of the retail sector has a very low plateau of possible improvement in the supply of goods to the population, unless the wholesale sector is previously, or at least simultaneously, demonopolized and made to perform at a higher level of efficiency.

This is not the place to decide this controversy, and our survey contains only limited information bearing on this issue. It should be

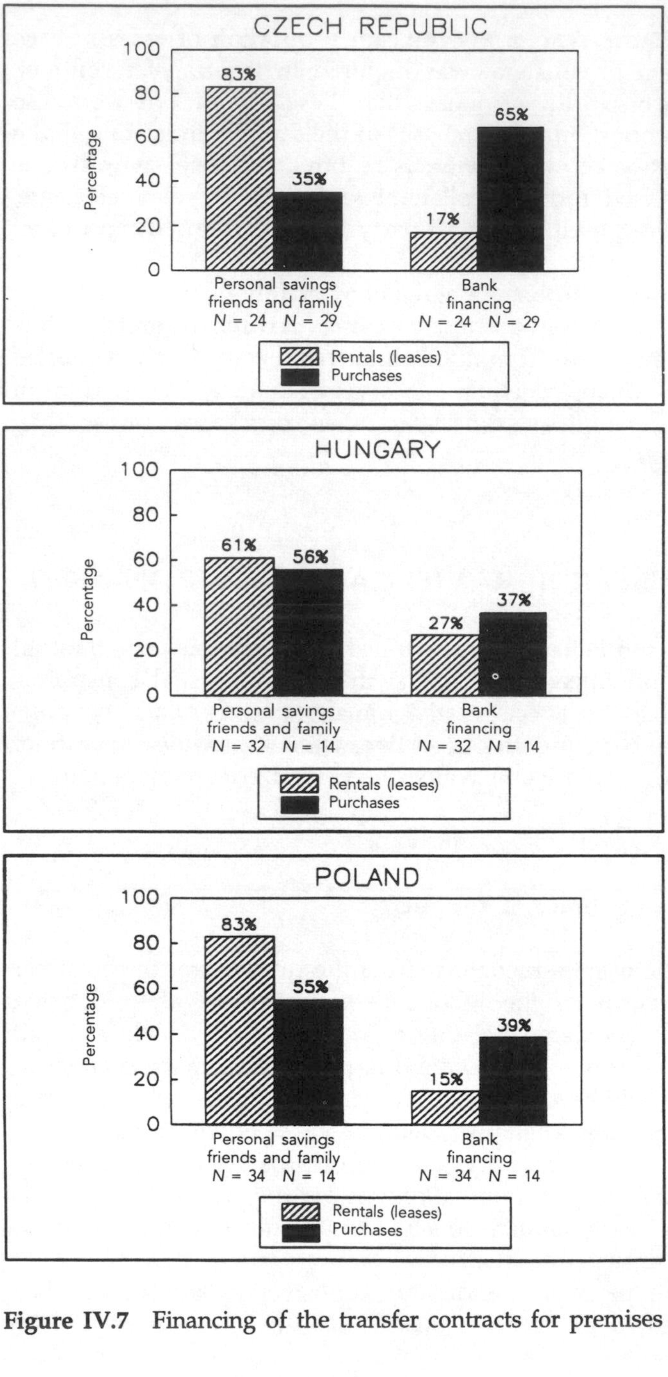

Figure IV.7 Financing of the transfer contracts for premises

noted, however, as a caveat to our description of the changes in the retail area, that the process of reform in all three countries we examine has proceeded simultaneously in the retail and the wholesale sectors. For this reason, some of the results detected in our sample may not be easily reproducible in other countries of the region, where resistance to the reform of the wholesale sector may be stronger and change may be slower in coming.

Having said this, we should add that our survey is not without implications for the debate about the relative priorities of the reform in the retail and wholesale sectors. In fact, it provides some evidence for both points of view, although the evidence for the "upstream push" by the reform of the retail sector is somewhat more direct and perhaps stronger.

The strongest evidence for the existence of "upstream push" is contained in Figure IV.8, which reports the proportions of supplies delivered to the retail units in the sample through various means of transportation.

The most striking feature in the graph is, of course, the proportion of supplies delivered in the vehicles owned by the units themselves. This figure, which reaches 65 percent in Poland, shows that, if all else fails, private retailers themselves are able to organize a very powerful substitute for a functioning system of wholesaling. The extent to which they are able to do this depends, of course, on the availability of means of transport, and in this case the Polish story is also instructive. Apparently, in the wake of the tightening of the budget constraint of state enterprises, as a result of the Balcerowicz stabilization plan of 1990, many enterprises, strapped for cash, sold off a part of their stock of trucks to private individuals. This increase in supply of transport vehicles made possible a very rapid expansion of the new private wholesale sector. While we have no information on the source of the large number of private trucks in use in Hungary and the Czech Republic, the universality of the phenomenon indicates that the very fact of "upstream demand" may be a significant factor in generating increased supply.

Under conditions of unconstrained choice, the retailers' perceptions of the quality of various sources of supply drive the shifts from one source to another. It was important, therefore, to examine the way in which retailers in the three countries viewed the relative merits and demerits of private and state suppliers. For this purpose, respondents in each country were asked to evaluate each source of supplies (state, cooperative, and private) along five dimensions: price, timeliness, assortment of

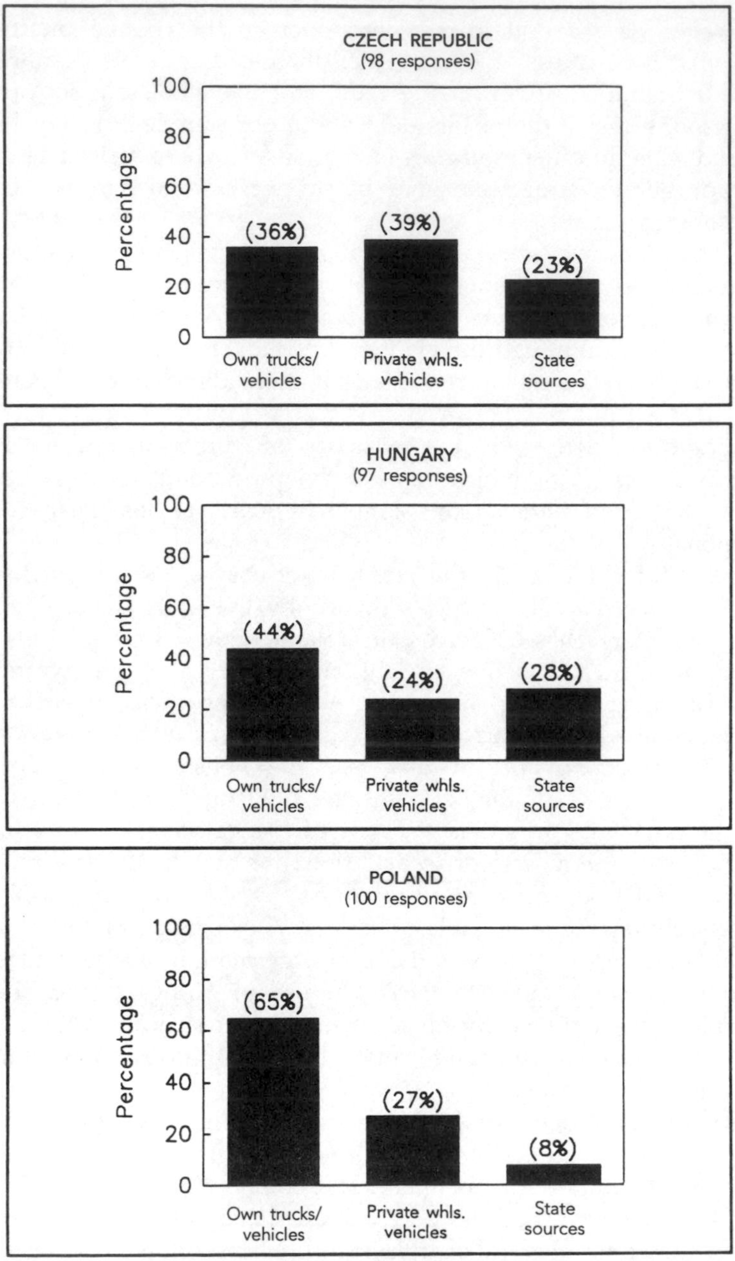

Figure IV.8 Mode of transport used for supplies

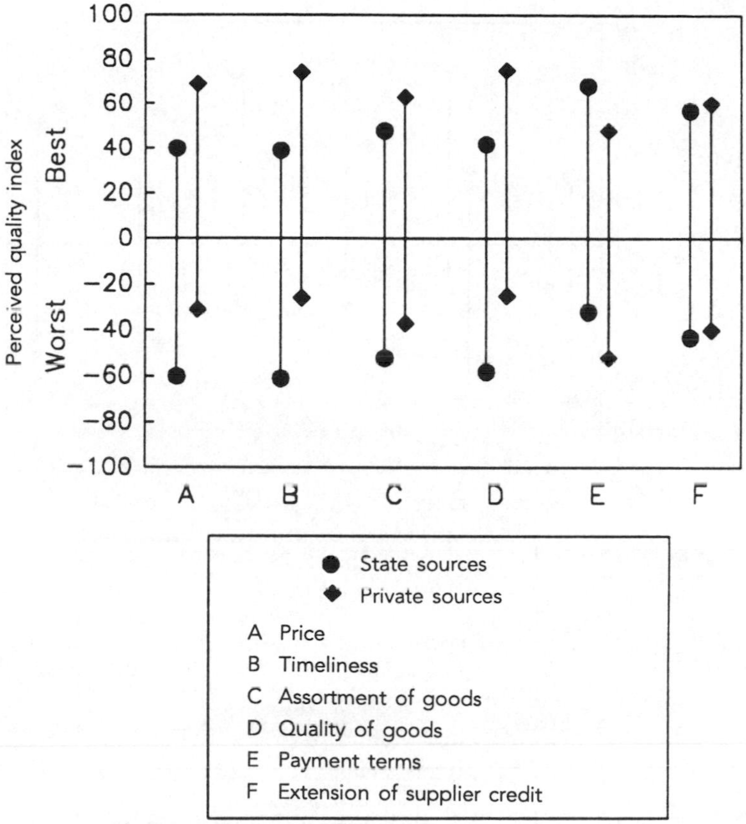

Figure IV.9 Perceived quality of suppliers according to various criteria: Czech Republic

goods, quality of goods, terms of payment, and extension of supplier credit.[22] Each supplier could be ranked as "best" or "worst" on each of the dimensions. The results of this examination of the relative merits and demerits of state and private suppliers are presented in Figures IV.9–IV.11.[23] The top of each vertical bar on the graphs points to the number

[22] The difference between the last two categories is that extension of supplier credit refers to extension of payment terms once the customer fails to make timely payments.
[23] The cooperative suppliers were omitted because of the small number of responses.

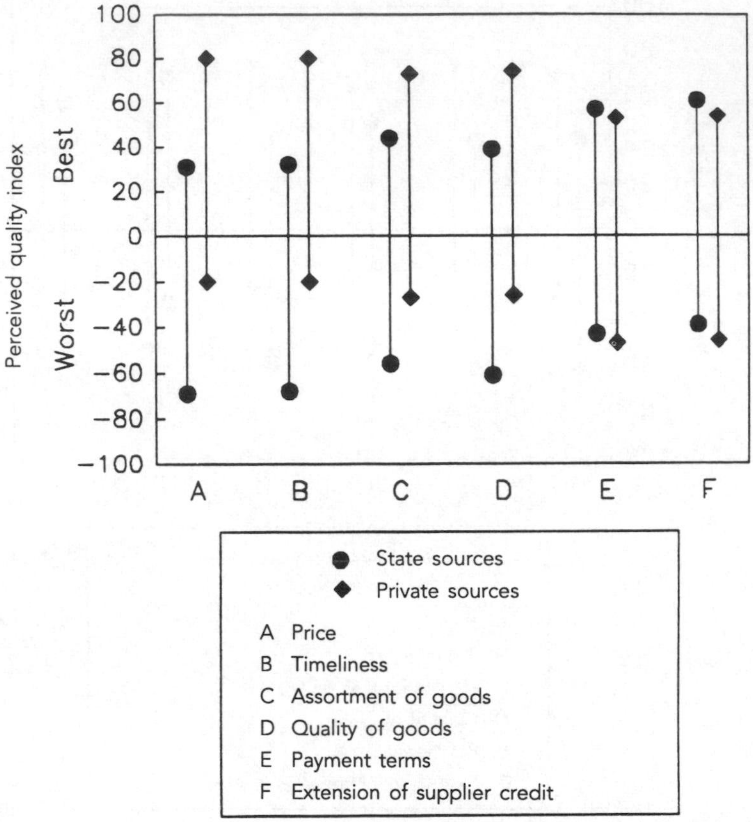

Figure IV.10 Perceived quality of suppliers according to various criteria: Hungary

of "bests" received by a given supplier along a given dimension as a proportion of the sum of all "bests" and "worsts." The lowest point of each bar points to the proportion of "worsts" to the same total, so that the higher the position of the vertical bar, the higher the overall evaluation of the supplier along that dimension.

A rather interesting fact comes to light when the results reported in Figures IV.9–IV.11 are compared with those in Figure IV.12. In all three countries, the respondents, as a group, nearly uniformly ranked private suppliers above state suppliers on all dimensions – indeed, only in one

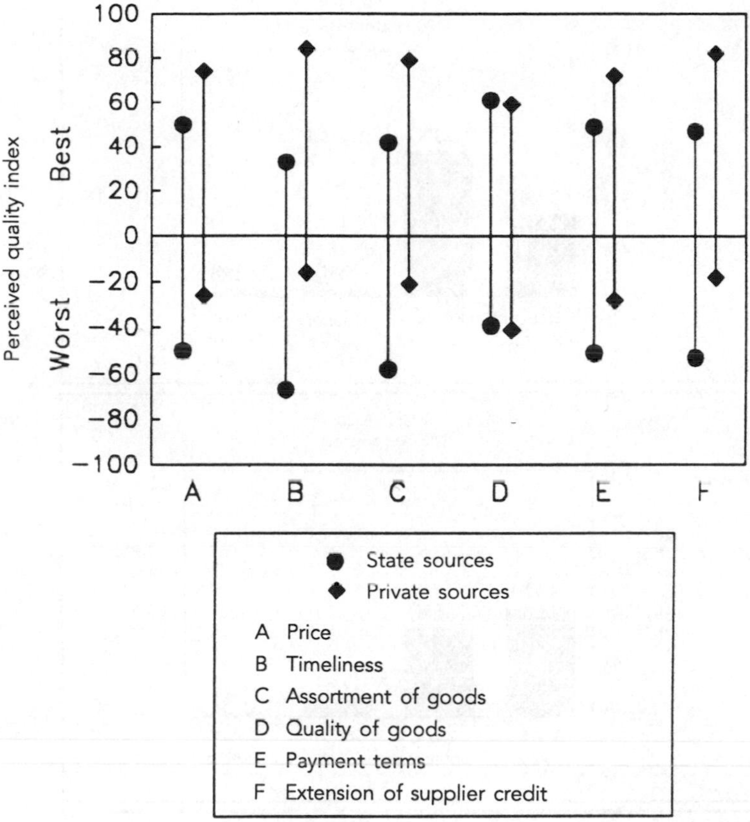

Figure IV.11 Perceived quality of suppliers according to various criteria: Poland

case and on one dimension (extension of credit in the Czech Republic) were state suppliers ranked significantly higher than the private ones. The rankings of private suppliers become even higher when only previous outsiders are polled, which points to the slower pace at which the old managers in the state sector change their minds. But some of the highest ratings of private suppliers on all counts other than those relating to payment terms and extension of credit can be seen in Hungary, and even on these two dimensions the state and private suppliers are quite comparable. Yet, Hungary is the country with the

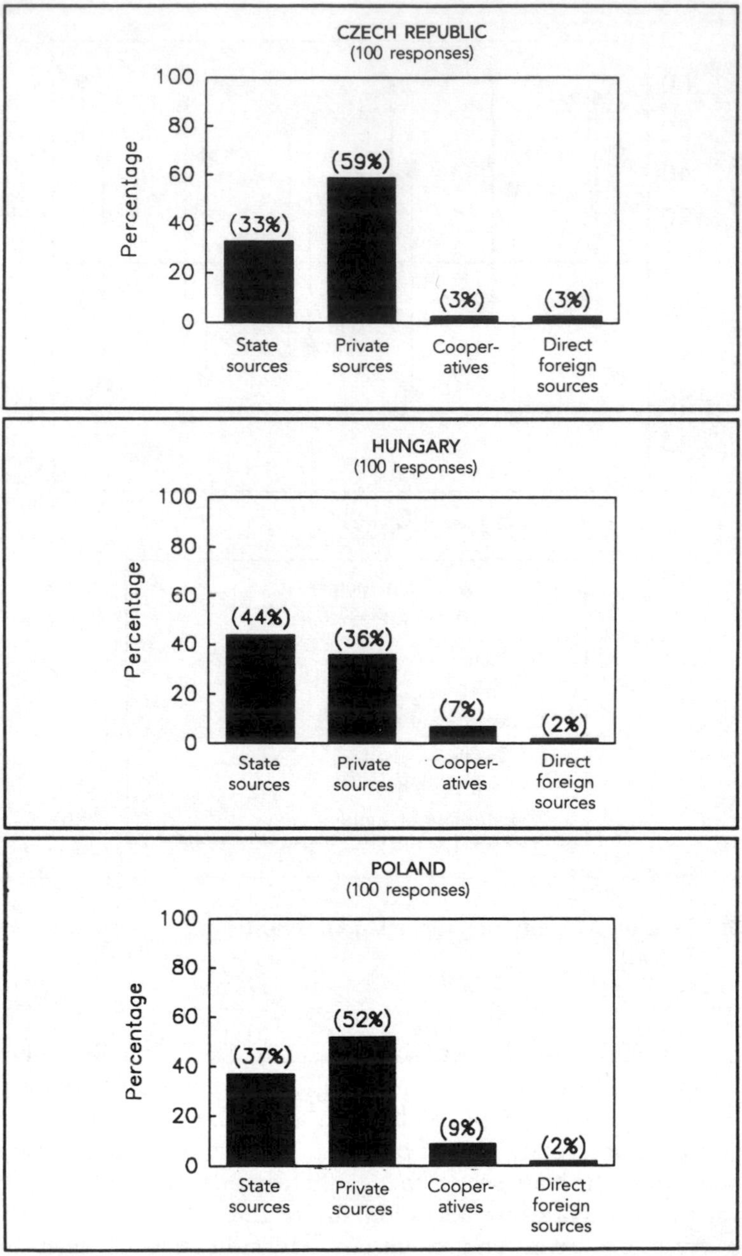

Figure IV.12 Percentage of supplies obtained from different sources

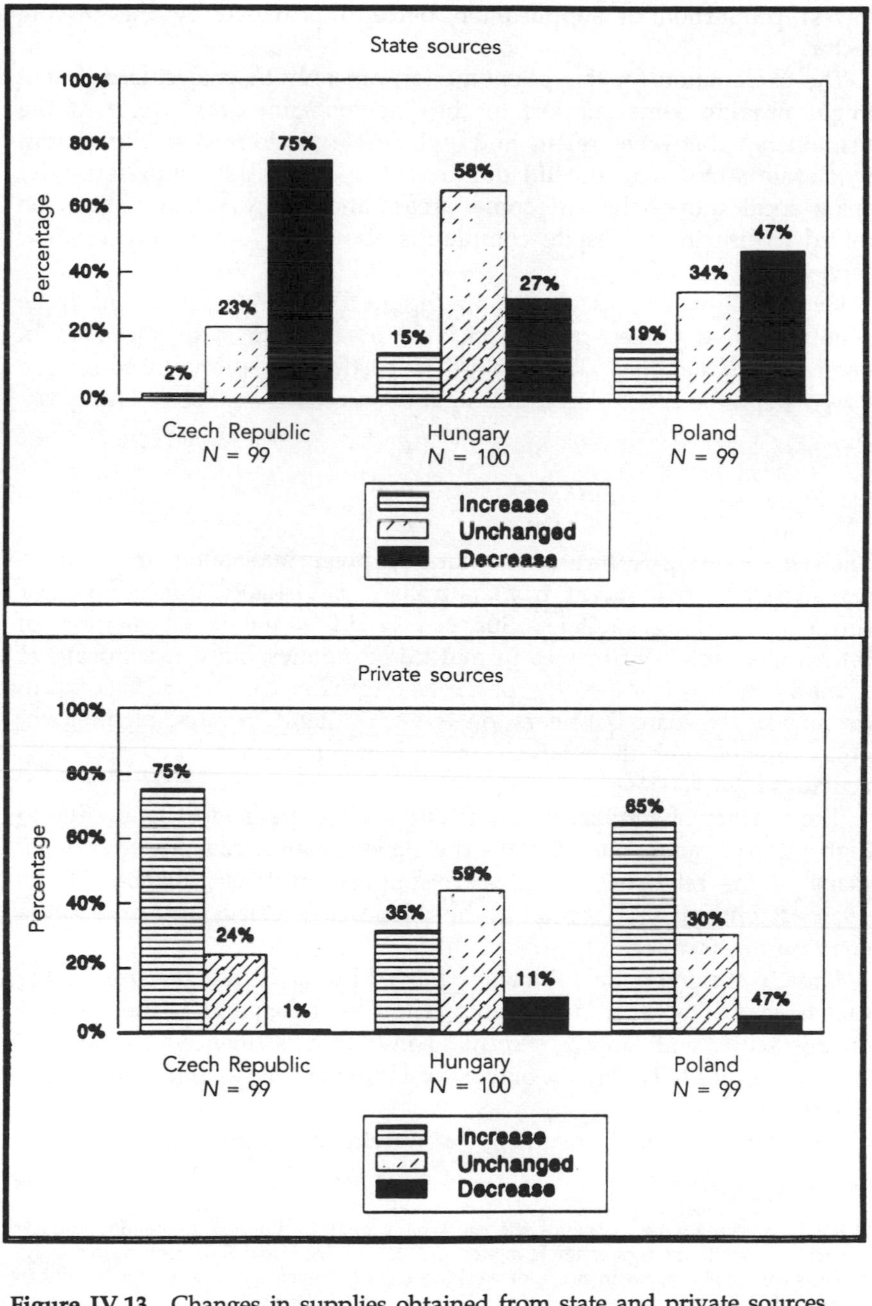

Figure IV.13 Changes in supplies obtained from state and private sources

lowest proportion of supplies (36 percent) provided by the private sector.

The explanation for this phenomenon can only be conjectured, but it might provide some support to the "downstream drag" view of the relationship between retail and wholesale sectors: the Hungarian wholesale sector may be still dominated by large state suppliers who enjoy local monopolies in some areas, and many retailers may be forced to use them, despite complaints about the low quality of their services.

Overall, however, as shown in Figure IV.13, retailers in all three countries have moved quite decisively away from state suppliers in favor of private ones. The change is particularly pronounced in the Czech Republic and Poland, and again somewhat weaker in Hungary.

5.2. Financing of operations

The most striking feature of the data on postprivatization financing in the survey is that credit from suppliers is virtually unavailable for financing working capital.[24] Supplier credit is the usual method of financing of retail businesses in mature economies, since monitoring of small businesses is too costly for banks and other creditors in relation to the size of the loan. Suppliers, on the other hand, because of their ongoing relation with the retailers, are in a better position to oversee their activities.

The absence of supplier credit in Eastern Europe is most likely due to high interest rates coupled with the newness and transitional state of many of the relationships between suppliers and new owners of the retail establishments. Turmoil in the wholesale sector is also probably a contributing factor.

Equally striking is the minor role played by the banking system in the financing of long-term investments. The Czech Republic is the weakest on this score, with only 9 percent of investments financed by banks.[25] The figures are only slightly higher for Hungary (18 percent) and Poland (26 percent).

The scarcity of bank financing for investment purposes appears to be

[24] In our Czech sample, none of the working capital is reported to be financed by suppliers, while the figures for Hungary and Poland are 5 and 7 percent, respectively.
[25] Not surprisingly, bank financing of working capital is even more limited: 4 percent in the Czech Republic, and 11 percent in Hungary and Poland.

one of the important factors affecting investment levels and ownership structure of small businesses in the area. In a situation in which bank financing is unavailable and private wealth is small, individuals wishing to expand their businesses must turn to other equity contributors and change the structure of ownership of their businesses. This effect is very pronounced in our sample, where partnerships in Poland and Hungary[26] were found to invest significantly more in the remodeling of their units following privatization: while individual owners invested, on the average, $4,199, partnerships invested $6,349. The difference is still more pronounced when only outsider owners are considered, and the sample mean of investment for partnerships skyrockets to $8,224. At the same time, as shown in Figure IV.14, partnerships formed by insiders do not show significant growth in posttransfer investment levels, and the explanation probably is that the motivation with which they are formed has more to with the need to share preferential acquisition terms, rather than the pooling of investment resources.

The fact that partnerships may be an imperative of properly funded business may modify the usual assumption that single- or family-owned businesses managed by the owners themselves are optimal for most shops and catering establishments in the region. But the encouragement of shared ownership also potentially creates some problems for the governance structure of small businesses and its effects should be further investigated.

5.3. Employment patterns

Figure IV.15 presents the average employment per unit in each country. The larger average of the Hungarian stores is in part due to the fact that the sample contained eleven stores with over twenty employees, but even the elimination of a few outliers would leave the average size of a Hungarian unit somewhat larger than in the other two countries. Another interesting fact is that in both Hungary and the Czech Republic the average employment per unit in the sample is growing, but this is not the case in Poland, where the number of both managerial and nonmanagerial employees is smaller than it was at the time of transfer.

[26] There were no partnerships in our sample in the Czech Republic.

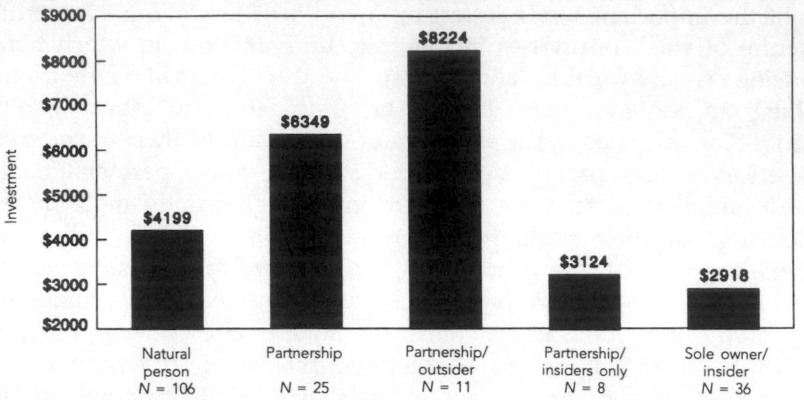

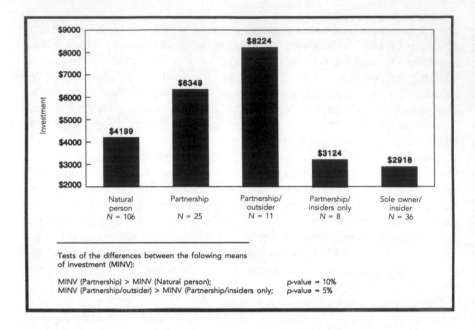

Tests of the differences between the folowing means of investment (MINV):

MINV (Partnership) > MINV (Natural person); p-value = 10%
MINV (Partnership/outsider) > MINV (Partnership/insiders only; p-value = 5%

Note: The tests reported in the figures of this chapter refer to the standard t-tests for the differences in the means. In order to compute the value of the test statistic and the number of degrees of freedom, the t-tests were accompanied by the test of equality of variances of the tested populations.

P-values are reported only if they are smaller than 20%. For sample sizes *smaller than 30* these results should be treated with caution, since the exact validity of the t-tests for small samples requires normality of the underlying populations. Although small samples preclude statistical tests of normality, the underlying population is unlikely to be normally distributed. Many of the investments are likely to be bunched at lower values, making at least the lower tail "too fat."

Figure IV.14 Partnerships and investment in remodeling of premises

(This result obtains despite the highest number of former insiders in the Polish sample.) The changes over time in the average number of employees per unit should not, however, be taken as an indication of the overall changes of employment in the sector; in fact, the number of units in all countries grew exponentially in the wake of the reforms, and the consumer sector represents one of the few dynamic areas of growth in the three economies.

A strong increase in the ratio of managerial to nonmanagerial

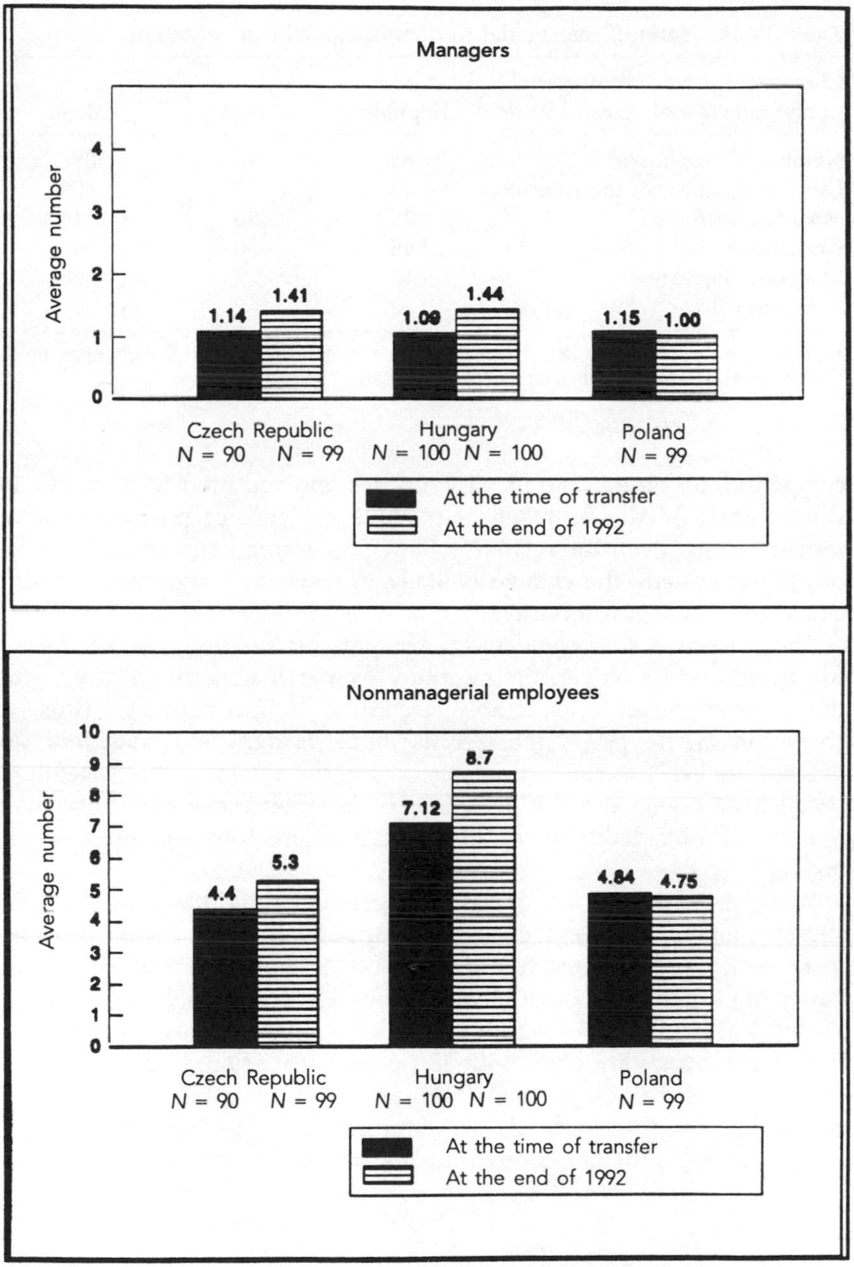

Figure IV.15 Average employment (per unit)

Table IV.14 Ratio of managerial to nonmanagerial compensation

Changes of ratio of managerial to non-managerial compensation	Czech Republic	Hungary	Poland
Number of responses[1]	85	78	85
Large increase since the transfer	13	3	5
Moderate increase	23	18	34
Unchanged	48	50	39
Moderate decrease	1	7	7
Large decrease	0	0	0

[1] Number of interviewees who responded to the question about the changes in the compensation structure in their establishments.

compensation, observable in all countries and reported in Table IV.14, should undoubtedly be taken as positive evidence of postprivatization restructuring. Given the relatively flat compensation curve characteristic of the old system, the change is likely to result in a significant modification of managerial incentives.

The survey also provides information about the fate of former managers and employees. How many former managers get fired after the transfer varies considerably according to the country. Thus, as shown in Figure IV.16, the Czechs, both insiders and outsiders, are much more likely to fire old managers, and the outsiders are particularly brutal in applying the axe. By contrast, in Poland, even in units taken over by the outsiders, the rate of retention of previous managers is very high.

While the retention rate of old managers in Poland has been high, the survey contains some evidence of a search for a more rational employment policy on the part of the small units. Both the employees and newly hired managers must have been fired at a very high rate, since, as shown in Figure IV.17, overall labor turnover in the units sampled in Poland has been very high, with 43 percent of managers and 76 percent of nonmanagerial employees fired since the transfer. This may be considered as evidence of restructuring and perhaps also as an indication of a shift of power from the workers to the managers.[27]

[27] There is even some evidence that former managers of state units fire more workers after transfer than do outsider owners in Poland.

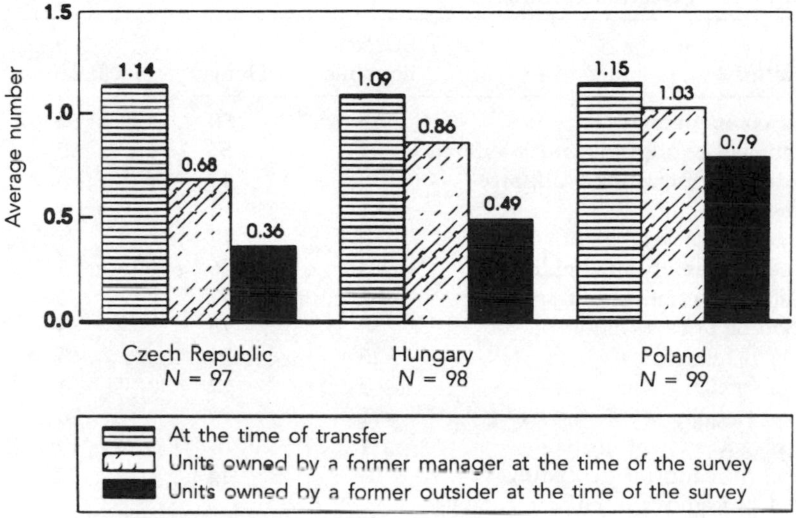

Figure IV.16 Average number of former managers

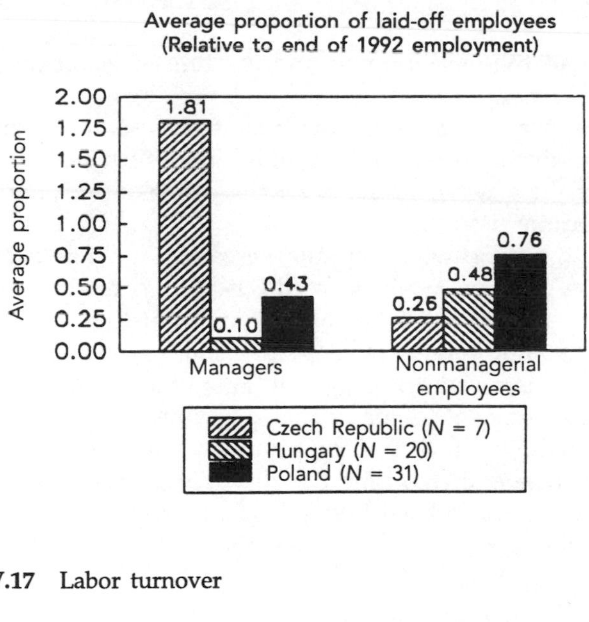

Figure IV.17 Labor turnover

Table IV.15 Perceived constraints

Constraint	Czech Republic	Hungary	Poland
Strong competition[1]	13	50	50
Government regulations and interference	54	51	10
Poor quality of existing workforce	15	13	8
Shortage of labor	11	12	4
High cost or lack of credit	83	77	74
Limited availability of supplies	23	16	4
Problems with delivery of supplies	22	11	4
Inflation or price stability	58	78	83
Lack of demand	25	59	65
Lack of foreign exchange	0	2	4
Political stability	11	19	26
Corrupt government officials	14	8	13
Difficult bureaucratic procedures	53	44	24
Lack of procedures to enforce contracts with customers and suppliers	11	7	7
Legal uncertainty	31	30	64

[1] The table shows the number of respondents who listed a given constraint as a critical one affecting their operations.

5.4. Perceptions of the environment and the role of government

The respondents' perceptions of the constraints imposed on them by the environment in which they have to operate, presented in Table IV.15, confirm some of the analysis in the previous sections of this survey and raise other interesting issues.

The two most significant constraints perceived by the respondents were clearly the lack of available credit (which correlates with our discussion of the financing of operations) and inflation (which could also be related to high interest rates of financing). Rather interestingly, strong competition is a serious concern in Poland and Hungary, where complaints about lack of demand for goods is also a subject of complaint, while both of these appear much less important in the Czech Republic, where, at the time the survey was taken, the changes in the sector may not have been fully felt yet. Perhaps surprisingly, not many respondents complain about the availability and delivery of supplies.

Table IV.16 Ownership structure and government assistance (pooled data)

Type of assistance	Sole owner/ insider	Sole owner/ outsider
Number of responses[1]	69	93
Number of units reporting to have received government assistance	3	0
Number of responses[2]	69	88
Number of interviewees alleging preferential treatment by state agencies of their state-owned competitors	10	20

[1] Number of interviewees (insiders or outsiders) who responded to the question about government assistance.
[2] Number of interviewees (insiders or outsiders) who responded to the question about the preferential treatment of their competitors.

A whole new set of issues is raised by the perceptions of the legal system and governmental actions. The respondents evidently do not see government corruption or political instability as very important factors, but both Czechs and Hungarians worry about governmental interference and bureaucratic obstacles (both of which seem to be relatively minor concerns to the Poles). Contrary to the concern of many Westerners, the respondents do not seem to be very worried by difficulties with contract enforcement, but they do worry considerably (especially in Poland) about "legal uncertainty," by which they most likely mean the insecurity of property entitlements. Former insiders, who often acquired their property on preferential terms, may be particularly worried about the insecurity of property rights, and the survey contains evidence that the insiders who complain of legal uncertainty also invest less in postprivatization restructuring.

Additional information concerning perceptions of the role of government is presented in Table IV.16, which shows that a substantial proportion of respondents believes that the government still favors state enterprises competing with newly privatized units. Further examination of responses in individual countries also shows a near total absence of government-sponsored training. A significant gloss on the question of government assistance is that in all the Polish cases it was rendered to a former insider.

6. BEHAVIORAL IMPLICATIONS OF THE TRANSFER CONTRACT

This and the next two sections will focus on the effect of various features of the transfer process and postprivatization ownership structure on the behavior of privatized units following the transfer. The study will be centered primarily around one outcome variable – the level of investment in the wake of privatization – defining a crucial feature of the restructuring process in Eastern Europe.

The survey was originally designed to develop a number of additional outcome variables, such as profit rate, labor market flows, revenues, assortment of goods, and debt restructuring. Unfortunately, only limited use could be made of most of these additional variables, because of the paucity of answers – apparently a large number of respondents refused to divulge information concerning some basic facets of their business, such as revenue or profits – or because of too small variation in the data, not allowing for a level of differentiation required for relating the answers to other important facets of the transfer process.

6.1. Levels of investment and restructuring in the sample

Investment in the remodeling of premises in the wake of privatization is used in this study as a proxy for long-term investment in the unit. The physical stock of the consumer trade and service outlets under the old regime was run down and woefully inadequate to satisfy the needs of the population. While the elimination of shortages and an increase in the assortment of goods was the most pressing need in countries such as Poland, a sizeable investment in the remodeling of premises, improving their appearance and functionality, and furnishing them in accordance with the standards customary in advanced Western countries was necessary to bring the consumer trade and service sector up to par.

In using levels of investment in remodeling as a proxy for post-privatization restructuring, we had to make a decision whether the value of this variable should be scaled, so that investment should be measured in relation to some proxy for the size of the business. The most obvious candidate here was the floor-space occupied by the business, but other variables, such as the number of employees, could also be contemplated.

In the event, we decided against scaling of the investment variable. A technical reason was that the data from our sample concerning floor-space seemed to us unreliable in some respects, and the floor-space of many businesses was changing precisely as a result of remodeling. Similarly, employment did not seem to be a proper measure, since most businesses in our sample employed very few people and the resulting differentiation would not be sufficient. Furthermore, other factors, such as the line of business of the remodeled units, requiring very different types of adjustments, were clearly important in determining the size of postprivatization investment, so that it was not clear that looking at investment in terms of any one or another measure of size would be appropriate.

There were also other, more general reasons against scaling the investment variable. To begin with, investment in remodeling was uncorrelated with floor-space in our sample, which confirmed our doubts about the advisability of using it as a scaling variable. Most importantly, we did not believe that investment in remodeling, under the postprivatization conditions in Eastern Europe, was essentially a marginal decision. Instead, we saw it as a major turn-around step, with the new owners, constrained by their human capital, inertia, and financial resources, making a judgment pertaining to the aggregate level of restructuring for a given small unit.

Another problem we faced in using investment in remodeling as a proxy for postprivatization restructuring was that even for this variable, despite attempts at reinterviewing, some of the responses were either clearly not representative of the units in the region, or were simply unreliable. While the median level of postprivatization investment in our sample was below \$3,000, some respondents listed figures in excess of \$100,000 for establishments with 30 square meters (330 square feet) of display space. Since such levels of investment seemed completely out of line with those reported by over 80 percent of units in our sample, their inclusion would bias the results. Therefore, in order to preclude *ex post* data-mining and the possibility of the bias, we decided, *prior to the analysis and without knowing whom we excluded,* to eliminate from the sample all units reporting investment levels over \$30,000.

At the lower end of the range of values of investment figures, some interviewees gave figures as low as \$100, which hardly qualify as proxies for a restructuring variable and probably refer to a type of

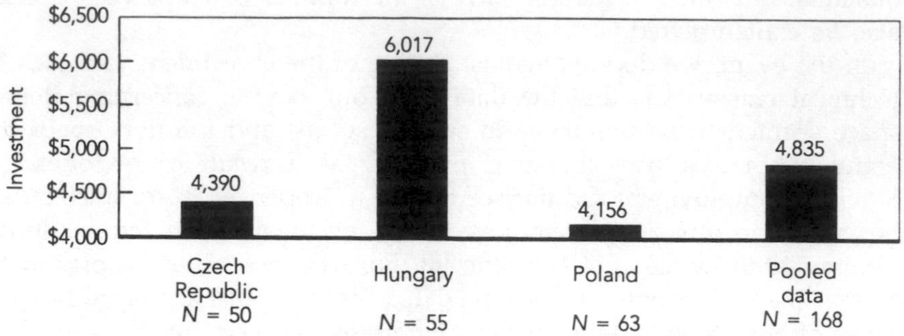

Tests of the differences between the following means of investment (MINV):

MINV (Hungary) > MINV (Poland); *p*-value = 5%
MINV (Hungary) > MINV (Czech Republic); *p*-value = 5%
MINV (Czech Republic) = MINV (Poland)

Figure IV.18 Investment in remodeling of premises

expense other than genuine remodeling. In order to minimize the possibility of a selection bias, we therefore eliminated from our sample all units reporting "investment" levels of less than $500.

In addition to excluding the outliers by the mechanical rules described above, closer examination of the data revealed that five units in the sample were purchased by their former managers at very high price ratios and showed very high posttransfer investment levels. These units, all of which were in the Czech Republic, probably represented special cases involving particularly attractive businesses and they raised the sample mean of investment in the Czech Republic by approximately 40 percent. Anecdotal evidence from the Czech Republic also indicated that many insiders in such situations were merely "fronts" for "silent partners" (usually foreigners) who were the real principals. Since the levels of investment by new insider owners of these five units were clearly not representative of the usual behavior of insiders in our sample, their inclusion would seriously bias the results. We have therefore decided to exclude them from the sample in all the subsequent discussions. A further examination of the sample revealed three similar cases of outsider owners (one in each country), and these were also eliminated.

Figure IV.18 shows the sample means of the levels of investment in remodeling (in US$)[28] in each of the three countries.[29]

6.2. Debt and its impact on investment

One of the decisions to be made in the context of small privatization is whether units in the sector should be liquidated and their assets sold to private parties, or whether they should be privatized as going concerns. One of the arguments against privatization of going concerns is that saddling new owners with the obligations of old state businesses may interfere with their restructuring efforts.

Although a question concerning precisely the issue of the assumption of debts at the time of transfer was included in the questionnaire, the responses cast some doubt on whether all interviewees properly understood what was being asked. From various pieces of circumstantial evidence, it appears that some respondents included the bank debt with which they financed the transfer as the debt assumed, and others may have done the same in connection with their taking over some supply or inventory from previous owners. But even if the correct and incorrect answers cannot always be distinguished, the important factor in this context is the very fact of indebtedness, rather than its source.[30]

However, as shown in Figure IV.19, the survey did not yield conclusive results concerning the impact of indebtedness at the time of transfer. Although the sample mean of investment for units with no financial obligations is much higher than for the indebted units, the difference is not statistically significant.

6.3. The impact of contract uncertainty and lease restrictions

Another important feature determining the level of investment is the degree of uncertainty of the title to the most important assets of the

[28] The following exchange rates were used in this study: Csk 28 = $1, Ft 75 = $1, Zl 13,000 = $1.

[29] About 25 percent of the respondents did not report the levels of investment in their units. The units with missing observations were excluded from the analysis.

[30] In addition to the burden of debt, taking over a going concern may also have other negative features, such as a lock into existing labor contracts, and the difficulty of overcoming the inertia of the old ways of doing business.

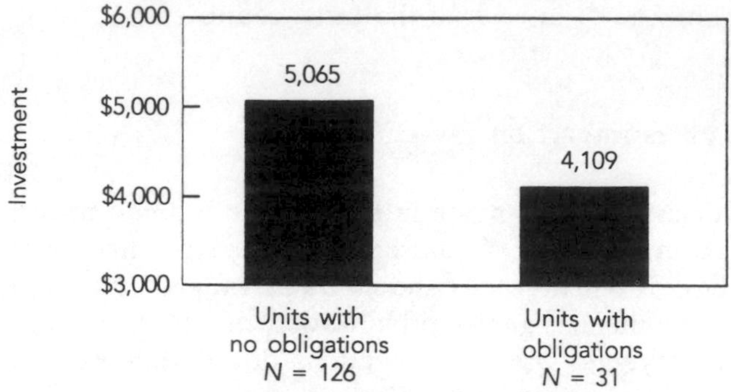

Test of the difference between the following means of investment (MINV):

MINV (Units with no obligations) = MINV (Units with obligations)

Figure IV.19 Indebtedness at the time of transfer and investment in remodeling of premises

business; in this case, the premises. As shown in Figure IV.20, when the pooled sample for all three countries is considered, *the respondents have a pronounced preference for outright ownership over lease contracts*, and the businesses that own their premises show much higher mean levels of postprivatization investment. Even an option to purchase raises the mean level of investment in our sample, but this result is not statistically significant. The strong preference for purchases over leases is somewhat surprising. As we have pointed out before (in the section on gmina privatization in Poland), one would ordinarily expect businesses leasing their premises, even if they had reasonable security of renewal at ordinary market rates, to be somewhat less certain about the cost of their lease, and thus to have a preference for outright ownership. But, after all, most shops in the West are operated on leased premises and this does not seem to have a very pronounced effect on either investment or other desirable business behavior. In some countries of Eastern Europe, however, the behavior of tenant-businesses stands in such a marked contrast to that of businesses that own their premises that other factors are likely to be involved.

There are several possible explanations of the preference for purchases

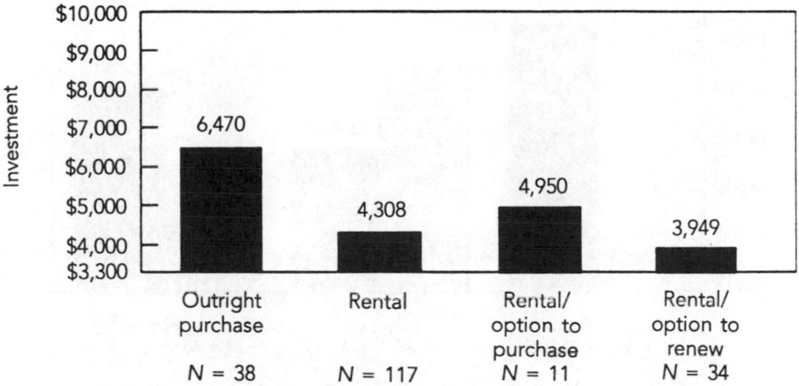

Test of the differences between the following means of investment (MINV):

MINV (Outright purchase) > MINV (Rental); *p*-value = 3%
MINV (Rental/option to purchase) = MINV (Rental/option to renew)

Figure IV.20 Effects of contract uncertainty on investment in remodeling of premises: pooled data

over leases. One is the tenant's weak bargaining position *vis à vis* his or her landlord, who is often a municipality or a powerful state institution, frequently with a near monopoly on the real estate of a given kind. In this situation, it is likely that the new businessmen do not expect their landlords to behave like ordinary market participants, but rather anticipate that they might use their market position to extract all kinds of unexpected concessions.

But there may also be another explanation: the fact that rentals, especially in Poland and the Czech Republic are usually of very short duration (sample mean of four years, with a large number of under two years).[31] Indeed, a closer examination of our sample, Figure IV.21, reveals that the preference for rentals over leases is very pronounced in Poland and the Czech Republic, but not in Hungary, where the average length of rental is seven years.

[31] Cf. Table IV.9.

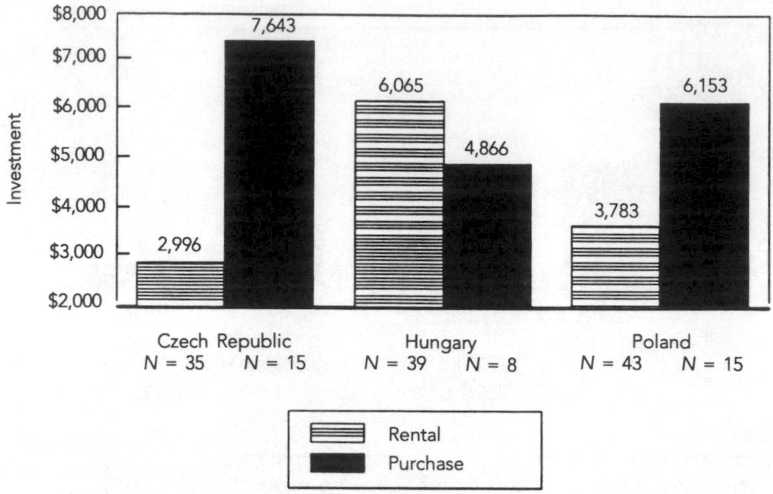

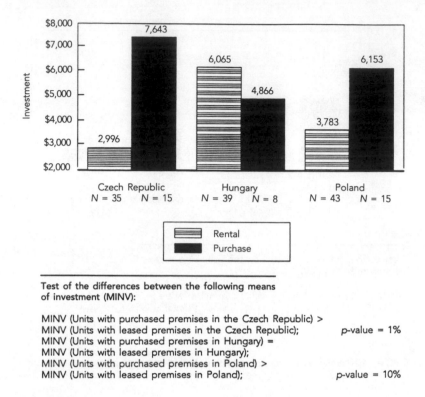

Test of the differences between the following means of investment (MINV):

MINV (Units with purchased premises in the Czech Republic) >
MINV (Units with leased premises in the Czech Republic); *p*-value = 1%
MINV (Units with purchased premises in Hungary) =
MINV (Units with leased premises in Hungary);
MINV (Units with purchased premises in Poland) >
MINV (Units with leased premises in Poland); *p*-value = 10%

Figure IV.21 Investment in remodeling of rented or purchased premises

Independent evidence in our study also shows that *contract duration is one of the crucial driving forces of postprivatization investment*: as shown in Figure IV.22, units with leases with terms longer than five years had, on the average, more than double the investment rate of the units with leases shorter than five years.[32]

Unfortunately, because of the size of the sample and the limited number of valid responses, no firm conclusions could be drawn with respect to the impact that restrictions on sublet and resale may have on the levels of postprivatization investments. While there is some evidence that units without restrictions on sublet or resale invest more than those

[32] There appears, however, to be some lack of monotonicity for durations of less than five years. It is not clear whether this fact is due to sample variation or other factors affecting contracts with short durations.

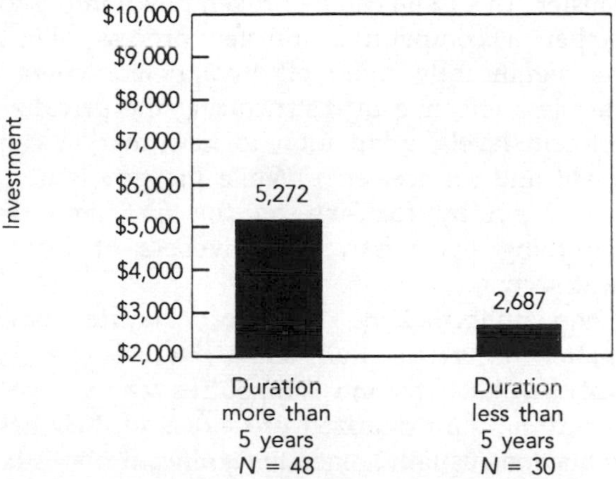

Test of the difference between the following means of investment (MINV):

MINV (Duration more than 5 years) > MINV (Duration less than 5 years);

p-value = 1%

Figure IV.22 Duration of rental contracts and investment in remodeling of premises: pooled data

with such restrictions, the average investment in the restricted units is still higher than the overall average, which suggests that perhaps the restrictions are imposed on the more valuable properties in the first place.

7. BEHAVIORAL IMPLICATIONS OF THE COMPETITIVENESS OF THE MODE OF TRANSFER

Perhaps the most often debated issue, and one of the most important questions for policymakers, in the context of small privatization is whether granting preferences to former employees in the acquisition of the privatized units adversely affects the behavior of the those units in the wake of the transfer. This issue can be broken down into two related problems: 1) whether a competitive transfer process allocates the privatized units to significantly more effective new owners, and 2) whether insiders are less effective in restructuring the privatized units (in terms of investment levels, adaptation to new market conditions, improving assortment and service, etc.). While the two issues are not unrelated, we shall begin by focusing on the first, and defer the considerations concerning the relative effectiveness of insiders and outsiders to the next section.

Commentators and policymakers in many countries have often assumed as a matter of course that using market-type allocation procedures, such as open auctions and competitive tenders, is the most effective way of allocating the privatized properties to their best users. Even though open auctions usually generate significant opposition from insiders threatened with loss of control and possible unemployment, which may, in some countries, slow the process or perhaps even doom it to failure, there has been significant pressure to use them in all small privatizations.

7.1. The effect of open vs. closed procedures

Open procedures (auctions and open tenders), when looked at only from the point of view of whether they result in a better allocation of the privatized units, seem to be significantly preferable to transfers with no outsider participation (closed procedures), since, as shown in Figure IV.23, *investment in units transferred through open procedures*[33] is, on the average, significantly higher.

Figure IV.24 in turn parcels out the binary division between open and closed procedures among three categories: that of auctions, open tenders, and closed procedures (which may or may not be competitive), and looks at their effect on investment. Perhaps surprisingly, the figure shows that open tenders yield, on the average, the highest investment levels of all the modes of transfer in our sample. One reason for this

[33] In order to achieve a large group of relatively homogeneous cases and allow for a clearer interpretation of the factors behind the results, we have eliminated from our sample the cases of sales of premises, and limited our analysis to the cases of rentals. Given the small number of sales in many categories of transfers, the inclusion of sales would make it very difficult to separate the effect of sales from that of other factors.

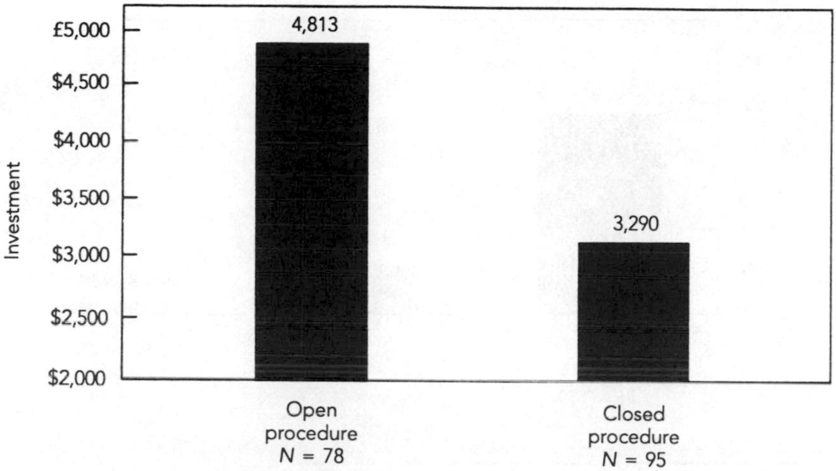

Test of the difference between the following means of investment (MINV):

MINV (Open procedure) > MINV (Closed procedure); *p*-value = 5%

Figure IV.23 Competitiveness of the transfer process and investment in remodeling of premises: pooled data

may be that a promise of high postprivatization investment is one of the criteria used for choosing the winners of open tenders. The other side of the same coin may be that prices paid in open tenders may be lowered in exchange for promises to invest, thus lessening the problem of the shortage of capital, which is one of the factors responsible for low postprivatization investment.

7.2. Auctions

Another surprising result in Figure IV.24 is that *auctions are not clearly superior to closed procedures*: although the mean investment level for auctions is numerically higher, the difference is not statistically significant. This result is all the more striking, given the fact that contracts obtained through auctions are, on the average, of significantly

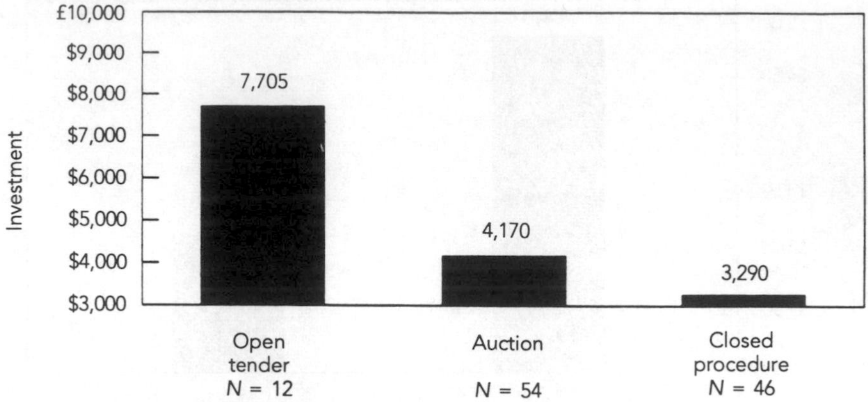

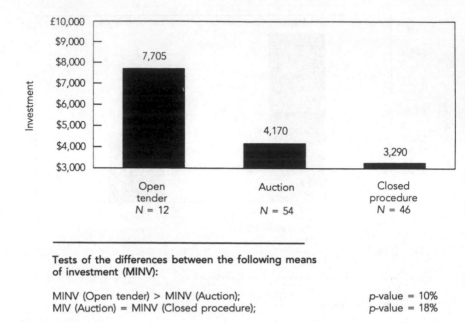

Tests of the differences between the following means of investment (MINV):

MINV (Open tender) > MINV (Auction);	*p*-value = 10%
MIV (Auction) = MINV (Closed procedure);	*p*-value = 18%

Table IV.24 Investment in remodeling of premises and the mode of transfer of rental contracts: pooled data

longer duration than those entered into as a result of closed procedures.[34] Since contract duration is a strong factor in increasing postprivatization investment levels (see Figure IV.22), longer contracts should boost the effect of auctions on investment. Despite this, however, the effect of auctions remains inconclusive (with a *p*-value of 18 percent).

A large body of evidence outside the survey points to certain disadvantages of auctions and other highly competitive procedures. We have noted in the section on gmina privatization in Poland that auctions often led to exorbitant prices and consequent bankruptcies of new businesses. Similar evidence is also anecdotally available for the Czech Republic,[35] and our survey confirms that auctions have led to higher

[34] In fact, the difference between the average length of auction contracts (5.28 years) and closed procedure contracts (3.82 years) is significant at 0.3 percent. (We may also note parenthetically that the difference in mean duration of open-tender contracts and auction contracts is not statistically significant, and thus the higher investment levels in open tenders cannot be attributed to the influence of duration.)

price ratios in our sample. One might have expected, therefore, that auctions would reveal an inverse relationship between price ratios[36] and postprivatization investment, since highly competitive pricing under conditions of capital shortage would be likely to lead to lower investment. Our survey contains only indirect and inconclusive evidence on this point. The survey does contain strong evidence that, across all modes of transfer, higher price ratios are associated with lower postprivatization investments.[37] Since the survey also shows that auctions lead to higher price ratios, these two facts combined suggest the effect of diminishing investments in auctions as well. But no such effect was obtained directly.[38]

8. BEHAVIORAL IMPLICATIONS OF POSTPRIVATIZATION OWNERSHIP STRUCTURE

We have now come to perhaps the most important factor affecting postprivatization restructuring revealed by our survey: the difference between former insiders and outsiders as owners of the privatized businesses. As shown in Figure IV.25, *outsiders, on the average, invest much more than insiders*. Moreover, this result, which is statistically significant at a very high level (0.5 percent), is not solely due to the presence of outside co-owners presumably brought in to improve the financial position of the business, since single outsider owners also invest significantly more than single insider owners.

The superiority of outsider owners is not surprising. To begin with,

[35] Some of this evidence was presented by the architect of the Czech small privatization program, Dusan Triska, at a conference held at the World Bank in June 1993.

[36] For price ratios as a measure of price levels, see above section 4.6.

[37] Mean investment at ratios below 1.25 equals $3,408, while the figure for ratios above 1.25 is $5,639. This result, which is significant at the 4 percent level, could be due to a selection bias, since people may bid higher for properties that do not require postprivatization remodeling. (We owe this point to Professor Randi Ryterman.) The likelihood of such selection bias is in turn lessened by the fact that, as explained in section 6.1, above, the particularly low investment rates (which presumably pertain to premises that did not require remodeling) were treated as outliers and eliminated from the sample prior to the analysis.

[38] Another inconclusive piece of evidence was the fact that insiders who acquired their premises through closed tenders have, on the average, invested less than those whose contracts resulted from closed noncompetitive procedures. While the difference was numerically large ($2,486 vs. $3,822), it was not statistically significant.

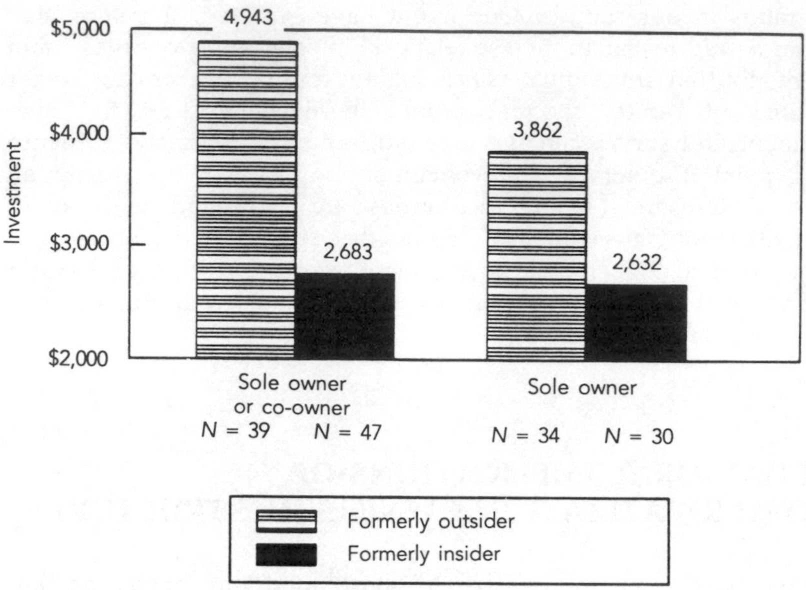

Tests of the differences between the following means of investment (MINV):

MINV (Sole owner or co-owner/outsider) > MINV (Sole owner or co-owner/insider);	*p*-value = 0.5%
MINV (Sole owner/outsider) > MINV (Sole owner/insider);	*p*-value = 7%

Figure IV.25 Outsiders' and insiders' investment in remodeling of premises: pooled data

outsiders, being a self-selected group of entrepreneurs, probably have more capital than former employees in what was traditionally a low paid sector in Eastern European economies. Also, the outsiders are less likely to be set in the old ways of doing business, and this makes it more likely that they would institute changes, such as those in the line of business,[39] that naturally lead to a greater amount of remodeling.

[39] In Poland, which is the only country with a sufficient amount of change to measure the relative frequency of changes in the line of business among the insiders and the outsiders, outsiders change the line of business 2.5 times more often than the insiders.

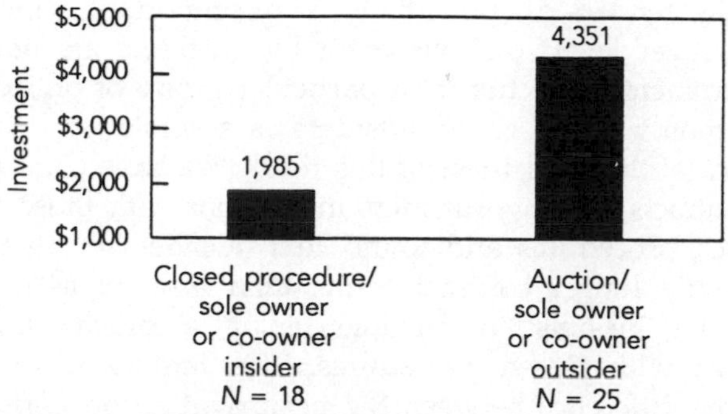

Test of the difference between the following means of investment (MINV):

MINV (Sole owner or co-owner/outsider) >
MINV (Sole owner or co-owner/insider); *p*-value = 1%

Figure IV.26 Outsiders' and insiders' investment and the mode of transfer: pooled data

Given the fact that auctions do not seem to lead to significantly higher levels of investment, it was important to examine whether the high levels of investment by outsiders are not due to the fact that they dominate open tenders, which in turn lead to much higher levels of investment. To test this possibility, we have compared the average levels of investment of outsiders who acquired premises at auctions with those of insiders who obtained premises through closed procedures. The result, presented in Figure IV.26, shows that investment by outsiders following auctions was significantly higher than that by insiders following closed procedures.[40]

The fact that the positive effect of outsider participation is felt in

[40] It is interesting why, given the relatively high levels of investment by outsiders following auctions, auctions still do not lead to significantly higher levels of investment than closed procedures (see section 7.2). The reason for this is twofold: First, the insiders who win auctions do not invest more than insiders in closed procedures, and they drag down the auction performance. Second, perhaps unexpectedly for the proponents of competition, the absence of competition among insiders in closed non-competitive transfers leads to numerically much higher levels of investment, which boosts the performance of closed procedures.

auctions as well as tenders is potentially very important, since it indicates that the higher levels of investment by outsiders are not an artifact of the government's selection of a particular group of outsiders, but rather are common to the class of outsiders as a whole.

As a further check of the robustness of this result, we have compared the durations of contracts won by outsiders in auctions with those won by insiders in closed procedures and found that outsiders in auctions have very significantly longer contract terms than insiders in closed procedures, and that insiders in auctions enjoy a much smaller advantage compared with closed procedures. This finding raises the question whether the difference between the postprivatization performance of outsiders and insiders is not simply an artifact of contract duration.

In order to examine this question we performed a simple multivariate analysis of the relationship between investment in remodeling of premises, duration, and postprivatization ownership arrangements, as well as other factors considered in this and the previous sections: the mode of transfer, price ratios, purchases vs. rentals, country specific dummies, etc.

All variables except the dummy variables for long and short duration and postprivatization ownership arrangements turned out to be insignificant.[41]

The estimated regression model, retaining only significant variables for the sample of rentals, is as follows:

$$\text{Investment in remodeling of premises} = \underset{(0.0436)}{4{,}972} + \underset{(0.0416)}{2{,}211 \cdot \text{SMSO}} - \underset{(0.007)}{2{,}947 \cdot \text{DURX}}$$

where,

DURX[42] = 1, if duration > 5
= 2, if duration $\leqslant 5$

SMSO = 1, if the establishment is solely owned by its former manager
= 2, if the establishment is solely owned by a former outsider

[41] Perhaps the only surprise is that open tenders did not turn out to be significant. This needs to be further investigated, and it is probably due the inclusion of an insider–outsider dummy in the regression, which captures the effect of tenders on investment.

[42] Since the relationship between duration and investment appears to be non-linear, this dummy variable was used to estimate approximate effects of long- and short-term leases.

As is clear from the *p*-values (noted in parenthesis under the coefficients), both dummy variables are highly significant. Therefore, even after the effect of duration on investment is controlled for, and despite the finding that outsiders' rental contracts have longer durations, the effect of outsider ownership on investment in remodeling of premises following privatization remains significant.

9. CONCLUSIONS: OWNERSHIP STRUCTURE AND THE MODE OF TRANSFER

There is an apparent tension between our findings concerning the optimal mode of transfer and the decisive advantage that bringing in outsiders has with respect to postprivatization restructuring. Open procedures are clearly superior to closed ones in as much as they facilitate the entry of outsiders into the retail trade and consumer service sector in the wake of privatizations. But both kinds of the most commonly used open procedures, auctions and tenders, have their disadvantages as well, primarily in raising the opposition of the powerful insiders to the privatization process. In addition, tenders, while perhaps the most effective way of raising the levels of postprivatization investment, are also quite slow and subject to procedural irregularities. Auctions, on the other hand, when conducted under conditions of heightened uncertainty, may lead to overbidding and the "winner's curse" syndrome.

It thus seems that the tension between the need to bring outsiders into the process of small privatization and the tendency of open procedures to increase the opposition to privatization is a tension between the quality of individual transformations and the scale of privatization that may be important to bring about a sufficient "critical mass" of reform. One of the devices used to reconcile these two elements is a widely encountered system of special preferences for insiders, designed to provide them with incentives to cooperate with more open privatization processes. Although insider preferences may in some cases lessen resistance to privatization, there are obvious limitations to this method. If the preferences are weak, they are likely to have only a limited effect. If, on the other hand, they are strong, they are simply a way of assuring future insider control. The experience of countries, such as Hungary and Russia, where some forms of insider preferences have been used, seems to confirm that they are no panacea.

Still, given the overwhelming importance of bringing outsiders into the process of small privatization, keeping the process as open as possible is certainly very important. This means that auctions, perhaps with some discounts for the insiders, should be used whenever feasible. But it is also possible that the insistence on open procedures in initial privatizations of the existing stock of retail and service establishments has been somewhat over-emphasized, to the neglect of other potentially effective methods of bringing outsider participation.

The reason why what may be the most important method of bringing outsiders into the sector is not fully attended to is that privatization is usually understood too narrowly to refer to the ownership transformation of the existing businesses. But it must be remembered that privatization of the existing stores is, above all, a conveyance of rights to real estate on which these stores are located, and that, in this sense, it is not much different from the creation of new businesses, since the latter, in as much as they obtain the use of real estate previously monopolized by the state, are also the beneficiaries of small privatization. Insofar as the greatest change in the sector may come from the increase in the number of new businesses, rather than merely the restructuring of the old ones, the entry of outsiders can naturally be facilitated by a policy of making commercial real estate widely available to new entrepreneurs. Moreover, it is here that the use of market mechanisms may be particularly important, as much as in the auctioning of the existing stores, since the replacement of the state's rigid monopoly on commercial premises by a genuine real estate market is among the main preconditions of sectoral reform.

The reason for this last statement is that the creation of a commercial real estate market not only facilitates the entry of new entrepreneurs into the retail trade and consumer service sector, but also creates the foundation of genuine property rights in the most important assets of retail trade and consumer service establishments in the period of transition. As we have seen from the survey (especially sections 4.1–4.3 above), the rights conveyed to the new owners of the privatized businesses in Eastern Europe, in so far as real estate is concerned, are often of a limited nature. The short terms of most leases, the uncertainty of renewal, and the lack of alternative locations are among the main reasons why new entrepreneurs, insiders and outsiders alike, hesitate to invest large amounts in their businesses. And with respect to all of these concerns, the state monopoly on real estate serves as an aggravating factor, which will persist until the state transfers its rights over most commercial real estate into private hands and allows the market to operate.

The final point related to the creation of the real estate market is the importance of the creation of secondary markets for the privatized businesses and the possibility of a postprivatization reallocation of retail trade and consumer service resources. While our survey, concentrating on the effects of original privatizations, was unfortunately unable to document the extent of secondary market transactions in the three countries, the importance of these markets in the transition economies is additionally heightened by the insider domination of many privatization procedures. To the extent that the insiders who gain ownership control of their stores are locked into them in the long run, either because of the existing restrictions on resale and subletting or because of other market imperfections, the entry of outsiders and the speed of restructuring is compromised. But if the property rights conveyed in the initial privatizations are relatively unencumbered, secondary markets may also constitute an important method for outsiders to enter the process, and thus lessen the pressure for the sometimes ineffective use of market mechanisms in the original transfer of the privatized assets.